R4

FILM REVIEW

1981–82

FILM REVIEW
1981–82

edited by F. Maurice Speed

W.H. Allen · London
A Howard & Wyndham Company
1981

This book or parts thereof may not be reproduced in
any form whatsoever without permission in writing.
Printed and bound in Great Britain by
Mackays of Chatham Ltd, for the Publishers,
W.H. Allen & Co. Ltd,
44 Hill Street, London W1X 8LB

ISBN 0 491 02825 3

CONTENTS

Introduction

A few years ago, as you may recall, it was the Theatre which was being gloomily written off by the pundits. Television, they suggested, coming on top of all else, had sent it spinning into its death throes and its time was short. In fact, the Theatre today, in spite of recession, tight purse-strings, terrifyingly high-priced seats, VAT and all the other burdens appears to be in reasonably good heart and not really in any worse shape than it was at the time of those convinced prognostications.

Certainly one seldom now reads any forecasts of the Theatre's immediate, or indeed even long-term, demise, and it is the turn of the Cinema to be written off as all but finished by a number of seers on both sides of the Atlantic, who see a future – not too distant – when films will only – or at least primarily – be made for television, the video-cassette and cable TV. The surviving cinemas, they suggest, will be reduced to chains of small, specialist 'art' houses for the screening of old films, foreign movies and other odd productions not considered suitable for the mass audience. The audiences by this time will have been reduced to a hard-core of film buffs, and youngsters who for a while may want to escape from their parents and the family's TV choice to hold their girl-friend's hand or whatever in the comforting, anonymous darkness of the intimate cinema!

And if at this point you ask me what I think of all this I shall have to borrow that famous Eric Morecambe comment of 'Rubbish'. I just won't accept all this gloom and doom stuff about our neighbourhood cinemas. I won't – indeed, cannot – ignore the fact that cinema audiences in many countries, including America and our own, are falling, nor can I gloss over the fact that 1980 was the worst year ever in British cinema history with its total of 104 million admissions as against the figure of 112 million the previous year. In America things were not so bad. Although the 1980 figure of one billion is low by their standards (in 1946 four billion seats were sold) it is still pretty impressive and actually as much as 25% up on the early 1970s' totals.

The reason for the gradual slide downward in cinema attendance is only partly due to the advent and increased coverage and choice of TV. Football attendances are likewise declining, and here again it would be unfair to blame the fall entirely or even primarily on television, although obviously it is a contributory cause. In contrast, other sports and other forms of entertainment are drawing considerably enlarged followings. Look, for instance, at the enormous crowds that trail around the golf courses these days at every major tournament – quite unthinkable just a few years ago. Look at the current increasing popularity of snooker, basketball, tennis and the like (admittedly all popularised by television, without which it is highly doubtful that they would ever have attained their present boom in public interest). All these, and the emerging video-cassette, *are* drawing the people and the money away from the cinema and the football stadium.

The basic problem here is that there is only so much money in the public's pocket and only so much time to be spent on amusement, so that if one form of entertainment rises then another must, logically, fall. As more and more attractions become available so the struggle between the competing forms of amusement for the public's lolly becomes more intense and the jam becomes spread lighter over a larger area.

As an illustration I quote a restaurateur friend's remarks to me recently in reply to my suggestion that he wasn't quite so busy as in the past. He explained that the number of potential patrons of first-class restaurants are limited, so that every time a new place opens it must draw its clientele from other, longer established restaurants. Inevitably as new places open so others must close – in roughly the same ratio. This same basic rule must apply to the entertainment business generally. If one form of public amusement grows in popularity and financial success, another must wane. And today, with everything costing so much and – at least in theory, in practice it appears arguable on the evidence – with less spare cash available in the public's pockets, the struggle for success, indeed for survival, becomes ever more intense.

The cinema is in the forefront of this struggle and it has to fight back. It must become consistently good enough in terms of the entertainment value of the films it shows, to hold not only its present proportion of the entertainment business but somehow manage to claw back a larger ration from the opposing forms of amusement.

One of the greatest evils of today's cinema is the ludicrously soaring price of film production. It is quite astonishing to me that at one point last year the head of Paramount studios had to line up his producers to tell them that in future their budgets must *not exceed £5 million per picture!* That was, in fact, about the average cost of producing a movie during 1980, but with costs spiralling again Hollywood is quite calmly accepting that by the end of the year that figure will have probably climbed to the £10 million mark. Today the average American movie must take £8 million to break even and *gross* £20 million to get its complete investment back! If the gap seems a little puzzling let me refer you to Jack Valenti, President of the Motion Pictures Association of America, and his statement that 'a £5 million expenditure on a film must be seen against an additional budget of a like amount for prints, advertising and marketing the movie'.

A large proportion of these inflated budgets is due to the often ludicrous payments made to the stars. A number of 'box-office names' now demand as much as a million pounds before they'll even start discussing a deal and no star in the world *earns* that kind of money, even if they can get it. Burt Reynolds is rumoured to have been presented with a cheque for £2.5 million for his role in *The Cannonball Run* and Barbra

Streisand is reputed to have pulled in a like amount for her contribution to *All Night Long.* Such payments are, admittedly, headline-making, but others only a little less ridiculous are not all that rare. It is not only the players who are getting away with such undeserved rewards: for directing his latest epic *One from the Heart,* Francis Ford Coppola is said to be getting £1.5 million *plus* a percentage of the profits. However, not everyone in Hollywood is happy about this money madness. Director Martin Scorsese is reported (in *Time*) to have said in public what many others are apparently thinking in private: 'We're working ourselves right out of a job. I'm concerned that the industry is being destroyed.' It is Scorsese, by the way, who recently said gloomily, 'Movies are on the way out.'

Moviemaking has always been a gamble but in today's climate the stakes have become terrifyingly, ridiculously high. Though really big profits are still possible for the fortunate few (*Every Which Way But Loose,* which cost something around £7 million to make, is finally expected to show a 'take' of little short of £30 million; *Kramer vs Kramer* which in today's costs context must be considered a cheap production at around a mere £3 million is expected to show a final gross figure of £130 million; and *The Empire Strikes Back* took nearly £5 million the first week of its showing in America alone), the financial cost of a single big flop can be completely ruinous. *Heaven's Gate,* which was made by Michael (*The Deer*

Hunter) Cimino at about £20 million proved such a dire failure on its initial release that within a week or two it was withdrawn to undergo a multi-million-dollar re-vamping before further exposure. It didn't turn out to be Cimino's year. Even the re-vamped version of his epic met with further critical cruelty when shown in America, added to which the cruelty to animals in the movie (five horses were apparently killed during production, one actually being blown-up, and there's a cock-fight which the British censor asked to be pruned) brought out the pickets right across the United States. And it is possible to see a connection between this and the £400 million MGM deal in May with United Artists, whose film* *Heaven's Gate* was. A similar thing happened with Disney's *A Way in the Woods,* which after an opening disaster was trundled back to Pinewood Studios for a £250,000 re-shaping, unusual for the normally highly successful Disney people, with their string of unfailing popular successes.

But in giving these figures one must, to be scrupulously fair, take into consideration the ravages of inflation. In a recent fascinating *Variety* exercise, production and profit figures were up-dated to today's terms. Thus it was reckoned that *Gone with the Wind,* which in 1939 was produced at a cost

*Perhaps significantly, soon after the MGM takeover of UA the latter announced 8 new productions, the first 4 of which were to be made on budgets ranging between £3 million and £6½ million – all well within the £7½ million ceiling that MGM had previously announced would be operating.

of £2.45 million would today cost £15 million and its, then, income of £38.35 million would be £142 million. 1963's *Cleopatra,* which nearly ruined Fox at a cost of £22 million would now at £55 million set any studio spinning into a red abyss (according to these figures it is reckoned that even today the film has only recovered £13 of that original £22 million). Other interesting items from this comparison list: *Jaws* cost £6 million to make in 1975 and to date has shown a return of nearly £67 million. Biggest disaster, *Waterloo,* made in 1971 at a cost of £12.5 million has so far only earned the odd half-million in revenue.

Somewhat surprisingly – in view of the amounts they demand for appearing in front of the cameras – actors who turn directors or producers or whatever are not the most lavish of spenders. Though Warren Beatty is certainly no skinflint with his still uncompleted *Reds* (so far he has spent £15 million and two years of his time on the project), Robert Redford claims it is still possible to make *good,* money-making movies at modest cost and points to his own record as proof. It seems he brought *The Candidate* in for well under £1 million, and his latest, Oscar-winning production, *Ordinary People,* he made for just over the £3 million mark, paying himself only £26,000 as director and his entire cast a total of £300,000. Robert Benton, writer-director of the similarly Oscar-awarded *Kramer vs Kramer* agrees with Redford. He is on record as saying that: 'The cost of movies now is astronomical and that's dangerous. It

makes it difficult to take creative risks. If it continues fewer pictures will be made.' Supporting this suggestion was the news from United Artists that they would concentrate on 'larger, more commercial movies' in the future. If the actual production figures dropped in America in 1980 – and though they've kept busy in 1981 the ground lost that year hasn't been regained – it was largely due to the strike of actors and actresses which, beginning in July and lasting through to the end of October, hit the studios hard, causing postponement of many films and cancellation of others. It all began when the Guild (the players' trade union) demanded a 35% rise in salaries with a three-year contract and the producers countered with an offer of a 12% rise the first year and subsequent 8% rises for the following two years. (At that time the basic pay for actors and actresses in Hollywood was £112 a day or £400 a week.) Eventually the Screen Actors Guild voted to accept the new compromise contract offered by the Association of Motion Picture and TV Producers by a total of 18,577 for and 3,697 against, so ending a dispute which was reckoned to have cost the film and television industry some £20 million for every week it lasted, with a final total of well over the £250 million* mark. As yet it is difficult to see the final result of this unhappy bleeding but it may turn out to be something of a blessing in disguise. *Variety* claimed that it had brought the industry up against reality with a jerk and what at the time the players saw as a victory

may in the long run turn out to be rather less than that. It certainly gave some of the producers a chance to see the amount of waste that had been going on, revealing for instance that too much costly work goes on production of films which never get as far as the studio. In extreme cases it was realised that of every ten films planned and to some extent worked on, only one ever got as far as actual production. In the long term the realisation of this kind of thing will almost certainly mean a pruning of staff and a tightening of purse-strings. One point in the moviemakers' favour this year has been the continuation of the trend noted last year of the swing away from the exploitation of nudity and general pornographic content in productions, the reversal of a trend which climaxed a couple or so years back. Today nudity in films when it occurs is generally justifiable and there's a much more healthily balanced attitude towards it. But the foul language content of scripts, even if slightly less and somewhat less foul, continues and one can only hope that

*The Hollywood screenwriters went on strike in April 1981 and at the moment, eight weeks and more later, they are still refusing to take up their pens. They were originally asking for 2.75% of producers' gross income from home video sales, but the producers wanted 10 days' playing time in each year on each Pay-TV broadcasts before passing anything on to the writers. And as the argument went on there was a distinct threat of the directors going on strike, too, for similar reasons, but this was averted in late June by a last-minute agreement with the producers which won them a 12%, 12% and 11% earnings rise respectively over a three-year period, as well as benefits from Pay-TV showings of their movies.

DIRECTORS AT WORK
Clint Eastwood explains a scene to the
late Scatman Crothers during the
filming of Warner's *Bronco Billy*, in
which Eastwood did a fine job both in
front and behind the camera.

John Cassavetes tells John Adames
how he wants him to play the next
scene in Columbia's *Gloria*, which he
both directed and wrote and which
starred his wife, Gena Rowlands.

British director Joseph Losey with
singer-star Ruggero Raimondi (in the
title role) during the shooting of *Don
Giovanni*, his remarkable screen
version of the Mozart opera (an
Artificial Eye release).

this too, like nudity and all the other unfortunate film fashions that appear inevitable from time to time, will gradually improve. Perhaps the fact that some of the year's most successful movies have not used this kind of unpleasant and needless language will be noted by writers, directors and producers.

As a footnote to this subject, an interesting decision was made by the Rank film bookers when they decided they would not show UA's *Raging Bull* (which, it turned out, was really not that much worse than many movies which had previously been given wide showings) because of its bad language and violence. Although in view of the film's content it was a controversial decision it was to me a most welcome stand against this kind of thing which I would like to see copied by others. Generally triggered off by one big box-office success, almost every year in the cinema is dominated by a special kind of movie – those inevitable cycles which wax, and finally wane as the get-rich-quick boys jump on the profitable band-wagon and ruin it with shoddy product. So we've had in the past the spectacle/disaster cycle and the space wars cycle etc. This year the screen has been considerably dominated by the less subtle kind of 'horror pic' (as *Variety* puts it). Now in spite of all the reasonable psychological and metaphysical explanations that may be advanced by the experts I've never really understood – or at least sympathised with – the popular box-office-proved taste for bloody horror as cinema entertainment. Why

anyone should be prepared to pay today's pretty stiff admission charges to see, for instance, a head cleft from a blood-spouting body or a close-up of a chain-saw killing is quite beyond me. But the fact is that this year's flood of blood-dripping spine-chillers and eye-averters have been drawing some of the largest attendances. It must prove something but exactly what I shudder to think.

But there were signs in early 1981 that the cycle that really began with *Halloween* (a good thriller) having waxed mightily may be coming to an end, as reaction towards the baser kind of 'gore and guts' movie builds. Said one cinema executive: 'All they want is blood pouring off the screen. I question the mental balance of people making and buying (exhibiting) this stuff.' And another buyer is on record as saying: 'The old Hammer stuff was good clean horror which could be related to real life. Now sadistic horror which can be emulated is the vogue . . . some are so bad that scrupulous distributors are holding out against them. One film I've seen was obviously made by a mental defective for the mentally defective.'

One of the more reputable producers of thrillers (Bill Rebane) while admitting to being 'drawn in' to the making of bloodier versions of terror-suspensers complained that 'They've gone to such extremes that the art of the classic horror picture has gone.'

The groundswell against the worst kind of blood-curdler is growing in America, where feminists are joining in

the chorus (on the grounds that so many of these movies depict attacks on women). It all boils down to the old movie-making practice of every producer trying to out-do his predecessors, be it in sex, violence, pornography and everything else. One can only hope that the time has come for the cycle – as happens with every movie cycle – to step over the limit to box-office disaster (as has happened so often in the past), the only lesson the moviemakers seem able to accept. Turning to the technical front, once again this year we haven't seen much that has been startling, in the way of innovations or inventions. Last year I was asking whatever had happened to the various methods of making and showing 3-D movies – without having to wear special glasses – which had been announced from time to time during the past few years but about which nothing more has been heard. So it is with some slight sceptism one notes this year's announcement of yet another method. This came from the United Artists Theatre Circuit which claimed that they had perfected and patented a revolutionary 70mm panoramic three-dimensional production and exhibition process which it was said would make all other previous 3-D systems appear primitive in contrast.

This system (named Sterospace – combining stereoscopic sight and phonic sound) is filmed by twin cameras, representing the right and left human eye, and then exhibited by two linked projectors in the same way. The addition of the system is said to increase a film's budget only by about 8% and converting a cinema to show such films would cost only something between £10,000 and £20,000.

A report in *Variety* said 'The Process lived up to and came close to exceeding Vetter's (Richard Vetter is the principal developer of the system) claims in the demonstration screening. There was none of the distortion, fuzziness or eyestrain associated with previous 3-D systems. Colour, depth and definition were flawless . . .'

However, we are not likely to see Sterospace (which costs £1.5 million and took four years to perfect) until at least the middle of 1982. At the moment the first of three such films is being planned, a psychic thriller (what else!) 'in which ghosts will come to within 15in of the viewer'. Well, we'll see if this one, in contrast to all those other promised 3-D systems, will actually get off the ground on to the screen. For fun's sake I hope so. Incidentally, the first 3-D production to be televised in the United States was shown on Pay-TV there in December 1980; a filming of a three-dimensional *Sadie Thompson*. But if this appears revolutionary it must be noted that Japan has been beaming 3-D cartoons over the air for more than three years now and something along similar lines has been going on in Mexico.

In the summer of 1980 Martin Scorsese raised something of a storm about the instability of colour over a period. It was claimed – a claim that was supported by a number of well-known Hollywood personalities – that even at the end of five years the blue in *Jaws*

was becoming obviously paler just as the reds appeared to be increasing in strength. The suggestion seemed to be that within a period of years a film would become quite different – colourwise – to the one originally screened and could lead to some bizarre visual results.

A technical marvel was accomplished by Alan Douglas, whose firm created a full-length coherent new Laurel and Hardy feature – *The Dance of the Cuckoos* – from bits of the couple's black-and-white shorts. Basically the process (developed by BJA Productions), says Douglas, entails the transferring of the original film to videotape, then transforming it into 1,000-line colour tape – using a friendly computer – and then transferring it back to 35mm film stock. By clever editing the film will have a continuous story. A new soundtrack will be added – but retaining the comics' voices – and you can expect to see this funny marvel sometime in 1982.

Another interesting gimmick to look forward to in the same period is used in MGM's *Brainstorm*. Called the Show-Scan process it – briefly, and for the less technical – adds to the realism of a movie by using a camera which shoots more frames per second. Presumably this is something like the 360 fps Photosonic's 35-4E Super High Speed Camera used by Samuelson Film Services for a special glass-breaking scene in their trailer for *Breaking Glass*. This camera, already used by the military for experimental purposes, runs at three times the usual camera speed.

Adding some £8 million to the £15 million budget, the new Electronic process used by Francis Ford Coppola for his *One from the Heart* is claimed to be the 'biggest technical step forward since the advent of sound in 1927'. Still in the development stage this process, according to a long report in *Screen International*, allows for the 'pre-visualisation of a film'. Months before the start of shooting, storyboard sketches are transferred to video discs, then the film's dialogue, music and sound can be added, so producing a pictorial and audio form of the script which gives a clear picture of how the film will finally appear.

Technical details! 'The Electronic Cinema consists of three main centres of operation inter-connected by cables. From the sound stages where video cameras are attached to the film cameras with a standard beam-splitter video tape and to individual Sony Betamax recorders with connecting monitors, the performance is fed to the Image and Sound Control vehicle. 'Fulfilling dual production/editing functions, transmissions are both sent and received from this vehicle. Here the director can view and control the action from source monitors corresponding to the cameras and stage monitors as well as make a 'first impression' edit. In this chamber an audio composite condensed from an eight-track dialogue recording is mixed with sound effects and music and added to the video.'

From all this (and more!) it seems that the director/producer can more completely than previously build the

Writer-producer-director Stanley Kubrick (right) at work on a chilly scene in his Warner thriller *The Shining*.

Producer Tony Bill made a big impact with his debut as a director in the Fox release *My Bodyguard*, one of the most thoroughly pleasant movies of the year.

Roman Polanski (right) discusses the next shot with his cameraman and his star, Nastassia Kinski (as Tess) in his beautiful adaptation of the Hardy novel '*Tess of the d'Urbervilles*' – Columbia's *Tess*.

films to its final print as it goes along, allowing the film-makers continually to preview their production so far. All this considerably reduces post-production editing time, saving money! Quote from Coppola: 'We're on the edge of something which will make the Industrial Revolution look like a small out of town try-out. I can see a communication revolution that's about movies and art and music and digital electronics and satellites but above all human talent – and it's going to make the masters of the cinema, from whom we inherited this business, believe things that they would never have thought possible.'

In contrast to the United States where admissions last year – as previously mentioned – though down were not all that bad*, Britain has certainly been badly hit by the depression. Yet though the *admissions* fell to an all-time low the *money* taken at the box-office thanks to inflation was actually up. According to *Variety* 1980's £167 million compared with 1979's £143 million. Another paradox was that while attendances dropped the number of screens – as apart from actual cinemas – increased†.

The British Production story for 1980–81 was not all that cheering. January 1981 proved to be the worst

*In fact the last two weeks in June 1981 were the best in United States box-office history and so restored the position that by the end of the month the figures actually showed a small advance in last year's total at the same period.

†But the situation altered when in June 1981 Rank announced they were closing 29 unprofitable and unviable cinemas during the coming months, including 13 in Greater London.

month ever for British production with only one film *The Great Muppet Caper* in production. Again in contrast to the United States, where at least at the turn of the year studio space was at a premium, with every major studio working to capacity and even in some cases leasing additional space from outside – a situation likely to continue it was thought well into the summer and autumn of 1981 at least – a spring round-up of the British Studios showed that, though Pinewood had actually more space booked than at the same time the previous year, only about half the available space would be taken up until the middle of 1981, after which the situation was not clear. The EMI studios at Elstree more cheerfully anticipated being fully occupied until the autumn and, with a little luck, well into 1982. In contrast Shepperton not only had nothing on the floor but had no future bookings at all. At Twickenham there was also nothing in production but at least there was hope of several movies likely to be made there late in 1981 and early 1982*. Among more optimistic news about British production plans was the summer announcement that the British Film Institute would be making three feature films during the 1981–2 period, with a £680,000 budget. £140,000 to go to Ed Bennet's *Ascendancy*, £120,000 to a Peter Greenaway subject and – presumably – the balance to be spent

*Surprise announcement made in late June by the government was that they had decided to slash the quote from 30% to 15% in future. In spite of various angry reactions it was an entirely logical move in view of the few British films now being made.

on a film starring Julie Christie. Just after the Rank bombshell of announcing they would no longer continue film production (see the extended feature on the subject by Iain McAsh on a later page) there was a happier news story about a group called Goldcrest Films International which with a kitty of some £8 million (financed from among other sources by the National Coal Board's Pension Fund of all things!) intended to produce six British films a year over a five-year period. The plan was to limit the investment to 20% of the net capital in any one production and never to provide more than 50% of that production's total budget. Well, here's hoping.

Incidentally in April 1981 Francis Ford Coppola made a bid to buy Pinewood Studios from Rank, who announced that the bid would of course be put up to the directors though it was unlikely to be accepted.

Another 'Depression' blow to British Film Production came with the announcement that the National Film Finance Corporation would be tightening its belt in 1981. With an income of only about £1 million annually in future from the Eady Fund, Managing Director Mamhoud Hassan announced that the Board would be 'redefining its responsibilities'. He said there was no purpose in the Corporation acting as a low-funded film company nor would it be useful to make small, token contributions to a large number of productions. Instead, they would give financial assistance to those (obviously

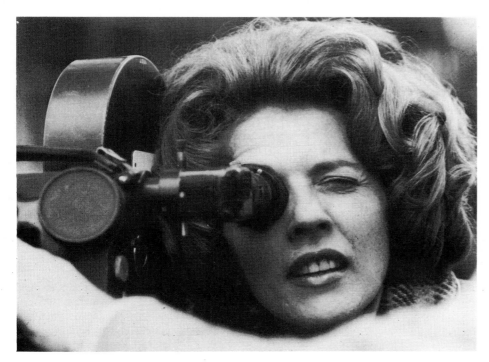

France's Nelly Kaplan, who started her career as assistant to the great Abel Gance, and is now a highly regarded European director, though far less well known in Britain, something London's Scala cinema tried to correct with a season of her work this year.

report only twenty-three films have resulted from the Anglo-French production pact signed in 1965; ten films from the Anglo-Italian pact signed two years later; five from the 1974 Anglo-German agreement. Some of those films have been major box-office and artistic successes, proving this kind of production *can* be achieved. So why not more often? A rather strange new trend (in the United States) during the period has been the increasing backing of stage shows by the film companies. Warner, for instance, backed the production of Arthur Miller's *The American Clock* and it was Universal's money that brought *The Best Little Whorehouse in Texas* to the footlights (they are going to make it into a movie). Other film companies were behind the production of George Furth's *The Supporting Cast* and Henry Guettel's comedy *Twigs*. More recently some film companies have extended their interest in stage shows from financing to actually producing them. Of course, it is reasonable to imagine that at the back of at least most of such ventures is the intention of at some time or another making them into movies. That's nothing new: most of the biggest Marx

few) films which sought a wide audience but which the industry considered to be too risky to support. And even for these films the Corporation would only put up the minimum amount of cash to get the film into production.
Disappointed with the Government's low level of NFFC funding under the Films Act of 1980, and their decision to end direct support of the Corporation, Hassan said: 'We wanted dynamite but with the funds made available to us our role (in future) will be merely the fuse.'
It was decided to reserve about 10% of the annual NFFC's budget for a

National Film Development Fund to provide support for script-writing and pre-production work. Incidentally, the Board's loss for the year 1980 was just over £1.25 million.
What, by the way, has happened to the promise of prosperity offered by British-European co-production? Nearly every 'foreign' film shown in Britain today is a result of collaboration between France, Germany, Spain and Italy in some sort of combination. Why aren't the British moviemakers doing more in this direction, spreading their production costs and greatly enlarging their potential audiences?
According to a *Screen International*

Brothers' screen successes were 'tried out' as stage productions by Paramount, and there are plenty of other examples of such testing of material eventually destined for the screen.

So to the bits and pieces; news and other items worth recording to produce an overall picture of the cinema year. For instance, the big success of the 1980 London Film Festival was, ironically enough, Abel Gance's 1927 production of *Napoleon*, which got a standing ovation at the end of its five-hour showing. Reconstructed by Kevin Brownlow with loving care, the movie was shown to orchestral accompaniment and confirmed its position as one of the greatest masterpieces of the silent – or, come to that, any other – era. Another successful revival was that of John Huston's remarkable World War II documentary *Let There Be Light*, an hour-long account of the psychiatric recuperation of shell-shocked soldiers in an Army hospital, which upon its completion thirty-six years ago was suppressed by the authorities as being unsuitable for public exhibition. In fact now seen for the first time, it has been hailed in the US as a masterpiece and one of Huston's greatest triumphs.

In America there's been a rash of switching film directors at the beginning or during the actual production of a movie. Of 110 films produced during the period 15% of them suffered (or possibly were improved?) by such switches. And somewhat disturbingly the trend has been to replace seasoned movie

directors with new and usually untried talent from TV.

The good old Western – once the movie always sure to make money – has been suffering an eclipse recently. Apparently such more recent Westerns as *The Long Riders, Bronco Billy, Tom Horn* and even Travolta's Western-style *Urban Cowboy* have not done too well at the box-office. The Spanish-Italian source has long since dried up and you won't find many – if any – Westerns on the current schedules of American companies. Blame has been put on TV for overdoing the genre. It's a pity because the Western is the most consistently watchable kind of movie even when it's only done on the old 'B' scale.

On the other hand the strip-cartoon movie has been given the Big treatment recently with such major movies as *Superman I* and *II*, *Popeye* and *Flash Gordon*. And more are planned.

Already well established the other side of the Atlantic, the British Government agreed this year to allow Pay-TV to be re-introduced in Britain. (It was somewhat tentatively tried out in the 1960s but the experiment was terminated when it turned out to be less than a success at the time.) The licence will be for a two-year experimental period and no film will be allowed to be shown until after it has been available for cinema showings for not less than twelve months.

Incidentally, I wonder if you find it as ironical as I do that the very large and very expensive Soviet-British production of *The Blue Bird* which was made for but never shown in British

cinemas, apparently because it was considered not to have enough even minority appeal, was premiered on television this year to *that* great captive audience.

Finally a marvellously scathing, hard-hitting article in a May issue of *Screen International* by Quentin Falk is worthy of comment I feel and offers a neat way of rounding off this review of the film year.

'Years of greed, self-interest, restrictive practice and sheer complacency allied to a stunning disregard by government for the enormous potential of a healthy British film industry are the main contributors to its current plight. Add to this a flagellatory attitude by critics and film illiterate media, and it can be understood why all spheres of the industry are in such dire straits.' And a lot more in the same vein, with the worthwhile idea of making people think and act and unite and drag the industry, by the scruff of the neck if needs be, back to success. It needs both government and self help. We have all the talent necessary, all the film-making facilities, all the know-how; we have made and can make movies which combine entertainment with art, such as Australia is now doing with wonderful consistency. It is up to the industry, yes, and the government and those that love the cinema to show that all this current gloom and doom prophecy about the demise of the cinema is so much rubbish. Let's never forget Alfred Hitchcock's dictum, that it is *ideas* and not *money* that makes good movies.

Releases
of the Year
in Pictures

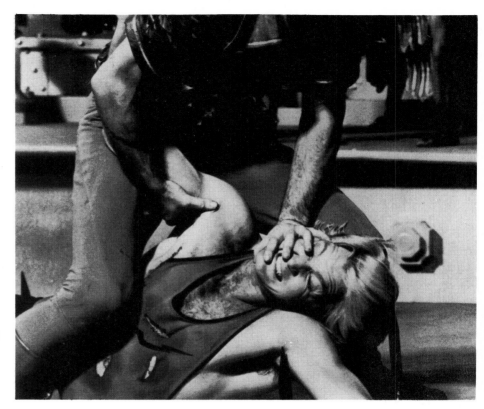

The films illustrated in the following pages are those from America, Great Britain, Canada, South Africa and Australia. Films made in any other country than these will be found similarly illustrated in the following section, that devoted to and headed 'The Continental Film'. In both cases all films have had a general or a floating release between the beginning of July, 1980 and the end of June, 1981. Full cast and other credits will be found in 'Releases of the Year in Detail' section on a later page.

One of the more interesting – and some may find significant – recent trends in the movie business has been the interest that producers have shown in yesteryear's comic strip and former film serial characters; basing large, spectacular and expensive features on them, such as the EMI release of *Flash Gordon,* in which former American football player Sam Jones played the intrepid hero who alone can stop the villainous outer space Emperor from

blasting our earth into little bits from his evil planet of Mongo! Once there, Flash has to endure a duel to the death with a local Prince (Timothy Dalton) (*top left*) and the considerable nubile charms of the Emperor's daughter, shapely Ornella Muti (*right*).

Sympathetic surgeon Anthony
Hopkins shows the members of the
London Pathological Society the
hideously deformed body of John
Merrick (John Hurt), known as 'The
Elephant Man', in the EMI release of
that title – which was based on the true
facts of this Victorian sensation.
Beautifully acted, and for the most part
directed in a low key, the movie
emerged as an often moving and always
superior production.

Thrillers, of one kind or another and of varying standards, made much of the news – and took a lot of money at the box-office – during the period under review (this particular subject you will find discussed at greater length in the Editor's Introductory notes on a previous page), culminating in Stanley Kubrick's in many ways controversial Warner release *The Shining*. A mixture of subtlety and old-fashioned grand guignol, it gave Jack Nicholson – marooned with his frightened wife in a snowed-up mountain hotel for the winter – the opportunity to pull out all the stops as he gradually reveals his madness.

Though not quite up to the standard of his best work, Brian De Palma's contribution to the 1980 thriller quota in ITC's *Dressed to Kill* was still a superior example, with flashy sequences alternating with quite brilliant ones as it told a story about a transvestite killer with a taste for razor killings – terrified victim about to get the bloody chop is pretty Nancy Allen.

Another master of the screen thriller – he made that outstanding example of the genre, *Halloween* – John Carpenter included enough to satisfy most horror addicts in his Avco-Embassy/Rank release *The Fog,* in which some long-drowned sailors return from their watery graves (*left*) to take revenge on the wrecker ancestors of the townsfolk who, by moving the guide-beacon, ensured the ship's sinking on the rocks. And among the most threatened and terrified, local radio station operator Janet Leigh and real-life daughter Jamie Lee Curtis (*below*).

Tricky moment for Caitlin O'Heaney, struggling to escape the unpleasant intentions of a psychotic killer in MGM-CIC's *He Knows You're Alone*, the story of a young bride-to-be who becomes convinced that it's a toss-up whether she is going to be killed or married first!

More psychotic killings in Fox's *Terror Train*, with a mysterious murderer among the guests of what starts out as a happy end-of-term college party, held on a specially hired train, but ends in a welter of blood and corpses and confusion as the axe-wielder settles old scores. (*Right*)

There was a nice, old-fashioned, almost Hammer-like atmosphere in EMI's *The Awakening*, an adaptation of a Bram Stoker novel based on stories about the very nasty things that are supposed to happen to those misguided enough to break into the tombs of the Kings and Queens of Ancient Egypt. It certainly brings little happiness to dedicated archaeologist Charlton Heston (*left*) or to his pretty assistant Stephanie Zimbalist (*right*) (who in this scene is showing her psychiatrist what's wrong with her in a rather over-graphic manner!)

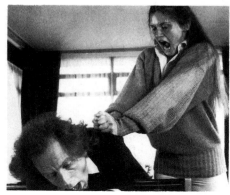

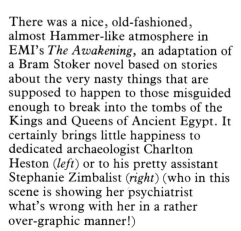

Releases of the Year in Pictures

Though it may be a little difficult to credit, this nasty looking, special-effects-department-conceived creature, about to chew up some innocent beach campers, is a salmon that has escaped from some experimenting scientists' tank and grown up a bit oddly – and quickly! – during the night! And it was all explained at grisly length in UA's *Monster*.

George C. Scott and Trish Van Devere are confronted by the 'thing' which haunts the house which the University have loaned Professor Scott for his 'quiet' hours of musical composition during his lecturing stay on their campus. It all boiled up to one of those raging, holocaust endings beloved of directors since the *Exorcist* set the pace. This time it happened in Brent Walker's *The Changeling*. (*Top right*)

One of the least ambitious but certainly more easily believable of the year's thrillers was UA's Fred Walton film, *When a Stranger Calls*, which related the story of an insane child murderer who, when he escapes from his asylum prison, tracks down the baby-sitter who escaped from him when some years back he murdered her charges. Nicely held tension and a nice portrait of a terror-struck girl by Carol Kane.

Some of the walking horrors in Target International's George A. Romero thriller *Zombies – Dawn of the Dead,* in which several worried live humans are besieged in a supermarket by a hungry collection of the undead, keen on getting some of their only possible sustenance – human flesh and blood. And it was all just a bit *too* nasty.

Scared Betsy Palmer prepares for the worst in Warners' *Friday the Thirteenth,* in which a mad killer spills plenty of blood, and the thunder roars, during a long night of terror at a lonely lakeside holiday camp where the new owner and his several young helpers are getting the place ready for summer opening.

Fun was mixed with the thrills in Rank/Avco-Embassy's *A Man, a Woman and a Bank* (at one time titled 'A Very Big Withdrawal' in the United States), which was a fairly minor effort about some thieves who build their own fail section into the bank's newly installed fail-safe system! With his hands on the £2,000,000 haul, greedy Donald Sutherland.

A rather odd if quite entertaining Australian-set story about a mysterious stranger (Robert Powell – *right* – who may – but on the other hand may not – have supernatural powers) who makes a political impact of a sort on the senator (David Hemmings – *centre*) and certainly an impact of another kind on the senator's wife (Carmen Duncan – *left*) in Hemdale's *Harlequin*.

With that face like a very expressive withered apple, Walter Matthau gave another outstanding comedy performance in Universal-CIC's *Little Miss Marker*. In this Damon Runyon story adaptation Matthau played the cantankerous New York bookie who grumpily accepts a punter's six-year-old daughter (Sara Stimpson) as a form of IOU and is then slowly broken down into a warm and loving human being by her wiles.

Little Darlings Tatum O'Neal (*left*) and Kristy McNichol having some slapstick fun at the holiday camp in which they are competitors in a race to lose their virginity – a case of nice performers in a rather nasty story – made and released by Paramount-CIC.

The moving hand . . . typically British sex scene in ITC's typically British comedy *George and Mildred,* based on the popular TV series of the same name, with Brian Murphy as George. (*Centre left*)

And typically (modern style) American humour of the 'Animal House' crazy-type was the keystone of Warners' *Caddyshack,* into which were tossed a collection of vulgar, sick and similar jokes to embroider a basically pleasant enough story about a young caddy's aspirations to further education. Bill Murray was one of the main 'comics' and the mechanical gopher he is about to try to catch was one of the few really funny things in the film. (*Centre right*)

Universal-CIC's *Smokey and the Bandit Ride Again* was virtually a re-run of the original Smokey film, the considerable financial success of which made a sequel almost inevitable. This time around The Bandit's (Burt Reynolds) cargo is a pregnant elephant, his mate again Jerry Reed, his pursuer again Sheriff Jackie Gleason and his girl again Sally Field, and again one of the comedy(?) highspots was the mass destruction of large numbers of motor vehicles.

A more polished, superior Burt Reynolds vehicle was Paramount-CIC's *Rough Cut*, in which he played a highly successful and wealthy diamond thief who is persuaded into attempting a multi-million-dollar heist by the lovely – blackmailed – bait (Lesley-Anne Down) dangled before him by retiring Scotland Yard Inspector David Niven whose machinations provide the delightfully amusing little twist in the movie's tail.

Perhaps less than vintage Neil Simon, Columbia's *Chapter Two* was a lot funnier than most of the year's comedy movies. An adaptation of one of Simon's stage plays, the fun came from the somewhat familiar situation of a man's devotion to the memory of his first wife seemingly spoiling his chances with his second – and the couple were played, quite delightfully, by James Caan and Marsha Mason.

It was the American version of the Franco-German feature cartoon *Jungle Burger* which was released in this country by Entertainment Films. It admitted to being 'lewd, crude and outrageously rude', but it also had the saving grace of being quite amusing as it poked fun at 'Tarzan' and sundry other targets.

In contrast to the preponderance of X-certificated movies more or less dominating our screens, Walt Disney's delightful 'U' production *The Last Flight of Noah's Ark* was a perfect family film, with its story about a penniless pilot, a pretty girl, several children and a number of animals wrecked on a desert island on which they find the only occupants are two very friendly Japanese survivors from the long-over war. Elliot Gould was the pilot, Genevieve Bujold the girl, Ricky Schroeder and Tammy Lauren the children, all of whom combine efforts to build their very 'original' escape craft (*below*).

Owing something to *Hellzapoppin'* and something to *Animal House* (whose directing-writing team were responsible) Paramount-CIC's *Airplane!* was a 'Disaster' spoof which with wild, and sometimes successful, abandon tossed into the script a series of witty, black, bad taste, and pretty uproarious situations, and lines, in telling the story of an airplane disaster in which Lloyd Bridges (*above left*) and Robert Stack (*above right*) attempt to 'talk down' the crippled liner initially piloted by Peter Graves and Robert Hays (*left*) but later by a lustful 'mechanical pilot' and terrified air hostess!

Another film which was almost a carbon copy of a previous big commercial success was Warners' *Any Which Way You Can,* in which fighting truck driver Clint Eastwood carried on where he left off in *Every Which Way But Loose,* except that this time he is blackmailed by crooked bookies – who hold girl-friend Sondra Locke (*centre*) prisoner until he has fought the opponent they have selected to face up to him. A little more vulgar than the original film, the follow-up again included the driver's mate (Geoffrey Lewis) and Ma (Ruth Gordon) in the cast.

A far better movie was Warners'
Bronco Billy, with Clint directing
himself as star and making a very good
job wearing either cap. A tongue-in-
cheek return to the style and
atmosphere of the 1930s, the story
concerned urban-born cowboy Clint's
struggle to keep his company together
and his Wild West show on the road in
spite of misfortune and the changing
public tastes. And his girl-friend was
played with a nice sense of humour by
Sondra Locke.

Steve McQueen in his last film role, prior to death from cancer in late 1980, in Paramount-CIC's *The Hunter*, the story of a modern bounty hunter who still believes in and achieves the final object of bringing his man in – dead or alive. While highly unlikely, the fast pace of the story's direction by Buzz Kulik and the injection of a steady vein of humour made it all very well worth while.

Even more unlikely – in fact downright impossible! – was the story told in Universal-CIC's *The Island*, in which nosey newsman Michael Caine gets caught and tortured by a band of bloodthirsty pirates who have survived, unsuspected for centuries, on their small Caribbean island, their forays from which have bolstered the legends of the mysterious vanishing ships in the so-called 'Bermuda Triangle'.

A rather weird mixture of sex, sadism and music, James Toback's Gala release *Fingers* had a certain style as it related the story of an unbalanced New York gangster's son who divides his time between doing his father's dirty work (viciously beating up dad's debtors) and practising for his hoped-for Carnegie Hall piano-playing debut. Harvey Keitel played the part for all – and considerably more – than it was worth. The debtor 'paying-up' is Lenny Montana.

Weird was the right word, too, to describe UA's *The Final Countdown* in which Kirk Douglas as the CO of a modern American aircraft carrier suddenly finds they have broken through into time-past and can alter history by alerting the US Navy of the impending Japanese Fleet's attack on Pearl Harbour! Good old-fashioned hokum, with lots of fine flying sequences.

Roy Scheider (*centre right*) in Bob Fosse's semi-autobiographical Columbia musical *All That Jazz*, which was fine as long as it stayed that way and followed the fun and games of show business but became a lot less steady on its feet when it strayed off into rather over-simple symbolism. With star Scheider in this spectacular number: Leland Palmer, Ben Vereen and Ann Reinking.

There were also some pretty spectacular musical numbers in Alan Parker's MGM-CIC release, *Fame*, which tried (without any sensational success) to combine documentary and movie-musical styles in a story about some half-dozen pupils of the Manhattan High School of Performing Rights from their acceptance to graduation. Here the pupils spill out into the street for a pretty unlikely – and very loud – musical rave-up. And marring the proceedings more than somewhat, the dreary repetitious use of four-letter words in the dialogue.

A roller-skating tour of New York's famous Greenwich Village by tower Valerie Perrine and skater Steve Guttenberg was one of the more spectacular numbers in EMI's bright and lively rock musical *Can't Stop the Music*, which recaptured something of the atmosphere of the classic old screen musicals and included civilised and four-letter-word-free dialogue to enhance its wide all-ages appeal.

Dan Ackroyd and John Belushi as Universal-CIC's *The Blues Brothers*, which was a pretty wild comedy with music relying for a lot of its laughs on the hardly uproarious antics of Belushi and the destruction of vast numbers of motor cars – an ever increasing, misguided fad of Hollywood producers. One of the best things in the film was the appearance of that great veteran of jazz and 'scat' singing, Cab Calloway – seen *right*.

Though he was balanced enough to escape the tragic ambition that has ruined so many of his comic fellows – the hankering after intellectual achievement and dramatic fame (the old saying about the clown wanting to play Hamlet is based on proven truth) – there is no doubt that the late Peter Sellers saw something deeper than his usual screen role in Lorimar-ITC's *Being There*, the amusing story of a very intellectually limited gardener whose wise comments about the plants he tends are taken up to Presidential heights (Melvyn Douglas played the President, as the judgments and forecasts of a sage, and accordingly take him towards the White House hot seat itself!) A beautiful penultimate performance by Sellers in a witty, satirical movie.

Universal-CIC's *Xanadu* was Olivia Newton-John's second movie, in which she played a Greek Goddess who comes down to earth to do good turns to restless young artist Michael Beck, (*left*) and frustrated older (business) man Gene Kelly.

The only real interest in Orion/Warners' *The Fiendish Plot of Dr Fu Manchu* was that it was Peter Sellers' final performance, for the movie showed something of the way it had been dogged by bad luck (and other detriments) during production. But there were some gloriously funny individual sequences in the uneven whole, one of which was this preparation – with assistant Helen Mirren – of the elixir which keeps the 168-year-old Dr Fu fiendishly ticking over.

GTO's *Breaking Glass* was really a show case for composer-singer Hazel O'Connor, playing a pub group lead vocalist who rises to fame and fortune, is exploited, cracks up and at last begins to come to terms with life. Her remarkable punk-style make-up, and her rebellious songs gave this tired old story something of a new impetus. The sax player was Jonathan Pryce, and he contributed a memorable supporting performance.

Real punk was the motivation of Virgin Films' *The Great Rock 'n' Roll Swindle*, a compilation of various live performances by Sid Vicious and his notorious Sex Pistols group.

Brent Walker's *McVicar* told the basically factual but considerably fictionalised story of the notorious criminal of that name – played by Roger Daltrey – who managed to break out of Durham's top security jail (*top left*) to continue his crime career but when finally recaptured by the police turned to writing as a safer job. While on the run a pal – Georgina Hale – offers him shelter and service. (*Top right*)

A little bit of Orgy in Bob Guccione's large, lavish, star-studded, controversial sex extravaganza *Caligula*, adapted from an original screenplay by Gore Vidal. This concentrated considerably on the less pleasant side of Roman history, and caused cinema censors to break out into a cold sweat wherever it was shown; though after some initial uproar it settled down to make a lot of money during its premier London run.

Roger Moore and Gregory Peck were among the stars of Euan Lloyd's Lorimar-Rank release *The Sea Wolves*, a story of an almost unknown and certainly quite incredible – though true – mission carried out by some India-based veterans of the Calcutta Light Horse Regiment who managed to sink a German spy ship interned, but dangerously active, in a Portuguese harbour during a time when in the last war British shipping was taking a terrible beating from German U-boats. Lots of excitement, tension, stars, and polish, added up to highly entertaining hokum.

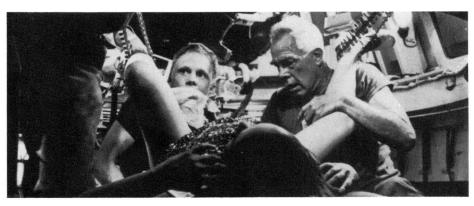

One of the best and certainly funniest scenes in ITC's *The Big Red One* was the one in which the tough old sergeant (Lee Marvin) and some members of his youthful squad take time out from World War Two in order to deliver a local girl's baby in their tank. A mixture of bloody battles and lighter scenes, such as this, the movie was apparently based on veteran director-writer Samuel Fuller's own war-time experiences.

John Travolta as the farm boy who comes to the big city – Houston – to make his (oily) fortune in Paramount-CIC's *Urban Cowboy*, which was essentially a boy-meets-girl story seen against a Country-and-Western background.

One of the more unpleasant films of the period was William Friedkin's (he both wrote and directed) Lorimar-ITC release, *Cruising*, all about a New York cop (Al Pacino) working under-cover in order to find the killer responsible for a series of brutal homosexual murders.

David Peterson as the *Skip Tracer*, or
ruthless debt collector, in the
remarkable Canadian production of
that title which, made in twenty-eight
days on a shoestring budget by
director-writer-editor Zale Dalen, was
a marvellous example of how top-class
films *can* still be made without vast
expenditure. The movie richly
deserved its many international
awards. (A Contemporary Films
release in Great Britain.)

A similarly brilliant example of modest-budget movie-making was another Contemporary release, this time from South Africa, *Marigolds in August*, which told a moving tale about the friction between an old, black gardener and the hungry, workless youngster who appears on the scene and tries to capture some of the old fellow's jealously guarded jobs. Winston Ntshona (who has since died) played the old man, John Kani the young, and screenwriter Athol Fugard (*right*) contributed a delightful performance as the philosophical old 'coloured' snake-catcher.

Once again the Australian films that reached us were among the most impressive movies of the year, from any source. A good example was the Enterprise release *Breaker Morant*, the story of a court martial of three members of the Bushveldt Carbineers towards the end of the Boer War, when they were accused of murdering a captured Boer prisoner and in their defence claimed they were acting on the unwritten orders of Lord Kitchener. A fine script, assured direction and an outstanding performance by Jack Thompson (*left*) as the men's defence lawyer, strongly supported by Edward Woodward, Bryan Brown, and Lewis Fitz-Gerald, added up to an outstanding and convincing, little-known chapter of the history of an almost forgotten war.

A wonderfully effective, modestly made, example of suspense movie was Bordeaux Films International's Australian import *The Long Weekend*, a story of a not too happily married couple who drive to the beach for a camping holiday – not knowing they are driving to their deaths. Without any subsidiary characters, John Hargreaves and Briony Behets had to carry the entire film on their shoulders – which they did most creditably.

Another modestly made gem, one of the most completely visually poetic films of the year, was UA's *The Black Stallion*, the story of a boy (Kelly Reno) and the horse he loves who are the only survivors of a shipwreck and are stranded on a small desert island where each saves the other's life.

Claimed to be the first 'American' Martial Arts movie, Warners' Golden Harvest release *The Big Brawl* was a brutal and violent but also sometimes quite funny film showcasing the fighting skills of young Jackie Chan, seen in a story of a mass, nothing-barred struggle for big prize supremacy in Chicago in the 1930s.

Space epics came a lot fewer and further between this year, but we did have George Lucas's second 'Star Wars' episode from Fox, *The Empire Strikes Back*, which was sub-titled 'Star Wars Episode 5' (the original *Star Wars* movie now carrying the additional title tag of 'Episode 4') all of which underlines Mr Lucas's announced plans to make many more additions to the series, not necessarily to be made or presented in correct sequence. All the old favourites were to be found in the new film including the tin soldiers and black-hearted (and visored) villain (*above left*), laser-beam duels (*below left*) and that comic scene-stealing duo of Artoo Detoo and See Threepio (*above right*). Big, expensive, spectacular fun.

Island chieftain Dayton Ka'ne and Mia Farrow, as the US Governor's daughter determined to marry him, are the only buffeted survivors of the *Hurricane* which gave the film its climax and title. A De Laurentiis–ITC re-make of the big 1937 success. (*Near right*)

Newcomer Eric Roberts as the Gypsy Crown Prince not too keen on accepting his heritage in Paramount-CIC's *King of the Gypsies*. (*Far right*)

Columbia's *Wholly Moses!* looked very much like America's answer to Britain's Monty Python satire on religion, and certainly achieved the same kind of tastelessness. In this scene, would-be prophet Dudley Moore is confronted by Angel-of-the-Lord Paul Sand. (*Near right*)

Maybe he's not easy to recognise but that second rider from the right is Burt Lancaster, playing the leader of the Doolin-Dalton gang in Hemdale's semi-comic Western *Cattle Annie and Little Britches*, the story of two teenage girls who insist on joining in with the gang's law breaking. (*Far right*)

Far more serious, UA's *The Long Riders* was the story of the combining of several infamous gangs in a series of raids and hold-ups. Its main bid for novelty was director Walter Hill's gimmick of having actor brothers play the outlaw brothers. Thus James Keach as Jesse James (*left*) and Stacy Keach as brother Frank (*centre*) in this scene. *Right*: Randy Quaid.

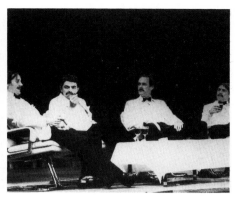

The mass suicide scene in Barber Rose International's *Guyana – Crime of the Century*, a rather tasteless reconstruction of the headline-making news story about 800 followers of a Rev. James Johnson's religious sect who died by their own – or others' – hands when the unhappy conditions of the commune were seen by a visiting United States congressman – who was murdered to try and prevent the leak.

The – very well – British made, Osiris-released *Babylon* was a gloomy picture of London's black community which, made on a small budget and entirely on location, presented the cops as brutally biased, the black youngsters as thugs, the young hero unable to obtain suitable work, and all this against a background of racial prejudice, hopeless housing conditions and a simmering, threatening violence. (*Top left*)

Tigon's *The Secret Policeman's Ball* was a straightforward film record, made on the spot, of the 1979 Amnesty International stage Comedy Gala with (*left to right*) comics Michael Palin, Rowan Atkinson, John Cleese and Terry Jones in the cast of an uneven but spottily brilliant production. (*Top right*)

Trevor Howard made the most of his role in Charisma's crazy, often crude, and certainly lively screen version of the Vivian Stanshall creation, *Sir Henry at Rawlinson End*, which had previously enjoyed considerable success as radio serial, record album and, most recently, book. (*Centre left*)

John Maybury models evening wear as Miss Winscale Nuclear Reactor in Tigon's *The Alternative Miss World*, a straightforward film record of Andrew Logan's fun show presented on London's Clapham Common in 1978. (*Centre right*)

A family fight in Orion/Warner's *The Great Santini*, with the US Marine air ace martinet father (Robert Duvall) losing his temper with his argumentative son (Michael O'Keefe) and being restrained by his wife (Blythe Danner, *left*) and younger daughter (Julie Anne Haddock, *right*). A well observed study of the inability of most people to communicate even with their own families, it showed that beneath all the superficial friction there is often a deep if awkwardly or even unexpressed love.

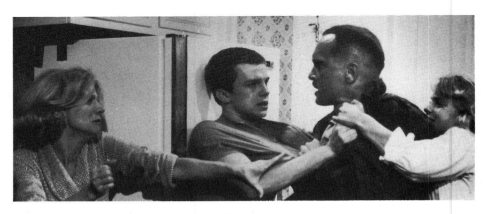

More family misunderstandings and consequent friction in Fox's *Tribute*, the father in this case being an irritating but loving theatrical press agent father (played by Jack Lemmon, a magnificent performance, repeating his stage success in the role) who finds it impossible to break down his son's (Robby Benson) disapproval of him even when he learns that his father is dying. Also contributing a fine performance, Lee Remick as the ex-wife who retains a deep affection for her former husband.

In the entire history of the movies few sequels have measured up to their originals and Universal/CIC's *More American Graffiti* proved no exception. Following up the stories of the several youngsters so delightfully presented in the original *American Graffiti* film, it showed them coming to terms with more adult life and its problems, including the Vietnam war. Among the young players involved, Paul Le Mat, Cindy Williams, Candy Clark and Charles Martin Smith.

Prisoner Robert Redford reveals to a discomforted predecessor that he is in fact the new prison governor and has been investigating the corrupt jail conditions the hard way, by posing as a prisoner. A performance of some considerable integrity, it lifted Fox's *Brubaker* into a bracket otherwise unlikely to have been reached.

Interrogation in space . . . in Orion/Warner's somewhat minor addition to the Space Wars cycle, *Battle Beyond the Stars*. Plenty of the now familiar space hardware, rainbows of colour, fierce gun-ship fights in a struggle between black-hearted villains, heroic heroes, and assorted robot retainers added up to something of a treat for junior – or any parent with a young heart and taste for cartoon-strip-style fun.

Ernest Borgnine gives orders and saves the life of his men midst shot and shell in ITC's routine re-make of the renowned Erich Maria Remarque anti-war novel *All Quiet on the Western Front,* which long ago provided material for one of the screen's all-time classics when directed by Lewis Milestone in 1930.

Another re-make, but this time of a very different kind of subject, was Columbia's re-filming of H. de Vere Stacpoole's charming story *The Blue Lagoon*, with Brooke Shields (the girl who made her sensational debut in Louis Malle's controversial *Pretty Baby*) and athletic newcomer Christopher Atkins as the girl and boy wrecked on a desert island and learning all the facts of life during the years they are stranded there.

White mercenary leader Shannon – Christopher Walken at the wheel of the Jeep – takes his men into battle against the black dictator's troops in UA's *Dogs of War*, a straightforward adaptation of the Frederick Forsyth novel about an international cartel's self-interested interference with the political affairs of a mis-ruled African state.

Big business was again the villain of the piece in MGM/CIC's *The Formula*, in which the oil cartel's large and expansive chief executive (Marlon Brando) is quite ready to include murder in his determination to retain the Nazi secret formula of making synthetic oil fuel from coal. The story, apparently, did have a basis of fact although it emerged on the screen confusingly unlikely.

In a year noteworthy for the number of star actors who made their directorial debuts, James Caan achieved a pretty good standard with his MGM/CIC release *Hide in Plain Sight*, which was founded on a true story about an ever-loving father who unrelentingly tracks down his children who, along with their mother and her new husband, have been spirited away by government agents in order to protect the man from possible revenge dangers.

Pamela Sue Martin suffers from an attack by the corrupt prison wardress in Barber Rose's *The Lady in Red*, the story of a naive young farm girl who in the Roaring Twenties went to Chicago and became the girl-friend of the period's Public Enemy No. 1, John Dillinger, and when he was shot to death at her side by the cops, went into the bank-raiding business on her own account.

ITC's *Raise the Titanic* deserved something of a better fate than it had, for although a rather fanciful tale about the salvaging of the famous old wreck when the Americans get the idea that some advanced atomic secrets are hidden somewhere in the hold (a premise shared by the Russians, who do their best to thwart the 'raisers') it was very well done, quite spectacular and reasonably tense. Among the technical crew of the expedition, Jason Robards (*centre*).

By far the best thing about Fox's *The Stunt Man* was Peter O'Toole's bravura portrait of a ruthless film director whose machinations include the harbouring of a young criminal on the run in order to blackmail him into attempting various stunts the like of which have already killed his predecessor. These stunts were brilliantly staged and gave an extra dimension to an uneven but intermittently brilliant movie.

Performance, too, was the most outstanding quality of EMI's otherwise not so outstanding *Times Square*, with two girl newcomers, Trini Alvarado and Robin Johnson, both giving very promising performances as 'The Sleaze Sisters', contrastingly backgrounded young rebels against society. The story's odd ethical standpoint, and far too much use of four-letter words, couldn't spoil the obvious talent of the two girls.

Osiris's *Dance Craze*, was obviously firmly aimed at the younger Pop generation, with its collection of recordings of a number of live performances by various groups, such as that illustrated – Bad Manners.

One of the outstanding performances of the year and certainly the best thing she has yet achieved on the screen was Sissy Spacek's playing of real-life Country-and-Western star Loretta Lynn in Universal-CIC's *Coal Miner's Daughter*, in which she was utterly convincing as she aged and changed from the ill-dressed little daughter of a coal miner working in the primitive conditions of the Kentucky hills (*bottom left*) to the sophisticated and successful singing star with her legions of loyal fans (for this performance she won the 1981 Oscar).

Yet another re-working of a famous old film was EMI's *The Jazz Singer*, with Neil Diamond now in the old Al Jolson role of the cantor's son who refuses to follow in his old dad's footsteps and goes off to find success with more popular songs. Laurence Olivier played the horrified old father who sees his son as going to the devil.

Alan Arkin, in *Simon*, as the brain-washed human guinea-pig, the object of an experiment by a group of American professors who persuade him he's a visitor from another planet and when this idea is suitably implanted in him, sit back and watch the results and public reaction.

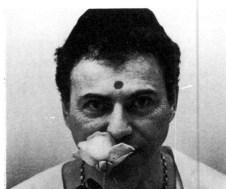

Friendly enemies KGB agent Herbert Lom and his CIA counterpart Walter Matthau take a tot together in Avco-Embassy's *Hopscotch*, a highly unlikely but consistently amusing comedy-thriller about a disillusioned American agent who responds to his sacking after a life-time in the spy business by arranging to publish his explosive memoirs, writing and delivering them chapter by chapter as he keeps one step ahead of the department's 'hit men' ordered to keep him quiet, quickly and finally! The role provided Matthau an opportunity to add one more delightful addition to his diverse personal portrait gallery.

Though well covered here, the ladies are some of the cast of New Realm's amusing *The First Nudie Musical*, which was a comedy, with music, about the making of a pornographic movie.

One of the more consistently pleasant films of the period, Fox's *My Bodyguard*, was about a smart young lad's novel answer to some of the more brutal and bullying pupils at the new school he attends when he switches from private to public education. It was all so heart-warming to see the youngster – played with charm by fifteen-year-old Chris Makepeace – finally get his own back.

Below the usual Disney high standards, *The Devil and Max Devlin* was a mildly amusing story concerning Elliot Gould's bargain with the Devil to sign up three willing souls for Satan in return for his own escape from purgatory. In this scene Gould tries to get the signature of Julie Budd while dark devil's advocate Bill Cosby looks on with interest.

With other male stars turning directors, delightful Goldie Hawn swung the changes by turning producer of her own Warner comedy release *Private Benjamin*. The movie stood the old story about the naive Army recruit's misadventures on its head by making the rookie a lady – Goldie! And underlying all the fun – mainly provided by Miss Hawn's performance – was a more serious theme about all men, including those hand-kissing continental charmers, being male chauvinist pigs at heart. With Goldie in this scene, mother Barbara Barrie.

Eagle's *Penitentiary* was a very rough, very tough prison drama about a young black unjustly convicted of killing a white man who literally learns to fight his way out of jail – legitimately.

Barber International's *Middle Age Crazy* was a mild little comedy about a man who gets the forty-year-itch but eventually learns that for lasting happiness it is necessary to control it. Bruce Dern played the itchy one, Ann-Margret his wife.

The killer about to strike again – in Barber Rose International's *Prom Night*, a thriller in which a crazed murderer puts a bloody damper on the jollities of the high school's annual dance as he lurks in the shadows picking off his selected victims.

More mayhem in Alpha Film's *The Exterminator*, which had Christopher George as the ex-Vietnam war veteran who takes awful revenge on the gangster killers of his black pal in such various horrid ways as forcing one of them through a meat-grinder!

Sunn Classic's *The Bermuda Triangle* was a semi-documentary based on Charles Berlitz's book about the strange and long term series of disappearances in that part of the Caribbean of men and ships – and airplanes, too. The very various explanations put forward included seafarers (Clement St George in this case) being hypnotised by visiting UFOs!

Somewhat less violent thrills and certainly more easily watchable was Warner's extremely good Australian thriller *The Chain Reaction*, which had as its highly topical theme the potential dangers of a leak of lethal atomic waste. About to enter the decontamination chamber, husband and wife, Steve Bisley and Anna-Maria Winchester.

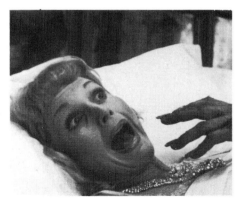

Understandably, Carol Lynley isn't too happy about that threatening, horrid hand in the third adaptation of the famous old whodunnit thriller *The Cat and the Canary* (Gala).

His sourest movie to date, a comedy which took a sidesweep at some of the people who have helped him to his present top star position, Woody Allen's United Artists release *Stardust Memories* was intermittently both visually (it was in black-and-white) and verbally amusing as it commented obliquely on the 'penalties' of success, and it all looked very much like another delving into Allen's own experiences. Co-star was Charlotte Rampling.

Katrina Hodiak, Sean Young and Nancy New in Contemporary's *Jane Austen in Manhattan*, another original effort from that remarkable international trio of moviemakers, director James Ivory, producer Ismail Merchant and writer Ruth Prawer Jhabvala. This time their fancy was to build a fictional story of stage rivalries and romance on the factual sale a few years back of the manuscript of a novel written by Miss Austen when she was only twelve years old.

The path from Europe to Hollywood success is strewn with the bleaching bones of the many failures and the highest rate of non-success has been in the ranks of directors. But France's Louis Malle proved to be one of the few triumphant exceptions, making the transition from his native France to adopted America first with the controversial but memorable *Pretty Baby* and then with the Enterprise Pictures release *Atlantic City*, in which against a marvellously atmospheric background of the East Coast playground he presented a series of remarkable portraits, drawing some outstanding performances from his cast, including one of the finest, in-depth performances ever by Burt Lancaster as the 'retired' small-time gangster who, to his own surprised delight, commits a double murder in order to protect his girl-friend – Susan Sarandon.

Also socially concerned with the subject of prostitution, Mainline Pictures' *Prostitute* was the story of a Birmingham whore who goes to London to make more money but soon finds herself becoming involved in the seamiest side of the business. Eleanor Forsythe played the role.

Carolyn Pickles played the murdered prostitute in *Brothers and Sisters* which, made on a minute budget-grant from the British Film Institute, was an interesting if not quite successful effort to tell two intertwining stories illustrating the theme that for the girl's murder all men must share the guilt!

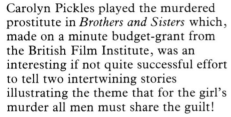

Paul Michael Glaser – of TV's 'Starsky and Hutch' fame – made his feature film debut as an experimental psychiatrist whose patients meet violent deaths when their 'cures' fail in Barber Rose's *Phobia*, a sort of whodunnit, well below the standard we have come to expect from director John Huston.

The lady with the gun, and every intention of using it (as indeed she does several times with devastating effect) is Gena Rowlands, who gave a magnificent performance in husband John Cassavetes's Columbia release *Gloria*, as a woman who fights back against the gangsters with their own weapons. The film was easily the most commercially successful of all this director's work to date.

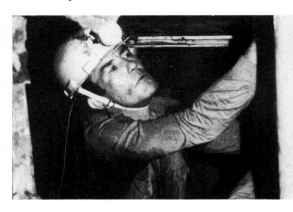

'Brains' Albert Finney and 'bent' architect assistant Martin Sheen bore their way upward from the London sewers into the bank vault with its treasures in Brent Walker's thriller *Loophole*, a story strongly paralleling the facts of a French gang break-in to a Nice bank some years back, when they successfully helped themselves at leisure to a multi-million fortune. But the French didn't have to contend with the storm waters that provide the excitement of the escape (*centre*) and several other unexplained puzzles in the movie.

A minor film in terms of budget and pretention but a major achievement of film art, Richard Pearce's *Heartland* (Contemporary) was a marvellously real and convincing story – based on two books written by a woman who went out West at the beginning of the century – about a plump and cheerful cook-housekeeper to a dour Scots immigrant farmer on the dreary Wyoming plains. A completely different off-beat kind of Western, its highlight was a terrible winter which kills off half the farmer's stock and nullifies ten years' work. Shown in this group, the main characters *left to right:* Lilia Skala as the wise old neighbour, Conchata Ferrell as the housekeeper, Rip Torn, the farmer, Megan Folsom as the small daughter and Barry Primus as the hired hand.

Robert De Niro gave of his best – and won a 1981 Oscar – as the abrasive and unpleasant character, champion boxer Jake La Motta in UA's *Raging Bull*. Though the actual fight scenes were few they were explosive both in terms of sight and sound.

Eddie Constantine, Helen Mirren and Bob Hoskins line up against a London Thames-side background in Handmade Films' *The Long Good Friday*, a tough and violent but critically highly acclaimed British gangster thriller.

Agatha Christie's unconventional crime investigator Miss Marple (played on this occasion by Angela Lansbury) points out some interesting landmarks to her Scotland Yard Inspector nephew Edward Fox (*far left*) in EMI's *The Mirror Crack'd*, a typical Christie whodunnit set, in this instance, in and around the local manor house taken over by some moviemakers, among which are plenty of suspects. Among them, director Rock Hudson – flanked by his two stars, Kim Novak and Elizabeth Taylor.

Hero John Terry gets the better of villain – and brother – Jack Palance thanks to his Excalibur-like magic sword in Chips/ITC's *Hawk the Slayer*, a fairy tale with so much violence that it seemed rather dubious entertainment to offer the kids.

Last year it was wars in space that occupied a great deal of moviemaking attention, this year the celluloid band wagon has been bloody horror and we've been subjected to a whole series of rather similar movies in which, generally, teenagers suffer horrible, eye-averting fates at the hands (cleaver, knife and whatever) of psychotic killers. And such films have been making a lot of puzzling money: who wants to pay to be sickened? Typical was UA's *Motel Hell*, in which the motel owner uses some of his guests to provide the famed piquancy of his pies, storing his victims – with vocal chords severed to keep them quiet – buried up to their necks until he needs some more supplies! Attacking victim Nina Axelrod, chain-saw-wielding, porkine-masked villain Rory Calhoun.

Rightly claimed as sensational, and certainly a sensational commercial success, David Cronenberg's *Scanners* was a rather horrid horror story about an elite with telepathic powers who use it to get their own way, ending with a dual between two similarly trained killers in which eyes pop out of their sockets and veins swell to leaking point. Duelling to the death, Michael Ironside and Stephen Lack.

Prepared to defend herself from the unknown menace, Karen White in Barber-International's *The Howling*, the latest addition to the cinema's considerable stock of werewolf celluloid, and it was well up to standard.

The who-can-it-be? killer strikes again and another teenager bites the (coal) dust down the mine where they've gone to have fun in Paramount/CIC's *My Bloody Valentine*, in which the killer tears out the hearts of his victims and sends them to the sheriff as tasteful red-ribbon-wrapped gifts!

The happy beginning and the awful end to a 'dare' when four youngsters decide to spend a night in a fair sideshow and are there trapped, hunted down and murdered one by one by a mad mutant. *The Funhouse* (a Universal-CIC release).

Lovely young American Egyptologist Lesley-Anne Down has her first glimpse of the golden boy statue which is at the root of all the adventure that follows in Orion/Warner's *The Sphinx*, a thriller, with fascinating Egyptian backgrounds, which advances steadily to incredibility but was always worth watching – as was Miss Down.

Marvellously – and so, unfortunately, topical – Bordeaux International's *The Kidnapping of the President* was premiered in Britain within a day or so of the attempt on President Reagan's life. Terrorist Miguel Fernandes takes the opportunity of the US President's (played brilliantly by Hal Holbrook) visit to Canada to kidnap and force him into a van full of hair-trigger explosives, where he holds him while bargaining for the vast cash ransom demanded. Two of Hollywood's Golden Age stars played supporting roles, Van Johnson and Ava Gardner (*far right*).

A jittery Dennis Lipscomb waits in his office and wonders when he'll be apprehended for the murder of the man who stole his bottles of milk and whose body he has hidden in an adjoining empty flat. There was something of an Edgar Allen Poe atmosphere in Mainline's *Union City*, a modest thriller which achieved its purpose in a black comedy way.

Christopher Reeve about to take off again in Salkind/Warner's *Superman II*, which continued the flying fun and thrills which made such an impact in the first 'Superman' film. In this episode our hero is up against three powerfully equipped nasties from Outer Space who decide when they arrive here that they'll stay around and take over the earth, preferably over Mr Reeve's dead body! Luckily our hero has something still up his sleeve, even if it's not immediately apparent from

the close-fitting uniform he dons whenever he changes from modest newspaper man to national hero.

Jack Nicholson (a very carefully measured but fascinating performance) and Jessica Lange (superbly sensual) shared top billing in Lorimar/ITC's *The Postman Always Rings Twice*, the fourth, and arguably best, filming of the James M. Cain story of over-riding sexual greed which leads to murder and final ironic retribution.

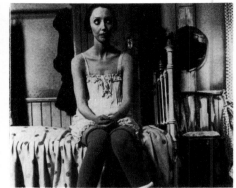

Another strip-cartoon favourite character brought to celluloid life was the famous spinach-powered, mighty-muscled E. C. Segar creation *Popeye*, played by Robin Williams – shown (*top left*) putting an end to Peter Bray's pugilistic pretentions. But the chief scorer in this Paramount/Disney release was Shelley Duvall, (*top right*) whose 'Olive Oyl' was a marvellously amusing creation.

A worried Roy Scheider, having had a message proving he's been followed from his New York home to Princeton University by his unknown enemy and is still threatened, asks Professor John Glover (hand-in-hand with Janet Margolin) to assist him in trying to unravel the puzzle in UA's thriller *The Last Embrace*.

Don Adams as the bumbling yet remarkably successful Secret Agent 86 is out-gunned and out-numbered in this scene from Universal/CIC's *The Nude Bomb*, a sort of James Bond spoof with lots of bizarre gadgets, weird effects and fast action.

Peter Ustinov as the oriental sleuth Chan in UA's *Charlie Chan and the Curse of the Dragon Queen*, a comedy whodunnit and a tribute to all those 'Chan' mysteries of the 1930s–1940s, when Warner Oland became famous as the always ultimately successful Chinese solver of deadly puzzles.

Small and getting smaller, Lily Tomlin as *The Incredible Shrinking Woman*, a comedy changed-sex re-hash of the same company's quarter-century ago science-fiction success *The Incredible Shrinking Man*. It was radiation that reduced *his* statue; it is supermarket detergents that trigger *her* vanishing trick.

Lily Tomlin again, this time as one of the three office workers – others, Dolly Parton and Jane Fonda – who get so fed-up with their intolerable boss that they kidnap him and hold him prisoner in his own house in Fox's thoroughly enjoyable comedy *Nine to Five*.

UA's *Foxes* presented a depressing picture of American youth, with its four girl pals (Cherie Currie, Jodie Foster, Marilyn Kagan and Kandice Stroh) devoted apparently to booze, dope and sex, not necessarily in that order! And only very occasionally did the film suggest that behind the superficial facade there might be a moral point to put across.

Richard Pryor and Gene Wilder getting their first glimpse of the jail to which they have been sentenced to work out their 125-year sentences (for a crime of which they are actually innocent) in Columbia's comedy *Stir Crazy* which, obviously erected around the talents of the two stars, mixed gags with giggles and far too many foul words.

Helen Burstyn – marvellous – as the very down-to-earth Kansas widow who after healing herself finds she has the gift to heal others in Universal/CIC's carefully balanced *Resurrection*, a splendid treatment of a difficult subject. This was one of several of the year's films that deserved a far wider showing than it had.

Long and slow and never particularly riveting, Barber International's *Inside Moves* was about a couple of cripples, pals who finally fall out over a girl. The trio were played by John Savage and Amy Wright and newcomer David Morse.

Universal-CIC's *Somewhere in Time* was a pleasant throwback to the romantic cinema, with Christopher ('Superman') Reeve as the young man who falls in love with the photograph of a beautiful girl (Jane Seymour) and travels back through time to find her.

Tatum O'Neal and Richard Burton share a chequered Spring-Autumn romance in Bordeaux International's Canadian production *Circle of Two*, with artist Burton finding the girl's parents understandably less than happy about the liaison.

The warm and charming performances of Mary Beth Hurt and John Heard, under writer-director Joan Micklin Silver's guiding hands, overcame the rather dubious moral of the story about the young man's passion for a married woman and his unceasing efforts to woo her away from her husband and child, in UA's *Head Over Heels*.

With something of the situation but little of the finesse of *Jules et Jim*, Orion/Warner's *Heart Beat* was a story of a friendly human triangle, with Sissy Spacek sharing her favours between author John Heard (*left*) and the less stable Nick Nolte; and the background was America's post-war 'Beat' generation.

CIC's *Ordinary People* marked the quite sensationally successful – artistically and commercially, winning several Oscars including one for best directed film of the year – directing debut of Robert Redford. A story of family trauma it starred Donald Sutherland and Mary Tyler Moore as the parents of Timothy Hutton (seen with his psychiatrist Judd Hirsch) who blames himself for his brother's drowning in a boating accident and causes all sorts of family problems by his guilt complex, allied to the fact that his mother in her heart also blames him for the loss of her favourite.

Black and white victims of the Klu Klux Klan shake hands and decide to fight on the same side in Enterprise's *Freedom Road*, a story of the post-Civil War American Deep South, in which Muhammed Ali gave a dignified performance as the negro driven beyond endurance by the white stealers of his land. Kris Kristofferson played the white neighbour.

Writer William Peter Blatty (he wrote *The Exorcist*) had a far less great success with his debut behind the camera, and his *The Ninth Configuration* (ITC) was a very odd and not very pleasant story about a crowd of ex-Vietnam war problem soldiers housed in a gloomy, thunderstorm-assaulted old castle where the new psychiatrist is eventually revealed as a notorious (martial) killer – played gloomily by Stacy Keach.

So far CIC's *Nijinsky* has had a pretty poor showing, which makes it another of the sadly undervalued movies of the year. With its marvellous Edwardian decor, visual beauty and very good taste, it was a fascinating picture of the love affair between the great ballet impresario Diaghilev (played by Alan Bates) and his star Nijinsky (George de la Pena – debut); and the tragic results that followed the break-up of the affair.

Adulation. The new pop star sensation is artfully launched to screaming success in UA's *The Idolmaker*, a film about the way that these youthful idols are manufactured. It had the factual background provided by a man who should really know about this sort of thing – Bob Marucci, who after himself managing a stable of such performers was employed to advise the makers of the movie.

Pool star James Coburn shows a pretty pupil how it should be done in the Rank Release *The Baltimore Bullet*, a mixture of comedy and drama about the rivalry between Mr Coburn and Omar Sharif, both anxious to prove to the world that *they* are the greatest wizard of the cue.

Third screen version of the renowned Frances Hodgson Burnett novel, Rosemont/GTO's *Little Lord Fauntleroy* was another superbly staged period piece with little Ricky Schroeder as the young milord who suddenly finds himself switched from Brooklyn slum to English Stately Home on the orders of his grandfather, who decides the little lad shall be trained to take over the Earldom when he dies. Alec Guinness had to pull out one of his most polished performances

to meet the challenge of the remarkable little lad with the blonde hair and blue-eyed charm. A well written script, witty direction, and fine acting added up to one of the more superior movies of the year.

British films were few and far between this year but at least some of the few were as good as they come: notably

Fox's *Chariots of Fire*, a splendid re-creation of the motivation and eventual success, for divergent reasons of Olympic medal winning star runners Harold Abrahams and Eric Liddell, the first running to avenge slights on his Jewish blood and the second because he felt he should develop his idea that he had God's gift. Several comparative newcomers to screen stardom gave very impressive performances, including Ben Cross and Ian Charleson as the runners.

Another attempt to emulate the classic *Jules et Jim* situation in terms of America today, Fox's *Willie and Phil* was a story about a triangle friendship between a girl and two boys (Margot Kidder, Michael Ontkean and Ray Sharkey) which eventually gets too tangled to be sustained. All highly immoral but not unamusing and certainly nicely performed.

Usually Neil Simon's screenplays are adaptations of his stage successes but Columbia's *Seems Like Old Times* was written directly for the screen and very wittily funny it was, too, with its crazy story about the sudden arrival at a lady lawyer's (Goldie Hawn) home of her former husband (Charles Grodin) who hopes she will help him out of the difficult position of being wrongly accused of bank robbery – just at the moment that her current husband is about to become Attorney General.

Paul McCartney leads his 'Wings' Group in Miracle's *Rock Show*, a straightforward recording of a concert that the Group gave to 70,000 fans at Seattle as a grand finale to their ten-country tour in 1976.

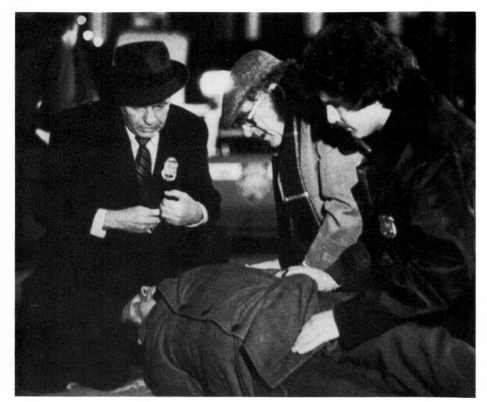

Confrontation, between Charles Bronson (*below left*) as a trapper framed for murder and the 'Mountie' who has the task of bringing him in (Lee Marvin with assisting Andrew Stevens, in Fox's *Death Hunt*, a chase story based on one of the more famous Royal Canadian Mounted Police cases.

After a decade away from the screen Frank Sinatra chose the same kind of detective role for his return to it that had brought him success in the late 1960s (*The Detective, Lady in Cement* etc) and showed in CIC's *The First Deadly Sin* that the intervening years had taken little toll of his appearance – and none at all of his expertise – as he played the New York police officer who on the edge of retirement tracks down a killer and makes sure that justice shall be done, even if not seen to be done. (*Above*)

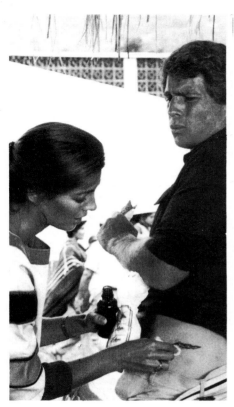

Oooh, it hurts! Ryan O'Neal gets first-aid treatment from lovely Anne Archer after being winged by a bullet in ITC's large-scale adventure spectacular *Green Ice*, the title referring to the vast hoard of emeralds that the lady's man friend Omar Sharif keeps guarded in his tower and which O'Neal plans to steal, with the help of a trio of hot air balloons!

Lots of fun, loud pop, and some genuine thrills in ITC's entertaining *The Monster Club*, a sort of spoof on all those Draculean epics, in which nice old vampire Vincent Price relates three macabre stories to his friendly victim John Carradine, while they sip, respectively, their glasses of blood and tomato juice at a club for ghouls and suchlike.

Sylvester Stallone and Billy Dee Williams, as a sort of Starsky-and-Hutch team of undercover New York cops, who after combatting muggings, dope-pushers and the like are suddenly assigned to bring in, dead or alive, a notorious international terrorist who is in hiding on their 'patch'. And Universal-CIC's *Nighthawks* had plenty of action!

Bette Midler belts out 'The E Street Shuffle' with the backing of The Harlettes in Warner's *Divine Madness*, a recording of one – or more – of her stage shows.

Change partners and dance! Shirley MacLaine as the professor's wife who, when she learns of husband Anthony Hopkins's affair with one of his prettiest pupils (Bo Derek – in bed, and inviting), jumps into the arms of the first man who knocks at the door (Michael Brandon) and asks him to accompany her between the sheets in Warner's *A Change of Seasons*. In spite of its apparent immorality, in the end it appeared to be proving that such marital diversions merely lead to eventual unhappiness for all concerned.

Lauren Bacall (*centre*) as the famous stage star, with her ex-husband (James Garner) at her side, shows detective Hector Elizondo the threatening letters she has had from the fan whose obsession about her has developed into a murderous onslaught on those around her and now threatens her with death in Paramount-CIC's *The Fan*.

The old psychiatrist (Glenn Ford) tries to find out if his young patient (Melissa Sue Anderson) is guilty or not of the series of horrid murders of some of her fellow pupils which occur at her exclusive private school in Columbia's *Happy Birthday To Me*.

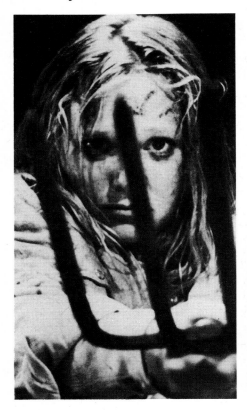

Recall those horrid murders of holiday-camping youngsters in *Friday the Thirteenth?* Well, in Paramount-CIC's *Friday the Thirteenth Part 2*, a new lot of hopeful teenagers move into the camp – and into a similarly unpleasant situation, with a crazy killer determined to decimate them.

007 Bond (Roger Moore) beats villain Krisatos (Julian Glover) in the finale of the climactic race to obtain the piece of highly secret equipment which in the wrong hands could control our fleet of atomic submarines and is the key to all the considerable action in UA's *For Your Eyes Only*, a vastly entertaining mixture of laughs, thrills and quite incredible stunts shown against superbly photographed international scenic backgrounds. The lady dashing to James's aid, by the way, is willowy French beauty Carole Bouquet.

The Continental Film

The films illustrated in the following pages are those from any country other than Great Britain, the United States of America, South Africa, Canada and Australia, which have been shown in this country between the beginning of July 1980 and end of June 1981. Wherever possible the name of the country of origin has been included (or is obvious) in the captions. Fuller details about these films will be found in the 'Releases of the Year in Detail' section on a later page.

One of the more unusual imports of the period was Chantal Akerman's Franco-Italian-German co-production (which she wrote as well as directed), *Les Rendezvous d'Anna,* a slow but consistently enthralling story of a film star (Aurore Clément) and her cross country train journeys while publicising her latest film – a remarkably memorable portrait of a lonely woman painted against cold and impersonal backgrounds.

The Continental Film

Another fine comedy performance by Jean Rochefort, paired with the ever-lovely Catherine Deneuve, helped to make the Yves Robert comedy *Courage – Let's Run – Courage Fuyons* one of the most amusing French films of the year. The story of the passionate love of a middle-aged Parisian chemist for a dazzling young international singing star, it threaded a slight skein of mystery through the fun.

Critically undervalued, at least in Great
Britain, Gala's *Peppermint Soda –
Diablo Menthe* was a remarkable first
film by Diane Kurys, who both wrote
and directed this modest production,
with its story (based on her own,
fifteen years since, school experiences),
of a year in the lives of two sisters,
beautifully played by Odile Michel and
Eléonore Klarwein. In France it
received the coveted accolade of the
Louis Delluc award for the best motion
picture of the year.

François Truffaut's *The Green Room –
La Chambre Verte* was very much a
personal film in that he wrote and
directed and then played the leading
role in it. It was a somewhat gloomy
but beautifully made portrait of man
obsessed with his dead wife. Not
exactly black film but very dark grey.

Very black indeed, however, and
surrealistic too, was Bertrand Blier's
(he both wrote and directed) Gala
release *Buffet Froid*. Without any
clearly observable story thread, it was
about a succession of motiveless
murders, centred on a new and almost
empty tower block of flats in which
the few tenants include a strange police
inspector (Bertrand's father, Bernard
(*below right*) and an unpredicatable
out-of-work waster (Gérard Depardieu
– with Genevieve Page) (*below left*).

Unfortunately dubbed (in the London-shown version) into awful Americanese, Bernard Queysanne's Gala release *Lover Boy* was an often amusing story of a lovely high-class Parisian call-girl (Mimsy Farmer) who after seducing a sixteen-year-old boy (Pascal Sellier) for the fun of it, then finds herself becoming uncomfortably romantically attached to him.

One of the year's best films, warm, funny and beautifully acted, Bertrand Tavernier's Curzon Films release *Une Semaine de Vacances*, was a basically serious and thoughtful story of a young woman teacher (Nathalie Baye) who suddenly has doubts about her life and work and takes a week off from school to think, during which she meets a charming cafe owner (the parent of one of her pupils – played beautifully by Philippe Noiret) who falls in love with her. And the marvellously atmospheric backgrounds were of Lyons in sad mid-winter.

Also one of the year's best, most unusual and imaginative French productions was Alain Resnais's *My American Uncle – Mon Oncle d'Amerique*, which marvellously successfully managed to blend a serious lecture on human behaviour by a famous French Professor – Henri Laborit – with a fascinating fictional story illustrating his points of argument. Among the players, Nicole Garcia and Roger Pierre.

Bulle Ogier with a couple of her clients in the long held-up (by censorship troubles) 1975 French film *Maîtresse*, which was a highly unpleasant story of a Madame who caters more especially for sado-masochistic clients – whose weird desires and satisfactions were often shown in revolting close-up. It was shown, understandably still without any censor's certificate, in London in 1980, imported by Mainline Pictures. (*Below left*)

After something like a seven-year absence from the cinema – during which time television had the dubious delight of his attention – Jean-Luc Godard turned up with a new film this year called *Slow Motion – Sauve Qui Peut (La Vie)* (an Artificial Eye release) in which he showed that he has not changed at all, presenting an almost incomprehensible mixture of political allusions, personal obsessions and sexual unpleasantness, which even his many fans must have found difficult to enthuse about. (*Below right*)

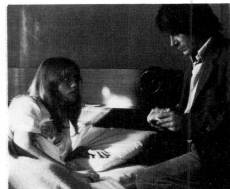

Made by the producers of that Italian 'sleeper' *The Last Snows of Spring*, GTO's *Last Feelings* was in the same vein, with its story about a 14-year-old boy who earns the opportunity to compete in the European Swimming Championships and actually wins his race before the terminal illness from which he is suffering takes its final toll. The lad was played by Carlo Lupo.

Franco Brusati's *Forget Venice – Dimenticare Venezia* was a remarkable film: a subtle, intricate and delicate story of a small and closed group of characters who for the most part are withdrawn from the present and feeding on memories of the past, while living in a lovely, isolated old house near Venice. A film of intense visual beauty: often in colour and shape like a fine old painting brought to life. Shy lovers are Mariangela Melato and David Pontremoli.

Hanna Schygulla as Maria in Rainer Werner Fassbinder's *The Marriage of Maria Braun,* which is probably his most commercial movie yet, with its story about a girl who, marrying a soldier during a Berlin air-raid, subsequently takes a Negro lover, this leading to a rather confected but dramatic ending.

Wolfgang Peterson's West German film *The Consequence – Die Konsequenz* (a Kampas Films release) was the story of a homosexual love affair between a pretty boy and an elder man (Ernst Hannawald and Jurgen Prochnow) which starts in a prison cell and continues in freedom. Though well made, it was rather tasteless and unconvincing in its apparent intention to suggest that the final tragedy is caused by social prejudice.

Tengiz Abuladze's Georgian/Russian movie *The Wishing Tree* was an initially ironically amusing but increasingly bitter story of a love drama set in a small village at the turn of the century; the cruel pillorying of a girl who rejects local social codes by taking a lover after being made to marry a man she does not love. The unfortunate girl was beautifully played by Lika Davtaradze. Made in 1976, released now by Artificial Eye Films.

One of the year's celluloid treasures from abroad was Goran Paskaljevic's satirical comedy from Yugoslavia, *Special Treatment*, a story about an official alcoholics' clinic run by a hypocritical doctor, who when he takes some of his 'cured' charges to a brewery to stage a temperance lecture/play, himself becomes inebriated, seduces the boss's secretary and then finds his whole cast is reeling drunk!

A superb and extremely daring Hungarian film, *Angi Vera* poked fun at rigid (and hypocritical) Communism with its public confessions, its clap-trap and petty party officials, all leading to general unhappiness. Angi's (Veronika Papp, *left*) confessing to her love affair with a married party official leads to his disgrace and her elevation to a job in journalism.

Though cut by twenty minutes since it was shown (and took first prize) at the Cannes Film Festival, Akira Kurosawa's *Kagemusha – The Shadow Warrior* (released in GB by Fox) still ran for 159 minutes and was one of the very few films to do so without for a moment boring the viewer. With a slim story – based on fact – about a sixteenth century warlord and the 'double' (Tatsuya Nakadi) he trains to take his place on occasion – it was a masterpiece of visual spendours, a sprawling yet always tightly controlled example of film art, with unforgettable scenes, marvellous use of colour and fine acting. A stunning movie about a bloodily brutal time and place.

Lady with a sword – and she shows how to wield it, too – in Osiris Films' *The Valiant Ones*, a superior martial arts film made in Hong Kong in 1974 with Mandarin dialogue, a story based on historic fact, and some delightfully balletic fight sequences.

A nasty moment for the villain in *A Touch of Zen*, a 1969 martial arts movie made in Hong Kong and Taiwan and set in the Ming Dynasty.

Movieworld's *Dynasty* claimed to be the first Kung Fu movie to be made in 3-D – with all the implications of suffering in the stalls!

A Franco-Italian-West German co-production, Joseph Losey's *Don Giovanni* was musically (with noteworthy isolated exceptions) pretty well faultless and though it sometimes strained painfully after contrived political straws it was, with its gorgeous backgrounds, a worthy example of movie-opera. The Don was played by Ruggero Raimondi, seen with Malcom King as Masetto.

Artificial Eye's *Loulou* was an odd and
disappointing French film in that
through Maurice Pialat's direction was
of a high level of technical excellence,
the content was less than interesting,
with its aimless and unelevating story of
a highly sexed lazy layabout and his silly
little girlfriend who works to keep him.
Isabelle Huppert and Gérard Depardieu
played the roles – and are seen in this,
one of the happier scenes in a generally
gloomy movie.

The highly dramatic, tragic end to Lina
Wertmüller's stark *Blood Feud* (ITC
release), with Sicilian widow Sophia
Loren crying over her two dead lovers;
the professor (Marcello Mastroianni,
right) and the gangster (Giancarlo
Giannini, *left*) both of whom have
returned to the island from long stays
abroad – the gangster from Chicago, the
professor from Rome – to fall in love
with the revengeful widow and, as her
supporters, fall out with the fascists.

One of the happier moments from Rank's Russian import, *The Orlovs*, when Anatoly Semyonov as the temporarily reformed drunkard is congratulated for his good work during the outbreak of cholera in the village. Smiling onlooker is his wife (Nina Ruslanova) who finds fulfilment in nursing the victims and through the experience rises to the position of village schoolteacher while her relapsed husband slides downhill. Superb performances, wonderful atmosphere and photography, plus fine direction by Mark Donskoy gave the film the full flavour of the Maxim Gorky story.

Another Russian import, Connoisseur/Contemporary's Andrei Tarkovsky film *Stalker*, was one of the most complex, confusing and at the same time fascinating films from any country to be seen this year. Something of a science-fiction story, it made endless, ambiguous ethical and social allusions in a story about three men who venture into the 'forbidden zone', moving tentatively towards a wrecked house where it is said wishes come true. Absorbing, and extremely demanding in that it needed constant, entire and intelligent concentration to be anything like understood. In this scene the trio are about to start their journey; the guide (the Stalker) Aleksandr Kaidanovsky; the writer Anatoly Solonitsyn and professor Nikolai Grinko.

The Continental Film

Cinegate's *The Blood of Hussain* was written, produced and directed by Jamil Dehlavi largely in Pakistan but had to be completed in Britain when after having to surrender his passport he managed to escape to this country: the trouble being that, although made before the military took over in Pakistan, Dehlavi critically pictured just that situation in his film, which told the story of a modern martyr who dies, like his namesake the Prophet Mohamad's nephew did in 680 AD, because he refuses to acknowledge what he considers to be an illegal regime.

Though the story was naively romantic and there were other weaknesses, Lino Brocks's *Manila* (from Cinegate) had charm and attractive performances; it also had a rarity value in being made in the Philippines. Rafael Roco played the country boy who follows his girl friend to the Big City to find her working in a brothel.

In the movie business success spells sequel and nobody could have failed to expect, after the worldwide triumph of the Franco-Italian *La Cage Aux Folles*, to see it quickly followed up by *La*

Cage Aux Folles II, released in this country by UA. This time around, the two homosexual partners of a Nice nighterie, played superbly by Michael Serrault and Ugo Tognazzi, become involved with secret agents, valuable microfilms and sundry other comical complications. Though the impact of the original No. 1 comedy was lost, No. 2 was still a very funny and thankfully tasteful comedy – and no prize for guessing who M. Serrault is impersonating in this scene.

Surprisingly, considering it was made in France by a Polish director with a German star and an international cast, Roman Polanski's screen adaptation of Thomas Hardy's very English novel *Tess of the d'Urbervilles* worked marvellously well. *Tess* (released in Britain by Columbia) was considerably enriched by the late Geoffrey Unsworth's camera-work (he died during the film's production and it was finished by Ghislain Cloquet, winning the 1981 Oscar for best photography) which was stunningly beautiful, as was new star Nastassia Kinski in the title role.

Bertrand Tavernier, who has made several very fine movies including the classic *Watchmaker of Lyon*, came up with a very peculiar piece indeed in his Contemporary French/West German release *Deathwatch*. Set in Scotland and in the future and made entirely on location there (in Glasgow and the Western Highlands, though never a Scots accent is heard and never a Scots player seen), it was about a man who agrees to have a TV camera implanted in his head so that a ghoulish producer can show on the screen the final days and agonies of a dying woman that the human camera, who intrigues to become her friend, watches in minute detail. And at least, if incredible, it was intelligent and contained plenty of ideas and wry comment. Germany's lovely Romy Schneider was the woman, Max Von Sydow the (Swedish) first husband she seeks final solace with, and the human camera was played by America's Harvey Keitel.

Julianna Nyako as the sixteen-year-old delinquent always trying to get away from the reformatory in the Hungarian film *Sunday Daughters – Vasarnapi Szulok* (Cinegate) and always being brought back to hateful incarceration.

In France and elsewhere his greatest commercial success, winner of ten of the dozen Cesars (France's equivalent to America's Oscars) and L'Academie Francaise's Grand Prix, Francois Truffaut's Gala release *The Last Metro – Le Dernier Metro* was set in Paris in 1942 and was about the efforts of a dedicated, Jewish, thespian to keep his 'Theatre Montmartre' open in spite of the Nazis, with most of the worry being borne by his non-Jewish wife, who has to do the business during the day, star on stage in the evening, join and comfort her hidden husband at night and try to avoid the amorous advances of her co-star; roles played by Catherine Deneuve and Gerard Depardieu.

There was plenty of bitter political comment (enough and strong enough to make it something of a miracle that it could have been made, and shown, in a Communist country) in Andrzej Wadja's Polish Artificial Eye release *Rough Treatment – Bez Znieczulenia*, which was all about an honest journalist whose comments during a TV interview bring subsequent official displeasure, loss of friends and wife, disillusion and death. Zbigniew Zapasiewicz played the victim, here musically accompanying his daughter.

In his latest (made in Germany) movie *From the Life of the Marionettes*, Ingmar Bergman once again meditated on the agony and stupidity of the human condition as he has so often done in his past films, but now presents his always stimulating ideas in a visually severe and unstimulating way, concentrating almost obsessively on close-ups of faces. The story into which he weaves his arguments is about an apparently sane man (Robert Atzoen, seen here during a sleepless night with his wife, Christine Buchegger) who murders a prostitute and subsequently slips down into dumb insanity.

For Whom the Gong Tolls – 1936–1980: The History of Rank Film Productions

by Iain F. McAsh

Ken Richmond strikes the great Rank Gong – the company's famous trade mark.

For almost forty-five years, the Rank name has been synonymous with top quality British film entertainment. Wherever there's a cinema, the Man with the Gong has proudly sold his ware to eager audiences around the world. He was a cinematic symbol to millions for more than four decades, becoming nearly as well known as MGM's Leo the Lion. To world-wide moviegoers Rank *was* the British Film Industry, its hundreds of films produced over that period appearing to represent the best, and most dependable, way of British life. Around the world millions of people learned about the English and our customs and traditions, past and present, by what they saw of Rank films on their screens.

Now, sadly, all that has come to an end. In June 1980, Rank announced their withdrawal from production. It was a death blow, if one which had been expected for some time. Failure to crack the major American market, spiralling costs and being unable to keep tabs on current trends with the free-spending youngsters who constitute two-thirds of today's market were given as official reasons. But delve deeper beneath the surface and any number of other reasons would be revealed in the post mortem. With hindsight, Rank certainly might have been more venturesome with their choice of subjects during their last years of production. Titles for their current product in the trade press all too often resembled a forty-year-old programme. Re-makes of such British classics as *The Thirty-Nine Steps* and *The Lady Vanishes*, entertaining as they were, were not the ingredients to offer the dwindling audiences as the film industry entered into the 1980s. Undaunted, Rank latched onto a David Essex motorbike drama, *Silver Dream*

Racer, which failed to make the first lap with his fans, while Nicolas Roeg's *Bad Timing* proved all too prophetic as the company's gong knelled for the last time on its once proud production division.

But it is surely better for a film organisation to have had a glorious past than no past at all, and in that respect at least Rank was for many years a shining name which will certainly be recorded in the film history books with the best of them. Rank bravely carved an era in British movie productions. Stars and directors made their names, as well as international reputations, under the Rank banner. The company ceased active production with a whimper rather than a bang, with a loss of £1.6 million, chicken feed compared with today's escalating budgets, but for Rank it was the end of the road. They cut their losses and announced they would be making no more films.

Traditionally, the British Film Industry has always been in a state of the doldrums ever since the late 1920s.

The front entrance to Pinewood studios – gateway to the stars for some forty-five years of moviemaking.

The advent of sound threw the native production industry into panic. Already completed films were hastily re-dubbed from silent to the new novelty of talking pictures. Acting careers were made and broken according to their vocal capabilities. Audiences flocked to hear the new attraction of Sound. It was the era of the Depression and cinemagoing generally boomed on both sides of the Atlantic. In the mid-1930s the British Film Industry was dominated by Alexander Korda, the Hungarian-born movie magnate who brought a touch of class to his lavish productions. His predominance at this time was challenged by a Yorkshire flour miller named Joseph Arthur Rank, a staunch Methodist and Sunday school teacher who began his career in the industry by producing a series of religious films. The earliest Rank titles are recorded as *Mastership* and *Turn of the Tide* in 1934. Korda towered over the British cinema of his time with a cheque book in one hand and a Union Jack in the other. He brought a touch of Hollywood

spectacle to his high-budget productions which most of hs contemporaries found hard to match, let alone beat. It was into this atmosphere that Rank chose to make his bid for celluloid glory. Korda had his own studio at Denham, then reputed to be the best in Europe. Rank realised that if his plan was to stand any chance of success then he, too, would have to acquire his own studio base.

In 1934, J. Arthur Rank met Charles Boot, chairman of a building concern, who had tried to establish his own Hollywood-style studio in Britain some ten years earlier. He had acquired Heatherden Hall, a vast Georgian mansion situated in the heart of 158 acres of verdant Buckinghamshire countryside mid-way between Denham in one direction and Uxbridge in the other. The Hall had a long and impressive history. Vast sums had been spent from time to time to keep it in good order. Certainly its previous owners had not been lacking for money, as its past occupiers included a

certain Dr Drury Lavin in the late nineteenth century and, at the turn of the present century, its owner was Lt Col Grant Morden, a Canadian financier and Member of Parliament for Brentford and Chiswick. Still later, Heatherden Hall became the impressive home of K. S. Ranjitsinhji, the famous Sussex and England cricketer.

Politicians had always been attracted to Heatherden Hall. The Irish Free State Treaty was signed within its walls on 3 November 1921, the signatories being Lord Birkenhead, Viscount Younger, Sir Malcolm Fraser and Col Morden. The Colonel continued his political activities, as well as a very busy private life shooting grouse and pheasant on the estate, until his death in 1934. It was then that Charles Boot stepped in and bought Heatherden Hall. With J. Arthur Rank as his partner, the foundations were laid for what was destined to become a production headquarters to make British films known and respected throughout the world.

The name chosen for the new enterprise was Pinewood Studios. It was here at the former Heatherden Hall, 'situated in the Ecclesiastic Parish of Iver Heath in the County of Buckingham', that Mr Boot handed over the opening key to Dr E. L. Burgin, Parliamentary Secretary to the Board of Trade, before more than 1,000 guests. The date was 30 September 1936, and the chairman of the newly-formed company was J. Arthur Rank.

Pinewood became a magnet for highly respected producers almost as soon as it was fully operational. Herbert Wilcox was the first to work on its stages, completing *London Melody* for Rank, starring Anna Neagle. Carol Reed was the director with the distinction of the first wholly Pinewood-made film, titled *A Man With Your Voice*, Rank became a name to be reckoned with in British film-making circles as Pinewood flourished and its reputation grew. Up until that time, Rank had continued to make his films in such London-based studios as Highbury, Gainsborough at Islington, Gaumont-British at Lime Grove, Shepherd's Bush.

Pinewood had been in business only three years at the advent of World War II. The sound stages were silenced and used for stockpiling food until the Royal Mint also moved in to produce copper coins. But two years later the studio was back again in the film-making business, in 1942 turning out wartime propaganda and documentaries for the RAF and Crown Film Units.

At the war's end, production control of Pinewood was taken over by The Rank Organisation. A new era of optimism began for the company which had previously kept the British production banner flying high throughout the long dark years of European conflict with such fine films as *Madonna of the Seven Moons* (1944) followed by *The Man in Grey, A Place of One's Own* and *The Seventh Veil* (1945). Even at the tail end of World War II, Rank embarked on a programme of costly and

Lord Rank talks to Noel Coward on the set of *The Astonished Heart* during its shooting at Pinewood in 1949.

prestigious films aimed at the world market, headed by the mammoth *Caesar and Cleopatra* and the still more ambitious *Henry V*. That these, and other equally significant British films made under the Rank banner, had indeed captured international interest and acclaim was proved by the fact that several of them won top awards in the coveted Hollywood Academy Award stakes.

Other independent British producers were quick to see the benefits to be gained from a liaison under the Rank production umbrella. After the war, Cineguild (comprising David Lean, Ronald Neame, Anthony Havelock-Allen, Noël Coward), Wessex (Ian Dalrymple), Individual (Frank Launder and Sidney Gilliat), Gainsborough, Two Cities and The Archers (formed by the enterprising team of Michael Powell and Emeric Pressburger) worked together closely and, for the most part, harmoniously under the Rank aegis.

At this period, the question arises of what constitutes a Rank film. How to define this? First of all it is necessary to determine what is a Rank film, as opposed to co-productions, shared financial-distribution projects and other pick-up deals for domestic distribution in the UK as well as certain other territories. For the purposes of this article, which would otherwise far outrun the space allotted here, I have decided to concentrate as far as possible on what could be termed as wholly Rank-produced films.

In 1946, *Black Narcissus* moved into Pinewood with a prestigious cast headed by Deborah Kerr, David Farrar, Jean Simmons, Kathleen Byron and Sabu. Although the story was set in a convent situated in the Himalayas, the mountains were matte paintings by Peter Ellenshaw and the stars and production crew never moved out of the studio's back lot. That same year, *Green for Danger* and *Captain Boycott* (starring Stewart Granger and Kathleen Ryan) were also completed at Pinewood, as was part of the Dickens classic *Great Expectations*, directed by David Lean for Cineguild. In fact, the thriller *Green for Danger*, starring Sally Gray, Trevor Howard and Alastair Sim, had been the studio's first post-war feature production.

During the war years, Rank had built up an enviable roster of home-grown box-office stars who had brought the crowds flocking to cinemas throughout the British Isles and also seemed set at last to crack the coveted American market. Foremost of these were James Mason, Stewart Granger, Margaret Lockwood, Dennis Price, John Mills, Patricia Roc, Jean Kent, Deborah Kerr, Valerie Hobson and Phyllis Calvert. Of these, only Mason, Granger and Miss Kerr were destined to find Hollywood fame, but J. Arthur Rank was nonetheless determined to foster and groom budding film talent at home. In 1946, he formed the famous so-called Rank 'Charm School' at Highbury Studios where many embryonic stars of the future were given a thorough training in such essentials as acting, speech, deportment and camera technique. Many of the graduates were to become household names, such as the young Jean Simmons, Sally Gray, Joan Collins, Christopher Lee, Diana Dors, Petula Clark and countless other starlets, many of whom were to shine brightly in later years.

But it wasn't only acting talent that Mr Rank was determined to develop. He also established the *This Modern Age* documentary series, in addition to an ambitious cartoon studio. Animation has always been a particularly tough nut to crack in Britain, but under the guidance of David Hand a team of British artists was set up at Cookham. Hand, an American who had worked at the Disney Studios in Hollywood, created his own pen-and-ink characters headed by a squirrel named Ginger Nutt to supplement his *Musical Paintbox* series of short cartoons praising the pictorial beauty of Britain. The immediate post-war years emerged as a period of great activity for Rank. The atmosphere was right for providing the type of entertainment that audiences, starved for six years of such glamorous fare, were willing to

Lord Rank, the Yorkshire flour miller and Methodist School teacher who founded a great British film empire.

pay to see. Product ranged from the classics of Dickens and Shakespeare to domestic comedies, the inevitable war dramas, lavish costume pieces and crime thrillers. Valerie Hobson and Stewart Granger starred in *Blanche Fury,* while a young stage actor named Dirk Bogarde made an impressive screen debut in *Esther Waters* and Alec Guinness made a memorable impression as the skulking Fagin in *Oliver Twist.* These films were made in black-and-white, as were most productions of this cost-conscious era, but some subjects would have been unthinkable in anything but colour. One of the most ambitious of these was *The Red Shoes*, starring Anton Walbrook with an enchanting newcomer named Moira Shearer, a ballet film which endeared itself to the hearts of millons and earned fresh plaudits for British film craftmanship. Olivier's black-and-white version of *Hamlet* won more prestige at home and, more particularly, in the vast American market where Hollywood voted it Best Picture in the Academy Award ceremonies. Films such as these were the first to gain for Rank an entry into the rich American domain. Bookings at the country's largest theatres were secured for *Great Expectations* at New York's mammoth Radio City Music Hall, while a lesser British offering, *Odd Man Out*, was screened at a leading Times Square cinema.

It had long been Rank's cherished ambition to see his films widely shown in the United States. This was an encouraging start and he went all out to promote and encourage it. At home, Rank had already secured maximum domestic distribution through his vast chain of Odeon and Gaumont cinemas. From small beginnings, he had gradually expanded his horizons to include theatres in Ireland, Canada, Australia, New Zealand, South Africa, Holland, Italy, Egypt and Singapore. To release and market his films he had his own distribution arm in Wardour Street, General Film Distributors (later to become more widely known as Rank

Sir John Davis, who for so long guided the fortunes of the Rank entertainment empire.

Edmond Chilton, who for a number of years was Chairman of the vastly spreading Rank Leisure group of companies, only resigning in January 1981, coinciding with Rank's withdrawal from film production.

Film Distributors). In time, Rank Overseas Film Distributors was also formed with a fully trained and experienced sales staff to look after his many overseas interests. Several Rank films underwent subtle changes of title to make them more acceptable for the tastes of audiences in a variety of foreign territories. But it was still the vast and even more lucrative American market which presented Mr Rank with his biggest challenge, as indeed it did to all British producers. Rank never

completely found total success in the United States, although latterly the majority of his most prestigious pictures were seen by American audiences. In the mid-1940s, he had planned to open a 2,500 British flagship to première his films on Broadway, but this never came to fruition. He did, however, strive to present Rank films to the maximum number of American audiences throughout the rest of his remarkable career.

Meanwhile, back home, Rank continued to forge ahead with a programme as varied as almost anyone could reasonably wish for. Launder and Gilliat's Individual Pictures produced *The Blue Lagoon* as their last film for Rank, with Jean Simmons and brawny newcomer Donald Houston cast as the romantic young castaways. Powell and Pressburger continued to keep the flag flying high for Rank who released their prestigious *I Know Where I'm Going* (starring Roger Livesey and Wendy Hiller) and *A Matter of Life and Death* (with David Niven, Roger Livesey, Raymond Massey and Kim Hunter), honoured as the first Royal Performance Film in 1946 (it was seen by American filmgoers as *Stairway to Heaven*).

For several years the famous Gainsborough Lady had been the logo for films produced by the company, such as the costume epics *The Wicked Lady, They Were Sisters* and *Caravan* (1946). Consequently, Rank thought that a similar trade-mark should be created to present an easily recognisable identity for their ever-increasing production programme. General Film Distributors was the first company to utilise the Man With the Gong as its corporate symbol in 1935. The first Gong Man was Bombardier Billy Wells, British champion heavyweight boxer and one of the greatest fighters of the twentieth century. Phil Nieman and Ken Richmond, who was British amateur champion wrestler for five years, superseded Bombardier Wells when the famous logo was re-filmed in later

years. (A fourth attempt, early in 1978, with stuntman Martin Grace, intended to carry an updated Man With the Gong image, was produced in three separate screen ratios but never released).

From 1948 onwards, Rank continued to produce an average of ten or twelve of their own productions each year at Pinewood. Dirk Bogarde quickly sprang to the foreground in many of these. Vintage titles from this productive period include *Passionate Friends, Once a Jolly Swagman, Once Upon a Dream, Fools Rush In, Dear Mr Prohack, Obsession, Warning to Wantons, Floodtide, Golden Salamander, Boys in Brown, Madeleine, The Spider and the Fly, The Astonished Heart, Prelude to Fame,* and *So Long at the Fair,* starring David Tomlinson and Jean Simmons.

The 1950s were ushered in with a veritable floodtide of Rank films headed by *Waterfront, Tony Draws a Horse,* W. Somerset Maugham's *Trio, The Clouded Yellow, The Woman in Question, Highly Dangerous, Blackmailed, The Browning Version, Night Without Stars* and *White Corridors.*

Hot on their heels came *Hotel Sahara, High Treason,* Maugham's *Encore, Appointment with Venus, Hunted,* Compton Bennett's *The Card,* starring Alec Guinness, and an all-star version of Wilde's classic comedy *The Importance of Being Earnest* with Michael Redgrave, Joan Greenwood and the splendid Dame Edith Evans. The ensuing years saw *Penny Princess* (Yolande Donlan), *The Planter's Wife* (Jack Hawkins), *The Long Memory*

(John Mills), *Venetian Bird* (Richard Todd, Eva Bartok), *Something Money Can't Buy, Meet Me Tonight, It Started in Paradise, The Net, Desperate Moment, The Final Test, The Key, The Malta Story, Turn the Key Softly,* and the contemporary *Made in Heaven.* Any year which produced that racy British-to-the-core comedy *Genevieve* (1952) must be regarded as an exceptional one. Under the inspired direction of Henry Cornelius, an expert team of laughtermakers led by Kenneth More, John Gregson, Kay Kendall and Dinah Sheridan participated in the annual 'old crocks' automobile race from London to Brighton with hilarious results. Their combined antics had audiences in stitches from Bangkok to Wapping, proving that there is no universal barrier in the comedy stakes. The following year, Rank enjoyed another world-wide comedy success with *Doctor in the House* (1953), starring Dirk Bogarde, Kenneth More and Donald Sinden as trouble-prone medical students created in the first of Dr Richard Gordon's richly funny novels which was to inspire a successful series for the company.

The mid-1950s was a halcyon period for Rank. The studios were bustling with activity and creativity. Box-office bells were ringing with a programme as varied as anything they ever produced: *A Day to Remember, You Know What Sailors Are, The Seekers, The Beachcombers, The Young Lovers, Mad About Men, Passage Home* and *Above Us the Waves.* *The Kidnappers* (1953) won a special Hollywood Academy

Award for its juvenile star, Vincent Winter (who, in later years, became a successful assistant director). Norman Wisdom made his first Rank comedy, *Trouble in Store* (1953) at Pinewood. A mermaid named *Miranda*, played by Glynis Johns, had audiences rolling in the aisles, demanding a sequel entitled *Mad About Men*. Serious drama was catered for in *Simba*, *A Town Like Alice*, *Lost* and *The Black Tent*. For romantics there was *The Young Lovers*, *A Woman for Joe* and *To Paris, With Love*. Comedy was well to the fore throughout this most prolific era with such offerings as *An Alligator Named Daisy*, *Value for Money*, *Simon and Laura* and *All for Mary*. The great Jack Buchanan made his last film at Pinewood, a lighthearted romantic comedy called *As Long as They're Happy* (1954). Naturally, the aftermath of World War II was still strong in everybody's mind, and the Rank film-makers were not slow in making this the main theme for many of their best dramas. They hit the public pulse with the Douglas Bader story, *Reach for the Sky* (1955), which provided Kenneth More with one of his most memorable dramatic roles as the legless Battle of Britain fighter ace. Stiff upper lips were again called for in *The Battle of the River Plate*, *Ill Met by Moonlight*, *The One That Got Away*, *Carve Her Name With Pride*, *Nor the Moon by Night*, *Seven Thunders*, *Sea of Sand*, *SOS Pacific*, *Conspiracy of Hearts*, *Above us the Waves*, *House of Secrets* and countless others.

Over the years, Rank had built up a stable of leading stars who did Trojan

Dirk Bogarde and Ernest Jay in the early 'Doctor' film *Doctor at Large*, which helped to set Bogarde on his distinguished acting career.

A (young) Michael Craig with Geoffrey Keen and Barbara Bates in the 1956 Rank production *House of Secrets*.

Stephen Murray, Dorothy Tutin, Dirk Bogarde and Athene Seyler in Betty Box's 1957 production for Rank of the Charles Dickens classic *A Tale of Two Cities*.

service and became household names (and faces) in a wide assortment of films. As always with the British cinema, men dominated the list but in those days there were quite a few female stars to counterbalance the distaff side. During the 1940s James Mason, Stewart Granger, John Mills, Dennis Price, Margaret Lockwood, Jean Kent, Patricia Roc, Phyllis Calvert and Jean Simmons had won cinemagoers' hearts. In the 1950s a new stable had been carefully nurtured with such Rank stalwarts as Dirk Bogarde, Peter Finch, Kenneth More, Jack Hawkins, Donald Sinden, John Gregson, Alec Guinness, Stanley Baker, Anthony Steel and Keith Michell. Coming along fast on the outside rail were promising young newcomers like Stephen Boyd, Michael Craig and Patrick McGoohan. Kay Kendall, Muriel Pavlov, Virginia McKenna and Diane Cilento were foremost of our leading screen actresses. No Rank comedy of this period would be complete without that ferociously bearded Scots character actor James Robertson Justice, while Noel Purcell had cornered the market in Irish priests and ship's cooks from the Emerald Isle. A talented young juvenile named Richard O'Sullivan (later to become a popular TV star in 'Man about the House' and the 'Dick Turpin' series) made his film debut for Rank in the Irish comedy *Jacqueline,* followed by a period swashbuckler called *Dangerous Exile*.

At its peak, Rank had one hundred artistes under contract. As the company's fortunes declined, through overspending on lavish productions, the economic climate, and fast dwindling audiences, this list was cut to a mere twenty-five. Among the favoured ones who enjoyed the security of a weekly pay cheque from Rank were Anne Heywood, Joan Rice, Belinda Lee, June Thorburn, Eunice Gayson, Jill Ireland, June Laverick, Ronald Lewis, Terence Longdon, David McCallum, Patrick McGoohan, Mary Ure, Maureen Swanson, Jane Hylton and Tony Wright. Some went on to greater glory, but others seemed to glow momentarily and then fizzle out. Other Rank contractees included Gerda Larsen, Elvi Hale, Beth Rogan, Susan Beaumont, Beverly Brooks, Philip Gilbert, Anna Gaylor, Shirley Eaton, Betta St John, Barbara Murray, David Knight and Marla Landi, all of whom enjoyed some measure of early success in Rank films.

No tribute to the history of Rank productions would be complete without special mention being made to the immense contribution of that most prolific producer-director teams, Betty E. Box and Ralph Thomas. For more than two decades, their offices at Pinewood turned out an amazing amount of comedies and dramas, made new stars and created careers.

Producer Box began her film career in 1942 working on the preparation of some two hundred short subjects for Verity Films. In later years the company turned to feature productions and Betty worked on *The Seventh Veil* and *The Years Between* before moving to Gainsborough Studios. There, as a producer, she made *Dear Murderer,*

When the Bough Breaks, Miranda, The Blind Goddess and the popular *Huggett* family series. Her partner, director Ralph Thomas, was a former journalist and entered films as a humble clapper boy, working his way up through the various grades of assistant editor and eventually editor. After military service in the Western Desert, Thomas joined The Rank Organisation's Trailer Department in 1946 and, three years later, moved over to Gainsborough where his first feature-film in the director's chair was *Once Upon a Dream*. It was around this time that he first met Betty Box and, as a team, they both played a major part in Rank's production history.

Betty recalls that her first film made at Pinewood for Rank Productions was the period mystery melodrama, *So Long at the Fair*. The year was 1949 and outdoor filming took place on the back lot on exactly the same spot where the giant James Bond/Superman stage now stands. Since then, she and Ralph Thomas have made over thirty films for Rank in one of the industry's happiest and most successful partnerships. In particular, the famous *Doctor* series (originally starring Dirk Bogarde as young Dr Simon Sparrow, superseded in later years by Michael Craig and Leslie Phillips) was a comedy landmark in their joint careers. But it wasn't all laughter, for the team also turned to thrills with the Bulldog Drummond adventures, with our hero played on two occasions by Richard Johnson in *Deadlier than the Male* and its sequel, *Some Girls Do*. Among the most famous Box-Thomas films are

Above us the Waves, Campbell's Kingdom, A Tale of Two Cities, The Wind Cannot Read, The Thirty-Nine Steps (the Kenneth More version), *Upstairs and Downstairs, Conspiracy of Hearts, Doctor in Love, No Love for Johnnie, The Wild and the Willing* (which introduced then newcomers Ian McShane, John Hurt and Samantha Eggar), *Doctor in Distress, The Captain's Table, Hot Enough for June, The High Bright Sun, Doctor in Clover, A Pair of Briefs, Nobody Runs Forever* and *Doctor in Trouble*. Additionally, the pair had an eye for glamorous new female talent and male filmgoers have cause to thank them for bringing to Rank such shapely newcomers as Brigitte Bardot (in *Doctor at Sea*), Claudia Cardinale, Odile Versois, Elke Sommer, Camilla Sparv, Daliah Lavi, Sylva Koscina and Mylène Demongeot, to name but a few.

As the years progressed, Rank joined in the then fashionable habit of importing big American stars as 'names' to lure patrons to the international box office. One of the first to arrive at Pinewood in the mid-1950s was Gregory Peck, who made two films for the company in quick succession (*The Million Pound Note* and *The Purple Plain*). Hot on his heels were Howard Keel (for *Floods of Fear*), Rod Steiger (*Across the Bridge*), Anthony Quinn (*The Savage Innocents*), Lauren Bacall (*North West Frontier*) and Yul Brynner (*The Long Duel*). Rank also reached to the continent in their quest for important foreign stars who would appeal to the vast European market: French

heart-throb Louis Jourdan for *Dangerous Exile*; Melina Mercouri, the fiery Greek actress, for the period melodrama, *The Gypsy and the Gentleman*. Two big German stars added to their fame at Pinewood: Hardy Kruger played Franz von Werra, the only German to escape from a World War II British POW camp in *The One That Got Away*, while Curt Jurgens appeared with Orson Welles in *Ferry to Hong Kong*.

It was around this time, in the mid-1950s, that I made my first visit to Pinewood. As a young publicist-journalist, I can still vividly recall the excitement of seeing the bustling activity of a major studio at its creative peak. Every office and corridor seemed to be occupied by famous names and faces. In production, or just completed at that time, were *Above us the Waves, Passage Home* and *As Long as they're Happy*. Even today, looking back with a fair amount of nostalgia as I write this piece, I can remember the famous bar and restaurant full of familiar, easily recognisable faces. Pinewood was different from other studios. For a start, its old-world mansion façade cast it apart from the more commonplace image of rival contemporary celluloid dream factories. With its hundred plus bustling acres, surrounded by green fields, man-made lake and aura of pastoral well-being, just being there was an experience in itself.

In those halcyon days, production at that time came under the control of Earl St John, an American domiciled in Britain who had previously managed cinemas in the provinces as well as

London's West End. On an average day at Pinewood, conversation could be swapped with producers Hugh Stewart, George H. Brown, Maurice Cowan, Julian Wintle, Daniel Angel, Betty, Sydney and Muriel Box in addition to then resident directors like John Paddy Carstairs, George Pollock and Ralph Thomas. American Joseph Losey made one of his earliest British films for Rank, *The Gypsy and the Gentleman*, before going on to become a cult figure on the continent. In later years, the names of producer Peter Rogers and director Gerald Thomas, those merry funsters responsible for an endless stream of *Carry Ons*, could be added to the list. An old-time publicist with whom I later worked would never tire of showing me the table for four on the raised dais which had been a regular for Bernard Shaw when he was engaged on *Pygmalion* at the studio before the war.

In 1957, Pinewood celebrated its twenty-first year of active film-making with a full scale party embracing those showbusiness luminaries, both past and present, who had lent their talents to films made at the studio. Lord Rank (now elevated to the peerage) and his right-hand man, Sir John Davis, acted as affable hosts to the hundreds of celebrities and Pressmen who assembled to mark the occasion in its famous grounds and sound stages. Anne Heywood cut the large birthday cake as hundreds of camera flash-bulbs popped. Watched by many of the higher Rank echelons from overseas, it was indeed a day to remember with pride and mixed perhaps with nostalgia for all that had gone before.

At its peak, Pinewood had produced twenty films a year. But in the past, Rank had known bad times as well as good. In 1949 severe measures were called for when the Film Production Division reported a loss of £3.35 million for that year. The immediate result was that David Hand's animation studio at Cookham was disbanded, and *This Modern Age* documentaries ceased production. It was the end of the Charm School's training scheme with the closure of Highbury Studios and the announcement that all future feature films would be concentrated on Pinewood, where a financial ceiling of £150,000 (far lower than the final cost of *Henry V* and *Hamlet*) was imposed. At home, Rank was accused of holding a monopoly on the theatrical exhibition of films through his control of the Odeon and Gaumont circuits, then by far the largest chain of cinemas operating in Britain. The government's quota system dictated that forty-five per cent of the product shown on these screens should be produced domestically. This meant a boom period for British production and Rank led the field. Naturally, to keep pace with such an output, there was at first an almost inevitable decrease in overall quality. The new demands put everyone concerned with production under considerable strain as writers, producers and directors manfully tried to shoulder the impossible burden. Cash was low, and many of these home-produced efforts suffered from lack of funds – and looked it. But it

was a time when financial strain called for further creative ingenuity on otherwise shoestring budgets.

The National Film Finance Corporation was formed late in 1948 to offer assistance to British producers to at least partly off-load their monetary problems. Other major companies took advantage of this new offer, but Rank continued to finance their films their own way. Production kept afloat, mainly at Pinewood, with smaller 'B' pictures made at lesser studios, until the early 1950s. The middle of that decade saw Rank emerge triumphant once more with such quality films as *The Spanish Gardener, Hell Drivers, Across the Bridge, Robbery under Arms* (with locations in Australia), *Campbell's Kingdom* (in Canada), *The Wind Cannot Read* and *Carve Her Name With Pride*, as well as bread-and-butter offerings such as *Jacqueline* (based on Catherine Cookson's best-seller), *Rooney, The Naked Truth, True as a Turtle* and *Miracle in Soho*, among others. The quality productions which made this era outstanding included *Reach for the Sky, The Battle of the River Plate, The One That Got Away, Carve Her Name With Pride* and *A Night to Remember*. Rank embarked in 1958 confidently enough with *Nor the Moon by Night, Sea Fury, Rockets Galore, The Passionate Summer, Floods of Fear, Sea of Sand, Bachelor of Hearts, Operation Amsterdam, Too Many Crooks, Ferry to Hong Kong, Whirlpool* and *Sapphire*. But they also produced the John Buchan adventure classic *The Thirty-Nine Steps*, starring Kenneth

More and Taina Elg, on location in Scotland and, more importantly *Tiger Bay*, which introduced a brilliant new child star in Hayley Mills.

The next year was also to be remembered for *The League of Gentlemen, North West Frontier* (an Indian adventure starring Kenneth More with Hollywood's Lauren Bacall), *The Savage Innocents* (an Eskimo tale starring another Hollywood import in Anthony Quinn) as well as the World War II drama, *Conspiracy of Hearts*. Rank entered the 1960s with such above-average offerings as *The Singer, Not the Song* (which presented another worthwhile role to Dirk Bogarde), *No Love for Johnnie* (a political drama with Peter Finch well cast), *Flame in the Streets* (an inflammatory story of contemporary racial tensions in London) and, particularly, *Whistle Down the Wind* (in which Alan Bates and Hayley Mills won critical raves under Bryan Forbes' inspired direction) and another accomplished performance from Dirk Bogarde as a barrister with homosexual tendencies in *Victim*. Later, *Seance on a Wet Afternoon* teamed Richard Attenborough with American actress Kim Stanley under Forbes' direction. A film version of Anouilh's *The Waltz of the Toreadors* saw the strange casting of Peter Sellers with French beauty Dany Robin, while James Mason travelled to the South Seas for Ivan Foxwell's *Tiara Tahiti*. Val Guest directed *80,000 Suspects* for Rank, and the year also produced such above average dramas as *All Night Long, A*

Life for Ruth, Bitter Harvest, A Place to Go and also *The Beauty Jungle*, intended as a serious exposé of beauty contests starring former child star Janette Scott with Ian Hendry and erstwhile Hollywood heart-throb Edmund Purdom. The prolific Box-Thomas team continued to keep active with such diverse films as *A Pair of Briefs, The Wild and the Willing, Doctor in Distress, Hot Enough for June* (a spy spoof) and *The High Bright Sun*, a political thriller set in Cyprus starring Dirk Bogarde with American imports George Chakiris and Susan Strasberg. Also in 1964, Michael Caine portrayed for the first time the laconic Cockney spy, Harry Palmer, in a screen version of Len Deighton's espionage novel *The Ipcress File*.

But it wasn't all serious dramas and adventure thrillers. The company also built up a big reputation for domestic comedies. Norman Wisdom was a comedy sensation in Russia, as well as many other unexpected foreign territories, proving that there is no substitute for universal knockabout-style humour. The little man in the jump suit first made his screen debut for Rank in *Trouble in Store*, directed in 1953 by John Paddy Carstairs. Such was his instant success that he went on to star in another dozen comedies for Rank, each tailored to his individual style, over the next twelve years: *One Good Turn, Man of the Moment, Up in the World, Just my Luck, The Square Peg, Follow a Star, The Bulldog Breed, On the Beat, A Stitch in Time, The Early Bird*, and *Press for Time*.

In the mid-1960s, Rank successfully lured another famous team of comics to the big screen. Morecambe and Wise made their film debut at Pinewood in 1965 in *The Intelligence Men* (a spy spoof perhaps suggested by the then current success of *The Ipcress File*). Their repuation, built initially to perfection as a team on the music-halls and, latterly, the television screen, seemed to rest uneasy when translated to wider cinematic dimensions. Although they brought their own scriptwriters, Dick Hills and Sid Green, Eric and Ernie somehow failed to find the same audience response in movies. Their second Rank film was *That Riviera Touch* (1966), while a third endeavour titled *The Magnificent Two* (shown as *What Happened at Campo Grande?* for overseas exhibition), a comedy featuring the famous pair involved with revolutionary goings-on in a mythical South American country, brought their big screen careers to an untimely halt. In 1965, Rank backed another all-star comedy *The Sandwich Man* (*That Swinging City* overseas), a vehicle designed for popular TV comedian Michael Bentine, in which virtually the tiniest supporting role was played by a recognisable face. Bentine failed to have the same charisma in movies, and has not since ventured back onto the big screen, although his television following remains undiminished. That film made little impact at home or overseas, but infinitely more successful financially were the ever-increasing *Doctor* series from Betty E. Box and Ralph Thomas. The sequels had less

class than the original *Doctor in the House*, and fell more into broad slapstick of the trouser-dropping variety. Seventeen years separated such titles as *Doctor at Sea* (still with Bogarde at the helm), *Doctor at Large, Doctor in Love, Doctor in Distress, Doctor in Clover* and, finally, *Doctor in Trouble* (1970), which brought the once-popular series to a close. Although many of the stalwart supporting cast remained the same (James Robertson Justice, Joan Sims, etc), the series had latterly lacked lustre when the main role of Dr Simon Sparrow was taken over, successively, by Michael Craig and Leslie Phillips. The *Doctors* had clearly outstayed their welcome. It was the end of an era, and the cinemagoing tastes of the British public had changed. The product for the mid-1960s was mixed and catered for most tastes. 1965 saw the World War II drama *The Heroes of Telemark*, starring Kirk Douglas and Richard Harris. John Mills made his debut as director on *Sky West and Crooked*, in which his now teenage daughter Hayley scored another notable success. Michael Anderson directed another Hollywood import, George Segal, in *The Quiller Memorandum*, a spy thriller set in Berlin for producer Ivan Foxwell. Yul Brynner also visited our shores to play a bandit chieftain of the Indian North-West Frontier period, opposite Trevor Howard, in *The Long Duel*, which Ken Annakin directed on Spanish locations for Rank. That same year, Hayley Mills was off to the Far East for a romantic drama *Pretty Polly*, while the Box-Thomas team starred Rod Taylor, Christopher Plummer and Lilli Palmer in a contemporary political thriller with a London background, *Nobody Runs Forever*.

The year 1967 saw Rank re-enter the comedy stakes in a big way. It was a case of 'Carry On Rank' as the company inherited this famous, saucy laughtermaking series from Anglo-Amalgamated who had instigated what was to become a British comedy institution with *Carry On Sergeant* back in 1958. The first of the Rank record-breakers did not even have the magic words *Carry On* in its title. It was *Don't Lose your Head*, a French Revolutionary farce, with the welcome addition of imported French beauty Dany Robin as the only true Gallic member of the cast. Next in line was *Follow that Camel*, described as a 'Beau Jest', and was the first in the series to break with an all-British acting tradtion by featuring an American comedy star, Phil ('Sergeant Bilko') Silvers. For the ensuing dozen years, under the Rank banner, the familiar team of producer Peter Rogers, director Gerald Thomas and scriptwriter Talbot Rothwell continued to churn out a further sixteen of these near-the-knuckle rib-ticklers. Among the titles were: *Carry On up the Khyber* (critically received as the best in the long-running series), *Carry On Camping, Carry On up the Jungle, Carry On Loving, Carry On Henry, Carry On at your Convenience, Carry On Doctor, Carry On Matron, Carry On Abroad, Carry On Girls, Carry On Dick, Carry On Behind* and *Carry On England*. In

keeping with modern tastes, each film became increasingly more crude and the laughs were few and far between although the veteran repertory team (headed by Sidney James, Kenneth Williams, Jim Dale, Kenneth Connor, Hattie Jacques, Joan Sims, Barbara Windsor and Charles Hawtrey) worked harder than ever to raise the guffaws. The last title in the series, keeping in touch with contemporary trends, was the dire *Carry On Emmanuelle* with which Rank was happily not associated. *Carry On Yanks* failed to get into production, while the indefatigable Rogers-Thomas partnership have since threatened to come right up to date with *Carry On Dallas*. Several of the original funsters are now dead, so whether this will ever materialise (or indeed be for Rank release!) remains to be seen.

On rare occasions, between *Carry Ons*, Rogers and Thomas produced and directed modern thrillers for Rank. There was *Revenge*, a drama starring Joan Collins, and *Quest for Love*, which again starred Ms Collins opposite Tom Bell. The company released the sex thriller *Assault*, starring Suzy Kendall and a very young future star named Lesley-Anne Down. Also on the schedule were *All Coppers Are . . .* and a grisly spinechiller, *Nothing but the Night*, starring British horror kings Peter Cushing and Christopher Lee. Rank turned to the then fashionable TV spin-off with the comedy *Please, Sir!* starring John Alderton as the luckless young schoolteacher of the Fenn Street gang. More surprisingly, the year saw an unexpected return to

The late Sidney James and Hattie Jacques, co-stars of an earlier, 1970, Carry On, *Carry On Loving*.

historical romance with *Kidnapped,* based on the Robert Louis Stevenson classic, with Cockney Michael Caine making a brave stab at a Scots accent as the heroic Alan Breck.

An earlier departure for Rank had been the disastrous space-age musical *Tomorrow* (1969), intended to be a starring vehicle to launch a new 'pop' group called Tomorrow. The film failed on every count. Not surprisingly, the group split up soon after and, one of its member, pretty songstress Olivia Newton-John, went solo and on to greater glory in Hollywood.

Another Rank film of this period was *When Eight Bells Toll,* directed by Frenchman Etienne Périer, starring Anthony Hopkins and Jack Hawkins. It was a workmanlike job, but little more than an above-average spy thriller. Horror continued then, as now, to dominate cinema screens during the early 1970s and Rank were quick to form a distribution link wth the world-famous Hammer house of horror. Their first joint effort was the vampire shocker *Countess Dracula,* starring horror queen Ingrid Pitt in the title role. Then came *Hands of the Ripper,* starring Eric Porter and then newcomer Angharad Rees as the ill-fated daughter of Jack the Ripper who followed her father's unfortunate tendencies with horrifying results. Then followed *Vampire Circus* and *Twins of Evil* under the Hammer pact, and later, *I Don't Want to be Born,* directed by Peter Sasdy. Around this time they also formed a deal with producer Kevin Francis of Tyburn Film Productions, another Pinewood-based independent with a reputation for chilling spines, the liaison resulting in *The Ghoul* and *Legend of the Werewolf.*

Lord Rank, who had been living in retirement for several years, died at his magnificent home at Sutton Scotney in 1972. He had seen the company he founded flourish and expand to include, as well as film production, a processing laboratory, hotels, dance-halls, banqueting suites, bowling alleys, a yacht marina and the famous Rank Xerox copying machines as part of the vast leisure industry. His second-in-command, Sir John Davis (knighted in 1971), was a financial wizard who had been at Lord Rank's right hand since 1939. He remained within the Organisation as a powerful force, taking drastic action wherever necessary to keep the company afloat in the stormy seas of the fast diminishing British Film Industry.

Throughout the 1970s, Rank continued to distribute a number of quality independent productions such as *The Belstone Fox,* based on David Rook's charming country life novel, as well as more routine pot-boilers like *What Changed Charley Farthing?* and the Reg Varney farce, *Go for a Take,* in which he played an inept movie stuntman. They also released the inappropriately titled *That Lucky Touch,* a luke-warm comedy teaming Roger Moore and Susannah York with Hollywood stalwarts Shelley Winters and Lee J. Cobb, which Christopher Miles directed. In 1976, Rank came in for much criticism over their handling of *Bugsy Malone,* an off-beat musical from David Puttnam's Goodtimes Productions enacted entirely by a cast of 200 juveniles, written and directed by a promising new talent named Alan Parker. After being initially rejected by the authorities, *Bugsy* was eventually shown as Britain's only official entry at Cannes that year, where it scored a resounding success and quickly became the hit of the festival. The film was sold to nearly all major overseas territories at Cannes, but at home Rank were unsure of how to market

Morecombe and Wise with Francis Matthews in their 1964 Rank comedy *The Intelligence Men.*

the picture which didn't fit into any conventional category. Its subsequent British release pattern may have gone a long way towards independent producer-directors such as Parker losing faith in the company and pointing the way to Rank's eventual demise as a production source in their own right. As events turned out, *Bugsy* proved to be one of the year's most successful releases for their distribution arm.

Full of renewed optimism, Rank now seemed determined to turn the tide of fortune flowing in their direction. Early in 1977, Rank's production division, so long dormant, announced its intention to return to movie-making in a big way. Edmond Chilton, then Chairman of Rank's leisure activities, confidently called a Press conference to announce his company's ambitious plans for renewed vigour and hope. He revealed that just before Christmas the main board of the Organisation took a decision to step up their production investment to double what it had been before. They were evidently anxious to make full use of all their costly film facilities which included Pinewood Studios and their newly-modernised laboratories at Denham. Now they were looking for good projects and worthwhile scripts that Rank could invest in and market successfully overseas. After watching with interest and not a little trepidation the changing tide and new development of the vast American market, they were bent on re-establishing themselves as a major force to be reckoned with as an important production company with

films intended to appeal not only to the vital sixteen to twenty-four age group, but also all family and social groups. As part of the new entrenchment in production, Rank went boldly on to announce an impressive line-up with one of Britain's foremost independent producers, Michael Klinger. The four major titles concerned in the deal were *The Chilean Club;* Wilbur Smith's best-seller *Eagle in the Sky; The Limey* (a project tailored for Michael Caine); and James Leasor's World War II novel, *Green Beach*. As events turned out, none of these films were ever made despite the elaborate production plans and stellar cast announcements. Rank were, however, involved with one Klinger project which went before the cameras. It was the psychological thriller *Tomorrow Never Comes,* an Anglo/Canadian co-production shot in Montreal locations starring Oliver Reed, Susan George and Raymond Burr under the direction of the late Peter Collinson. Of Rank's own productions, Betty Box and Ralph Thomas were waiting to go ahead with advanced plans for *The Red Hot Ferrari*, to have starred Roger Moore and Raquel Welch, as well as *The Persian Ransom*, from the best-selling spy novel by Evelyn Anthony, when both projects were cancelled at the last moment and effectively ended their long-time association with the company.

Rank, for so long an obvious absentee at Cannes, chose the annual film-makers' jamboree in May 1978, to announce still more ambitious plans. The higher echelons of Rank

descended on Cannes with an impressive show of force, including their own yacht, and used their hospitality suite to tell the world's Press of how Rank was back in a big way with solid proof that they intended going places as mainstream producers. They reminded their audience that over the previous year they had already fulfilled part of their promise by putting into production four new pictures. They were *The Shout,* directed by Poland's Jerzy Skolimowski, starring Alan Bates, Susannah York, John Hurt and Robert Stephens based on a Robert Graves short story. The film was well received, although largely on an intellectual level, and went a certain way to revive producers' faith in Rank. In 1977, they

John Gregson, Kathleen Ryan and (children) Jacqueline Ryan and Richard O'Sullivan in the 1956 Rank drama set in Belfast, *Jacqueline*.

also went ahead with *Wombling Free,* based on the popular children's TV puppet series created by Elisabeth Beresford. Although the director was Lionel Jeffries (closely associated with family entertainment since his brilliant work on EMI's *The Railway Children*), the film only received a minimal release through Rank Film Distributors, thus failing to live up to expectations. Over a period of two years, producer-director David Cobham had been patiently filming *Tarka the Otter,* based on Henry Williamson's wild-life classic, on various West Country locations. It was now completed and ready for showing, with Peter Ustinov as the story-teller, and like many of the Disney features it could be released again and again at holiday time for years to come. And finally, Rank had also given the go-ahead to a new version of that old adventure thriller, *The Thirty-Nine Steps,* directed by Australian veteran Don Sharp. With a cast headed by Robert Powell, David Warner, Eric Porter, Karen Dotrice and John Mills, it surprised not a few pessimists by gaining generally good reviews and performing not only well at the domestic box-office but also with impressive results from overseas.

Both *The Shout* and *Wombling Free* had started filming on the same day in late June 1977. Budgeted at half-a-million pounds (chicken feed by today's vastly inflated standards), the latter was the first totally Rank-financed project in the company's current line-up. Said *Wombles'* producer Ian Shand: 'It's very important to all of us that the film should do well. Not just for me, but

for everyone. It's the first film project that Rank has invested in one hundred per cent in a long time. If it's not a big hit, they're going to be very cautious about putting money into any other films and that would be a great shame for the whole British Film Industry.' Unlike the Wombles on Wimbledon Common, the film failed to clean up at the British box-office due to its restricted release pattern and, looking back, Shand's words now seem fatally prophetic. But the Man with the Gong was on the march again, with Anthony Williams established in the hot seat as Head of Production at Pinewood, and a close working relationship existing between Rank Film Productions and Rank Film Distributors in Wardour Street. Chairman Chilton announced with confidence that the company had eight million pounds to invest in films over the next two years. Certainly, they had fulfilled their promise to complete four pictures by the end of 1978. They had a fifty per cent stake in *The Shout* (which became Britain's official entry at Cannes and won a special jury prize) and also *The Silent Flute,* made in Israel. Looking ahead, future projects included *Bengal Lancers,* to be shot on location in India; *Mistress of the Seas,* the true story of woman pirate Ann Bonny; and a contemporary sci-fi subject called *Skyfall.* All were aborted before the first cameras rolled.

But, despite this set-back, Rank's fortunes seemed to be on the rise. They had achieved their best-ever results at Cannes in 1979, with record sales of $4 million. Also in the pipe-line was a film of Erskine

Childers' World War I espionage classic *The Riddle of the Sands* starring Michael York, Jenny Agutter, Simon MacCorkindale and Alan Badel. With youth at the helm, apart from its cast, the producer was Drummond Challis (son of veteran British cinematograph Christopher Challis) and director Tony Maylam, fresh from other recent successes. Also completed was an ambitious production of another old cinematic classic, *The Lady Vanishes,* this time given a new lease of life by American co-stars Elliott Gould and Cybill Shepherd, with staunch support from Herbert Lom and Angela Lansbury as the disappearing nanny, Miss Froy. Shot partly on breathtaking locations in the Austrian countryside, the thriller was made in association with Hammer Films with Michael Carreras as Executive Producer and Anthony Page directing. It followed hard on the impressive heels of *Eagle's Wing,* a British Western produced by Peter Shaw in authentic locations around Durango, Mexico. The international cast was headlined by Martin Sheen and Sam Waterston, with Stéphane Audran and Harvey Keitel. The film received outstanding critical acclaim, yet failed to ignite that vital spark with audiences. Undaunted, Rank went ahead and announced its 1979 production programme was to begin with a project from one of the industry's most respected cameramen-turned-directors, Nicolas Roeg. Originally titled *Illusions,* its cast was headed by singer-actor Art Garfunkel, Harvey Keitel and an American newcomer of

Belinda Lee and Anne Heywood in the 1957 romantic Rank drama about Franco-British relations two hundred years ago, *Dangerous Exile*.

with a top box-office calibre cast comprising Gregory Peck, Roger Moore, David Niven and Trevor Howard, based on James Leasor's now-it-can-be-told factual account of a true incident in Goa, India, which helped turn the tide of warfare for the Allies in 1943. Lloyd's films were tailored for international audiences and were for Rank a much-needed, if only temporary, shot in the arm.

The final blow fell in June 1980, when Rank dramatically announced their

undoubted talent named Theresa Russell. A modern psychological romantic drama of an American university professor in Austria whose very physical love affair leads to an attempted murder, Roeg's film attracted considerable attention but ultimately proved too high for many brows. It also underwent an unfortunate title change to *Bad Timing* (there was already another well-known novel called 'Illusions') which did nothing to enhance its box-office chances.

Finally, it must have been with considerable optimism that Rank announced in 1979 their plans for a large-scale motorcyle racing film to star David Essex. It was well-known to his many fans that Essex was in real life an enthusiastic bike racer, so *Silver Dream Racer* should have been a certain winner, especially with Americans Cristina Raines and Beau Bridges imported to add international appeal. Despite the obvious star power of Essex (it was a non-singing role, apart from the obligatory title song) and

fast-paced direction by David Wickes, David's fans failed to turn out in sufficient force to lead it to victory and the film was right off the box-office track.

Apart from their own productions, Rank also became involved with Otto Preminger's ill-fated *The Human Factor*, based on Graham Greene's modern espionage novel. The famed producer-director ran into heavy financial trouble mid-way through production which almost proved disastrous and, despite a workmanlike cast headed by Nicol Williamson, it made little impression on audiences. More successful was independent British producer Euan Lloyd, who made two action films in association with Rank (who had previously released his *Paper Tiger*). The first was *The Wild Geese*, a contemporary story of modern mercenaries set in Africa, with a spectacular cast headed by Richard Burton, Roger Moore, Richard Harris and Hardy Kruger. In association with Lorimar, he followed this up with *The Sea Wolves*, again

Alan Bates and Susannah York in the acclaimed movie *The Shout* made at Pinewood in 1978.

withdrawal from production. Although far from unexpected by close observers of the company's affairs, the end was sudden. Taking full blame for Rank's lack of success in this area, Edmond Chilton admitted: 'Our returns were just not good enough. We didn't succeed in cracking the US market with our product, although I wouldn't have thought that the quality of at least two or three of the films was anything less than good. Inflation and the US distribution policy has defeated us.' Added another Rank spokesman, Rodney Ryecroft: 'The time lapse between the end of production and of the last batch of films and the starting of a new one seemed like a good point to discuss the future. With all the other sections of Rank making a profit, it was inevitable that the film side had to go.'

So for Rank Film Productions, the axe had fallen. Chilton, 51, resigned from the company at the beginning of January 1981, after stating: 'Obviously I feel extremely sad and I take all the blame. I suggested that we get back into film production, I controlled what happened during the three years and I recommended that we came out of it. So the fault is entirely mine.'

Brave words, indeed, but if Rank's fortunes had fallen the other way it might have been a very different story. As things were, various producers who had been developing their projects for Rank were left disappointed and tried to resurrect their films elsewhere with other companies. But, on an optimistic note, before his departure Mr Chilton added that the company would be increasing their investment via Rank Film Disbributors by releasing between ten and fifteen new films per year, rather than struggling to finance a handful of their own making. This is, admittedly, a point which most people in the midst of Rank gloom have chosen to ignore.

So it was the final curtain for the Man with the Gong. It is doubtful whether, in the present recession and economic climate, Rank will ever re-establish themselves as majors in the production field. Only time will tell, but what a rich legacy they have left behind them with hundreds of films which have given pleasure to countless millions around the world during these past forty-five years.

Will Rank ever rise again? It now seems unlikely in this fast changing era of video cassette recorders and discs, but in show-business one never can tell. An announcement of the re-entrenchment of Rank as leaders of a prospering new British Film Industry? Now there's an upbeat story I would very much like to write some day . . .

Letter from Hollywood

by Anthony Slide

1980 was a momentous year for Hollywood for one major reason, a Hollywood star, or to be more precise former star, Ronald Reagan was elected the President of the United States. There was also a lot of talk of Reagan bringing a touch of Hollywood to Washington; cartoonists hinted at an Oscar being placed on the tip of the Capitol Dome and *The New Yorker* suggested Warner Brothers should now bill itself as moviemakers to the President.

Hollywood's awards season got underway on 26 January with the annual Golden Globes presentation, at which the Hollywood Foreign Press Association recognised the best in motion pictures and television. As a precusor to its Academy Award, *Kramer vs Kramer* was named Best Picture, and the film also received awards for Best Actor (Dustin Hoffman), Best Screenplay, and Best Supporting Actress (Meryl Streep). Bette Midler received two Golden Globes – for Best Female Performance in a Motion Picture Comedy or Musical and as New Female Star of the Year – and took the opportunity to repeat a Joan Crawford remark

concerning golden globes of another type. Dustin Hoffman announced that 'awards are very silly' and then proceeded to use the word 'shit' for possibly the first time on prudish American commercial television. Jack Lemmon presented Henry Fonda with the Cecil B. DeMille Award for lifetime achievement, Fonda's daughter, Jane, received the award for Female World Film Favourite and Roger Moore received a similar award for World Male Film Favourite. Thanks largely to the comments of Hoffman and Midler, it was a fun evening.

Not quite as much fun was the American Film Institute's annual Life Achievement Award, going this year to James Stewart. There was a note of pomposity and pretension surrounding the event, although it was nice to see the ever dignified and gracious Beulah Bondi making what was to be her last major public appearance (she died in January 1981).

The Los Angeles International Film Festival, Filmex, came round for three weeks in March, opening not with a new American film as in previous years but with *The Tin Drum*. The film was not exactly a cheerful opening to the festivities, but festival director, Gary Essert, did his best to enhance post-film fun by having guests walk between rows of small children banging tin drums and then be welcomed at the buffet supper by dwarfs with balloons. The highlight of the festival was a week of screenings of Treasures from Eastman House, including James Whale's 1931

production of *Waterloo Bridge*, featuring a stunning performance by Mae Clarke, and a special screening of the 1924 version of *Peter Pan*, accompanied by a live orchestra, to which I had the honour of escorting one of the film's stars, Mary Brian.

The Emmy Awards, honouring the best in American television, were marred in 1980 by the non-appearance of virtually every television actor thanks to the long-running strike by the Screen Actors Guild and the American Federation of Television and Radio Artists. Paradoxically, it was *Lou Grant,* the television series starring Ed Asner, one of the most outspoken leaders of the strike, which won the most awards.

Other major events of Hollywood's year included the removal of the American Film Institute from its rented mansion in Beverly Hills to a new, larger home at the former Immaculate Heart College on the outskirts of Hollywood, and the sale of Pickfair, the fabulous home of Mary Pickford and Douglas Fairbanks, for five-and-a-half million dollars to real estate developer and sports entrepreneur, Jerry Buss. The contents of the home were sold at public auction in February 1981.

In 1980, Hollywood lost an actor – to the Presidency – and it also lost one of its most colourful personalities – to death. Mae West, one of the last great superstars passed away during 1980, and Hollywood is certainly the poorer without her wisecracks and her frequent appearances at Hollywood premières.

The Academy of Motion Picture Arts and Sciences: More Than Just Oscar

by Anthony Slide

A little over fifty years ago, on 4 May 1927, the Academy of Motion Picture Arts and Sciences came into being, when thirty-six leading members of the film community – including Louis B. Mayer, Mary Pickford, Douglas Fairbanks and Cecil B. DeMille – organised the Academy as a non-profit corporation, dedicated to the ideal of enhancing the cultural, educational and technical progress of the motion picture. It has come a long way since then. From that small group, the Academy has risen to an organisation with 4,000 members, representing twelve branches of film-making, from acting to directing, from cinematography to film editing, and from composing to public relations. The Academy is, of course, best known for its annual awards – the Oscars – without question the most famous of all show business honours, equivalent to the Pulitzer Prize in the field of literature. (In fact, there are probably many in the film industry who would value it higher than the Nobel Peace Prize, although that number would certainly not include George C. Scott

and Marlon Brando!). Oscar has not changed in size or height since it was first conceived back in 1927 by Cedric Gibbons. It weighs eight-and-a-half pounds and, including its base, stands thirteen-and-a-half inches tall. Today, the gold-plated statuette is made from a metal called britannium, and costs a little over £50 to manufacture. Each Oscar is numbered, and each year only a sufficient number to cover all the likely winners at the Academy Awards ceremony are struck.

The origin of Oscar's name is shrouded in mystery. There are many who claim that Bette Davis so named it in honour of her first husband. The official Academy explanation is that it was named by Margaret Herrick, the organisation's first librarian and long-time executive director, who remarked, in the hearing of a journalist, that it reminded her of her uncle Oscar. As yet, the Academy has not come forward with an explanation as to why Margaret Herrick should have produced a mental picture of her uncle Oscar naked and covered in gold plate – or, for that matter, as Dustin

Hoffman noted at last year's Academy Awards ceremony, minus his genitals. The Academy of Motion Picture Arts and Sciences was created at a time of great change in the film industry. The 'scandals' involving 'Fatty' Arbuckle and Wallace Reid were past, but the memory lingered on. There was internal strife between the various branches of the industry. There was much talk of introducing film censorship on a national and state level. And, above all, a revolution was about to sweep through the industry – talking pictures, which the Academy was quick to recognise at its first Awards banquet with a special award to *The Jazz Singer*.

The original declaration of intent for the Academy stated in part: 'The Academy of Motion Picture Arts and Sciences is an organisation uniting into one body all branches of motion picture production . . . In a word, the Academy proposes to do for the motion picture profession in all its branches what other great national and international constructive bodies have done for other arts and sciences and industries. . . . The time has come, we

The reading room in the Margaret Herrick Library.

believe, when we should no longer remain inactive but should present a solid front, all branches united in a common cause. The time has come when unjust condemnation without defence on our part should no longer prevail. Therefore, to the end that the arts and sciences of the industry and the dignity and honour of the profession may be advanced to their rightful standing among the creative institutions of mankind, we have sponsored the Academy of Motion Picture Arts and Sciences.'

In its formative years, the Academy was heavily involved in trade and labour activities, but with the rise of the various guilds – such as the Directors Guild and the Writers Guild of America – the Academy moved out of that area, and, in so doing, assured itself a healthy future, untouched by the more sordid of industry disputes. The Academy's byelaws now prevent its involvement in economic, labour or political matters. Today, the Academy's activities are many and varied, rivalling those of the American Film Institute, and it is well to

point out that unlike the Institute, the Academy receives no public money, but is totally reliant on the income it receives from membership dues and from the Academy Awards Show for the continuation of its varied programmes. (In answer to an oft-posed question, membership requirements are three recent screen credits and nomination by two members of the branch the prospective member wishes to join. However, any non-member nominated for an Academy Award in any category is generally automatically invited to become a member.)

The Academy has two major ongoing publications. The best-known is *The Academy Players Directory*, a casting directory which has become almost a bible for actors and casting directors, and which began publication in 1937 as *The Players Directory Bulletin*. Nowadays, actors must have an agent to be included in the Directory, but back in the 1930s rumour has it that prostitutes would use the Directory's low rates to advertise themselves with photographs and phone numbers.

To be eligible for an Academy Award in most categories – the exceptions are documentaries, shorts and the Best Foreign Language Film – a film must have played the Los Angeles area for seven consecutive days. The Academy has staff people whose job it is to keep track of all films playing in Los Angeles and to compile a list of the eligible films at the end of each year. Out of that work came *The Annual Index to Motion Picture Credits*, which provides complete player and technical credits for the 200 and more new films playing Los Angeles in a given year. In addition, the Index breaks down the information by individual and by category.

In the educational field, the Academy sends out its members to speak, without charge, at colleges and universities on the art and craft of film-making. Through the American Film Institute, it makes grants available to enable students to intern with major film directors on current motion pictures. In 1973, the Academy presented its first annual student film awards, and since then the competition has grown in strength. Today, co-sponsored by the Bell Telephone system, the contest involves more than 250 student film-makers across the country who submit entries to six regional centres. The winning entries from each of those regions are then submitted to the Academy for final judging by its members. Winners are invited to receive their trophies and cash awards at the Academy, and, in addition, have the satisfaction of seeing their films included in a compilation which is sent out free of charge to colleges and universities across America. The Student Film Awards programme is administered like a mini-Oscar ceremony, and, in 1980, the presenters included Arthur Hiller, Colin Higgins, Susan Anspach, and Ned Beatty.

When the Academy moved to its new seven-storey headquarters at 8949 Wilshire Boulevard in Beverly Hills in the Autumn of 1975, there was little question that the focal point of the building was the Margaret Herrick Library, embracing two floors, and including more than 12,000 books and pamphlets, four million still photographs, and files of newspaper and magazine clippings on 50,000 films and several thousand film personalities. It is not an exaggeration to describe the Academy's Margaret Herrick Library as the greatest film research centre in the world.

Virtually all of the books are on the open shelves, as are the runs of the various film periodicals, including *The Moving Picture World, Daily Variety, The Hollywood Reporter, Sight and Sound, Films and Filming, Films in Review,*

The foyer of the Samuel Goldwyn Theatre. Here on display throughout the year are various exhibitions, open to the public free of charge. During 1980 such exhibitions included a tribute to Jesse L. Lasky, the Musical Film and a tribute to W. C. Fields which included the comedian's famed pool table.

Some of the founders of the Academy: standing left to right – Cedric Gibbons, J. A. Ball, Carey Wilson, George Cohen, Edwin Loeb, Fred Beetson, Frank Lloyd, Roy Pomeroy, John Stahl, Harry Rapf. Seated are: Louis B. Mayer, Conrad Nagel, Mary Pickford, Douglas Fairbanks Sr., Frank Woods, M. C. Levee, Joseph M. Schenck and Fred Niblo.

Motion Picture Herald, Photoplay, American Cinematographer, and *Monthly Film Bulletin.* In addition to its books and files, the Margaret Herrick boasts a magnificent group of special collections, including Paramount still books and scripts from 1914 through 1960, the MGM stills collection, the RKO stills collection, the personal files of Hedda Hopper, the stills and script files of Mack Sennett, the scrapbooks of Robert Z. Leonard, Jean Hersholt, Louella Parsons, and dozens of other film personalities, forty-eight volumes of clippings relating to the career of Richard Barthelmess from 1916 to 1936 compiled by his mother, almost one hundred albums of stills from Thomas H. Ince productions, eighty-five volumes of scripts from the Lux Radio Theatre from 1936 to 1953, and the papers of George Stevens, George Cukor, William Selig, Frank Borzage, J. Searle Dawley, and many others.

The Margaret Herrick Library is open to the public at no charge, from nine to five, Monday, Tuesday, Thursday, and Friday. In addition, for those unable to visit the Library in person, the Academy operates the National Film Information Service, offering Xeroxes and copies of stills, etc, by mail. The head librarian is Mrs Terry Roach, while the National Film Information Service is coordinated by Val Almendarez. The address for both operations is 8949 Wilshire Boulevard, Beverly Hills, CA 90211. The first three floors of the Academy's building house the Samuel Goldwyn Theatre, named in honour of the pioneer producer who died in 1974. With a seating capacity of 1,100, the theatre is equipped to handle stereophonic sound, as well as quadraphonic sound, quintaphonic sound, Sensurround, Todd-AO, and Dolby sound, and the projection booth contains 16mm, 35mm and 70mm projectors. It is the perfect place to view films, and here, every Sunday, the Academy members see all the new features just prior to their release.

But the Samuel Goldwyn Theatre is not merely an elitist viewing facility. For here, for the past five years, I, as the Academy's resident film historian, have been privileged to present many – I hope – interesting and unusual programmes devoted to the history of the cinema. In past years, I can look back with pride on tributes to Mary Pickford, Yakima Canutt, Groucho Marx, Pete Smith, Will Rogers, and Best Dance Direction. During 1980, I coordinated a varied group of screenings, which included two rare Frank Borzage features, *Liliom* and *Moonrise*, as a tribute to the UCLA Film Archives and a programme of films honouring Southern California on Film. Penny Singleton introduced an evening of film clips from musicals of 1929 and 1930. Peggy Ann Garner and Margaret O'Brien introduced a tribute to the Outstanding Juveniles who received Academy Awards from the 1930s to the 1950s. Gale Storm, Francis Lederer and others paid tribute to Jesse L. Lasky on the occasion of the 100th anniversary of his birth. Ken Murray introduced his 'all-bird' feature, *Bill and Coo*. Ralph Edwards introduced an evening of *This Is Your Life* shows which featured film personalities. In addition, there was a Saturday afternoon programme of silent serials, attended by Spencer Gordon Bennet, who had doubled for Pearl White and later became a serial director himself, a evening of trailers and exploitation reels and a tribute to Maurice Chevalier. All of these special programmes are open to both Academy members and the general public.

Perhaps the most important programme that I produced for the Academy during 1980 was the tribute to W. C. Fields in honour of the 100th anniversary of the comedian's birth, and which also included the first day of issue ceremonies for a special commemorative stamp from the US Postal Service. On hand was the Postmaster General and Ernest Borgnine, who, aside from being a fine actor, is also a stamp collector. Reminiscing about Fields were Madge Kennedy, Buddy Rogers, Mary Brian, Grady Sutton, Constance Moore, and Gloria Jean. Even President Carter sent a message of congratulation.

But, of course, the highspot of the Academy's year was the fifty-second Awards presentation which took place at the Dorothy Chandler Pavilion of the Music Center, in downtown Los Angeles, on Monday, 14 April 1980. As usual there were the miscellaneous array of Hollywood stars (Jane Fonda, Charlton Heston, Gene Kelly, Ann Miller, Mickey Rooney, Jack Lemmon) and not-quite stars (Farrah Fawcett, Robert Hays, Kristy McNichol) serving as presenters. Thankfully, there was Johnny Carson again serving as master of ceremonies. The highspots were both provided by Dustin Hoffman, with his presentation of an Honourary Academy Award to Sir Alec Guinness, and his own acceptance of the Oscar for Best Actor for his work in *Kramer vs Kramer*. Needless to say, through the years there have been many moments at Academy Awards presentations which, in hindsight, seem amusing. Claudette Colbert was about to board a train when she learned she had won an Academy Award for Best Actress for her performance in *It Happened One Night*. The departure of the train was delayed to allow her to race to the Biltmore Hotel, receive her Award and make the obligatory thank-you speech. And talking of thank-you speeches, the longest recorded was by Greer Garson, who spoke for one hour after receiving her Best Actress Award for *Mrs Miniver*. One wit at the time commented that her speech was longer than the film.

We all remember Goldie Hawn's 'Oh, my God . . .' after opening the famous envelope and discovering the George C. Scott had won the Oscar for Best Actor in 1971, and Marlon Brando's rejection of the 1973 Best Actor Award in protest at the treatment of the American Indian. They were not the first expressions of outrage at receiving Academy Awards. In 1938, George Bernard Shaw received an Oscar for his screenplay for the film version of *Pygmalion* and termed it 'an insult'. He went on to exclaim it was 'as if they had never heard of me before – and it's very likely they never had'. The streaker at the 1974 Awards who caused Elizabeth Taylor to comment, 'That's a pretty tough act to follow', or Edgar Bergen's Charlie McCarthy looking at the line-up of Oscars in 1937 and asking, 'What is this, an auction?' Spencer Tracy's Oscar going off to be

Winners of the Best Actor and Best Actress Oscars for 1980, Dustin Hoffman (for *Kramer vs Kramer*) and Sally Field (for *Norma Rae*).

Miss Piggy expresses her outrage that although millions would have nominated her for an Oscar, the rules make her ineligible for what so many thought would have been a well-deserved honour! Sympathetic companion: Johnny Carson.

Ron Fields (grandson of the comedian), Mary Brian, Madge Kennedy and Gloria Jean at the 100th anniversary tribute to W. C. Fields.

Sir Alec Guinness accepts his honorary Oscar at the 52nd annual Awards ceremony.

Former child stars Margaret O'Brien and Peggy Ann Garner at the Outstanding Juveniles Tribute presented by the Academy during 1980.

inscribed and coming back labelled Dick Tracy. Bob Hope's description of the 1939 Awards, at which David O. Selznick's *Gone with the Wind* swept the board, as 'a benefit for David Selznick'. All are part of the history of the Academy Awards, just as 1980s presentation has become part of history. From those first Awards given at banquets at various Los Angeles hotels, to the later Awards presentations at various theatres and auditoriums, beginning with the 1944 show at Grauman's Chinese Theatre, the Academy Awards have become the social event of the season for the Hollywood film community and the most important day of the year to millions and millions of filmgoers throughout the world. It may be a sad reflection on our society, but there were probably more people interested in the names inside those secret, sealed envelopes – first introduced in 1941 – than there were interested in who was elected president of the United States in 1980.

Awards
and Festivals

An initial word of warning – repeated at the beginning of this feature every year: It is *not* claimed to be a *complete* record of every International Film Festival and every prize awarded. In fact it is not intended to do more than offer a comprehensive record of the year's major Film Festivals, with some of the minor occasions of special interest added. The full list of Festivals and other various Award Ceremonies which have been, are, or will be taking place during the period covered by this book amount to something like 200 – according to the list periodically published in the American showbiz weekly *Variety* – including small, highly specialised occasions devoted to such subjects as Film Music, Sport, Agriculture, Mountains, the Dental Profession, Historical Subjects and Maritime Documentaries, none of which would be likely to hold any great interest to *Film Review* readers.
  Not all Festivals are competitive of course; the highly respected London and New York Film Festivals offer no prizes or in any way pass judgment on

the films shown, though even the selection of a film carries a useful commercial accolade. If for any reason you would like to see the – hopefully – complete list of such shindigs I dare say *Variety* would – on payment! – be pleased to send you a copy of the issue in which their feature last appeared.

Awards at the 16th annual Chicago Film Festival: announced 21 November 1980
Gold Hugo for Best Film: *Amator – Camera Buff*, directed by Krzysztof Kieslowski (Poland); with Special Gold Hugo to *Eugenio*, directed by Luigi Comencini (Italy).
Silver Hugo: *Opera Prima*, directed by Fernando Trueba (Spain).
Bronze Hugo: *Nous Etions Un Seul Homme – We Were One Man*, directed by Philippe Valois (France).
Gold Plaque for Best Screenplay: to *Solo Sunny* (East Germany) co-directed by Conrad Wolf and Wolfgang Kohlaase – who also scripted.

The Australian Institute Film Awards for 1980: presented 22 September 1980
Best Film: *Breaker Morant*.
Best Direction: Bruce Beresford for *Breaker Morant*.
Best Cinematography: Don McAlpine; Best Editing: William Anderson; Best Screenplay: Jonathan Hardy, David Stevens and Bruce Beresford – all for *Breaker Morant*.
Best Actor: Jack Thompson in *Breaker Morant*.
Best Actress: Tracy Mann in *Hard Knocks*.
Best Supporting Actor: Bryan Brown in *Breaker Morant*.
Best Supporting Actress: Jill Perryman in *Maybe This Time*.

The San Sebastian Film Festival: 13–24 September 1980
Critics Award: *The Conductor*, directed by Andrzej Wajda (Poland).
The £5,000 Prize for the film by best new director: *Hazal*, by Ali Ozgenturk (Turkey).

Awards and Festivals

The Cork International Film Festival: 10-17 October 1980

Award for Art Direction: Jiri Hlupy for *Hordubal* (Czechoslovakia).

Award for Editing: Thomas Schwalm for *Babylon* (GB).

Award for Music: Cameron Allen for *Stir* (Australia).

Award for Camera: Victor Svoboda, for *Hordubal* (Czechoslovakia).

Special Mentions: *Elephant Man* (GB) for effective use of black-and-white photography which enhanced both period and subject; *Criminal Conversation* (Ireland) and *Manganinnie* (Australia).

Best Documentary: *Please Don't Leave Me* by Ned McCann (Australia).

Best Animation: *Life and Death of Joost Roelofsz*, by Roger Proper and Delphine du Pury.

Awards at the 12th Festival International de Cinema (Shorts), at Nyon, Switzerland: 11-18 October 1980

Golden Sesterce (Grand Prix): *The Trials of Alger Hiss*, by John L. Lowenthal (USA).

Silver Sesterces: *Verdronker Land – Flooded Land*, by Chris Brouwer (Netherlands); *Finsternis – Obscurity*, by Marcus Fischer (Switzerland); *They Call Me Chamar*, by Loksen Lalvani (India).

Honourable Mentions: *This Shattered Land*, by Phil Lewis and Jim Laurie (USA); *Vital Statistics*, by Gina Newson (GB); *Numero Zero*, by Raymond Depardon (France). Jury's Special Prize to the American documentary director, the late James Blue.

The 4th Annual Montreal World Film Festival Awards: 22 August – September 1980

Grand Prix of the Americas: *The Stunt Man*, directed by Richard Rush, (USA) and, (shared) *Fontamara* directed by Carlo Lizzani (Italy).

Best Actor: Robert Duvall in *The Great Santini*.

Best Actress: Ana Torrent in *El Nido – The Nest* (Spain).

Film with most Moral Value: *Sunday Daughters*, directed by Janos Rozsa (Hungary).

Ottawa 1980 – The 3rd Ottawa International Animation Festival Awards: 23-28 August 1980

Grand Prize: *Ubu*, directed by Geoff Dunbar (GB).

Most Popular Film: *A Bogar – The Bug*, directed by Ferenc Rofusz (Hungary).

Best film under 3 minutes: *History of the World in Three Minutes Flat*, directed by Michael Mills (Canada).

Best film over 3 minutes: *Shazka Shazok – The Tale of Tales*, directed by Yuri Norstein (USSR).

The Venice Film Festival Awards: September 1980

Golden Lion, 'Quality for the Masses' Award: *Gloria*, directed by John Cassavetes (USA) and – shared – *Atlantic City, USA* directed by Louis Malle (France/Canada).

Golden Lion, 'Emerging Cinema': *Alex the Great*, directed by Theodoros Angelopoulos (Greece).

Golden Lion, 'First Work': *A Special Day*, directed by Peter Gothar (Hungary).

Special Jury Mentions: *The Rescuer*, directed by Serghei Solovie (USSR), *The Other Woman*, by Peter Del Monte (Italy), *Guns*, by Romert Kramer (France) and *Lena Rais*, by Christian Rischert (W. Germany).

The 'Evening Standard' Film Awards: presented 25 November 1980

The Peter Sellers Memorial Award 'for a performance of Special Significance': Leonard Rossiter for *Rising Damp*.

Best Film: John Schlesinger's *Yanks*.

Best Actor: Denholm Elliot in *Rising Damp*.

Best Actress: Frances de la Tour in *Rising Damp*.

Best Comedy Direction: Joe McGrath in *Rising Damp*.

Best Newcomer – Actress: Wendy Morgan in *Yanks*.

Best Newcomer – Actor: Jonathan Pryce in *Breaking Glass*.

Special Award to David Niven.

Awards at the Festival of Nations at Taormina: 16-26 July 1980

Grand Prize: *The Blood of Hussain*, by Jamil Dehlavi (Pakistan).

Special Jury Prize: *Radio On*, by Christopher Petit (GB).

Third Prize: *Anthracite*, by Edward Nierman (France).

Best Actress (shared): Fernanda Montenegro and Zeze Moto, in *Tudo Ben*, by Arnaldo Jabor (Brazil).

Best Actor: Dom De Luise in *Fatso*, by Anne Bancroft (USA).

Jury Certificates: *On the Nickel*, by Ralph Waite (USA) and *L'Avertimento*, by Damiano Damiani (Italy).

The 7th Annual Science-Fiction Film Awards made in Hollywood: July 1980
Best Sci-Fi film: *Alien*.
Best Fantasy Film: *The Muppet Movie*.
Best Horror Film: *Love at First Bite*.
Best Direction: Ridley Scott for *Alien*.
Best Writing: Nicholas Meyer for *Time After Time*.
Best Actor: George Hamilton in *Love at First Bite*.
Best Actress: Mary Steenburgen for *Time After Time*.

The David Di Donatello Awards: presented in Rome, June 1980
(These Donatello Awards are the equivalent of the American 'Oscars' and are made as the result of a voting system, a poll being taken among the Italian industry's leading figures and certain audiences in various big cities.)
Best Film: *Mani di Velluto – Velvet Fingers*, produced by Mario Gori; and Joseph Losey's operatic production, *Don Giovanni*.
Best Direction: Gillo Pontecorvo for *Ogro*; and Marco Bellocchio for *Salto Nel Vuoto – Leap Into the Void*.
Best Actress: Virna Lisi in *La Cicala – The Cricket*.
Best Actor: Adriano Celentano in *Mani di Velluto – Velvet Fingers*.
Best Foreign producer: Stanley R. Jaffe for *Kramer vs. Kramer*.
Best Foreign actor: shared between Dustin Hoffman for *Kramer vs. Kramer* and Jack Lemmon for *The China Syndrome*.
Best foreign director: Francis Coppola for *Apocalypse Now*.

The Oxford Film Festival: held 2–13 July 1980
Best Film: *Oblomov*, by Nikita Mikhalkov (USSR).
Best Actor: Oleg Tabakov in *Oblomov*.
Best Actress: Ilena Soloviev in *Oblomov*.
Best Cinematography: Pavel Lebeshew, for *Oblomov*.
Oblomov also won the best Film Award of the International Press Jury.
Best Screenplay Award (given by 'Screen International') *Tales from the Vienna Woods*, written by Maximilian Schell (who also directed) and Christopher Hampton (Austria).
Special Jury Prize to *Sir Henry at Rawlinson End*, by Steve Roberts.

The Karlovy Vary (Czechoslovakia) Film Festival: 27 June–10 July 1980
The Crystal Globe, Grand Prize: *The Fiancée*, by Gunther Reisch and Gunther Rucker (East Germany).
Special Jury Grand Prize (shared): *Signum Laudis*, by Martin Holly (Czechoslovakia) and *The Beads of One Rosary*, by Kazimierz Kutz (Poland).
Major Prizes: *Married for the First Time*, by Josif Heifits (USSR); *Johnny Larsen*, by Morten Arnfred (Denmark); and *Illusion*, by Lyudmil Staikov (Bulgaria).
Best Actress (shared): Anda Ones in *Gently Was Anastasia Passing*, (Rumania) and Brigit Doll in *Tales from the Vienna Woods* (Austria).
Best Actor (shared): Al Pacino in *And Justice For All* (USA) and Uelese Petaia in *Sons for the Return Home* (New Zealand).

Results of the 18th Annual Science-Fiction Film Festival, held in Trieste: 5–12 July 1980
Golden Asteroid: *La Morte en Direct – Death Watch*, by Bertrand Tavernier (France).
Special Jury Prize: *The Hotel*, by Grigori Kromanov (USSR).
Special Jury Prize for film with best atmosphere: *Quatermass Conclusion*, by Piers Haggard (GB).

The 4th Zagreb International Animated Film Festival: 16–21 June 1980
Grand Prize: *The Tale of Tales*, by Yuri Norstein (USSR).
First Prize for films not exceeding 5 minutes: *The Last Ray of Sunshine*, by Nikola Majdak (Yugoslavia).
Second Prize: *Seaside Woman* by Oscar Grillo (GB).
Third Prize: *Legacy*, by Will Winton (USA).
First Prize for films between 5 and 12 minutes: *Elbowing*, by Will Winton (Canada).
Second Prize: *Fisheye*, by Josko Marusic (Yugoslavia).
Third Prize: *Confessions of a Star Dreamer*, by John Canemaker (USA).
First Prize for films between 12 and 30 minutes: *The Three Inventors*, by Michel Ocelot (France).
Second Prize: *Ubu*, by George Dunbar (GB).
Third Prize: *Autobahn*, by John Halas (GB).

The German Film Awards (equivalent to the American 'Oscars') made in Berlin: June 1980
Silver Bands: *End of the Rainbow*, directed by Uwe Friessner (with Gold Band to film's leading actor Thomas Kufalh); *The Last Days of Childhood*, directed by Norbert Kueckelmann; *The Rebellion*, directed by Peter Lilienthal (with Gold Band to editor Siegrun Jaeger); *The Ortlieb Women*, directed by Luc Bondy (with Gold Band to Peer Raben for the film's music); *1 + 1 = 3*, directed by Heidi Genee (with Gold Band to leading actress, Adelheid Arndt); *Tales from the Vienna Woods*, directed by Maximilian Schell; *Lena Rais*, directed by Christian Rischert (with Gold Bands to actors Krista Stadler and Nikolaus Paryla). Various other 'Band' awards went to players and technicians and some veteran actors and actresses, including Marlene Dietrich, Ivan Desny and Martin Held.

The 38th Annual Golden Globe Awards were presented in Hollywood on 31 January 1981
Best Film: *Ordinary People*, directed by Robert Redford (Paramount).
Best Direction: Robert Redford for the same film.
Best Actor (in drama): Robert De Niro in *Raging Bull* (United Artists).
Best Actor (in comedy or musical movie): Ray Sharkey in *The Idolmaker* (United Artists).
Best Actress (in drama): Mary Tyler Moore in *Ordinary People*.
Best Actress (in comedy or musical):

Sissy Spacek in *Coal Miner's Daughter* (Universal).
Best Supporting Actor (also New Male Star of the Year): Timothy Hutton in *Ordinary People*.
Best Supporting Actress: Mary Steenburgen in *Melvin and Howard* (Universal).
Best Foreign Film: *Tess*, directed by Roman Polanski.
New Female star of the year: Nastassia Kinsky in *Tess*.

Results of the Avoriaz Festival of Fantastic Films, January 1981
Grand Prix: *The Elephant Man*, directed by David Lynch.
Special Jury Prize: *Resurrection*, directed by Daniel Petrie.
Terror Prize: *Terror Eyes* (sometimes called *Night School*), directed by Ken Hughes.
Critics' Prize: *Fade to Black*, directed by Vernon Zimmerman.
Golden Antenne Prize: *The Howling*, directed by Joe Dante and (shared) *Somewhere in Time*, by Jeannot Szwarc.

The result of the always interesting Quigley Poll in America, in which cinema managers and other executives place the stars which in their experience are most popular with the patrons and whose films draw the most cash into the box-office tills, was as follows: 1. Burt Reynolds; 2. Robert Redford; 3. Clint Eastwood; 4. Jane Fonda; 5. Dustin Hoffman; 6. John Travolta; 7. Sally Field; 8. Sissy Spacek; 9. Barbra Streisand; 10. Steve Martin. Of this half-score Mr Martin and Misses Field and Spacek appear in

the Top Ten for the first time. Woody Allen, in it last year, drops to 23rd place in the voting! Another of the 1980 'Ten' was Jill Clayburgh, who in the 1981 list is down to 15th; both Sylvester Stallone and Mel Brooks who were also in it, this year fail to get into the first 25!

Results of The Berlin Film Festival held in February 1981
Golden Bear (Best Film): Carlos Saura's *Di Presa, Di Presa – Hurry, Hurry* (Spain).
Silver Bear (Special Jury Prize): Mrinal Sen's *In Search of Famine* (India).
Silver Bear for Best Actor: Jack Lemmon in *Tribute* (USA) and Anatoli Solonitsyn in *26 Days in the Life of Dostoyevsky* (USSR) – shared.
Silver Bear for Best Actress: Barbara Grabowska in *Fever* (Poland).
Silver Bear for Best Direction and Screenplay: Markus Imhoof for *The Boat is Full* (Switzerland): this film also won the CIDALC Jury Prize. (Special mentions to: Seijun Suzuki's *Zigeunerweisen* [Japan] and *The Spacious Land of Alexis Droeven* [Belgium] for Georges Barsky's cinematography).
Golden Bear for Best Short: Michael Mill's *History of the World in Three Minutes Flat* (Canada).
Silver Bear for Best Short Direction: Paul Driessen for *On Land, At Sea and In the Air* (Holland).

The Annual French 'Cesar' Awards presented at the Palais des Congress in Paris on 3 February 1981
François Truffaut's *The Last Metro* took ten of the dozen awards on offer:

for Best Film, Best Direction, Best Actor (Gérard Depardieu), Best Actress (Catherine Deneuve), Screenplay (by Truffaut, Suzanne Schiffman and Jean-Claude Grumberg), Musical Score (Georges Delerue), Cinematography (Nestor Almendros), Sound (Michel Laurent), Editing (Martine Barraque), and Art Direction (Jean-Pierre Kohut-Svelko). The other two awards went to Jacques Dufilho as Best Supporting Actor in *A Bad Son* and Nathalie Baye as Best Supporting Actress in Jean-Luc Godard's *Every Man for Himself*. Best Foreign Film award went to Akira Kurosawa for his *Kagemusha*.

The American Academy of Motion Picture Arts and Sciences 'Oscar' Awards for 1980–81 awarded April 1981
Best Film: *Ordinary People,* directed by Robert Redford.
Best Actor: Robert De Niro, in *Raging Bull.*
Best Actress: Sissy Spacek, in *Coal Miner's Daughter.*
Best Direction: Robert Redford for *Ordinary People.*
Best Supporting Actor: Timothy Hutton in *Ordinary People.*
Best Supporting Actress: Mary Steenburgen, in *Melvin and Howard.*
Best Screenplay from another medium: Alvin Sargent for *Ordinary People.*
Best Original Screenplay: Bo Goldman for *Melvin and Howard.*
Best Cinematography: (The late) Geoffrey Unsworth & Ghislain Cloquet, for *Tess.*

Best Art Direction: Jack Stephens and Pierre Guffroy for *Tess.*
Best Costume Design: Anthony Powell, for *Tess.*
Best Foreign Language Film: *Moscow Does Not Believe in Tears* (USSR).
Best Editing: Thelma Schoonmaker for *Raging Bull.*

Actor Robert Redford made a distinguished directorial debut by winning the 1980–81 'Best Director' Oscar for his *Ordinary People* (CIC). One of the several stars who have moved from front to back of the camera – or who have doubled both roles, like Clint Eastwood and Burt Reynolds – Redford is shown explaining the set-up to star Mary Tyler Moore during the film's production.

Special Award for 'brilliant accomplishments' and 'his enduring contribution to the art of the motion picture' to Henry Fonda.
Best Short Animated Film: Ferenc Rofusz's *The Fly*.
Best Live Action Short Film: Lloyd Phillips' *The Dollar Bottom*.
Best Documentary Feature Film: Murray Lerner's *From Mao to Mozart: Isaac Stern in China*.
Best Documentary Short Film: Karl Hess's *Towards Liberty*.

The British Academy of Film and Television Arts Film Awards for 1980–81, April 1981
Best Film: Jonathan Sanger's *The Elephant Man*.
Best Direction: Akira Kurosawa, for *Kagemusha*.
Best Screenplay: Jerzy Kosinski, for *Being There*.
Best Cinematography: Giuseppe Rotunno, for *All That Jazz*.
Best Production Design/Art Direction: Stuart Craig for *The Elephant Man*.
Best Editing: Alan Heim, for *All That Jazz*.
Best Sound: Chris Newman, Les Wiggins and Michael J. Kohut, for *Fame*.
Best Actress and Most Outstanding Newcomer awards: Judy Davis, in *My Brilliant Career*.
Best Actor: John Hurt, in *The Elephant Man*.
Best Original Music: John Williams, for *The Empire Strikes Back*.
Best Short Film: Andrew Birkin's *Sredni Vashtar*.

Best Animated Film: Michale Ocelot's *The Three Inventors*.
Special Award to Jimmy Wright.
The Michael Balcon Award: Kevin Brownlow for his contribution to cinema.
The Academy's 1981 Fellowship to Michael Powell and Emeric Pressburger.

The New York Film Critics chose their 'Best' of 1980 as follows:
Best Film: *Ordinary People* (Paramount).
Best Direction: Jonathan Demme for *Melvin and Howard* (Universal).
Best Actor: Robert de Niro for *Raging Bull* (UA).
Best Supporting Actor: Joe Pesci in *Raging Bull* (UA).
Best Actress: Sissy Spacek in *Coal Miner's Daughter* (Universal).
Best Supporting Actress: Mary Steenburgen in *Melvin and Howard* (Universal).
Best Foreign Film: *My American Uncle*, by Alain Resnais.
Best Photography: Geoffrey Unsworth and Ghislain Cloquet for *Tess* (Columbia).
Best Screenplay: Bo Goldman for *Melvin and Howard*.
Best Documentary: *Best Boy*, by Ira Wohl.

The British Film Critics' Circle chose as their 'Best' for 1980 as follows:
Best Film: *Apocalypse Now*.
Best Foreign Language Film: *Angi Vera* and *The Marriage of Maria Braun* (shared).
Best Director: Nicolas Roeg, for *Bad Timing*.

Best Screenplay: Steve Tesich for *Breaking Away*.
Special Awards to Gillian Armstrong for her (first) film *My Brilliant Career* and the late Peter Sellers for his performance in *Being There*.

The Cannes Film Festival: May 1981
Palme D'or – Grand Prix: *Man of Iron*, directed by Andrzej Wajda (Poland).
Jury Prize – runner-up: *Light Years Away*, directed by Alain Tanner (France/Switzerland).
Best Actress: Isabelle Adjani in *Possession*, directed by Andrzej Zulawski (France/West Germany); and *Quartet*, directed by James Ivory (France/GB).
Best Actor: Ugo Tognazzi in *Tragedy of a Ridiculous Man*, directed by Bernardo Bertolucci (Italy).
Best Screenplay: Istvan Szabo and Peter Dobai for their *Mephisto* (Hungary).
Special Jury Tribute to Ettore Scola's *Passione D'Amore* (Italy).
Prize for artistic contribution: John Boorman for his *Excalibur* (Ireland).
Award for contemporary cinema to Ken Loach for his *Looks and Smiles* (GB) and Juliet Berto and Jean-Henri Roger for their *Neige* (France).
Best Supporting Actor: Ian Holm in *Chariots of Fire*, directed by Hugh Hudson (GB).
Best Supporting Actress: Elena Sovovei in *The Fact*, directed by Almantas Grikiavicius (USSR).
Camera D'or – The Critics' Award for best first feature film: Vadim Glowna's *Desperado City* (West Germany).

The British Quota Quickie

An examination and re-assessment

by William K. Everson

What is a 'Quota Quickie'?

The phrase 'quota quickie' is tossed about as promiscuously in discussing British films of the 1930s and 1940s as the phrase 'B Movie' would be in discussing American films of the same period. It is equally ambiguous, covering an equally diverse range of size and quality, but it is perhaps even more in need of explanation since so very few of them have survived for exhibition in Britain today. Indeed, archivally one of the best sources for the British quickie is American television, which bought them up *en masse* in the early days of TV before anything else was available, used and discarded them very quickly, and deposited a huge chunk of British film history in American storage vaults! The poor British quota quickie is perhaps the most maligned of all movie breeds, always spoken of in terms of absolute contempt, and now is as good a time as any to try to correct the record.

The problem started in 1925, when British cinema was at its lowest ebb. Only about fifty British films were made that year, and even the best of them were below average Hollywood standards.

British film makers were too cautious, reluctant to experiment and give new talent a chance, and content to turn out films that were imitative of Hollywood, re-makes of earlier British successes, and generally several years behind the times. This was one of Hollywood's peak periods, both commercially and artistically, and understandably British audiences were flocking to the American films and not supporting the home product at all.

The Government stepped in with two basic quota systems. British cinemas had, by law, to show a certain percentage of British films every year. And American distributors, operating in Britain, had to *produce* a certain percentage of British films every year. British governmental regulations governing these laws were both complex and escape-proof; supervision was rigid, and those who failed to live up to the imposed quotas could either be fined or have their operating licences suspended. Initially, the quota laws coming into effect in 1927 did a lot of good, at least in terms of giving employment and

promoting new talent. Because of the need for more films, new directors – particularly Alfred Hitchcock, Anthony Asquith and Victor Saville – were either given their first opportunities or allowed to advance and experiment at a rate that would not have been countenanced a year or two earlier. More films were made; and fortuitously the increase in quantity matched the mating of British films with a great deal of German talent. Such late 1920s films as *Moulin Rouge*, *The Informer* and *Piccadilly*, almost totally German in terms of directors, casts and key technicians, nevertheless for the first time enabled Britain to match Hollywood in size, gloss, and visual virtuosity. Alas, this moment of triumph was brief. The talkies arrived. Riding the crest of their recent success, British film makers were over-confident. They splurged on elaborate talkies, some of them made in multi-lingual versions, only to find that they were ill-received abroad. The pacing was off, they talked too much, and much of their talk was unintelligible to the non-British ear and difficult to subtitle. With the coming of sound, the quota quickie nightmare really began, and although to this day it has never disappeared, it reached its heights (or depths) of infamy in the 1930s.

The law stipulated that a feature was any film that ran more than 3,000 feet, and that it had to cost a minimum of one pound per foot. The result, of course, was a stream of films running about 3,001 feet, and costing £3,001. Generally 'dramatic' features aspired to be at least forty-five minutes in length; the thirty-one minute jobs were invariably documentaries or, as they were so misleadingly termed, 'interest' films. Non-British audiences only saw the cream of British documentary – *Night Mail* and films of that ilk – and thereby tended to inflate the achievements of the British documentary movement. British audiences were subjected to endless, snail-paced documentaries on the making of barrels, the breeding of horses or the training of dogs, all accompanied by bland narrations and stock musical scores.

A major problem was that while the American companies had to make British films, it was not required that they exercise their best efforts to sell them. Many American companies, especially MGM and Fox, merely considered their quota obligation a kind of nuisance tax. They made the films as cheaply as possible, thereby keeping within the law, and promptly forgot about them. Exhibitors would much rather play a good British film second or third run than risk boring their audiences with junk, and much of the

lesser-grade material never did get shown. Or if a distributor also happened to be an exhibitor (most of them had London showcase theatres) they would throw in a quota quickie to be shown only in the morning, before the regular programmes started. True, the public could come in and see it, but too often they knew what to expect in terms of quality – and, occasionally, in terms of competitive noise from cleaning ladies still using their Hoovers on the carpets. Nevertheless, a 4,000 foot film shown once every morning did add up to 28,000 feet of film a week, a worthwhile contribution to the final tabulation of percentages at the end of the year. And, to give them their due, some companies took their quota obligations seriously, and honestly tried to make good films. Warner Brothers, with good studios in Teddington, brought over American stars and directors to help, even re-made many of their American films, neatly reshaped to fit the British locale. All too few of the Warner British films still exist, and many of them were surprisingly good.

The real problem with quota quickies was that nobody wanted them. Exhibitors expected them to be bad, and played them only when there was no other way out. Audiences groaned through them or tried to avoid them. At least with the humble 'B' western there was always the knowledge that a market awaited it; even the cheaply made ones turned out by small companies like Resolute and Ajax were selling action and a star, and knew that audiences existed for them. But how frustrating it must have been to have laboured on

these films in Britain, knowing that your employer was making them only because he had to, and that audiences would either walk out on them, or greet them with contempt. Perhaps because of that, far fewer directors of note came out of the British quota quickie than, for example, the American 'B' western. For the most part, the quota quickie was a useful way for old-time directors and actors down on their luck to earn an honest if not very inspiring living. Albert Parker, who once had made big Hollywood specials starring Douglas Fairbanks and Gloria Swanson, ground out little mysteries for Fox, sixty minutes of talk and nothing else. George Pearson, once a mighty British director, in the silents a figure to be compared with Griffith and Feuillade, made little dramas and thrillers efficiently, but soullessly. It was only the newer directors, so in love with film that they savoured any chance to encase molehills in silk purses (if one may mix metaphors), that disregarded both the lack of money and the lack of interest in their finished films, and tried to make something out of nothing. It takes a thorough knowledge of all of the horrors of the quota quickies to realise the magnitude of some of their achievements – and if the films were watchable at all, it was an achievement. It is significant that these few directors who cared didn't stay in quota quickies for long. Basically there were only four of them. (Carol Reed made 'small' films at first, but they were far from quickies.) Norman Walker graduated from a whole string of quickies into 1935s *The Turn of the Tide*, a worthy companion-piece to

Michael Powell's *The Edge of the World*. Arthur Woods was a brilliant director of little thrillers, in the process of transferring to big thrillers, and had he not been killed in the early days of the war would have been the logical successor in Britain to Alfred Hitchcock. David MacDonald's career roughly paralleled Powell's; his particular quickie *tour-de-force* was a little film called *When the Poppies Bloom Again*. It was about as economical as they come – all of World War One was conveyed by the inside of a Red Cross tent and some sound effects of guns – yet, surprisingly, it was good, and directed with care and affection. MacDonald got out of quickies at about the same time as Powell, and went on to become a major director of both narrative and documentary films during the war years. And Michael Powell, of course, is the prime example of a director who cared, even when the material at hand seemed to offer nothing with which to work. One of his mid-1930s quickies was a little film called *Lazy Bones*. It had to be shot at night because the star, Ian Hunter, had to sleep in the mornings in readiness for afternoon matinees and evening performances of a London play. Being a light romantic comedy rather than a film *noir*, it had to stay inside the studio – and talk. Nevertheless, there are constant signs that Powell is trying to cover up his threadbare budget with interesting visual devices. Shooting through a string curtain in one sequence almost gives a saloon bar the exoticism of a Sternberg set; and a prosaic conversation is somehow given pep and pace by being staged around, and framed through, the action of a barmaid in constantly pulling the lever that fills the glasses with beer. Small things – but they make all the difference between a movie and just 5,000 feet of film.

A quota quickie didn't have permanent value. After a certain number of years, it ceased to count for quota, presumably so that a need for new product would remain. It was always British, of course, and had a neutral value. While it didn't build up an exhibitor's quota credit, it also didn't work against him, as a non-British film would. But certain British films, if considered of sufficient merit, could have their quota value renewed. Powell's *Phantom Light* was so regarded, and as a result was re-issued many times.

Both the best and the worst of the British quota quickies were made from the mid to the late 1930s, and their values today are often quite different from those they offered then. Many of the more ambitious little British films, bringing in Hollywood stars and directors (usually faded ones, but nevertheless representing something of a coup to the small British studio), merely emphasised the lack of know-how of the British in certain areas – specifically the musical comedy. The harder they tried, the more they stressed Hollywood's superiority. On the other hand, influenced by radio and its roster of established popular favourites, Britain made many 'big band' musicals in the 1930s – films like *Calling all Stars* (with Ambrose and his orchestra), *Everything is Rhythm* (Harry Roy) and *Music hath Charms* (Henry Hall). Virtually plotless,

sometimes quite accomplished in their staging, these little films today (when you can find them!) present a marvellous record of music-hall comedians and singing and dancing talents of the period. There's no equivalent group of American movies that does quite the same thing.

What is really surprising about the British quota quickie is how little it resembles both the methods – and the merits – of the American 'B' movie. Admitting that they contained a lot of junk, too, still the American 'B' evolved a kind of short-hand film-making in its typecasting, in its right-to-the-point dialogue, and in its speed. They are also often quite invaluable today for values quite transcending those of art or film history: They shot out of doors a great deal; they had neither the time nor the money to *recreate* a period, and they often, unwittingly, merely *reflected* it, thus literally holding up a mirror to their time. The British quickie, conversely, was stiff and artificial for the most part, and rarely got out of the studio except for establishing or linking shots, or the occasional chase. The main concern was to tell a story via people, dialogue and with a minimum of interior sets. Curiously enough, when British quickies partially evolved into British 'B' movies in the 1950s (there's a subtle difference between the quickie and the 'B', too involved to warrant amplification here, although the titular classifications in themselves are a tip-off) there was a greater stress on location work – though for the same reason that kept the earlier quickies indoors. By the 1950s, studio shooting had become much more expensive – and setting up cameras in the streets and parks, along seashores or aboard yachts, shaved many a budget. Unfortunately in many cases, and Terrence Fisher's interesting little thriller *The Flaw* is typical, the expanse of outdoor space merely emphasised how little was really happening in it! Curiously enough, it was the American-owned studios – who had no real stake in British films, other than a legal one – who turned out by far the better pictures. True, they had the benefit of Hollywood experience behind them. But they *didn't* have that all-important stimulus of hoping that good little pictures might lead to good big pictures, an attitude that seemed to be strangely lacking among independent British studios.

Warner Brothers, as mentioned earlier, made some of the best of the British quickies – and many of them were far more than quickies. One added factor in the quality of their British pictures was that they literally used them as screen-tests. To send a prospective new star over to Hollywood to make a test meant time and expense; putting him or her into a good showcase role in a British 'B' served a useful purpose at home – and then the whole film could be shipped to the States as a screen-test. Errol Flynn, Patric Knowles and James Stephenson all came to Hollywood Warner films via this route.

Warners had a particularly good record for slick, well-scripted little thrillers in the 1930s, and it is sad indeed that so many of these are no more. They made a marvellous film, *Twelve Good Men*, from a John Rhode mystery novel, in the mid-1930s. Sidney Gilliat scripted it, and I still remember the underplayed yet horrific climax, pre-dating the methods of Val Lewton, in which a murderer (with a fear of cats) is forced into a confession by being locked in a darkened room with a prowling feline!

Unfortunately all prints of this fascinating film seem to have been lost, and Warners themselves destroyed the bulk of their British negatives and prints only a few years ago. A handful were saved, including some vigorous Max Miller comedies and Arthur Woods' minor classic *They Drive by Night*, that curious mating of Fritz Lang and James Whale, and one or two were unexpectedly salvaged through being included in Warners' American TV package (this due entirely to the films in question having been given a US release originally, an honour accorded to very few of them), but far too many are either missing or generally unavailable, such as another fine Woods thriller, *The Nursemaid who Disappeared*.

Crown Versus Stevens, a really good Michael Powell-directed film of 1936, is an excellent example of how accomplished even the smallest of these Warner quickies could be – and how unfair that word 'quickie' is when applied to films like this. Although Warners were unusually conscientious with their British obligations, still a kind of filmic class distinction was employed. Some films, by virtue of plots and the utilisation of American stars and or directors, were thought to have qualities which would enable them to play top of the bill at smaller houses, and even to be offered for US release through the parent company. Films like William Beaudine's charming *Mr Cohen Takes a Walk* or Monty Banks' almost Lubitschian *The Church Mouse* fall into this category. Others, and a running time of no more than six reels was usually the tip-off, were intended only for unambitious home consumption, and *Crown Versus Stevens* certainly falls into this category. Nevertheless, it demonstrates how Warners, in England, had copied their Hollywood system of efficient, professional, assembly-line production. The sets here are either small or cramped, or revamped from bigger sets employed on other films. But they have a solid and atmospheric look to them, and excellent lighting and camerawork make them appear far more expensive than they must have been. A comparison of this film with the earlier-mentioned Michael Powell-directed quickie, *Lazy Bones* (made for Julius Hagen's studio at Twickenham) emphasises just how much disparity there could be even within the ranks of quickies, and how much Hollywood know-how, and even slightly upped budgets, could benefit the end result. As with so many of the stories used in Warners' British films, *Crown Versus Stevens* offers a very strong suggestion of input from Hollywood story properties. Added to the British story-line are incidents and characters borrowed from the Bette Davis-Paul Muni *Border Town*. Stage star Beatrix Thompson, making her film debut, even lights and smokes cigarettes in the approved Bette Davis manner, indicating that she at least knew where the inspiration was coming from! It's an interesting example too of the Warner ability to transpose high-powered Hollywood material into a far more subdued British suburban milieu. One can hardly imagine a Warner Brothers Hollywood hero of 1936 being worried about his entire future because of a £50 debt – but that amount to a low-salaried British worker of the 1930s would indeed be a matter for concern.

Buried in the now largely lost history of British quickies are *many* films like *Crown Versus Stevens* and *Twelve Good Men*. Also buried are some of the oddities like MGM's Fu Manchu rip-off, *Dr Syn Fang* with Harry Agar-Lyons, which I don't recall *ever* getting a single playdate *anywhere!* Unfortunately the best of the quota quickies were made by the bigger companies like Warners, who saw no percentage in preserving them, and who knew that any future revenues they might derive from them would be a pittance compared with the costs of storage and preservation. The ones that *have* survived tend to be those from the smaller companies and the individual producers to whom they probably represented a life's work and a life's savings, and who protected them zealously in the hopes of one day squeezing a few extra pounds out of them. Thus while the quota quickies of the 1930s can hardly be said to represent a major artistic cultural heritage, the bulk of those that have survived (and especially a plethora of appallingly unfunny 'comedies') are from the bottom of the barrel rather than the cream of the crop, and naturally tend to confirm all the unkind things we've always been told about quota quickies!

In 1937, the quota laws were amended somewhat in a partially successful attempt to rid the industry of these quickies. If a company turned out a particularly praise-worthy film, it could count as double or triple quota, thus eliminating the need to make so many cheap films. The immediate result was to spur major Hollywood-British co-productions, with genuinely big Hollywood directorial and star talent (not just the minor names that weren't particularly busy) joining forces with equally important British talent. MGM, with *Goodbye Mr Chips, A Yank at Oxford* and *The Citadel* was a pioneer in this field – a far cry from their earlier *Dr Syn Fang!* The war, however, prevented the continuance of this policy, though not before British production attained a new national identity and audiences really wanted British product. One side effect, not so salutary, was that Hollywood product generally was tending to get longer – and during the war, British cinemas strove to close earlier, so that audiences could get home before the nightly bombings began. This brought back the three-reel 'documentary' or simple musical omnibus with a vengeance, and the mental torture brought on by such films as *Sportlight On Dogs, Sweethearts Forever* and *The Dover Road* quite outweighed the lesser harassments of the blitz. Especially irksome in these films was the narrator's constant calling of our attention to 'an especially fascinating' footnote while he droned on with facts and figures of no importance or possible interest to anyone, and the pictorial quality of whatever he was describing in

such glowing terms was invariably ill-composed, ill-lit, poorly photographed, and often printed on the cheapest of stock! This particular form of cinematic horror is still a part of the British scene, perhaps more necessary than ever (to the exhibitor) since feature production is down so drastically. Now of course they are in colour, and in this permissive age have progressed from tours of barrel-making plants and fish canneries to strip-clubs and *cinema-verité* interviews with prostitutes. But quickies they still *are*, made to measure and carefully running just over the 3,000-foot mark. With production so precarious in Britain today, and the 'B' picture an economic impossibility, they do presumably fill a certain need. But audiences still groan through them, and the chances of them spawning another Arthur Woods or Michael Powell seem remote indeed!

IN MEMORIAM

Every year this feature devoted to the annual loss of cinema talent is full of famous names and this year's sad roster is no exception, with names like Mae West, Raoul Walsh, Peter Sellers, Steve McQueen and many others appearing, all of whom in one way or another are irreplaceable.

FRED (TEX) AVERY, who died in California on 26 August 1980, after a year's fight against cancer, was one of the screen's great animators, helping to create such favourite cartoon characters as Bugs Bunny, Daffy Duck, Droopy (the dog) and many others. Born in Dallas, Texas, Avery began his career at Universal under Walter Lantz and then, in 1936, joined Warners, where he was responsible for directing many of the *Looney Tunes* and *Merrie Melodies* cartoons. His final move was to MGM, where he did some of his finest work. Avery was the perfector of the gag cartoon, he was inclined to take craziness into the realms of surrealism: he was happiest, it appeared, when he was making satires like *The Isle of Pingo Pongo* (1938), which hilariously cut the travelogue down to size. He was 71.

BEULAH BONDI actually starred in only one film during her long and distinguished acting career (and that was in 1937, in Leo McCarey's *Make Way for Tomorrow*) but she contributed a great deal to numerous other movies as a supporting player. Aged 92 when she died, after a fall in her Hollywood home on 11 January 1981, Miss Bondi made her stage debut in 1901 in a production of *Little Lord Fauntleroy*. Thirty years later she made her screen debut in King Vidor's *Street Scene*. Some of Miss Bondi's finest work was to be seen in *Mr Smith Goes to Washington, The Gorgeous Hussy, Our Town, The Southerner, Trail of the Lonesome Pine, The Snake Pit*, and many other movies in which she maintained a very high standard of performance. Often playing nice old ladies, she could on occasion switch to very different roles, such as tough old Western women. As well as films, she appeared in a large number of stage plays and did quite a lot of television. She refused to accept old age, though so often playing it, and at the age of 90 set off on a voyage to Australia in a freighter.

BRENDA DE BANZIE, who died on 6 March 1981, at the age of 65, was a familiar feature player during the 1940–1960 period. Manchester born, dancer trained, she began to appear in repertory when she was 16. In 1939 she became a film extra and two years later made her feature debut, in *A Day to Remember*. Other films included *Hobson's Choice, Doctor at Sea, The Thirty-Nine Steps* (1959 version), *The Pink Panther* and, her final screen appearance, *Pretty Polly* in 1967. In between movies she did a lot of stage and television work. In 1958 she won Best Actress award for her role of the wife in John Osborne's *The Entertainer*.

Though he appeared in many movies, both as hero and villain, it was in television that RICHARD BOONE, who died of throat cancer in his Florida home on 10 January 1981, won greatest acclaim, being voted best TV actor of the year on three occasions. Born 63 years ago in Los Angeles, Boone had been an oil fields' worker, (unsuccessful) boxer, artist and writer

and served four years as a US Naval gunner before he turned to acting. His first job was as understudy to John Gielgud; in 1947 he reached Broadway; in 1951 he made his screen debut in Lewis Milestone's *Halls of Montezuma*. His 64 succeeding films included *The Desert Fox, Man Without a Star, Beneath the 12-mile Reef, The Alamo, The Shootist* and *The Big Sleep*. His 500-odd TV appearances included his lauded long-running *Have Gun, Will Travel*. At 63 he had retired to his Florida home to return to his old love of painting; he was also cultural ambassador for Florida. Tough, craggy and generally laconic, Boone was always at his best in Western roles.

RENÉ CLAIR (real name René-Lucien Chomette) one of France's most distinguished directors, died on 4 April 1980, at the age of 83. Son of a Paris soap merchant, he started writing poetry while still a child (and continued to write poems for almost all his life, though none have ever been published). Invalided out of the Army in 1917, for a short while he tried the monastic life. Then, in 1920, he turned to acting and changed his name, appearing in a couple of films that and the following year. But he hated acting and after studying cinema in Brussels for several months managed to secure his first directing-writing opportunity, writing *Paris qui dort* in a single night (it is said) and completing the film within the three subsequent weeks! He quickly developed an entirely original style in which comedy was always just a covering to his ironic

view of life, which grew into occasional bitterness in some of his later movies. His best films were made in France (his outlook, humour and expression was indelibly French) although a few of his English and American productions did have something of his unique touch: films like *I Married a Witch, The Flame of New Orleans* and *The Ghost Goes West*. But his great films were his early ones: *Sous les toits de Paris, Le Million, The Italian Straw Hat* and *Le Dernier Milliardaire*. His last film, made as a French-Rumanian co-production, was *Les Fêtes galantes* in 1965.

MADGE EVANS, who died at her New Jersey home, aged 71, from cancer, on 26 April 1981, had a long and successful career in show business, having made both her stage and screen debuts at the age of five. She also modelled extensively as a child. After appearing in *The Sign of the Cross*, she made a long succession of silent movies including *Zaza, Power and the Glory, On the Banks of the Wabash* and *Classmates*. The advent of sound had no terrors for her in view of her many stage appearances and she went on to star in *Son of India, Hell Below, Hallelujah I'm a Bum, Dinner at Eight* and many more until her last in 1938. She continued in the theatre, incidentally, until 1944, when she finally retired.

TERENCE FISHER, who was born (1904) and died (mid-June 1980) in London, aged 76, directed some forty-eight films during his career, which began in the cutting rooms at

the old Gainsborough studios in Lime Grove, Shepherd's Bush in 1933. As editor, he was responsible for some of the Will Hay comedies and such other famous films as *The Wicked Lady*. He made his directing debut in 1947 with *Colonel Bogey* and subsequently directed many of the most successful of the Hammer 'horrors' of the fifties and sixties. Specialising in screen thrills, his films include *Dracula, The Curse of Frankenstein, The Hound of the Baskervilles,* and *Phantom of the Opera*. One of his last productions was *Frankenstein Must Be Destroyed,* made in 1969. In 1955 he formed, with fellow director Francis Searle, his own company, Delta Films; and in later years he was involved with a number of TV films.

REGINALD GARDINER, who died at his Los Angeles home on 7 July, 1980, aged 77, from pneumonia after a long fight against illness, will always be remembered by moviegoers for his series of witty portraits of the 'true Britisher' in America. Born in

Wimbledon, Gardiner was a product of RADA and started his London stage career in 1923 with a small role in *The Prisoner of Zenda*. A number of increasingly important roles followed during the next five years, at which point Hitchcock offered him a part in his film *The Lodger*. When Gardiner was eventually lured across the Atlantic it was by a stage role, appearing on Broadway with Beatrice Lillie in *Home and Abroad*. He continued periodically to make stage appearances up to a revival of *My Fair Lady* in New York in 1964. He also did a number of successful cabaret seasons and during the war toured in USO shows. His first Hollywood film was *Born to Dance* in 1936; some of his other films include: *The Great Dictator, The Man Who Came to Dinner, Claudia, Back Street* (1961 version) and *Marie Antoinette*.

IMOGEN HASSALL, who died in her Wimbledon home from an overdose of drugs on 16 November 1980, at the age of 38, though at one time appearing with the Royal Shakespeare Company, never really 'arrived' or overcame her early glamorous starlet image. Among her films were *The Virgin and the Gypsy, When Dinosaurs Ruled the Earth* and *Carry on Loving*.

WANDA HENDRIX (real name Dixie Wanda Hendrix) who died of pneumonia in California on 1 February 1981, started to act in her birthplace's local theatre (the Jacksonville, Florida, Little Theatre) when she left high school and, seen there in a stage production of *Snow White*, was offered

her first screen role, in *Confidential Agent* (1945) at the age of 16. Later movies included *Nora Prentiss, Ride the Pink Horse,* and *The Black Dakotas*. Her final screen appearance seems to have been in *Stage to Thunder Rock* 1964, but she was kept pretty busy in several TV series. The first of her three husbands was Audie Murphy. Petite, dark and beautiful, her career never quite lived up to the initial promise and rather tailed off after several major into many minor movies. She was 52 when she died.

Spanish-born JOSE ITURBI was an infant prodigy, giving public piano recitals at the age of 7. His adult career started in London in 1928 with recitals and he was soon touring the world. In 1932 he started an eight-year contract as conductor of New York's Rochester Philharmonic. In 1942 he was persuaded to appear in his first film, *That Midnight Kiss,* and the debut was such a success that for the next few years Hollywood kept him busy with movies like *Anchors Aweigh, Thousands*

Cheer, Two Girls and a Sailor and *A Song to Remember*. But long after his last screen appearance he continued to give piano recitals, his last in March 1980, just three months before a heart attack killed him on 28 June at the age of 84.

ALLYN JOSLYN, who died from heart failure in a Hollywood hospital on 21 January 1981, appeared in more than one hundred movies but will possibly be best recalled as a dependably amusing comedy supporting player in a string of musicals such as *Hollywood Hotel*. He began his career as a chorus boy in the stage musical *Toot Toot* and did a number of Broadway shows before his screen debut in *They Won't Forget* (which also marked Lana Turner's film debut) in 1937. A few other titles of movies in which Joslyn appeared were: *Only Angels Have Wings, My Sister Eileen, Heaven Can Wait, The Jazz Singer* (first re-make), *The Fastest Gun Alive* and *Titanic*. His last screen appearance was in *Brother O'Toole* in 1972. Joslyn was also a busy TV actor and appeared in no less than 3,500 radio shows, some of which he also wrote. Born Milford, PA, 21 July 1905, he was 75 when he died.

JOHN LAURIE, who died in harness at the age of 83 on 23 June 1980, will almost certainly be best remembered for his role in the successful *Dad's Army* TV series, but that covers only a small part of a career which embraced a vast number of highly varied performances in plays and films. His stage debut in London was made under

Robert Atkins at the Old Vic, where he stayed for three years appearing in Shakespeare plays, returning to the theatre a few years later to star in productions of *Hamlet* and *Macbeth,* etc. His first film appearance was in *Juno and the Paycock* in 1930. Eventually he made around fifty films, including such famous productions as *Dangerous Moonlight,* the original *The Thirty-Nine Steps, Henry V, The Way Ahead, Hamlet, Richard III* and *Laughter in Paradise.* Born in Dumfries, Scotland, in 1897, Laurie at one time trained for a career in architecture.

British actor BERNARD LEE – who was probably best known for his playing of 'M', the MI5 chief in the James Bond movies – died of cancer in London on 16 January 1981, at the age of 73. Lee made his first appearance on stage with his father when he was only six. A graduate of RADA, he appeared in many plays before his screen debut in *Double Event* in 1934. He made nearly eighty movies, sometimes appearing in as many as five in a year;

among them were – *The Third Man, The Blue Lamp, Father Brown, The Angry Silence, 10 Rillington Place, The Raging Moon.* Chubby, reliably professional in all his work, Lee played villains and heroes with equal facility and conviction and added an extra dimension to every film in which he appeared.

SAM LEVENE (real name Samuel Levine) was the son of an East Side New York Cantor, and was born there in 1905. Initially in the local rag trade, he studied drama with the idea of becoming an expert salesman but turned to the stage for a career and made his Broadway debut in 1927 in *Wall Street.* He went on to be almost constantly employed in Broadway stage shows and in 1936 was signed up for his first movie, *Three Men on a Horse.* His subsequent thirty-odd movies included *Yellow Jack, Golden Boy, Brute Force, The Sweet Smell of Success* and *Slaughter on Tenth Avenue.* He was best known for his raffish, sharp, fast talking Jewish characters and he added that little bit extra to every movie in which he appeared. He was found dead, apparently from a heart attack, in his hotel room on Boxing Day 1980.

MARGARET LINDSAY (real name Margaret Kies) who died on 8 May 1981, at the age of 71, had the distinction of once having co-starred with today's President of the United States, Ronald Reagan! A pleasant, capable actress who never quite achieved the major stardom for which at one time she seemed destined, she

made her film debut in 1932 after some stage experience in London. Her first major film was *Cavalcade.* Her many subsequent movies included *The House on 56th Street, Jezebel, Hell's Kitchen, Scarlet Street* and *Cass Timberlane.* She also appeared in a number of the *Ellery Queen* series of whodunnits.

STEVE McQUEEN, who died (on 7 November 1980) from a heart attack following an operation for the removal of the cancer which he had been fighting for more than a year, had the distinction of being the highest paid star of the screen when he drew a three million dollar cheque for his role in his last film, *The Hunter,* subsequently putting it around that he would not even read another script unless it carried a five million dollar offer! Real name Terence Stephen McQueen, Indianapolis born, McQueen spent two of his youthful years in a sort of reform school, then ran away to sea, later doing all kinds of odd jobs before joining the US Marines at the age of 17. Discharged in 1950, he gravitated to Greenwich Village where after undertaking various jobs, including that of a barman, he was accepted by The Actors Studio (one of only five lucky ones out of 2,000 applicants!). The usual repertory, touring and TV work followed and in 1956 he reached Broadway (as a replacement for Ben Gazzara) in *A Hatful of Rain.* The same year saw him doing his first movie role in *Somebody Up There Likes Me* and getting a big TV success in the *Wanted, Dead or Alive* series. Several screen parts followed – none memorable – before he made his first real impact as a GI in *Never So Few*. His star status was quickly confirmed in such films as *The Sand Pebbles* (which brought him an Oscar nomination), *The Thomas Crown Affair*, *The Great Escape*, *The Magnificent Seven* and *Hell is for Heroes*. McQueen liked to do his own stunt work and was a magnificent driver (revealed in *Bullitt* and *Le Mans*) and was a collector of fast cars and motor-bikes. In one of his last

movies, the unfortunate *Tom Horn* (production troubles of which included several changes in directors, including McQueen himself for a few weeks), he appeared to show some of the signs of his disease but, ironically, appeared in much better shape in his final role in *The Hunter*. After he made a big success in *The Towering Inferno* (a tragically prophetic movie as the Las Vegas hotel fire disaster of November 1980 was to prove) McQueen began to hanker for more highbrow roles and with his own company (in which Barbra Streisand, Sidney Poitier and Paul Newman were partners) he made a film adaptation of Ibsen's *An Enemy of the People* – in which he was almost unrecognisable behind a vast beard – which was to prove a complete commercial disaster, with very few showings either side of the Atlantic. With his short hair, sharp blue eyes and an expression which seemed to suggest he found the world a satirically amusing place, McQueen's positive personality emerged from the screen strongly enough to set him apart. He never attained greatness but he will be long remembered with real affection. He was only 50 when he died.

GARY MARSH, who died at the beginning of March 1981, aged 78, made his stage debut in 1917 and for the next fifty years was seldom idle. Real name Leslie March Geranty, he made his first film, *Night Birds*, in 1930 and thereafter appeared in as many as a dozen movies in a year, his screen appearances adding up to a total of

110! As recently as 1968 he was still filming, in a short titled *Ouch!*

STROTHER MARTIN, who died after a heart attack early in September 1980, was an Indiana-born former swimming champion who appeared in a large number of films, many of them Westerns, several starring John Wayne.

Titles include *Cool Hand Luke*, *The Man Who Shot Liberty Valance*, *The Sons of Katie Elder*, *True Grit*, *Butch Cassidy and the Sundance Kid*, *The Wild Bunch* and *The Champ*.

LEWIS MILESTONE, who died, after a long illness, on 25 September 1980, in Los Angeles, just five days before his 85th birthday, was one of the cinema's most talented directors. Born in Odessa in the Ukraine, he left Russia at the end of his schooling and became an engineering student in Germany. He subsequently decided to go to America, arriving in New York in 1913 unable to speak a word of the language. After various odd jobs he enlisted in the US Army in 1917 and, luckily for him and his future, was assigned to a photographic unit. After the war he went to Hollywood and became film cutter for Henry King, later graduating to assistant director, film editor, and writer. It was Jack Warner who gave him his first actual directing opportunity – assigning Darryl F. Zanuck to him as his writer! In 1927 Milestone won one of the first Oscars ever presented with his *Two Arabian Knights*. Then came *The Betrayal* with Emil Jennings and *New York Nights* with Norma Talmadge and the young Jean Harlow. These were followed by his greatest triumph, the all-time classic *All Quiet on the Western Front* in 1930, which earned him another Oscar and worldwide critical acclaim. Other classic Milestone films include *The Front Page, Rain, The General Died at Dawn, Of Mice and Men* and *A Walk in the Sun*. His last completed film was the re-make of *Mutiny on the Bounty* (which he took over from Carol Reed). In 1962 he started to make *PT 109* for Warners but was sacked during the production. The following year he retired, suffering the ill-health which kept him confined to a wheel-chair for the final ten years of his life.

ARTHUR O'CONNELL died in California on 18 May 1981 after a long, progressive illness, at the age of 73. When he made his screen debut in the 1930s he already had London and Broadway stage success behind him. He made a big impact in *Picnic* in 1955 and among his many subsequent

appearances were those in *The Solid Gold Cadillac, Bus Stop, Anatomy of a Murder* and *The Poseidon Adventure*.

After appearing in something like fifty films, darkly beautiful GAIL PATRICK retired from acting to start a new career as TV producer in 1947, when with writer Erle Stanley Gardner she formed Paisano Productions and, ten years later, after a long period of gestation, presented the first of the

famous Perry Mason series, which kept its high place in the popularity ratings for the following ten years. Miss Patrick was a student of law when she went in for, and won, a Paramount beauty contest which took her to Hollywood to make a long series of movies which included *Artists and Models, The Plainsman and the Lady, Death Takes a Holiday, Stage Door* and *My Favourite Wife*. Aged 69, she died at her Hollywood home on 6 July 1980 from blood cancer.

GEORGE RAFT, who died of leukaemia in Los Angeles on 24 November 1980, aged 85, was the screen's No. 1 gangster. It all began with his role in the 1932 classic *Scarface*, in which he played the coin-flipping lieutenant of mobster Paul Muni, and for the rest of his long screen career he was called upon again and again to play a variation of this role. Born in New York's 'Hell's Kitchen' district, there was a period when he reportedly became involved

with the gangs and when he began his dancing-acting career was still working in the illicit liquor and protection rackets. After having failed as both boxer and baseball player, Raft, in 1927, was given the part of a dancer by Texas Guinan in her night club cabaret and it was said that the only time he was not wearing a gun under his coat was when he was on stage! Quite early in his film career Raft became so choosy (he dearly wanted to play other than the gangster roles he was generally offered) that Warner Brothers (who at that time owned his contract) suspended him. His films included *Night After Night, They Drive By Night, Johnny Allegro, A Bullet for Joey, Some Like it Hot, Casino Royale* and Mae West's last film *Sextette*, in which both appeared on the screen for the last time. Raft came to London in the sixties to help in the running of the Colony Sporting Club, but was later banned from this country by the Home Office, who said his stay here was 'not conducive to the public good'! Though on numerous occasions he voiced his irritation at being linked with the American underworld, *Variety* once quoted him as saying 'There are moments when I think my life would have been less painful if I had never come to Hollywood, but stayed on in New York and possibly become a big shot in the underworld'. Whatever the truth, there will never be another film gangster quite as suave, saturnine and convincingly cold a killer as was George Raft.

DUNCAN RENALDO (real name, Ranault Renaldo Duncan), who died in a Santa Barbara hospital in September at the age of 76, will always be best remembered as the Cisco Kid in the long-running film and TV series. Born in New Jersey in April 1904, he was educated in Versailles, earning his living in France as a portrait painter in the early twenties. Later he worked as art director on several films, subsequently turning with varying success to production, direction, screenwriting and acting, varying this with a number of stage appearances. His films as an actor include *The Bridge of San Luis Rey, Trader Horn, For Whom the Bell Tolls*, and *The Capture*.

Found dead in her own Los Angeles backyard, and judged to have taken some toxic fluid (accidentally or intentionally was not clear), RACHEL ROBERTS died on 27 November 1980 aged 53. Daughter of a Llanelly clergyman and born in that South Wales town, she was a graduate of RADA and began her professional stage career with the Shakespeare Memorial Theatre company in 1951. After her London stage debut two years later she joined the Old Vic company. Her screen debut was made in 1952 in *Valley of Song*. Later she appeared in *The Good Companions* and *Our Man in Havana*, prior to her first big success in *Saturday Night and Sunday Morning*, a performance which brought her the British Film Academy's Best Actress award. Three years later her role in *This Sporting Life* won her the same award and,

additionally, an Oscar nomination (a later Oscar nomination was for her role in *Yanks*). More recent films included *The Belstone Fox, Murder on the Orient Express, Picnic at Hanging Rock* and *When a Stranger Calls*. Her final screen appearance was in *Charlie Chan and the Curse of the Dragon Queen*. Between her filming she continued her stage work and she also appeared in a number of TV productions.

DORE SCHARY, who died at his New York home on 6 July 1980, at the age of 74, while undergoing treatment for cancer, had a highly successful career as stage actor, playwright, producer and director before he turned his attention to films in 1932, thereafter being involved in a great number of movies either as writer, director or producer, or sometimes all three. In 1947 he became production chief at RKO Radio and from the following year until 1956 as in charge of all MGM's output. In 1958 he formed his own production company. A few of the best-known films in which he had an important part in their production included: *Boys' Town, Journey for Margaret, Lassie Come Home, The Spiral Staircase, Mr Blandings Builds His Dream House, The Window, Bad Day at Black Rock, Sunrise at Campobello* and *Act One*.

Though it was primarily as a comedian that PETER SELLERS – who died after a massive heart attack in London, while on a visit to his old friends Spike Milligan and Harry Secombe, on 24 July 1980, at the age of 54 – made his

name and will always be best known, he was in fact an actor of wide range: his character performances were always outstanding in their feeling and detail and he could, as he occasionally proved, be a player of pathos. Born in Southsea on 8 September 1925, Peter Richard Henry Sellers was the son of show business parents and claimed descent – part Jewish – from a famous boxer (Mendoza) and a Victorian Prime Minister (Disraeli). After schooling in Highgate and appearances

as a drummer with a local band, Sellers joined the RAF and was quickly posted to the Entertainment Unit, subsequently making an appearance in *The Gang Show*. After the war he obtained an audition at the Windmill and was soon learning how to make people laugh the hard way at this famous little girlie show. In 1948, at the age of 22, he auditioned for the BBC and made an appearance in *Ray's a Laugh*, and then began his famous collaboration with Milligan and Secombe in the classic crazy series of *Goon Shows*, doing hundreds of voices and creating hundreds of characters, one of the best-loved of which was 'Bluebottle' whose 'Oh, you rotten swine' made radio history. Sellers also began to work for the films (once he was reputed to have dubbed seventeen voices in one movie!). Then came a role in *The Ladykillers* and the part, that of Fred Kite, the shop steward, which established him as both comedian and character-actor, in *I'm All Right Jack*. Initially married to Australian Anne Howe, he divorced her and in 1964 married Britt Ekland, later the same year suffering the first of his several serious heart attacks. His friends found Sellers a charming and amusing companion; to his fellow actors as both player and director he had the reputation of being 'difficult', possibly because he was a perfectionist; to his wives he was, it appears, not an ideal husband – by one of them once described as sometimes cold and indifferent. Success did not seem to bring him happiness: and his lavish expenditure on such material things as

cars, hi-fi sets and yachts revealed his restlessness. In interviews he admitted that the characters he had created swamped his own personality completely and he proved the point by switching from one to another of these characters when replying to the interviewer's questions. A complex character (far too complex to investigate here), a great performer and, almost certainly, a lonely and sometimes uncertain man. His many films include *Lolita*, *Dr Strangelove*, the *Pink Panther* films, *I Love You Alice B. Toklas*, *There's a Girl in My Soup* and *The Optimist of Nine Elms*, a small and now almost forgotten, sadly underrated movie in which I personally think Sellers gave his most memorable and in a subtle way best performance of all.

MILBURN STONE, who died, aged 75, in his sleep in a La Jolla, California, hospital on 12 June 1980, was a reliable character actor who appeared in all kinds of supporting roles in some 150 movies during a long career which started as a teenage actor in stage touring and repertory companies. In 1930 he became half the song-and-dance vaudeville act of 'Stone and Strain', two years later making his 'straight' Broadway debut in the Sinclair Lewis play *The Jayhawkers*. His first film was *Ladies Crave Excitement* (1935) and from then on was kept continuously busy in the studios. But perhaps his greatest claim to fame was made in TV where, as one of the orginal members of the *Gunsmoke* series cast, he appeared in 500 of the episodes as 'Doc'; this leading to a long series of personal appearances in rodeos and 'live' shows. When the series ended in 1975, Stone retired and lived quietly with his wife of forty years.

One of four actress sisters (Marina Vlady was the best known, others were Helene Vallier and Olga Poliakoff) ODILE VERSOIS (whose real name, incidentally, was Militza de Poliakoff-Baidarov) died in Paris on 23 June 1980, from cancer, at the age of 50. After a screen debut in *Les*

Dernières Vacances, at the age of 18 (a role which brought her a prize as the year's most promising young French screen actress) she went on to make more than thirty movies several of which were British productions, including *To Paris With Love, Passport to Shame, A Day to Remember* and *Checkpoint*.

RAOUL WALSH, who died on New Year's Day, 1981, in California, was one of Hollywood's Golden Age

directors whose output over a long period was both prolific and highly proficient. Born in New York on 11 March 1887, while still a lad he ran away to sea, his subsequent jobs including breaking horses in Texas. In 1910 he made his stage acting debut and two years later became D. W. Griffith's assistant. It was Griffith who gave him his first directorial assignment when he handed him *The Life of General Villa* in 1914. A year later, Walsh was back acting, playing John Wilkes Booth in Griffith's *Birth of a Nation*. He continued to wear both hats for a while but gradually ceased to appear in front of the camera as he was offered more directing assignments. He lost one eye while making *In Old Arizona* in 1929, and it was increasing blindness in his remaining eye which did a great deal towards his decision to quit the business in 1964. He wrote, directed and produced (sometimes combining two and sometimes three jobs) around 125 movies in his long carrer, including *The Bowery, Artists and Models, The Roaring Twenties, High Sierra, They Drive By Night, They Died With Their Boots On, One Sunday Afternoon, Captain Horatio Hornblower, The Naked and the Dead* and, his last, *A Distant Trumpet*.

JACK WARNER, who died in London in late May 1981, at the age of 86, will always be known as the perfect British Bobby, which part he created in *The Blue Lamp* in 1950 and was subsequently to play for many years in the long-running TV series. Brother of Gert and Daisy Waters, famous music

hall and radio entertainers, Jack Warner graduated to character roles after a career as concert radio and vaudeville entertainer. An endearingly simple and steady character, his obvious sincerity in everything he did earned him a very large and warmly appreciative following. Among his many (British) movies were: *It Always Rains on Sunday, Dear Murderer, My Brother's Keeper, The Ladykillers, Carve Her Name with Pride* and *Jigsaw*.

The real achievement of MAE WEST, that ageless sex symbol of the screen, who died in Hollywood on 22 November 1980, at the age of 87 (though various sources credited her with being anything from that to 90), was to bring fun into sex; she had the ability to make the most innocent of lines appear loaded with suggestions. Brooklyn born and raised (her father was a professional boxer, her mother a Bavarian-born model) she made her stage debut at the age of 5. At 8 she was playing the title role in *Little Nell* and was already known as 'The Baby Vamp'. In 1911 at the age of 17 she made Broadway, in a revue, and this was followed by vaudeville tours, night club appearances and stage shows. In 1926 she appeared as the star of *Sex*, which she both wrote and co-produced. It proved a sensation, running for some 350 performances before being closed down by the police, Mae subsequently having to spend a week in jail, being charged with 'corrupting the morals of youth'. Later she appeared as author-star of a number of very successful plays,

including *Diamond Lil* (in which she uttered the immortal words 'Why don't you come up and see me sometime?'). Her first film made in 1932, was *Night after Night* and later successful movies included *She Done Him Wrong* and *I'm No Angel*, which at a fee of £200,000 made her the highest paid Hollywood star. Mae wrote several novels and made several record albums – she was over 70 when she recorded a highly successful rock-'n-roll album. Her last two films were unfortunate flops, *Myra*

Breckinridge in 1970 and *Sextette* in 1978. Her figure and wit survived to the end: examples of the latter; 'Goodness, what lovely diamonds you have' – 'Goodness had nothing to do with it, my dear' and 'She climbed the ladder of success wrong by wrong'. At the very least, Mae West was unique. She was, incidentally a non-smoker, non-drinker and health food fan.

THE END-PIECE
Other deaths during the period covered by this volume include those of: GOWER CHAMPION, the male half of the famous – on stage and screen – dancing partnership of Marge and Gower Champion which enlivened a number of screen musicals. Gower, who made his screen debut in 1946 in *Till the Clouds Roll By*, also directed, his first film being *My Six Loves* in 1963. HUGH GRIFFITH, Anglesea born (30 May 1912) actor who made his screen debut in 1940 and went on to appear in some fifty films, becoming increasingly cast as a somewhat nutty comedy character. LILLIAN ROTH, born 1910, who started playing roles on the stage at six, later achieved six divorces and a sad spell of alcoholism, all related in her autobiography *I'll Cry Tomorrow*, which was turned into a very successful film starring Susan Hayward. After 44 years away from it, Miss Roth made a screen come-back in the late 1950s. Her final appearance was in 1977 in *Communion*. DAVID

JANSSEN, the gruff voiced and tough Nebraskan born (27 March 1931) actor (real name: David Meyer) who commenced his stage career at the age of nine. Some of his films; *The Green Berets, Shoes of the Fisherman, Away All Boats*, and, in 1979, *SOS Titanic*. Janssen achieved considerable TV success and played in several series as well as feature productions. SOL LESSER, born 1890 who died in Washington on 17 February 1980, started off as a cinema owner and only later went into production with films like *Our Town*, and *Stage Door Canteen*. In 1941 he became Executive in Charge of Production at RKO Radio and four years later formed his own production company, with which he made the *Tarzan* series and *Kon Tiki*.

Young Blood

by James Cameron-Wilson

Shamefaced, I admit that in last year's compilation of 'The Ten Most Promising Faces of 1980' I failed to include one English personality. And I shan't this year either. But with such

important English pictures as *Chariots of Fire* and *Excalibur* taking pride of place at the Cannes film festival – both of them boasting a roster of unfamiliar Anglo-Saxon faces – 1982 could be the year for the New British actor. Until then, Albion will have to find solace in producing more superstar film *directors* per foot than in any other country.

Of the ten I did nominate for stardom last year, Bo Derek is going from strength to strength and has now passed into household etymology, even if she failed to appear in a new film (bar the much-vaunted, but deceased *Tarzan, The Ape Man*). Paul Dooley managed to imitate the inimitable Wimpy in Robert Altman's *Popeye*, and later supported Burt Reynolds in *Paternity*. Lisa Eichhorn meanwhile met with more bad luck than Francis Coppola. Even before the disastrous reviews for *Why Would I Lie?* – with new hubby Treat Williams – trickled out, Ms Eichhorn was excused from the production of *All Night Long*, to be replaced by Barbra Streisand, no less. Her reviews for *Cutter and Bone* – as an alcoholic bitch – ranged from the respectful to the sadistic, but not too bad to prevent her being cast opposite Martin Sheen in Jeannot Szwarc's *Enigma*. But Lady Luck again dealt a dud hand, and she was replaced by Brigitte Fossey after becoming pregnant.

Talking of Francis Coppola, Frederic Forrest had his share of ill-fate when both his Coppola-backed films ran into trouble. The Dashiell *Hammett* thriller, produced by Coppola and directed by Wim Wenders, was delayed for months after initial photography had been completed, while the comedy-fantasy *One From the Heart* became the most publicised film in production when director Coppola shot over budget by £4 million. Thankfully, a wealthy Canadian bailed him out.

Bette Midler's notoriety multiplied with the release of her concert film *Divine Madness,* and will be followed by *Jinxed* with Don Siegel directing. 'But I'd like to do a film with Sylvester Stallone', she told me. 'I like my men big.' Who said Mae West was dead? Mariel Hemingway found herself top-billed in a film for the first time, with Scott Glenn in support, and Ricky Schroeder got cuter by the minute as *Little Lord Fauntleroy* – competing with Sir Alec Guinness in the acting stakes (there was talk on the set that he'd also do *Peter Pan*, with Guinness as Captain Hook). John Savage reinforced his stature as an actor by appearing in *Inside Moves*, going on to star in *The Amateur* in Canada and *Chamber Music* in England. Sigourney Weaver got excellent notices for *Eyewitness* as a Jane Fonda-type television reporter following up a murder, while *Popeye's* Robin Williams proved to the world 'he yis what he yis'.

Before I reveal this year's inevitably perfunctory top ten I would like to take an opportunity of looking at the promising personalities who were close contenders for the chart, and because of my gross misconduct last year *à propos* English absenteeism, I will start with the English. The aforementioned *Chariots of Fire* (from that enterprising gentleman David Puttnam) proffered several (almost) fresh faces, with Ben Cross heading the cast, his only previous film experience being a micro-role in Richard Attenborough's *A Bridge Too Far*. *Chariots* was also Ian Charleson's second film (his first was *Jubilee*) before he went on to work for Attenborough in *Gandhi*. Other faces from the Puttnam film included Nigel Havers and Cheryl Campbell, both from television, and Alice Krige, a young South African actress who played Lucie Manette in the recent film version of *A Tale of Two Cities*. Back to *Gandhi*, Royal Shakespearian actor Ben Kingsley took the most coveted title role of the decade, proffered previously to Brando, Tom Courtenay, Anthony Hopkins, John Hurt, an' everybody. Lucky chap, Kingsley. Another prestige British/Cannes epic was John Boorman's lauded and box-office-breaking *Excalibur*, with Nigel Terry cutting a dashing figure as Arthur of Camelot – a long shot from his snivelling Prince John in *The Lion in Winter*, his only other film. Others in Arthurian armour included Nicholas Clay as Lancelot, from *The Night Digger* and *Lady Chatterley's Lover*, the latter being another GB Cannes entry; Paul Geoffrey as Perceval; and twenty-one-year-old Robert Addie as Mordred, whose only previous claim to fame seems to have been a polo game with Prince Charles. Beautiful, talented Cherie Lunghi, again from television, made her screen debut as Guinevere. I expect great things from her.

Hardly a newcomer, Bob Hoskins nevertheless stunned audiences everywhere *The Long Good Friday* played, in his first starring film role (he previously played an American film producer in *Inserts* and was seen briefly, but to good effect, in *Zulu Dawn*). Jonathan Pryce stuck out impressively in two supporting performances, in *Breaking Glass* and *Loophole*, winning the *Evening Standard*'s most promising male newcomer award for the former. He will next be seen down under starring in *Kangaroo*, from the D. H. Lawrence novel, with Helen Mirren and Bryan Brown. Jeremy Irons, an engaging talent long seen on the British boards and box, stood out for the first time as Fokine in *Nijinsky*, and went on to take the male lead in *The French Lieutenant's Woman*, opposite Meryl Streep.

Not to deny our colonial stalwarts, Australia positively burst with new talent, throwing out Judy Davis ahead of the rest who walked off with Britain's BAFTA best actress award for *My Brilliant Career*. She has since starred in three Australian films, no less: Phil Noyce's *Heatwave*, *The Winter of Our Dreams* and Claude Whatham's *Hoodwink*. The male lead of *My Brilliant Career*, Sam Neill, fared no less well. He starred in the successful second sequel to *The Omen*, *The Final Conflict*, and also headed the cast of *A Man from a Far Country* (about Pope John Paul II), while joining Martin Sheen and Brigitte Fossey in *Enigma*. And Angela Punch McGregor, the slatternly bride of Tommy Lewis in *The Chant of Jimmie Blacksmith*, was busy, keeping Michael Caine captive on *The Island*, top-billing Louis Jourdan in *Double Deal* and fellow-Aussie Graeme Blundell in *The Best of Friends*. She also completed *We of the Never Never*, a true turn-of-the-century story filmed in Melbourne. John Hargreaves, Bryan Brown and Carmen Duncan were not to be overlooked lightly either. America, too, had its new blood and nominated most of it for Oscars. Most striking newcomer was Tim Hutton, who actually walked away with the Academy Award for *Ordinary People*. Judd Hirsch, also nominated for the film, may not have been exactly new, but he was a new face in England. Total newcomers Cathy Moriarty and Joe Pesci were nominated for *Raging Bull*, as was Michael O'Keefe for *The Great Santini* and Diana Scarwid for *Inside Moves*. Unknown to filmgoers, Eva Le Gallienne also collected a nomination, for her role in *Resurrection*, her third film and her first for twenty-two years. She is eighty-three!

One could go on indefinitely pointing out new talents from obscure films in small roles, but unfortunately there is just not the space, so before my final top ten, here are – quickly – some other names that show exceptional potential for future screen stardom, namely Lucie Arnaz, Albert Brooks, Kim Cattrall (from *Tribute*), Robert Ginty, Harry Hamlin, Robin Johnson (from *Times Square*), Gabe Kaplan, Cheryl Ladd, Christine Lahti, Martin Mull, Ray Sharkey and Jobeth Williams. I'll keep you posted.

The Ten Most Promising Faces of 1981:
KAREN ALLEN typifies a certain kooky, sexy, undergraduate, American woman until now represented exclusively by Margot Kidder and Brooke Adams. The gorgeous Ms Allen can be seen in *Raiders of the Lost Ark* and *Shoot the Moon*. Previous films: *The Wanderers; Manhattan; A Small Circle of Friends; Cruising.*

ROBERT HAYS. Dumb, good-looking (in an off-beat sort of way) comic actor in the Charles Grodin mould. Played the accidental pilot in *Airplane!* and hasn't looked back since. Other films: *Take This Job and Shove It!; Utilities.*

DAN AYKROYD. Trendy American comic with far-ranging experience incorporating all of video, vinyl and celluloid. Usually associated with John Belushi. Films: *1941*, *The Blues Brothers*. Next: *Neighbours*.

WILLIAM HURT. Sensitive-looking actor much in demand at the moment, playing a stricken scientist in Ken Russell's *Altered States*, an obsessed janitor in Peter Yates' *Eyewitness* and the lead in a new murder-mystery, *Body Heat*.

JAMIE LEE CURTIS. The Fay Wray, Elsa Lanchester or who-you-will of the 1980s, terrorised by bogey men, fogs, motorists and killers with bees in their collective bonnets. Fast becoming a cult figure. Beautiful, tall and elegant, she is the twenty-three-year-old daughter of Tony Curtis and Janet Leigh. Films: *Halloween; Prom Night; The Fog; Terror Train; Road Games.*

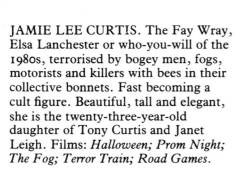

TIMOTHY HUTTON. Son of the late Jim Hutton, Timothy made his debut in Robert Redford's excellent *Ordinary People*, playing the son of Donald Sutherland and Mary Tyler Moore and shouldering the guilt of his brother's accidental death. Deservedly, he won an Oscar for his performance. Next film: *Taps*.

DEBRA WINGER. Attractive and talented foil for John Travolta in that actor's box-office comeback, *Urban Cowboy*. Hogging a considerable amount of the film's 135 minutes, Debra was next slotted into Steinbeck's *Cannery Row* after Raquel Welch was given the push (the latter consequently sued). This time Debra's leading man was hunky Nick Nolte. Her next will be Richard Gere in *An Officer and a Gentleman*. She is possibly the most envied woman in America.

STEVE MARTIN. Crazy comedian from US TV's 'Saturday Night Live', made a killing with his first starring role, as *The Jerk*, making him the tenth biggest American box-office star of 1980. Previous films: *Sgt Pepper's Lonely Hearts Club Band; The Muppet Movie*. Next film: Dennis Potter's *Pennies From Heaven*, with Christopher Walken.

NASTASSIA KINSKI. Stunningly beautiful daughter of German actor Klaus Kinski. After only two films (*To the Devil . . . A Daughter*, Wim Wenders' *The Wrong Move*), she shot to international fame as Roman Polanski's *Tess*. Subsequent films: *Stay As You Are; One From the Heart;* and *The Cat People*, with Malcolm McDowell.

JACLYN SMITH. Original *Charlie's Angel* who made her film debut in *Nightkill*, co-starring with Mike Connors and Robert Mitchum (Jaclyn got top-billing). Could surpass Fawcett.

Releases of the Year in Detail

Introductory Note: In this section you will find full details of the films released in Great Britain from 1 July 1980 to the end of June 1981 – the period covered by most of the features in the book. The precise dating of some of these releases is a little tricky in view of the decreasing rigidity of the release pattern, but where dates are given these refer to the *general* release and not the *pre-release* of the films in question.

When it comes to films which are sent out on a 'floating' release I have added, wherever possible, the date of the film's first London showing because usually this is also the first British showing.

The normal abbreviations continue to operate as follows: Dir: for Director; Pro: for Producer; Ex Pro: for Executive Producer; Pro Ex: for Production Executive; Pro Sup: for Production Supervisor; Co Pro: for Co-Producer; Pro Co-Ord: for Production Co-Ordinator; Ph: for Photographer; Ed: for Editor; Art: for Art Director; Pro Des: for Production Designer, and M: for Music.

Abbreviations for the name of film companies are also pretty obvious when used, such as Fox for 20th Century-Fox, UA for United Artists, Rank for Rank Film Distributors and CIC for Cinema International Corporation. Now that EMI have joined with the already collaborating Columbia and Warner companies for release of their films there is an additional complication here, but when I have it I have used only the name of the individual company concerned. Where known, the actual production company – or companies – is given first, the releasing company last.

When it comes to nationality of the film you will find that this is noted wherever it is possible to give it – those films without any mention of country of origin can be taken as being American – but in these days of increasing international co-productions between two, three and even four countries it is sometimes a little difficult to sort out where the major credit is due.

Finally, unless otherwise specified (ie in black-and-white), it can safely be taken that the film is made in Technicolor or some similar colour process.

Note: late decisions and revised schedules meant that it was not possible to include several of last year's late June releases in the 1980–81 *Film Review*, especially those that were generally released during the last few days of the month. They have therefore been included in this year's releases, below, with an asterisk before the title. The films in question are *The Day Time Ended, Friday the 13th; Guyana, Crime of the Century; Zombies – Dawn of the Dead* (all released on 29 June 1980); *The Inglorious Bastards;* and *Jungle Burger* (both released on 22 June). *Bad Timing, Hussy* and *The Great Rock 'n Roll Swindle,* which were all included in last year's releases as 'Floating Releases' were subsequently given fixed actual release dates; 8, 15 and 29 June respectively.

Adult Fairy Tales (shown in America in 1978 as *Fairy Tales*)

About the Prince who rambles through fairyland but finds that none of the nursery rhyme characters can raise his desire! A mixture of titillation, music and the very occasional smile. Cast: Don Sparks, Sy Richardson, 'Professor' Irwin Corey, Brenda Fogarty, Robert Staats, Martha Reeves, Nai Bonet, Angela Aames, Anne Gaybis, Bob Leslie, Linnea Quigley, Robert Harris, Simmy Bow, Frank Ray Perilli, Angelo Rossitto, Jeff Douchette, Lindsay Freeman, Lee Arries, Fred Deni, Moose Carlson, Idy Tripodi, Michael Hardin, Sherri Bragg, Melinda Utal, Joey Camen, Mariwin Roberts, Maritar Ditmar, Eveleyn Guerrero, James Waldman. Dir: Harry Tampa. Pro: Charles Band. Pro Co-Ord: Karen Dahl. Ph: Daniel Pearl. Screenplay: Frank Ray Perilli & Frances Schacht. Ed: Laurence Jacobs. Art: Jeremy Mitford & George Gizienski. Scenic Artist: Amanda Flick. M: Andrew Belling (who with Lee Arries wrote the songs). (Charles Band Productions-Productions Associates.) Rel: 14 June. 77 mins. Cert X.

Airplane!

A crazy comedy lampoon (bearing a distant but distinct relationship to *Hellzapoppin'*) which takes every cliché that ever was in the long trail of air disaster movies and holds them up – with varying success – to ridicule. A series of black, bad taste, witty, funny and neatly ironic gags tossed together by the 'Animal House' writing-directing team of Jim Abrahams and David and Jerry Zucker and adding up to an uneven but often pretty hilarious comedy. Cast: Kareem Abdul-Jabbar, Lloyd Bridges, Peter Graves, Julie Hagerty, Robert Hays, Leslie Nielsen, Lorna Patterson, Robert Stack, Stephen Stucker, Jim Abrahams, Frank Ashmore, Jonathan Banks, Craig Berenson, Barbara Billingsley, Lee Bryant, Joyce Bulifant, Mae E. Campbell, Ted Chapman, Jesse Emmett, Norman Alexander Gibbs, Amy Gibson, Marcy Goldman, Bobby Gorman, Rossie Harris, Maurice Hill, David Hollander, James Hong, Howard Honig, Gregory Itzin, Howard Jarvis, Michael Laurence, David Leisure, Zachary Lewis, Barbara Mallory, Maureen McGovern, Nora Meerbaum, Mary Mercier, Ethel Merman. Dir Ex Pro & Screenplay: Jim Abrahams, David & Jerry Zucker. Pro: Jon Davison. Assoc Pro: Hunt Lowry. Ph.: Joseph Biroc. Ed: Patrick Kennedy. Pro Des: Ward Preston. M: Elmer Bernstein. (Paramount-CIC.) Rel: 10 August. 89 mins. Cert A.

All That Jazz

Biographically inspired story of an actor-director-choreographer (as is the film's director, Bob Fosse) who overdoes his work and play so much that he suffers a major heart attack and, in the film, dies (though Mr Fosse obviously survived) and is lured to . . . heaven? . . . by a pretty young lady in flowing diaphanous draperies. Fine when at the beginning it concentrates on musical spectacle and backstage fun and games, but less so for the last part when we slide into Freudian symbolism about death and whatever. Cast: Roy Scheider, Jessica Lange, Ann Reinking, Leland Palmer, Cliff Gorman, Ben Vereen, Erzsebet Foldi, Michael Tolan, Max Wright, William Le Massena, Chris Chase, Deborah Geffner, Kathryn Doby, Anthony Holland, Robert Hitt, David Margulies, Sue Paul, Keith Gordon, Frankie Man, Alan Heim, John Lithgow , Sandahl Bergman, Eileen Casey, Bruce Davis, Gary Flannery, Jennifer Nairn-Smith, Denny Ruvolo, Leland Schwantes, John Sowinski, Candace Tovar, Rima Vetter, Trudy Carson, Mary Sue Finnerty, Lesley Kingley, P. J. Mann, Cathy Rice, Sonja Stuart, Terri Treas, Ralph E. Bernsten, Jan Flato, John Paul Fetta, Andy Schwartz, Robert Levine, Phil Friedman, Stephen Strimpell, Leonard Drum, Eugene Troobnick, Jules Fisher, Ben Masters, Catherine Sherriff, Joanna Merlin, Leah Ayres, Nancy Beth Fird, Harry Agress, C. C. H. Pounder, Tito Goya, Tiger Haynes, Lotta Palfi-Andor, K. C. Townsend, Melanie Hunter, Rita Bennett, Gary Bayer, Wayne Carson, Kerry Casserly, Judi Passeltiner, Steve Elmore, Nicole Fosse, Vicki Frederick, P. J. Mann, Minnie Gaster, Michael Green, Bruce MacCallum, Joyce Ellen Hill, I. M. Hobson, Edith Kramer, Barbara McKinley, Mary McCarty, Theresa Merritt, Gavin Moses, Mary Mon Toy, Wallace Shawn, Jacqueline Solotar, Sloane Shelton, Sammy Smith, Arnold Gross. Dir: Bob Fosse. Pro: Robert Alan Aurthur. Ex Pro: Daniel Melnick. Screenplay: Bob Fosse and R. A. Aurther. Ph: Giuseppe Rotunno. Ed: Alan Heim. Pro Des: Philip Rosenberg. Assoc Pro: Kenneth Utt and Wolfgang Glattes. Choreography: Bob Fosse. M: Ralph Burns. 'On Broadway' performed by George Benson; 'A Perfect Day' perf. Harry Nilsson; 'Take Off with Us', music & lyrics by Fred Tobias & Stanley Lebowsky; 'Everything Old is New Again' perf. Peter Allen; 'There's No Business Like Show Business' perf. Ethel Merman. (Columbia and 20th Century-Fox.) Rel: 19 October. 123 mins. Cert X.

All Quiet on the Western Front

A straightforward re-make of the 1930 Lewis Milestone classic movie based on the great Erich Maria Remarque anti-war novel about the young German volunteer who survives all four years of 1914–1918 horrors to die by a stray bullet just over a month before the Armistice. Still an ageless, topical and essential message always in danger of being bayed down by the dogs of war! A fine, strong performance by Ernest Borgnine as the professional survivor and a neat one by Richard Thomas as the young man finally outliving all his companions and being alienated from life by the seemingly endless war. Rest of cast: Donald Pleasance, Ian Holm, Patricia Neal, Mark Elliott, Dai Bradley, Mathew Evans, George Winter, Dominic Jephcott, Mark Drewry, Colin Mayes, Ewan Stewart, Michael Sheard, Katerina Lirova, Mary Miller, Denys Graham, Marie

Noelle-Barre, Dominique Varda, Arda Brokmenn, Mark Roemmich, Andrew Burleigh, Tomas Juricka, Bruce Purchase, Drahomira Fialkova, Veronika Jenikova, Ken Hutchison, Stephen Reynolds, Ian Hastings. Dir: Delbert Mann. Pro: Norman Rosemont. Ex Pro: Martin Starger. Screenplay: Paul Monash: based on the novel by Erich Maria Remarque. Ph: John Coquillon. Sup Ed: Bill Blunden. Ed: Alan Pattillo. Pro Des: John Stoll. Art: Karel Vacek. M: Allyn Ferguson. 2nd Unit Dir: Ernie Day. Assoc Pro: Ron Carr. Ex in charge of Pro: Richard L. O'Connor. (Lord Grade-Norman Rosemont-ITC.) Rel: Floating; first shown London (Empire) June 1980. 127 mins. Cert A.

The Alternative Miss World
A celluloid record of the Andrew Logan lark show on Clapham Common, London, in 1978: when a jury in a lion's cage judged a motley male/female collection of characters, leading the winner to an ass and directing the losers into a pit! Those taking part in one way or another: Andrew Logan, Divine, Luciana Martinez, Sophie Parkin, Nigel Adey, Ricardo de Velasco, John Thomas, Rosemary Gibb, Rebecca Du Pont De Bie, Jenny Runacre, Stevie Hughes, James Birch, Sarah Parkin, Golinda von Regensburg, Joanie de Vere Hunt, Jill Bruce, John Maybury, Emma Harrison, William Waldron, Janet Slee, John Hopwood, Stephen Holt, Bob Anthony, Maurice-of-Modern-Art, Bobby Claridge, Lynn O'Liam, Joan Bakewell, Lionel Bart, Duggie Fields, Michael Fish, Ulla Larsen-Style, Molly Parkin, Zandra Rhodes, Eric Roberts, Peter Logan, Kevin Whitney, Ken Grant. Dir & Pro: Richard Gayor. Ex Pro: Judy McDonald. Assoc Pro: Michael Davis, Simon Mallin & Toni Tye Walker. Ed: Bob Small. M: Title Song 'Beauty Queen' by Richard Hartley; lyrics, and sung, by Little Nell. (James Street Productions-Tigon.) Rel: Floating; first shown London (Classic, Chelsea) November, 1980. 89 mins. Cert X.

*Angi Vera
One of the most astonishing, perhaps significant, certainly hopeful films ever to come out of a communist country; the slow, bitterly satirical but still very human story of an idealistic, dedicated but uneducated young girl who is rewarded for her zeal and agonising public confession, of her one-night affair with a party official, by a journalistic post (!). A horrifying look at cruel Party sessions of self-criticism, comradely clap-trap and self-important officialdom. Cast: Veronika Pap, Erzsi Pásztor, Éva Szabó, Tamás Dunai, László Halász, László Horváth, Teri Bod, Agi Dávid, Franciska Györy, László Kanalas, Flóra Kábár, Antal Konrád, Cabi Koszta, György Kölfgyesi, Kati Marton, Imre Ráday, Tibor Varga, Zoltán Vadász, Ferenc Baracsi, József Bara, Vali Borbély, Laura Bökönyo, Eva Deák, Dezsö Füller, Pálma Gyimesi, Zsuzsa Högye, Péter Kerekes, László Lamanda, Éva Vadnsi, László Németh, István Pathó, Teréz Sántha, Gábor Schallinger, Annamária Szabó, István Szilágyi, Pál Szökem Mari Szür, Máté Tóth, Mátyás Usztics. Dir & Screenplay: Pál Gábor (the latter based on the novel by Endre Vészi). Pro Sup: Dezsö Koza. Ph: Lajos Koltai. Ed: Éva Kármentö. Pro Des: András Gyürky. Art: Vera Mattheidesz. M: Gyögry Selmeczi. (Mafilm, Objektiv Filmstudio-Cinegate. Rel. Floating: first shown London (Gate) June, 1980. 96 mins. Cert A.

Any Which Way You Can
Really a continuation, or extension, of *Every Which Way But Loose* rather than a sequel to it. Broader, more vulgar continuation of fighting truck driver Clint Eastwood's exploits, forced out of his 'retirement' by the mobster bookies who carry off girl-friend Sondra Locke and say they won't let her go until Clint has battled with the opponent of their choice. Rest of cast: Geoffrey Lewis, William Smith, Harry Guardino, Ruth Gordon, Michael Cavanaugh, Barry Corbin, Roy Jenson, Bill McKinney, William O'Connell, John Quade, Al Ruscio, Dan Vadis, Camila Ashlend, Dan Barrows, Michael Brockman, Julie Brown, Glen Campbell, Dick Christie, Rebecca Clemons, Reid Cruickshanks, Michael Currie, Gary Lee Davis, Dick Durock, Michael Fairman, James Gammon, Weston Gavin, Lance Gordon, Lynn Hallowell, Peter Hobbs, Art La Fleur, Ken Lerner, John McKinney, Robin Menken, Jack Murdock, George Murdock, Ann Nelson, Sunshine Parker, Kent Perkins, Anne Ramsey, Logan Ramsey, Michael Reinbold, Tessa Richarde, Jeremy Smith, Bill Sorrells, Jim Stafford, Michael Talbott, Mark Taylor, Jack Thibeau, Charles Walker, Bobby Porter, George Orrison, Jerry Brutsche, Orwin Harvey, Larry Holt, John Nowak, Walt Robles, Mike Tillman. Dir: Buddy Van Horn. Pro: Fritz Manes. Ex Pro: Robert Daley. Screenplay: Stanford Sherman; based on the characters created by Jeremy Joe Kronsberg. Ph: David Worth. Ed: Ferris Webster & Ron Spang. Pro Des: William J. Creber. Songs by various composers; supervision by Snuff Garrett with Steve Dorf conducting. (Warner.) Rel: 14 December. 115 mins. Cert A.

Atlantic City
Louis Malle triumphantly proves that unlike so many European directors whose work takes a dive when they go to work in Hollywood, he has marvellously survived the transition, first with *Pretty Baby* and then with this beautifully observed series of character studies against a finely atmosphered background of the famous Atlantic sea-side playground. The story of a small-time ex-gangster who suddenly finds himself a millionaire, thanks to his unexpected possession of a large haul of Mafia-bound drugs. And this leads to him becoming the lover of the girl with the lemon-rubbed breast and the happy killer of a couple of hoods! Beautiful performances by Burt Lancaster, Susan Sarandon and Kate Reid. Rest of cast: Michel Piccoli, Hollis McLaren, Robert Joy, Al Waxman, Robert Goulet, Moses Znaimer, Harvey Atkin, Eleanor Beecroft, Norma Dell'agnese, Louis del Grande, Cec Linder, Angus MacInnes, Sean McCaan, John McCurry, Wally Shawn, Sean Sullivan, Joyce Parks, Vincent Glorioso, Tony Angelo, Sis Clark, Gennaro Consalvo, Lawrence McGuire, Ann Burns, Marie Burns, Jean Burns, Connie Collins, J. Allmond, John Burns, Joe Galante, Danny Pucilli, Jack Allocco, Harry Madsen, Frank Ferrara. Dir: Louis Malle. Pro: Denis Héroux. Screenplay: John Guare. Ex Pro: Joseph Beaubien & Gabriel Boustany. Ph: Richard Ciupka. Ed: Susanne Baron. Pro Des: Ann Pritchard. M: Michael Legrand (song, 'Atlantic City, My Old Friend', comp. and sung by Paul Anka). Assoc Pro: Justine Héroux & Larry Nessis. Pro Co-Ord: Vincent Malle. (John Kemeny/Denis Héroux-Curzon Films Dist-Enterprise Pictures.) Rel: Floating; first

shown London (Curzon) January 1981. 105 mins. Cert AA.

The Awakening
Hammer-like horror! Nicely conventional adaptation of the Bram Stoker thriller *The Jewel of the Seven Stars* which in turn was probably inspired by the myths about the disaster and death which threaten those archaeologists brave and dedicated enough to break into and despoil the tombs of the Kings and Queens of Ancient Egypt. Charlton Heston and assistant Susannah York paying a high price for invading the 3,800-year-long privacy of the lovely but evil Queen Kara. Rest of cast: Jill Townsend, Stephanie Zimbalist, Patrick Drury, Ian McDiarmid, Leonard Maguire, Chris Fairbanks, Michael Halphie, John Rees, Nadim Sawalha, Ishia Bennison, Ahmed Osman, Miriam Margolyes, Bruce Myers, Madhav Sharma, Albert Moses, Michael Mellinger, Roger Kemp. Dir: Mike Newell. Pro: Robert Solo. Co Pro: Andrew Scheinman & Martin Shafer. Assoc Pro: Harry Benn. Screenplay: Allan Scott, Chris Bryant & Clive Exton. Ed: Terry Rawlings. Pro Des: Michael Stringer. Art: Lionel Couch. M: Claude Bolling. (Solofilm-Orion-EMI) Rel: 23 November. 105 mins. Cert X.

Babylon
British-made, shoe-string-budgeted movie about London's black community, presenting a gloomy picture of brutal and biased cops, young black thugs and a depressingly convincing background of racial prejudice, simmering violence and grey living conditions. Made entirely on location in South London and the West End. Cast: Brinsley Forde, Karl Howman, Trevor Laird, Brian Bovell, Victor Romero Evans, David N. Haynes, Archie Pool, T. Bone Wilson. Dir: Franco Rosso. Pro: Gavrik Losey. Screenplay: Martin Stellman & Franco Rosso. Ph: Chris Menges. Ed: Thomas Schwalm. M: Denis Bovell. (Chrysalis Group-National Film Finance Corp-Lee [Electric] Lighting–Osiris Films.) Rel: Floating; first shown London (Gate 2, Chelsea Classic and Brixton Ace) November 1980. 95 mins. Cert X.

The Baltimore Bullet
Old-fashioned style comedy-melodrama about pool hustlers climaxed by the final big game between rivals James Coburn and Omar Sharif to prove who is the best man with the cue. Rest of cast: Bruce Boxleitner, Ronee Blakley, Jack O'Halloran, Calvin Lockhart, Michael Learner, Paul Barselou, Jeff Temkin, Willie Mosconi, Cisse Cameron, Shep Sanders, Jon Ian Jacobs, Ed Bakey, Robert Hughes, Rocknee Tarkington, Shay Duffin, Thomas Castranova, Eric Laneuville, William M. Vint, Peter Jason, Edward Hoerner, Marco Rodriques, George Fisher, Charles Picerni, Walter Wyatt, John Alderman, Robert Acey, Alvin Maines, Lou Butera, Irving Crane, Richie Florence, Allen Hopkins, Peter Margo, Ray Martin, Jim Mataya, Steve Mizerak, Jim Rempe, Michael Sigel. Dir: Robert Ellis Miller. Pro: John Brascia. Ex Pro: William D. Jekel & Norman G. Rudman. Screenplay: John Brascia & Robert Vincent O'Neill. Assoc Pro: Ted Goetz. Ph: James A. Crabe. Ed: Jerry Brady. Pro Des: Henry Blumenthal. Art: Adrian Gorton. M: Johnny Mandel. (Rank Org.) Rel: Floating. 103 mins. Cert AA.

Releases of the Year in Detail

Battle Beyond the Stars
Fairly minor addition to the Space Wars cycle of movies; lots of remarkable outer-space hardware, macabre characters, robots, space battles, kaleidoscopic colours, cartoon-strip story and various other ingredients likely to at least make junior happy. Richard Thomas as the hero, John Saxon the black-eyed villain and Robert Vaughn as the in-between; with George Peppard contributing a comic 'Cowboy' character which surely comes from another film altogether! Rest of cast: Darlanne Fluegel, Sybil Danning, Sam Jaffe, Morgan Woodward, Steve Davis, Earl Boen, John McGowans, Laura Cody, Larry Meyers, Lynn Carlin, Jeff Corey, Julia Duffy, Eric Morris, Marta Kristen, Doug Carleson, Ron Ross, Terence McNally, Don Thompson, Daniel Carlin, Ansley Carlin, Whitney Rydbeck, Dallas Clarke, Dan Vincent, Rick Davidson, Ton Henschel, Brian Coventry, Kerry Frank, Dave Rekrut, Robert Reece, Nate Esformes, Dick Davilos, Lanny Broyles, Billy Akin, Willy Bagot, David D'Arnal, Casey Durkin, Keith Hartwig, Billy Hayes, Paul Lyle, Kevin O'Donnel, Jim Penwell, Alan Pulner, Jim Scanlon, Jude Soliz, Brad Thompson, Allen Wong. Dir: Jimmy T. Murakami. Pro: Ed Carlin. Ex Pro: Roger Corman. Screenplay: John Sayles; from a story by Sayles and Ann Dyer. Ph: Daniel Lacambre. Ed: Allan Holzman & R. J. Kizer. Assoc Pro: Mary Ann Fisher. Art: Jim Cameron & Charles Breen. M: James Horner. (New World-Orion-Warner.) Rel: 22 February. 102 mins. Cert A.

Being There
Yet another, beautifully moulded character study by the late Peter Sellers in a satirical comedy which is basically a single joke marvellously elongated by the talents of writer Jerzy Kosinski, director Hal Ashby and Sellers. The story of an entirely uneducated gardener whose only contact with life has been through TV (constantly switched from channel to channel without any absorption of content) who is literally by accident thrown into high political society and whose empty comments about plant culture are accepted up to US President level as being philosophical, metaphoric comment on the state of the nation and cures for its ills, and seems likely to take our idiotic innocent abroad right into the White House: in the land of the TV tube the idiot is king! Rest of cast: Shirley MacLaine, Jack Warden, Melvyn Douglas, Richard Dysart, Sam Wisman, Arthur Rosenberg, Gwen Humble, Fredric Lehne, Jerome Hellman, Ned Wilson, Alice Herson, James Noble, Richard Seff, Ruth Attaway, Arthur Grundy, Villa Mae, P. Barkley, Nell P. Leaman, Henry B. Dawkins, Richard Basehart, William Larsen, John Harkins, Fran Brill, Elya Baskin, Mitch Kreindel, Laurie Jefferson, Katherine DeHetre, Than Wyenn, Paul Marin, Sandy Ward, Dana Hansen, Janet Meshad, Hanna Hertelendy, Richard McKenzie, Melendy Britt. Dir: Hal Ashby. Pro: Andrew Braunsberg. Ex Pro: Jack Schwartzman. Assoc Pro: Charles Mulvehill. Screenwriter: Jerzy Kosinski: based on his novel. Ph: Caleb Deschanel. Ed: Don Zimmerman. Pro Des: Michael Haller. Art: James Schoppe. M: John Mandel. (Lorimar-ITC.) Rel: 5 October. 130 mins. Cert AA.

The Bermuda Triangle
A semi-documentary feature based on the Charles Berlitz book which sought to unravel something of the mysteries of the vanishing men, ships and airplanes in a certain section of the Western Atlantic, which have given rise to all sorts of weird and wonderful science-fiction and other theories. Dir: Richard Friedenberg. Pro: Charles E. Seillier Jr & James L. Conway. Screenplay: Stephen Lord. Ph: Henning Schellerup. Ed: John Link. Art: Charles Bennett. M: John Cameron. (Sunn Classic Productions [GB] Ltd.) Rel: 1 February. 93 mins. Cert U.

Best Boy
Feature documentary about a mentally retarded but not stupid fifty-two-year-old who has always lived with his parents but with the danger of their death becoming real, is trained to deal with life in an institution. The winner of the 1980 Academy Award for the best feature documentary. Dir, Pro & Ed: Ira Wohl. Designed & Ph: Tom McDonough. (Essential.) Rel: Floating; first shown London (Academy) March 1981. 104 mins. Cert U.

The Big Brawl
The first American-made Martial Arts movie, a brutal and violent and sometimes funny story of a skilled young Chinese unarmed combat expert who becomes involved with gangsters and is blackmailed by them into taking part in a gigantic no-holds-barred fighting contest in Chicago in the early 1930s. Starring popular Hong Kong martial arts master Jackie Chan. Rest of cast: Jose Ferrer, Kristine de Bell, Mako, Ron Max, David Sheiner, Rosalind Chao, Lenny Montana, Pat Johnson, Mary Ellen O'Neill, H. B. Haggerty, Chao-Lichi, Joycelyn Lew, Peter Marc, Marcus Mukai, Gene La Bell, Sonny Barnes, Stephen Merjanian, Phil Macado, Donnie Williams, Earl Maynard, Larry Drake, Helena Humann, Dolly Benjamin, Eugene Anderson, Steve Uzzell, Gene Rader, Big John Hamilton, Ken Hudgins, Talmadge Scott, John Martin, Gary Delaune, Hart Sprager, Craig Huston, Patricia Zapp, Frank Stewart, Robert Gottschall, Collie Eng, Charles Balcar, Dan Balcar, Loren Janes, George Fisher, Tom Morga, Nigel Binns, John Hall, DEBORAH Heldon, Darlene Langlois, Frank Macedo, Gwen Miller, John Parker, Ray Robles, Hill Farnsworth. Dir & Screenplay: Robert Clouse. Pro: Fred Weintraub & Terry Morse Jr. Ex Pro: Raymond Chow. Ex in charge of Pro: André Morgan. Pr: Robert Jessup. Ed: George Grenville. Art: Joe Altadonna. M: Lalo Schifrin. (Golden Harvest-Warner.) Rel: 26 October. 95. mins. Cert AA.

The Big Red One
Samuel Fuller, who made his name with some very acceptable action movies in the 1950s–60s period (such as *Pickup on South Street*) returns to work after a decade away from the studios with a World War Two story about four young soldiers and their tough sergeant literally fighting their way from the Eastern deserts, through Italy, to the Western Front and final cease fire. A series of bloody battles and a few more amusing scenes (notably the quintet's helping to deliver a baby in a tank) all based, it is said, on Fuller's own experience as a member of the US Army's 1st Infantry Division (The Big Red One of the title). Cast: Lee Marvin, Mark Hamill, Robert Carradine, Bobby di Cicco, Kelly Ward, Stephane Audran, Siegfried Rauch, Guy Marchant, Serge Marquand, Charles McCauley, Alain Doutey, Maurice Marsac, Colin Gilbert, Joseph Clark, Ken Campbell, Doug Werner, Perry Lang, Christa Lang, Howard Delman, Marthe Villalonga. Dir & Screenplay: Samuel Fuller. Pro: Gene Corman. Ph: Adam Greenberg. Ed: Morton Tubor. Art: Peter Jamison. M: Dana Kaproff (Lorimar-ITC.) Rel: 16 November. 112 mins. Cert AA.

The Black Stallion
Extremely beautifully photographed story of the love affair of a boy and a horse, only survivors of a shipwreck who each save the other's life while making their way to a small, idyllic, uninhabited island. The movie loses a little of its considerable artistic impact when it moves to America and follows the efforts of boy, horse and trainer to win the important (echoes of *National Velvet!*) race. Delightfully natural performance by Kelly Reno as the freckle-faced youngster and a restrained but equally good one by Mickey Rooney as the wise old trainer. Rest of cast: Teri Garr, Clarence Muse, Hoyt Axton, Michael Higgins, Ed McNamara, Dogmi Larbi, John Burton, John Buchanan, Kristen Vigard, Fausto Tozzi, John Karlson, Leopoldo Trieste, Frank Cousins, Don Hudson, Marne Maitland, Tom Dahlgren. With Cass-olé as the stallion. Dir: Carroll Ballard. Pro: Fred Roos & Tom Sternberg. Ex Pro: Francis Coppola. Screenplay: Melissa Mathison. Jeanne Rosenberg & William D. Wittliff; from the novel of the same title by Walter Farley. Ph: Caleb Deschanel. Ed: Robert Dalva. Art: Aurelio Crugnola & Earl Preston. M: Carmine Coppola. (Zoetrope Studios-UA.) Rel: 29 July. 117 mins. Cert A.

Blood Beach
Another 'monstrous' movie with the mysterious man-maiming and killing creature hidden beneath the sands of a Californian coastal resort. When finally blown to smithereens it seems likely to return – in some subsequent movie! – in mass, with every blown bit a whole new threat. Cast: David Huffman, Mariana Hill, John Saxon, Otis Young, Stefan Gierasch, Burt Young, Darrell Fetty, Lynne Marta, Eleanor Zee, Lena Pousette, Pamela McMayler, Harriet Medin, Mickey Fox, Laura Burkett, Marleta Giles, Jacqueline Randall, Don Barlow, David Wysong, Charles Rowe Hook, John Joseph Thomas, Julie Dolan, Julia Friebel, Christopher Franklin, Bobby Bass, Read Morgan, Barney Pell, Marcus Wyatt, Mary Jo Catlett, Ian Abercrombie, Robert Newirth, Lavelle Roby, James Ogg, Lynne Fienerman, Steve Finkel, David Jacob, Stefane Auerbach, Steve Ballard, Judy Walker, Muriel Bakcha. Dir & Screenplay: Jeffrey Bloom, from his own and Steven Nalevansky's story. Pro: Steven Nalevansky. Ex Pro: Sidney Beckerman. Assoc Pro: Neil Canton. Pro Ex: Carole Wilson. Pro Sup: Mel Dellar. Ph: Steve Poster. Ed: Gary Griffen. Art: William Sandell. M: Gil Melle. (Empress Productions-Miracle.) Rel: Floating; first shown London, March 1980. 90 mins. Cert X.

Blood Feud (Fatto di Sarigne fra due vomini per causa di una vedova – si sospettano moventi politici)
Classically dramatic Lina Wertmüller drama about the widow of a Sicilian Mafia victim who is determined to avenge the murder but finds herself loving the two men who can help her in her aim, a local lawyer returned after long absence in Rome and a cousin-by-marriage who comes back after even longer absence in New York, where he has become a gangster with a

twenty-five-victim tally. Finely acted by Sophia Loren, Marcello Mastroianni and Giancarlo Giannini, beautifully photographed, and directed with a fine sense of the story and scene. Rest of cast: Turi Ferro. Dir & Screenplay: Lina Wertmüller. Pro: Harry Colombo. Pro Sup: Gino Millozza. Ph: Tonino Delli Colli. Ed: Franco Fraticelli. Art: Enrico Job. M: Dangiò-Nando De Luca. (Liberty-ITC.) Rel: Floating; first shown London (Odeon, Kensington) January 1981. 100 mins. Cert X.

The Blood of Hussain
Beautifully photographed and in every way superior Pakistan film which, made before the event, foresaw the military taking over the country. The story of a modern martyr, the younger son (the elder accepts and works for the new regime) of a rich landowning family who rebels against the dispossessing of his villagers' land and dies with them when the soldiers fire on them. The story draws a parallel with the martyrdom of the Prophet Mohamad's nephew, who in 680 AD was murdered because he refused to acknowledge the Caliph who had usurped power. Dialogue partly in English and partly in Pakistan (sub-titled). Cast: Salmaan Peerzada (as both the brothers), Kika Markham, Durriya Kazi, Kabuli Baba, Mirza Ghazanfar Beg, Fauzia Zareen, Zil-e-Subhan, Dost Mohammed, Saqi, Alia Begum, Jamil Dehlavi, Khayyam Sarhadi, Mubila, Sanaulla Khan, Shoaib Hashmi, Perrin Cooper, Jehangir Khan. Dir, Pro Pro & Screenplay: Jamil Dehlavi. Ph: Walter Lassally & Jamil Dehlavi. Ed: Sue Collins and Jamil Dehlavi. Assoc Pro: Sandra Marsh & Shakira Masood. No other credits. (Cinegate.) Rel: Floating; first shown London (Gate), March 1981. 103 mins. Cert AA.

The Blood Spattered Bride – Novia ensangrentada
Brutal little Italian thriller based on the Sheridan Le Fanu novel about a bride who finds lots of nasty things happening in her hubbie's ancestral home when he takes her there for their honeymoon. Cast: Simon Andreu, Maribel Martin, Alexandra Bastardo, Dean Selmier, Rosa Ma Rodrigues, Monserrat Julio, Angel Lombarte. Dir & Screenplay: Vicente Aranda. Po Sup: Jaime Fernandez-Cid. Ex Pro: José Lopez Morena. Ph: Fernando Arribas. Ed: Pablo G. Del Amo. Pro Des: Juan Alberto Soler. M: Antonio Perez. (Morgana Films-Eagle.) Rel: 24 August. 101 mins. Cert X.

The Blue Lagoon
Pleasant, charming adaptation of H. de Vere Stacpoole's popular classic of yesterday about two children and an old sailor wrecked on an idyllic South Seas island where they have to come to terms with birth, death and all that goes between. Plenty of tasteful nudity, two delightful young stars, stunningly beautiful backgrounds. Cast: Brooke Shields, Christopher Atkins, Leo McKern, William Daniels, Elva Josephson, Glenn Kohan, Alan Hopgood, Gus Mercurio, Jeffrey Means, Bradley Pryce, Chad Timmermans, Geoff Jacoby, Alex Hamilton, Richard Evanson. Dir & Pro: Randal Kleiser. Co-Pro: Richard Franklin. Screenplay: Douglas Day Stewart; based on the novel by Henry de Vere Stacpoole. Ph: Nestor Almendros. Ed: Robert Gordon. Art: John Dowding. M: Basil Poledouris; played by the Australian Symphony Orchestra. Filmed in Fiji on Nanuya Island. (Columbia.) Rel: 4 January. 104 mins. Cert AA.

The Blues Brothers
A kind of loosely knit crazy comedy, with music, which seems to assume that if watching one cop car being smashed up is amusing, to watch a hundred being wrecked is hysterical! A story of a released convict (John Belushi, whose comic talents remain to be revealed to me) in trying to re-form their old jazz band in order to raise money for the threatened orphanage which raised them! Compensations include a string of fine rock, blues and jazz numbers, Cab Calloway (the 'King of Scat' in great form), Twiggy and Ray Charles. Rest of cast: Kathleen Freeman, James Brown, Carrie Fisher, John Candy, Murphy Dunne, Steve Cropper, Donald 'Duck' Dunn, Willie Hall, Tom Malone, Alan Rubin, Henry Gibson, John Lee Hooker, Walter Horton, 'Pinetop' Perkins, Willie 'Big Eyes' Smith, Luther 'Guitar Jr.' Johnson, Calvin 'Fuzz' Jones, Aretha Franklin, Matt Murphy, Lou Marini, Jeff Morris, Charles Napier, Steve Lawrence, John Landis, Steven Spielberg. Dir: John Landis. Pro: Robert K. Weiss. Ex Pro: Bernie Brillstein. Screenplay: Dan Aykroyd & John Landis. Ph: Stephen M. Katz. Ed: George Folsey Jr. Pro Des: John J. Lloyd. M: Ira Newborn ('God Music' by Elmer Bernstein). (Universal-CIC.) Rel: 2 November. 133 mins. Cert AA.

Breaker Morant
Outstanding Australian film based on an incident that occurred towards the end of the Boer War and centred on the court martial of Morant and two of his fellow officers of the Bushveldt Carbineers on a charge of murdering a captured Boer, something not denied by the prisoners, who claimed they were acting on indirect verbal orders from Lord Kitchener not to take any prisoners. But though brilliantly defended by a small-town Australian lawyer the verdict and death sentence is seldom in doubt, with the prosecutor so obviously determined to have them shot. Casually realistic, coolly ironic in its implications of the international politics involved, and brilliantly acted, the film fully deserved the way it swept the board at the Australian Film Awards ceremony, when it took top prizes for film, direction, photography, editing, screenplay, lead male performance (Jack Thompson) and supporting performance (Bryan Brown). Rest of cast: Edward Woodward, John Waters, Ray Meagher, Rod Mullinar, Lewis Fitz-Gerald, Charles Tingwell, Terence Donovan, Vincent Ball, Frank Wilson, Allan Cassell, Russell Kiefel, Judy Dick, Barbara West. Dir: Bruce Beresford. Pro: Matt Carroll. Screenplay: Bruce Beresford, Jonathan Hardy and David Stevens: based on the play by Kenneth Ross. Ph: Don McAlpine. Ed: William Anderson. Pro Des: David Copping. (No original music.) (South Australian Film Corp-The Australian Film Commission-The Seven Network-Enterprise Pictures.) Rel: Floating: first shown London (Classic, Haymarket) October 1980. 107 mins. Cert A.

Breaking Glass
Familiar story of a back-street pub-group lead singer who climbs to fame and fortune – and disc-publisher exploitation leading to disaster and breakdown. But given a fresh impetus and interest by Hazel O'Connor's singing of her own numbers, harsh social comment reflecting youthful rebellion against just about

everything. And the film does try to give a picture of this cynical and anarchical mood, with Miss O'Connor's extraordinary, punk-like make-ups and puppet-like movements. Rest of cast: Phil Daniels, Jon Finch, Jonathan Pryce, Mark Wingett, Gary Tibbs, Peter-Hugo Daly, Charles Wegner, Mark Wing-Davey, Hugh Thomas, Derek Thompson, Nigel Humphreys, Ken Campbell, Lowri-Ann Richards, Peter Tilbury, Patrick Murray, Richard Griffiths, Janine Duvitsky, Vass Anderson, Jim Broadbent, Michael Kitchen, Jonathan Lynn, Peter Cellier, Richard Hope, Kenneth MacDonald, Gary Olsen, Gary Holton, Christopher Driscol, Zoot Money, Paul McCartney, Rod Stewart, Victy Silva. Dir & Screenplay: Brian Gibson. Pro: Davina Belling & Clive Parsons. Ex Pro: Dodi Fayed. Ph: Kelvin Pike. Ed: Michael Bradsell. Art: Evan Hercules. Musical numbers devised and choreographed by E. G. Roberts. (Allied Stars – GTO Films.) Rel: 21 September. 104 mins. Cert AA.

Bronco Billy
Consistently entertaining, amusing, sometimes tongue-in-cheek up-dating of a typical 1930s–40s movie, with Clint Eastwood (who directed) as the craggy, upstanding cowboy (from the urban slums and a seven year jail sentence for killing his wife!) who takes his Wild West show around the small towns and in spite of all sorts of dramas manages to keep it on the road, ending up with an heiress as his loving assistant. All quite delightful. Rest of cast: Sondra Locke, Geoffrey Lewis, Scatman Crothers, Bill McKinney, Sam Bottoms, Dan Vadis, Sierra Pecheur, Walter Barnes, Woodrow Parfrey, Beverlee McKinsey, Douglas McGath, Hank Worden, William Prince, Pam Abbas, Edye Byrde, Douglas Copsey, John Wesley Elliott Jr., Chuck Hicks, Bobby Hoy, Jefferson Jewell, Dawneen Lee, Don Mummert, Lloyd Nelson, George Orrison, Michael Reinbold, Tessa Richarde, Tanya Russell, Valerie Shanks, Sharon Sherlock, James Simmerhan, Roger Dale Simmon, Jenny Sternling, Chuck Waters, Jerry Wills. Dir: Clint Eastwood. Pro: Dennis Hackin & Neal Dobrofsky. Ex Pro: Robert Daley. Assoc Pro: Fritz Manes. Screenplay: Dennis Hackin. Ph: David Worth. Ed: Ferris Webster & Joel Cox. Art: Gene Lourie. M Sup: Snuff Garrett ('Misery and Gin' sung by Merle Haggard; 'Cowboys and Clowns' and 'Bronco Billy' sung by Ronnie Milsap; 'Barroom Buddies' sung by Merle Haggard and Clint Eastwood; 'Bayou Lullaby' sung by Penny de Haven). (Warner.) Rel: 20 July. 116 mins. Cert A.

Brothers and Sisters
Initially arresting but finally rather lame British film which attempts to tell dual stories about the police investigation of the murder of a prostitute and the lives of a small commune which ends untidily with suspicion for the killing resting vaguely on several of the characters. Cast: Carolyn Pickles, Sam Dale, Robert East, Elizabeth Bennett, Jenifer Armitage, Barry McCarthy, Barrie Shore, Norman Claridge, Mavis Pugh, Fred Gaunt, Nick Jensen, David Threakston, Jack Platts, Mary Wray, Nelson Fletcher, Alexander Cruise, Leroy Mills, Bert Oxley, Ken Hastwell, Mitch Lewis, Ken Burgess, Brian Hibbard. Dir: Richard Woolley. Pro: Keith Griffiths. Ex Pro: Peter Sainsbury. Pro Sup: Jim Pearson. Screenplay: Richard Woolley – re-written in conjunction with Tammy Walker. No Ed

or Art credits. M: Trevor Jones (Song: 'Where Do You Think You're Going' by Mark Knopfler, performed by Dire Straits). (BFI) Rel: Floating; first shown London (ICA & Cinecenta) March 1981. 102 mins. Cert AA.

Brubaker
Robert Redford giving a performance of considerable integrity as the new Prison Governor who starts his job by becoming one of his own prisoners in order to find and root out the hard way all the corruption and evil practices rife in the place. And the story is based on fact. Rest of cast: Yaphet Kotto, Jane Alexander, Murray Hamilton, David Keith, Morgan Freeman, Matt Clark, Tim McIntire, Richard Ward, Jon Van Ness, M. Emmet Walsh, Albert Salmi, Linda Haynes, Everett McGill, Val Avery, Ronald C. Frazier, David D. Harris, Joe Spinell, James Keane, Roy Poole, Nathan George, Don Blakely, Lee Richardson, John McMartin, Alex A. Brown, John Chappell, Brent N. Jennings, Harry Groener, William M. Newman, Noble Willingham, Wilford Brimley, Jane Cecil, Ebbe Roe Smith, Young HwaHan, Vic Polizos, Jack O'Leary, James Dukas, J. C. Quinn, Jerry Mayer, Ivy Featherstone, Kent Broadhurst, Hazen Gifford, Elane Rower Richardson, John R. Glover, Bill McNulty, Linda Milligan, Rob Garrison, James E. Fraunfelter Jr, Ritch Brinkley, David E. Williams, E. J. Pearcy, J. K. Mahle, Vivian P. Bass, Greg Martin, Philip E. Combs, Richard L. Denny, Michael Holiday. Dir: Stuart Rosenberg. Pro: Ron Silverman. Ex Pro: Ted Mann. Assoc Pro: Gordon Webb. Screenplay: W. D. Richter; based on the story by Richter & Arthur Ross, and suggested by a book by T. O. Murton & Joe Hyams. Ph: Bruno Nuytten. Ed: Robert Brown. Art: J. Michael Riva. M: Lalo Schifrin. (Fox.) Rel: Floating; first shown London, (Leicester Square Theatre) September 1980. 130 mins. Cert AA.

Buffet Froid
Intriguing, puzzling, very black comedy in which the various characters kill, mostly without motive, without any pangs of conscience. It all starts when the unemployed Alphonse Tram kills a fellow passenger on the Metro and somebody else kills his wife, and it mostly all happens in or around the tower block where Tram's only neighbour is an understanding Chief Inspector of Police! A stylish exercise in the macabre. Cast: Gérard Depardieu, Bernard Blier, Jean Carmet, Geneviève Page, Denise Gence, Carole Bouquet, Michel Serrault, Jean Rougerie, Bernard Crommbey, Liliane Rovère, Jean Benguigui, Marco Perrin, Pierre Frag, Nicole Desailly, Maurice Travail, Eric Wasberg, Roger Riffard. Dir and Screenplay: Bertrand Blier. Pro: Alain Sarde. Ph: Jean Penzer. Ed: Claudine Merlin. M: The Bartók Quintet and Tatrai Quartet playing Brahms. (Sara Films/Antenne 2-Gala.) Rel: Floating; first shown London (Chelsea Classic) December 1980. 95 mins. Cert AA.

Cactus Jack
Very thin Western comedy (original American title: *The Villain*) about an incompetent outlaw hired by a local banker to stop the girl from getting through with the cash that will save her daddy's silver mine from being foreclosed. Cast: Kirk Douglas, Ann-Margret, Arnold Schwarzenegger, Paul Lynde, Foster Brooks, Ruth Buzzi, Jack Elam, Strother Martin, Robert Tessier, Mel Tillis, Laura Lizer Sommers, Ray Bickel, Jan

Eddy, Mel Todd, Jim Anderson, Ed Little, Dick Dickinson, Richard Brewer, Charles Haigh, Ron Duffy, Earl W. Smith, Mike Cerre, Lee Davis, Dick Armstrong, Sheldon Rosner, Budd Stout, Ott. Dir: Hal Needham. Pro: Mort Engelberg. Ex Pro: Paul Maslansky. Screenplay: Robert G. Kane. Ph: Bobby Byrne. Ed: Walter Hannemann. Art: Carl Anderson. M: Bill Justis. (The Villain Co for Rastar-Columbia.) Rel: 10 August. 89 mins. Cert A.

Caddyshack
In the 'Animal House' tradition, this comedy tosses together a collection of crude, ethnic, sick (literally) and other jokes in a story about a young caddy's aspirations towards further education by winning the Caddy Scholarship at the local Country Club; and the characters range from the inoffensive (Michael O'Keefe as the youngster and Chevy Chase as the shy miracle putter) to the outrageously offensive (Rodney Dangerfield as the Jewish vulgarian; Bill Murray as the mad greenkeeper). Rest of cast: Ted Knight, Sarah Holcomb, Scott Colomby, Cindy Morgan, Dan Resin, Henry Wilcoxon, Elaine Aiken, Albert Salmi, Ann Ryerson, Brian Doyle-Murray, Hamilton Mitchell, Peter Berkrot, John F. Barmon Jr., Lois Kibbee, Brian McConnachie, Scott Powell, Ann Crilley, Cordis Heard, Scott Sudden, Jackie Davis, Thomas Carlin, Minerva Scelza, Chuck Rodent, Kenneth Burritt, Bobbie Kostrin, Scott Jackson, Anna Uppstrom, Ron Frank, Patricia Wilcox, Debi Frank, Tony Gulliver, Kim Bordaux, Lori Lowe, Marcus Breece, Mark Chiriboga, Fred Buch, Frank Schuller, Mel Pape, Marge McKenna, Bruce McLaughlin, Dennis McCormack, Violet Ramis, Judy Arman, Dr Dow, Paige Coffman, Donna M. Wiggin, James Hotchkiss. Dir: Harold Ramis. Pro: Douglas Kenney. Ex Pro: Jon Peters. Screenplay: Brian Doyle-Murray & Harold Ramis. Ph: Stevan Larner. Ed: William Carruth. Pro Des: Stan Jolley. M: Johnny Mandel. Ex in charge of Pro: Mark Canton & Rusty Lemorande. Assoc Pro: Don MacDonald. Songs: 'I'm Alright', 'Lead the Way' & 'Mr Night' written and sung by Kenny Loggins; 'Something On Your Mind' written by Hilly Michaels & Morgan Walker, perf. Michaels; 'There She Goes' written by Paul Collins, perf. The Beat; 'Anyway You Want it' by Steve Perry & Neil Schon, perf. Journey; 'Summertime Blues' perf. Eddie Cochran. (Orion-Warner.) Rel: 17 August. 98 mins. Cert AA.

La Cage Aux Folles 11
Inevitably this Italian-French follow-up to the outrageous and uproariously funny original *Folles*, fell somewhat in standard, but was still extremely amusing; getting fun – in perfectly good taste – from the situation of an ageing homosexual couple who run a very smart night club in Nice with an all-male cabaret, and their (unwilling) involvement with secret agents, stolen microfilm rolls and (comic) chases. The couple, the magnificent Ugo Tognazzi and Michel Serrault, carried the unabashed farce with ease on their backs. Rest of cast: Mark Bodin, Bennie Luke, Gianrico Tondinelli, Marcel Bozzuffi, Michel Galabru, Giovanni Vettorazzo, Thomas Felleghy, Danilo Recanatesi, Nello Pazzafini, Renato Basso, Antonio Francioni, Nazareno Natale, Stelio Candelli, Giorgio Cerioni, Roberto Bisacco, Paola Borboni, Glauco Onorato, Lorenzo Danon. Dir:

Edouard Molinaro. Pro: Marcello Danon. Screenplay: Francis Veber, Marcello Danon & Jean Poiret. Ph: Armando Nannuzzi. Pro Des: Luigi Scaccianoce & Ramono Dandi. Ed: Robert Isnardon. M: Ennio Morricone. (UA.) Rel: 2 April. 99 mins. Cert AA.

Caligula
Bob Guccione's lavish, star-studded, controversial extravaganza about ancient Rome, concentrating very considerably on exploiting the twisted sexual and sadism angles. Notable in that after adverse American notices Guccione refused to invite the British press and critics to see his 'masterpiece' for free! Cast: Malcolm McDowell, Teresa Ann Savoy, Guido Mannari, John Gielgud, Peter O'Toole, Gianarlo Badessi, Bruno Brive, Adriana Asti, Leopoldo Trieste, Paolo Bonacelli, John Steiner, Mirella Dangelo, Helen Mirren, Richard Parets, Paula Mitchell, Osriride Pevarello, Donato Placido, Anneka di Lorenzo, Lori Wagner. Dir: Tinto Brass. Pro: Bob Guccione & Franco Rossellini. Additional scenes directed and photographed by Giancarlo Lui & Bob Guccione. Adapted from an original screenplay by Gore Vidal. Ph: Silvano Ippoliti. Ed: Nino Baragli. Art: Danilo Donati. M: Paul Clemente (with extracts from the works of Khatchaturian & Prokofiev). (Penthouse Films International/Felix Cinematografica-GTO Films.) Rel: Floating; first shown London (Prince Charles) November 1980. 150 mins. Cert X.

Can't Stop The Music
One of the very brightest and best of the Rock musicals; deafening and dazzling, with a mixture of new, young and old, tried and trusted performers, some good numbers belted over by The Village People group, a script thankfully free of four-letter words and altogether a highly successful recapture of the spirit of the old spectacular and fast-paced musicals of the 1930s transcribed into terms of today's pop era. Cast: Valerie Perrine, Bruce Jenner, Steve Guttenberg, Paul Sand, Tammy Grimes, June Havoc, Barbara Rush, Marilyn Sokol, Altovise Davis, Russell Nype, Dick Patterson, The Ritchie Family, Bobo Lewis, Paula Trueman, Denise Flamino, Greg Zadikov, Cindy Roberts, Maggie Brendler, Bradley Bliss, Rasa Allen, Gabriel Barre, Bob Peti, Russ Falcon, Portia Nelson, Kim O'Brien, Logan Carter, Victor Davis, Danone Camden, Jerry Lane, Terry & Darryl Ferges, Adam Mills, Albrie Selznick, Ed Jackman, Gary Kluger, Danny Nunez, Curtis Jones, Jonathan Porter, Todd Barrett, Timothy and Bradley Bogart, Adriano Rebora, Mark Miller, Leigh-Taylor Young. And The Village People – Alexander Briley, David Hodo, Glenn Hughes, Randy Jones, Felipe Rose, Ray Simpson, Dir: Nancy Walker. Pro: Allan Carr, Jacques Morali & Henri Belolo. Assoc Pro: Neil A. Machlis. Screenplay: Bronte Woodard & Allan Carr. Ph. Bill Butler. Ed: John F. Burnett. Pro Des: Steve Henrickson. Art: Harold Michelson. Choreographer: Arlene Phillips. M Ed: June Edgerton. (EMI.) Rel: 3 August. 123 mins. Cert A.

Capital City – A Portrait of London
Twenty-four hours of London Life, seen spaced out by Capital Radio programmes. Visits to the markets, the river, etc. With plenty of popular music in the background. (Warner.) Rel: 20 July. 39 mins. Cert U.

The Cat and the Canary
Fifth film based on the classic whodunnit thriller, set in a dark old house (outside of which an electric storm roars and rages!) where the possible heirs to the eccentric, deceased, owner gather to hear their chances of gaining a fortune and are soon being knocked off like flies by a mysterious killer. Cast: Honor Blackman, Michael Callan, Edward Fox, Wendy Hiller, Olivia Hussey, Beatrix Lehmann, Carol Lynley, Daniel Massey, Peter McEnery, Wilfrid Hyde-White. Dir & Screenplay: Radley Metzger; based on the original stage play by John Willard. Pro: Richard Gordon. Ph: Alex Thompson. Ed: Roger Harrison. Art: Anthony Pratt. M: Steve Cagan. (Grenadier Films-Gala.) Rel: Floating; first shown London (Kensington Odeon) February 1981. 98 mins. Cert AA.

Cattle Annie and Little Britches
Mildly amusing Western set at the turn of the century and against a background of the changing West, about two teenaged girls who join the Doolin-Dalton gang of outlaws and bring it some fun and games before they are – by arrangement – caught by the Law. Cast: Burt Lancaster, John Savage, Rod Steiger, Diane Lane, Amanda Plummer, Scott Glenn, Steven Ford, Ken Call, Redmond Gleeson, William Russ, Buck Taylor, Perry Lang, John Quade, John Sterlini, Tm Delaney, Matthew Taylor, Michael Conrad, Roger Cudney Jr., Chad Hastings, Yvette Sweetman, Mike Moroff, John Hock, Roger Cudney, Jerry Gatlin, Russ Hoverson. Dir: Lamont ohnson. Pro: Rupert Hitzig & Alan ing. Ex Pro: John Daly & Derek Dawson. Assoc Pro: David Korda. Screenplay: Robert Ward & David Eyre; based on the former's novel. Ph: Larry Pizer. Ed: William Haugse. Sup Ed: Robbe Roberts. Pro Des: Stan Jolly. M Sanh Berti & Tom Slocum with add. M. by Richard Greene. (Hemdale/UA Theatre Corp-Hemdale.) Rel: Floating. 98 mins. Cert A.

The Chain Reaction
Good, tense Australian thriller which has as its departure point the leak of some atomic waste into the water table and the fatal dose of radiation suffered by the man on duty at the time, who is then relentlessly tracked down by the organisation responsible with the idea of killing him before he can spread the dread news to the media. Meanwhile the contamination spreads from water to grass, from grass to cow, from cow to . . . Cast: Steve Bisley, Arna-Maria Winchester, Ross Thompson, Ralph Cotterill, Hugh Keays-Byrne, Lorna Lesley, Richard Moir, Patrick Ward, Laurie Moran, Michael Long, Margo Lloyd, Tim Burns, Arthur Sherman, Barry Donnelly, P. J. Jones, David Bracks, Jone Winchester, Joshua Ward, Ryan McKibbon, Kim Gyngell, Roger Ward, Sal Sarah, Frankie J. Holden. Dir & Screenplay: Ian Barry. Pro: David Elfick, Assoc Pro: Ross Matthews & George Miller. Ph: Russell Boyd. Ed: Tim Wellburn. Art: Graham Walker. M: Andrew Thomas Wilson. (Palm Beach Pictures in assoc with Victorian Film Corp. & Australian Film Commission-Warner.) Rel: Floating; first shown London, (Warner) December 1980. 92 mins. Cert AA.

A Change of Seasons
A would-be bright and cheery, but in fact often a little heavy handedly embarrassing, American sex farce in which amidst all the immorality a good old-fashioned moral point always seemed to be trying to make itself heard. About a fortyish professor who has a passionate affair with a pretty young pupil and carries on even when his faithful wife finds out; so she goes to bed with the first man who knocks at the door, and then all four repair to the professor's country cottage to carry on their liaisons and are surprised there by the couple's disgusted young daughter and the girl's father. In the end the rewards of sin don't look like being very happy ones for all concerned. Nice performances and some good laughs. Cast: Shirley MacLaine, Anthony Hopkins, Bo Derek, Michael Brandon, Mary Beth Hurt, Ed Winter, Paul Regina, K. Callan, Rod Colbin, Steve Eastin, Christopher Coffey, Albert Carriere, Billy Beck, Blake Harris, Karen Philipp, Paul Bryar, Anita Jodelsohn, Tim Haldeman, Paul Young, James Jeter, Stan Wright, Percy Davis, Steve Myers, John O'Connor, William Couch, Roger Creed, Bennie Dobbins, Robert F. Hoy, Joyce McNeal, John Moio, Conrad Palmisano, Lee Pulford, Tanya Samova, Greg Walker. Dir: Richard Lang. Pro: Martin Ransohoff. Ex Pro: Richard S. Johns. Assoc Pro: Cathleen Summers. Screenplay: Erich Segal, Ronnie Kern & Fred Segal; from a story by Erich Segal & Martin Ransohoff. Ph: Philip Lathrop. Ed: Don Zimmerman. Pro Des: Bill Kenney. M: Henry Mancini (song 'Where Do You Catch the Bus for Tomorrow'; lyrics by Alan & Marilyn Bergman; music by Mancini; sung by Kenny Rankin). Ex in charge of Pro: John W. Hyde. (Film Finance Group Ltd/Martin Ransohoff Production-Warner.) Rel: 17 May. 101 mins. Cert AA.

The Changeling
Another 'haunted house' psychic thriller in *The Exorcist* tradition, with Professor George C. Scott finding the quiet retreat the Seattle University has assigned him is full of weird noises and odd happenings as the ghost of the child long ago murdered in the house tries to enlist his aid in obtaining revenge. And it all gets further from any credibility as it travels reasonably smoothly to its confrontation and conflagration climax. Rest of cast: Trish Van Devere, Melvyn Douglas, Jean Marsh, Barry Morse, Bernard Behrens, Roberta Maxwell, Chris Gampel, Madeline Sherwood, James B. Douglas, Ruth Springford, Helen Burns, Eric Christman. Dir: Peter Medak. Pro: Joel B. Michaels & Garth H. Drabinsky. Exec Pro: Mario Kassar, andrew Vajna. Screenplay: William Gray & Diana Maddox; from a story by Russell Hunter. Ph: John Coquillon. Ed: Lilla Pederson. Art: Reuben Freed. (Chessman Park-Brent Walker.) Rel: Floating. 108 mins. Cert X.

Chapter Two
Neil Simon's own adaptation of his stage play; an amusing if familiar story about a writer who finds memories of his first wife spoiling the happiness of his life with his second. Not perhaps best Simon but still pretty good, lightly amusing entertainment. Cast: James Caan, Marsha Mason, Joseph Bologna, Valerie Harper, Alan Fudge, Judy Farrell, Debra Mooney, Isabel Cooley, Imogene Bliss, Barry Michlin, Ray Young, George Rondo, Cheryl Bianchi, Greg Zadikov, Dr Paul Singh, Sumant, Elizabeth Farley, Sunday Brennab, Danny Gellis, Cari Jonos, Henry Sutton. E. D. Miller, Howard Jeffrey, Marie Reynolds. Dir: Robert Moore. Pro: Ray Stark. Ex Pro: Roger M. Rothstein. Assoc Pro & Sup Ed: Margaret Booth. Screenplay Neil Simon.

Ed: Michael Stevenson. Pro Des: Gene Callahan. M. Marvin Hamlisch. (Song, 'I'm On Your Side' by Marvin Hamlisch, with lyrics by Carole Bayer Sager; sung by Marilyn McCoo). (Rastar-Columbia.) Rel: 28 September. 126 mins. Cert A.

Chariots of Fire
British and beautifully made, richly textured and artistically atmospheric story of real-life runners Harold Abrahams and Eric Liddell, who in the 1920s, driven on by contrasting ambitions – the first for his own and his Jewish race's prestige, the second because he felt he had God's gift – strove and sweated mightily and finally both achieved their Gold Olympic medals. A remarkably fine piece of filmcraft, superbly photographed and finely acted. Cast: Ben Cross, Ian Charleson, Nigel Havers, Nick Farrell, Daniel Gerroll, Cheryl Campbell, Alice Krige, John Gielgud, Lindsay Anderson, Nigel Davenport, Struan Rodger, Ian Holm, Patrick Magee, Dennis Christopher, Brad Davis, Robin Pappas, Ruby Wax, David Yelland, Peter Egan, Jeremy Sinden. Dir: Hugh Hudson. Pro: David Puttnam, Ex Pro: Dodi Fayed. Screenplay: Colin Welland. Assoc Pro: James Crawford. Ph: David Watkin. Ed: Terry Rawlings. Supervising Art Dir: Roger Hall. Art: Anna Ridley & Jonathan Amberston. M: Vangelis. (Allied Stars/Enigma-Fox.) Rel: 24 May. 123 mins. Cert A.

Charlie Chan and the Curse of the Dragon Queen
Revival of the Chinese screen detective character of the 1930s, created by Warner Oland, whose exploits stretched through a series of popular movies of the period. As now played by an oddly subdued Peter Ustinov, the film sadly failed as either serious tribute or successful send-up and fell back on knockabout farce, largely created by Chan's accident-prone, adulatory grandson Lee, played by Richard Hatch. A splendid idea but not developed along quite the right lines. Rest of cast: Lee Grant, Angie Dickinson, Brian Keith, Roddy McDowall, Rachel Roberts, Michelle Pfeiffer, Paul Ryan, Johnny Sekka, Bennett Ohta, David Hirokane, Karlene Crockett, Michael Fairman, James Ray, Momo Yashimia, Kael Blackwood, Jerry Loo, Laurence Cohen, Robin Hoff, Kathie Kei, James Bacon, Frank Michael, John Hugh, George Chiang, David Chow, Alison Hong, Dewi Yee, Joe Bellan, Garrick Huey, Duane Tucker, Don Parker, Kenneth Snell, Nicholas Gunn, Don Murray, Kai Wong, Miya, Gerald Okamura, Lonny Carbajal, Peter Michas, Vic Hunsberger, Larry Duran, Kay Kimler, Jim Winburn, Molly Roden, Pavla Ustinov, Trevor Hook, Paul Sanderson. Dir: Clive Donner. Pro: Jerry Sherlock. Ex Pro: Michael Leone & Alan Belkin. Screenplay: Stan Burns & David Axelrod; from a story by Jerry Sherlock. Ph: Paul Lohmann. Ed: Walt Hannemann & Phil Tucker. Pro Des: Joel Schiller. M: Patrick Williams. (American Cinema Productions/Jerry Sherlock Productions-UA.) Rel: 3 May. 97 mins. Cert A.

Chuquiago
One of the films in the forefront of a 'new wave' of 'social-realist' movies from Latin America: this one from Bolivia, examining life today in the country's capital city of La Paz, with its various races and social classes rigorously separated by the city's topography. Made in 1977. Cast: Néstor Yujra, Edmundo Villaroel,

David Santalla, Tatiana Aponta, Alejandra Quispe, Jesuua Mangudo, Fidel Huanca, Julia de Huanca, Raul Ruiz, Pablo Dávila, Julio Cesar Paredes, Tito Landa, Mario Castro, Vilma Arce. Dir: Antonio Eguino. Pro man: Carlos Sforzini. Screenplay: Oscar Soria. Ph: Antonio Eguino & Julio Lencina. Ed: Deborah Shaffer & Suzanne Fenn. M: Alberto Villapando. No art credit. (Grupo Ukamau-The Other Cinema.) Rel: Floating; first shown London (ICA) September 1980. 87 mins. No cert.

*Cinema Cinema
A fun history of the Indian cinema made by an expatriate Indian director – Krishna Shah – whose return to his native land after many years in America inspired the movie, which as well as film history concentrates on the amusing behaviour of the typical, uninhibited, involved and volatile native audiences (70,000,000 go to the cinema every week in India). Narrators: Dharmendra, Hema Malini, Amitabh Bachchan, Zeenat Aman. Cast: Kim, Mushtaque Merchant, Dinyar Contractor, Hoshidar Kambhatta, Kanchan Mattu, Sharad Bhagtani, Amar Sneh, Bishan Khanna, Hriday Lani, Momin Khan, Bobby Grewal, Phonsuk, Dharam Veer, Manmauji, Parvez, Payal Hijra, Babu, Shyam Awasthe Dev Sharma, Nadu, Charlie, Rishi Shankar, Shamsuddin, Aquil, Vijay Tandon. Dir. & Screenplay: Krishna Shah. Pro: Shahab Ahmed. Hindi Script: Kamleshwar. Ex Pro: Bhupendra Shah. Ph: K. K. Mahajan. Ed: Amit Bose. Pro Des: Ram Mohan. M: Vijay Raghav Rao. (Moroville Ltd.) Rel: Floating; first shown London (The Liberty, Edgware Rd.). May 1980. Colour and Black-and-White, 98 mins. Cert U.

Circle of Two
Autumn-spring romance between a middle-aged painter (Richard Burton) and the Toronto schoolgirl (Tatum O'Neal) who falls passionately in love with him; a true-love path not exactly smoothed by the sixteen-year-old's outraged parents. Rest of cast: Nuala Fitzgerald, Robin Gammell, Patricia Collins, Donann Cavin, Norma Dell'Agnese, Michael Wincott, Kate Reid, Leo Leyden, Elan Ross Gibson, Tanya Williams, Rebel Beard, Ann Louis Genet, Alysia Pascaris, Heather Graham, Sharon Lee, Mung Ling, Maggie Morris, Larry Ewanshen, Daisy White, Helen Carscallen, Pamela Hyatt, Yanka Van Der Kolk, Gordon Jocelyn, George Bourne Sr., George Touliatos, Pat Patterson, Bob Aarons, Ann Butler, Bill Yack, Bibi Caspari, Brendan McKane, Frank Ruffo, Morison Bock, Mack Dulgy, Les Carlson, Doug Smith, Craa Stevens, Jimmy Leone, Elias Zaron. Dir: Jules Dassin. Pro: Henk Van Der Kolk. Ex Pro: Wiliam Marshall. Assoc Pro: Bob Rodgers. Screenplay: Thomas Hedley; based on the book *A Lesson in Love* by Marie Terese Baird. Ph: Laszlo George. Ed: David Nicholson. Pro Des: Claude Bonniere. Art: Francois de Lucy. M: Paul Hoffert. (Bordeaux Films.) Rel: Floating; first shown London (Studio & Scene) May 1981. 113 mins. Cert AA.

City on Fire
A minor addition to the Disaster cycle, with a silly, sacked petroleum depot worker starting a fire which sweeps through a small American city more or less unchecked, and surrounding the hospital, escape from which, by patients and staff, gives the movie its spectacular fire-and-water climax. Cast: Barry Newman, Susan Clark, Shelley Winters, Leslie Nielsen, James Franciscus, Ava Gardner, Henry Fonda, Mavor Moore, Jonathan Welsh, Richard Donat, Ken James, Donald Pilon, Terry Haig. Cec Linder, Hilary Lebow, Jeff Mappin, Earl Pennington, Sonny Forbes, Bronwen Mantel, Janice Chaikelson, Steven Chaikelson, Lee Murray, Jerome Tibershien. Dir: Alvin Rakoff. Pro: Claude Héroux. Ex Pro: Sandy Howard & Harold Greenberg. Assoc Pro: Howard Lipson & Larry Nesis. Screenplay: Jack Hill, David P. Lewis & Celine La Frenière. Ph: René Verzier. Ed: Jean-Pol Passet & Jacques Clairoux. Pro Des: William McCrow. M: William & Matthew McCauley. Art: Claude Marchand. Special Effects: Cliff Wenger Sr. & Carol Lynn. Visual Effects: William Cruse. (Sandy Howard/Harold Greenberg-Astral Bellevue-Pathé-Rank.) Rel: Floating. 105 mins. Cert AA.

Coal Miner's Daughter
Sissy Spacek quite magnificent (she won a 1981 Oscar for the performance) in the true story of country-and-western singing star Loretta Lynn, a film which divides into two really quite separate parts; the brilliant early scenes set in the brutally poor Kentucky hills mining area and the more routine latter part when the singer rises to stardom, breaks down from overwork and makes a final triumphant return to her fans. Rest of cast: Tommy Lee Jones, Beverly D'Angelo, Levon Helm, Phyllis Boyens, Bill Anderson Jr, Poister Dickerson, Malla McCowan, Pamela McCowan, Kevin Salvilla, William Sanderson, Sissy Lucas, Pat Patterson, Brian Wharf, Elizabeth Watson, Robert Elkins, Bob Hannah, Ernest Tubb, Jennifer Beasley, Susan Kingsley, Michael Baish, David Gray, Royce Clark, Gary Parker, Billy Strange, Bruce Newman, Grant Turner, Frank Mitchell, Merle Kilgore, Jackie Lynn Wright, Rhonda Rhoton, Vernon Oxford, Ron Hensley, Doug Bledsoe, Aubrey Wells, Russell Varner, Tommie O'Donnell, Lou Headley, Ruby Caudrill, Charles Kahlenberg, Alice McGeachy, Ken Riley, Jim Webb, Dave Thornhill, Don Ballinger, Zeke Dawson, Gene Dunlap, Durwood Edwards, Chuck Flynn, Lonnie Godfrey, Bob Hempker, Danny Faircloth, Charles Gore, Doug Hauseman, Mike Noble, Daniel Sarenana, Billy West. Dir: Michael Apted. Pr: Bernard Schwartz. Ex Pro: Bob Larson. Assoc Pro: Zelda Barron. Screenplay: Tom Rickman; based on the autobiography of Loretta Lynn with George Vecsey. Ph: Ralf D. Bode. Ed: Arthur Schmidt. Pro Des: John W. Corso. M Sup: Owen Bradley. (Bernard Schwartz-Universal-CIC.) Rel: 15 March. 125 mins. Cert A.

*La Commare Secca
Interesting 1962 museum piece; the first feature film to be made by Bernardo Bertolucci. An intriguingly handled police investigation of a number of men suspected of possibly being involved in the murder of a prostitute on the banks of the River Tiber, with a lot of lies (often camera and dialogue simultaneously telling divergent stories) leading to the confession of the killer that he murdered her for her handbag. A very original

and unusual whodunit. *Note* Title literally translated means 'Dry Housewife' but in Roman dialect means death, 'The Grim Reaper'). Cast (of non-professionals): Francesco Ruiu, Giancarlo de Rosa, Vincenzo Ciccora, Alvaro d'Ercole, Romano Labate, Lorenza Benedetti, Emy Rocci, Erina Torelli, Renato Troiani, Marisa Solinas, Wanda Rocci, Alfredo Leggi, Carlotta Barilli, Santina Lisio, Gabriella Giorgelli, Clorinda Celani, Ada Peragostini, Silvio Laurenzi, Allen Midgette. Dir: Bernardo Bertolucci. Story & Screenplay: Pier Paolo Pasolini (latter with Sergio Citti & Bertolucci). Pro: Antonio Cervi. Ph: Gianni Narzisi. Ed: Nino Baragli. Art: Adriana Spadaro. M: Carlo Rustichelli. (Compagnia Cinematografica Cervi-Cineriz-Mithras Films.) Rel: Floating, first shown London (Everyman, Hampstead) June 1980. In Black-and-White. 88 mins. Cert AA.

The Consequence – Die Konsequenz
1977 West German film about a passionate homosexual love affair between a man and a boy which starts in jail and ends in tragedy. Writer-director Wolfgang Petersen attempts to enlist sympathy for the two main characters involved and suggests that they are victims of social prejudice, but fails to convince that the result would have been any different had the youngster been an under-age girl! Often pretty tasteless though otherwise well directed and beautifully photographed in black-and-white. Cast: Jürgen Prochnow, Ernst Hannawald, Walo Lüönd, Edith Volkmann, Erwin Kohlund, Hans Irle, Alexander Ziegler, Edwin Parker, Werner Schwuchow, Hans-Michael Rehberg, Elisabeth Fricker, Hans Putz, Wolf Gauitz, Thomas Haerin. Dir & Co-Scripted (with Alexander Ziegler, who wrote the book): Wolfgang Petersen. Pro: Bernd Eichinger. Ph: Jorg-Michael Baldenius. Ed: James Nickel. Art: O. Jochen Schmidt. M: Nils Sustrate. (Solaris-WDR-Kampus Films.) Rel: Floating; first shown London (Gate Cinemas) August 1980. 100 mins. In Black-and-White. Cert X.

*Courage – Let's Run – Courage Fuyons
Delightfully amusing comedy-farce (with a thread of mystery) by Yves Robert about the passionate romance of a middle-aged, much married Parisian chemist with an inherited broad yellow streak in his make-up, and a stunningly beautiful international chantreuse whose life isn't quite so simple as initially it appears to be. Deliciously acted by Jean Rochefort and Catherine Deneuve. Rest of cast: Dominique Lavanant, Michel Aumont, Philippe Leroy-Beaulieu, Robert Webber, Michel Beaune, Eliance Borras, Christian Charmetant, Christophe Bourseiller, Janine Souchon. Dir: Yves Robert. Pro: Yves Robert and Alain Poire. Screenplay: Jean-Loup Dabadie, Yves Robert. Ph: Yves Lafaye. Ed: Pierré Gillette. Art: Jean-Pierre Kohut Svelko. M: Vladimir Cosma: solo guitar, Philippe Catherine. (Productions de la Guéville-Gaumont-International-Curzon Dist.) Rel: Floating; first shown London (Curzon) June 1980. 97 mins. Cert AA.

Crazy Mama
In the 'road film' category (made 1975) this is a story about an oddly assorted little gang journeying from Long Beach, California, to Jerusalem, Arkansas, (and robbing and kidnapping along the way) with the idea of

regaining the farm from which they had been evicted (during which struggle, the father was shot dead) some twenty-six years previously. And the sound track used popular numbers of the period as background illustration. Cast: Cloris Leachman, Stuart Whitman, Jim Backus, Tisha Sterling, Ann Sothern, Don Most, Linda Purl, Bryan Englund, Carmen Argenziano, Merie Earle, Dick Miller, Sally Kirkland, Harry Northup, Clint Kimbrough, Ralph James, Dina Englund, Robert Reece, Mickey Fox, John Aprea, Cynthia Songey, Hal Marshall, Beach Dickerson, Barbara Ann Walters, Bill McLean, William Luckey, Warren Miller, Saul Krugman, Vince Barnett. Dir: Jonathan Demme. Pro: Julie Corman. Assoc Pro: Peter Cornberg. 2nd Unit Dir: Evelyn Purcell. Screenplay: Robert Thom; from a story by Frances Doel. Ph: Bruce Logan. 2nd Unit Ph: Tak Fujimoto. Ed: Allan Holzman & Lewis Teague. Art: Peter Jamison, M: Snotty Scotty and the Hankies. M Co-ordinator: Marshall Leib. New World-Barber International.) Rel: Floating. 80 mins. Cert AA.

Cruising
Nasty and not even very well made film about some actual homosexual murders which occurred in New York in the 1970s, with Al Pacino as the investigating undercover cop who finds the Gay world beginning to get under his skin more than it should . . . Rest of cast: Paul Sorvino, Karen Allen, Richard Cox, Don Scardino, Joe Spinell, Jay Acovone, Randy Jurgensen, Barton Heyman, Gene Davis, Annaldo Santana, Larry Atlas, Allan Miller, Sonny Grosso, Edward O'Neil, Michael Aronin, James Remar, William Russ, Mike Starr, Steve Inwood, Keith Prentice, Leland Starnes. Dir and Screenplay: William Friedkin (based on the novel by Gerald Walker). Pro: Jerry Weintraub. Pro Ex: Mark Johnson. Ph: James Contner. Ed: Bud Smith. Pro Des: Bruce Weintraub. Art: Edward Pisoni. M: Jack Nitzsche. M. Performed by The Cripples, Willy DeVille, Germs-GI, John Hiatt, Mutiny, Rough Trade & Madelyn von Ritz. (Lorimar-ITC.) Rel: 21 September. 99 mins. Cert X.

Dance Craze
Pop musical largely consisting of live recordings of concert performances by a large number of popular groups such as Bad Manners, The Beat, The Bodysnatchers, Madness, The Specials and The Selecter. Dir: Joe Massot. Pro: Gavrik Losey. Ph: Joe Dunton. Sup Ed: Ben Rayner. Music Pro by Clive Langer and Alan Winstanley. (Chrysalis-Osiris Films.) Rel: 15 March. 90 mins. Cert U.

*Dawson J
British film, made on a grant from the East Midlands Arts, which takes as its theme 'the power of the media in misrepresenting Trade Union struggles'. Cast: Roger Watkins, Harry Perscy, Bill Rourke, Fraser Kerr, John Joyce, Brian Hoskin, Roy Spencer, Jonathan Collinson, Liza Tramontin, Tamzin. Sound only: Alan McCelland, John Joyce, James Stephens, Keith Hazemore, Kitty Scopes. Made by Don Mason & Nicky Malleson. (The Other Cinema.) Rel: Floating; first shown London (ICA) June 1980. 35 mins. No cert.

*The Day Time Ended
Quite daft but amusing science-fiction contribution in which an unfortunate family are caught up in what one of the characters suggests is a 'Time vs. Space' war,

resulting in the appearance on their back doorstep of a magic green pyramid, a charmingly crinkled little fairy and various disturbing visual and sound manifestations of the quarrel. Cast: Chris Mitchum, Jim Davis, Dorothy Malone, Marcy Lafferty, Scott Kolden, Natasha Ryan, Roberto Contrevas. Dir: John 'Bud' Cardos. Pro: Wayne Schmidt. Ex Pro: Charles Band. Pro Ex: David Wolf. Assoc Pro: Steve Neill & Paul W. Gentry. Screenplay: Wayne Schmidt, J. Larry Carroll & David Schomoeller; from a story by Steve Neill. Ph: John Morrill. Ed: Ted Nicolaou. Art: Rusty Rosene. M: Richard Band. M Dir: John Watson (Compass-Manson-Transworld Communications.) Rel: 29 June 1980. 80 mins. Cert A.

Death Hunt
This film is based on a true story about a great manhunt of the 1930s, when a Royal Canadian Mounted Police trooper (Lee Marvin) was assigned to the tracking down and bringing in of a trapper accused of murder (Charles Bronson), only finally achieved after a forty-eight-day, 150-mile pursuit in temperatures of down to forty below zero. Rest of cast: Andrew Stevens, Carl Weathers, Ed Lauter, Scott Hylands, Angie Dickinson, Henry Beckman, William Sanderson, Jon Cedar, James O'Connell, Len Lesser, Dick Dalos, Maury Chaykin, August Schellenberg, Dennis Wallace, James McIntire, Rayford Barnes, Maurice Kowaleski, Sean McCann, Steve O. Z. Finkel, Dennis Lacroix, Tantoo Martin, Amy Marie George. Dir: Peter Hunt. Pro: Murray Shostak. Ex Pro: Albert S. Ruddy & Raymond Chow. Screenplay: Michael Grais & Mark Victor. Pro Sup: Andre Morgan. Ph: James Devis. Ed: Allan Jacobs & John F. Burnett. Pro Des: Ted Haworth. Assoc Pro: Robert Baylis. M: Jerrold Immel. (Fox.) Rel: 21 June. 97 mins. Cert X.

Death Watch
Macabre, difficult, and imaginative Bertrand Tavernier French/West German science-fiction movie about a man who allows some sort of TV camera to be installed in his head so that everything his eyes observe can be transmitted or recorded by a ruthless sensation-seeking producer planning to make TV history by following a dying young woman to her death in close-up. Not credible, of course; nor easy to follow; with so many questions asked but not answered; but original and fascinating. Made on location in Scotland. Cast: Romy Schneider, Harvey Keitel, Harry Dean Stanton, Max Von Sydow, Therese Liotard, Vadim Glowna, Bern Wicky. Dir & Screenplay (latter with David Rafiel): Bertrand Tavernier; based on the novel The Continuous Katharine Mortenhoe by David Compton. Ph: Pierre-William Glenn. Ed: Armand Psenny & Michael Ellis. Art: Tony Pratt. M: Antoine Duhamel. (Contemporary.) Rel: Floating: first shown London (Paris-Pullman) May 1981. 128 mins. Cert AA.

Defiance
Trite and familiar story about the reluctant hero – in this case a sailor forbidden the sea as punishment for being involved in a shipboard fight – who at first refusing to take part in local social troubles, is finally goaded to take up arms and the challenge of a confrontation with the Puerto Rican gang who are terrorising the locality. Cast: Jan Michael Vincent,

Theresa Saldana, Fernando Lopez, Danny Aiello, Santos Morales, Don Blakely, Frank Pesce, Rudy Ramos, Lee Fraser, Randy Herman, Alberto Vazquez, Church Ortiz, Art Carney, East Carlo, Lenny Montana, James Victor, Tom Reese, Ernie Orsatti, Marvin Katzoff, G. Anthony Sirico, Joe Campanella, Brian Dean, Pamela Gatell, Margarita Garcia, Phil Levy, Chino 'Fats' Williams, David Cadiente, Wendy Oates, Barabara Smith, Dawn Adams, James Oscar Lee, Victor Mendez. Dir: John Flynn. Pro: W. S. Gilmore Jr. & Jerry Bruckheimer. Ex Pro: R. J. Wunsch. Assoc Pro, Screenplay & Story (the last with Mark Tulin): Thomas Michael Donnelly. Pro Ex: Jere Henshaw. Ph: Ric Waite. Assoc Ph: Harvey Jenkins. Ed: David Finfer. Pro Des: Bill Malley. Art: Jack Cornwall. M: Basil Poledouris with add. M. by Gerard McMahon. (Necta-American International-ITC.) Rel: 13 July. 102 mins. Cert X.

Demon
A fantastic thriller – part science-fiction, part detection – about two opposing men with 'special powers', a cop and a villain, who after the latter has caused the violent deaths of several unfortunates who come under his power, meet for a duel to the death. Cast: Tony Lo Bianco, Deborah Raffin, Sandy Dennis, Sylvia Sidney, Sam Levene, Robert Drivas, Mike Kellin, Richard Lynch, Sammy Williams, Jo Flores Chase, William Roerick, Lester Rawlins, Harry Bellaver, George Patterson, Walter Steele, John Heffernan, Alan Cauldwell, Robert Nichols, Andy Kaufman, Al Fann, James Dixon, Bobby Ramsden, Peter Hock, Alex Stevens, Harry Madsen, Randy Jurgensen, Sherry Steiner, Jamkes Dukas, Mason Adams, William Bressant, Armand Dahan, Vida Taylor, Adrian James, Leila Martin, Michael Pendry, Dan Resin, Alexander Clark, Marvin Silbisher, Harry End. Dir, Pro & Screenplay: Larry Cohen. Ph: Paul Glickman. Ed: Arthur Mandelberg, William J. Waters, Christopher Lebanzon & Mike Corey. M: Frank Cordell. (Song: 'Sweet Momma Sweetlove' – lyrics by Janelle Webb, music by Robert O. Ragland.) (Larco Productions-Barber Rose.) Rel: 1 February. 89 mins. Cert. X.

Desperate Living
And a desperate dive into bad taste it is, too, by John 'Pink Flamingos' Waters, in a mix of murders, sex-change operations, rapes, penises cut off and sewn back again, disembowellings and cannibalism! Great fun – if you can take it like that. Cast: Liz Renay, Mink Stole, Susan Lowe, Edith Massey, Mary Vivian Pearce, Jean Hill, Brook Blake, Karen Gerwig, Jay Allan, Al Strapelli, George Stover, Turkey Joe, Willie Brooks, James Yeaton, David Klein, Ralph Crocker, Peter Koper, Sally Albaugh, Kenny Orye, Warren Newcomb, Roland Hertz, Pirie Woods, Damien Overholser, Ed Butner, H. C. Kliemisch, Paul Swift, George Figgs, Marina Melin, Cookie Mueller, Pat Moran, Sharon Niesp, George Hulse, Dolores Deluxe. Dir, Pro, Screenplay & Ph: (last with Thomas Loizeaux): John Waters. Assoc Pro: William Platt, David Spencer & James McKenzie. Ed: Charles Roggero. Art: Vincent Peranio. M: Chris Lobinger. (Charm City Productions-Oppidan Films.) Rel: Floating; first shown London (Ritzy, Brixton) July 1980. 91 mins. No cert.

Releases of the Year in Detail

The Devil and Max Devlin
Minor Disney comedy about a crooked landlord who when killed by a bus is given a chance by the Devil to have a new stretch of life if he can sign up three pure and innocent souls for future purgatory. Cast: Elliot Gould, Bill Cosby, Susan Anspach, Adam Rich, Julie Budd, Sonny Shroyer, David Knell. Dir: Steven Hilliard Stern. Pro: Jerome Courtland. Ex Pro: Ron Miller. Screenplay: Mary Rodgers; from a story by Jimmy Sangster & Miss Rogers. Ph: Howard Schwartz. Ed: Raymond A. de Leuw. Art: John B. Mansbridge & Leon R. Harris. M: Buddy Baker (Lyrics for 'Roses and Rainbows' by Carole Bayer Sager; for 'Any Fool Could See' by Allee Willis; music for both by Marvin Hamlisch). (Disney.) Rel: 22 February. 96 mins. Cert A.

Divine Madness
A Bette Midler showcase; a recording of one (or more) of her live shows in which she sings everything from soul to (shrieking) pop, tells raunchy jokes (of a dirtiness not previously heard in the cinema), does (pale) impressions of Sophie Tucker and Mae West, trips around the stage and even stands on her head, all with self-confessed vulgarity, terrifying vitality and a certain brash talent. Rest of cast: Jocelyn Brown, Ula Hedwig & Diva Gray (the Harlettes backing group); Irving Sudrow, Tony Berg, Jon Bonnie, Joey Carbone, Randy Kerber. The musicians: Chas Sandford (guitar), Tony Berg (guitar), John Pierce (bass guitar), Randy Kerber & Joey Carbone (keyboards), Art Wood (drums), David Shank (percussion), Rich Copper (trumpet), David Luell (saxophone/lyricon), Jon Bonine (trombone & bass trombone). Dir & Pro: Michael Ritchie. Ex Pro: Howard Jeffrey. Screenplay: Jerry Blatt, Bette Midler & Bruce Vilanch. Ph: William A. Fraker. Add Ph: Obby Byrne. Ed: Glenn Farr. Pro Des: Albert Brenner. M: arr. & supervised by Tony Berg & Randy Kerber. (The Ladd Company-Warner.) Rel: Floating; first shown London (Warner) January 1981. 93 mins. Cert AA.

The Dogs of War
Straightforward adaptation to the screen of Frederick Forsyth's novel about white mercenaries involved in African political upheavals. Christopher Walken as the battle scarred leader employed by an international cartel to stage a commando-style raid on a misruled African State with the idea of subsequently establishing their own puppet ruler and so ensuring their rights to mining all the rich minerals that it possesses. The careful planning pays off, the Amin-like ruler is killed, and then comes a neat, if, unfortunately, highly unlikely twist in the tail. Rest of cast: Tom Berenger, Colin Blakely, Hugh Millais, Paul Freeman, Jean-François Stevenin, Jo Beth Williams, Robert Urquhart, Winston Ntshona, Pedro Armendariz Jr, Harlan Cary Poe, Ed O'Neill, Isabel Grandin, Ernest Graves, Kelvin Thomas, Shane Rimmer, George W. Harris, David Schofield, Terence Rigby, Tony Mathews, John Quentin, Jean-Pierre Kalfon, Christopher Malcolm, Maggie Scott, Hugh Quarshie, Olu Jacobs, Christopher Asante, Thomas Baptiste, Eddie Tagoe, Kenny Ireland, Jim Broadbent. Dir: John Irvin. Pro: Larry De Waay. Ex Pro: Norman Jewison & Patrick Palmer. Screenplay: Gary Devore & George Malko; based on the novel by Frederick Forsyth. Ph: Jack Cardiff. Ed: Anthony Gibbs. Pro Des: Peter Mullins. M: Geoffrey Burgon (End title song sung by Gillian McPherson). (Silverworld-UA) Rel: 25 January. 119 mins. Cert AA.

The Dollar Bottom
Brilliant thirty-three-minute-long film which in that time with style and leisured completeness tells an amusing story of a bright pupil in a Scottish school who dreams up an ingenious insurance scheme among the pupils and, when it spreads to most of the other schools in Scotland and is rather reluctantly stepped on by the authorities, comes up with an equally ingenious way of solving his liquidation problems. Cast includes: Rikki Fulton, Robert Urquhart and Jonathan McNeil. Dir: Roger Christian. Ph: Lloyd Phillips. Screenplay based on a short story by James Kennaway. M: Trevor Jones. (CIC.) Rel: Floating; first shown London (Plaza) March 1981. 33 mins. Cert U.

Don Giovanni
Joseph Losey's French/Italian/West German (1979) production of the Mozart opera based on the plans, and assembled cast, of ex-Paris Opera producer Rolf Liebermann. A more or less conventional screening of the work – though with some rather silly straining after social significance which takes nearly all the fun out of the piece – seen against stunningly beautiful backgrounds of Italy's Palladian palaces and gardens. For the most part magnificently sung and musically impeccable, though with a few rather unhappy exceptions. Even with these flaws a remarkable and highly imaginative movie-opera. Cast: Ruggero Raimondi, Kiri te Kanawa, Edda Moser, Teresa Berganza, José Van Dam, Kenneth Riegel, Malcolm King, John Macurdy, Erid Adjani, and The Orchestra & Chorus of the Paris Opera con. Lorin Maazel (Harpsichordist: Janine Reiss). Dir: Joseph Losey. Screenplay/Adaptation: J. Losey, Patricia Losey & Frantz Salieri. Ph: Gerry Fisher. Ed: Reginald Beck. Art: Alexandre Trauner. (Gaumont/Camera One/OFP/Janus Films-Artificial Eye.) Rel: Floating; first shown London (Academy) September. 1980. 174 mins. Cert A.

Don't Answer the Phone!
Minor murder movie with a mentally sick photographer raping and killing various girls, including a prostitute, a hitch-hiker and model, in sexploitation sequence. Cast: James Westmoreland, Flo Gerrish, Ben Frank, Nicholas Worth, Pamela Bryant, Paula Warner, Denise Galik, Dale Kalberg, Susanne Secereid, Ellen Kay Karsten, Havoc Oliver, Stan Haze, Tom Lasswell, Chris Wallace, Victor Mohica, Gary Allen, Michael Castle, Ted Chapman, Deborah Leah Land, Mike Levine, Chuck Mitchell, Hugh Corcoran, Joyce Ann Jodan, Corine Cook, David Osterhout, Peter Fain, Jon Greene, Robin Oliver, Shirley Handelsman, Don Lake, Eileen Castle, Danny Disney. Dir, Screenplay & Pro: Robert Hammer (with (in last two) Michael D. Castle; based on Michael Curtis's novel 'Nightline'. Ex Pro: Michael Towers. Pro Co-Ord: Sharron Reynolds. Ph: James Carter; Joseph Fineman. Assoc Ed: Robert Gordon. Art: Cathy Cahill. M: Byron Allred. (Scorpion for Manson International-New Realm.) Rel: 15 February. 93 mins. Cert X.

Dressed to Kill
Generally flashy but often imaginative and occasionally brilliant (a marvellous long, silent sequence in a museum) thriller about a schizophrenic transvestite killer who likes to use an open razor to despatch his victims. But Brian De Palma's increasingly obsessive passion to pay homage to Hitchcock (whose heir he was at one time thought possibly to be) is overdone to the edge of becoming merely copycat. A fascinating example of cinematic style, all the same. Cast: Michael Caine, Angie Dickinson, Nancy Allen, Keith Gordon, Dennis Franz, David Margulies, Ken Baker, Brandon Maggart, Susanna Clemm, Fred Weber, Sean O'Rinn, Bill Randolph. Dir & Screenplay: Brian De Palma. Pro: George Litto. Exec Pro: Samuel Z. Arkoff. Assoc Pro: Fred Caruso. Ph: Ralf Bode. Ed: Jerry Greenberg. Pro Des: Gary Weist. M: Pino Donaggio. (Cinema 77/ Filmways Pictures-ITC.) Rel: 19 October. 104 mins. Cert X.

Dynasty
3D Kung Fu film introducing Bobby Ming. Dir: Chang Mei Chun. Pro: Frank Wong. No other details obtained. (Eastern Media Productions-Eagle Films). Rel: Floating; first shown London (Scene 2) July 1980.

El Salvador, Revolution or Death
Dutch-made documentary about the escalating troubles and social unrest in that South American country. Made by Frank Diamand. (Stitching Derde Cinema, Amsterdam-The Other Cinema.) Rel: Floating; first shown London (ICA cinema) September 1980. 41 mins. No cert.

The Elephant Man
Warmly compassionate and on occasion deeply moving film about John Merrick, who lived in the late 1800s in London and was so grotesquely deformed he became known as 'The Elephant Man' and was exhibited as a side-show freak at travelling fairs. But saved from this miserable life by an interested doctor who became his dedicated friend and mentor, he rose to become a Victorian social lion, courted by the gentry and visited by Royalty, dying while still young by suffocating when he tried to sleep normally in a bed. Finely polished performances by John Hurt (as 'The Elephant Man'), Anthony Hopkins (as the doctor), John Gielgud, Wendy Hiller and Anne Bancroft. Rest of cast: Freddie Jones, Michael Elphick, Hannah Gordon, Helen Ryan, John Standing, Dexter Fletcher, Lesley Dunlop, Phoebe Nicholls, Pat Gorman, Claire Davenport, Orla Pederson, Patsy Smart, Frederick Treves, Stromboli, Richard Hunter, James Cormack, Robert Bush, Roy Evans, Joan Rhodes, Nula Conwell, Tony London, Alfie Curtis, Hugh Manning. Dir: David Lynch. Pro: Jonathan Sanger. Ex Pro: Stuart Cornfeld. Screenplay: Christopher De Vore, Eric Bergren & David Lynch. Ph: Freddie Francis. Ed: Anne V. Coates. Pro Des: Stuart Craig. M: John Morris. In Charge of Production: Terence A. Clegg. Based on the life of John Merrick and not upon the play of the same title, or any other fictional accounts. (Brooksfilms-EMI.) Rel: 19 October. 123 mins. Cert AA.

The Empire Strikes Back – (Star Wars Episode 5)

George Lucas's sequel to his first *Star Wars* Outer Space Spectacular (now re-titled *Star Wars – Episode 4*) and designed as only one of a long series of such movies (maybe 1 to 10!) telling in detail the – fairy – story-history of a galaxy of 'long ago and far away'. This second in the series is as good as, if not better than the first, with plenty of fun, spectacle and remarkable invention, such as Yoda, the green-blue visaged elf with long ears, mysterious powers and much wisdom. And also present, such old tin favourites as Artoo Detoo and his robotian pal See Threepio. Cast: Mark Hamill, Harrison Ford, Carrie Fisher, Billy Dee Williams, Anthony Daniels, Frank Oz, David Prowse, Peter Mayhew, Kenny Baker, Alec Guinness, Jeremy Bulloch, John Hollis, Jack Purvis, Des Webb, Kathryn Mullen, Clive Revill, Kenneth Colley, Julian Glover, Michael Sheard, Michael Culver, John Dicks, Milton Johns, Mark Jones, Oliver Maguire, Robin Scobey, Bruce Boa, Christopher Malcolm, Dennis Lawson, Richard Oldfield, John Morton, Ian Liston, John Ratzenberger, Jack McKenzie, Jerry Harte, Norman Chancer, Norwich Duff, Ray Hassett, Brigitte Kahn, Burnell Tucker. Dir: Irvin Kerschner. Pro: Gary Kurtz. Story & Ex Pro: George Lucas. Screenplay: Leigh Brackett & Lawrence Kasdan. Ph: Peter Suschitzky. Ed: Paul Hirsch. Pro Des: Norman Reynolds. Assoc Pro: Robert Watts & James Bloom. M: John Williams. Special Visual Effects: Brian Johnson & Richard Edlund. Second Unit Dir: Harley Cokliss, Peter MacDonald & John Barry. Photographed on the Hardangerjokulen Glacier, Finse, Norway & EMI Studios. (Lucasfilm-Fox.) Rel: 17 August. 124 mins. Cert U.

The Evictors

Neat and nicely sustained suspense thriller about some very possessive characters prepared to lie, cheat and ultimately murder most foully any number of people in order to keep untenanted the house from which they were forced out of in a bloody battle with the authorities. It all gets a bit wild in the end but by then has achieved considerable thrill success. Cast: Vic Morrow, Michael Parks, Jessica Harper, Sue Ane Langdon, Dennis Fimple, Bill Thurman, Jimmy Clem, Harry Thomasson, Twyla Taylor, Glen Roberts. Dir, Pro & Screenplay: Charles B. Pierce. Assoc Pro: Steve Lyons. Ph: Chuck Bryant. Ed: Shirak Khojayan. Art: John Ball. M: Jaime Mendoza-Nava. (Samuel Z. Arkoff-American International-ITC.) Rel: Floating; first shown London, (Classic, Leicester Sq.) June 1980. 92 mins. Cert X.

The Exterminator

Violent, brutal and bloody thriller about ex-Vietnam war veteran who when his black pal is made a paraplegic by some gangsters during a robbery, sets out to even things up by killing off the villains in a giant meat-grinder, a flame-thrower and other less routine – more sadistic – ways. He becomes a sort of one-man vigilante force who ends up confronting both crooks and cops in a shoot-out which he survives – to almost certainly carry on in a sequel! Cast: Christopher George, Samantha Eggar, Robert Ginty, Steve James, Tony di Benedetto, Dick Boccelli, Patrick Farrelly, Michele

Harrell, David Lipman, Cindy Wilks, Dennis Boutsikaris. Dir & Screenplay: James Glickenhaus. Pro: Mark Buntzman. Ph: Robert M. Baldwin. Ed: Corky O'Hara. Art: Jane Herschcopf & Mark Slater. M: Joe Renzetti (Songs by The Tramps & Roger Bowling; guest perf by Stan Getz). (Interstar-Alpha Films.) Rel: 25 January. 101 mins. Cert X.

Fame

A not very successful effort to combine semi-documentary (and up-dated) old-time musical styles in one movie, which in several caption-headed segments attempts to follow a half-dozen pupils of the Manhattan High School of Performing Arts and New York City High School of Music and Art through from audition to graduation. Contrasting factual scenes of training (music, dance and drama) with set-pieces when the pupils spill into the streets for spectacular, lively (and loud) song-and-dance numbers. And for future actors and whatever most of the youngsters appear to have surprisingly constricted – mostly four-letter word – vocabularies. Not much like RADA! Cast: Eddie Barth, Irene Cara. Lee Curreri, Laura Dean, Antonia Franceschi, Boyd Gaines, Albert Hague, Teresa Hughes, Steve Inwood, Paul McCrane, Anne Meara, Joanna Merlin, Barry Miller, Jim Moody, Gene Anthony Ray, Maureen Teefy, Debbie Allen, Richard Belzer, Frank Bongiorno, Bill Britten, Eric Brokington, Nicholas Bunin, Cindy Canuelas, Nora Cotrone, Mbewe Escobar, Gennady Filimonov; Victor Fischbarg, Penny Frank, Willie Henry Jr., Steven Hollander, Sang Kim, Darrell Kirkman, Judith L'Heureux, Ted Lambert, Nancy Lee, Sarah Malament, James Manis, Carol Massenberg, Isaac Mizrahi, Raquel Mondin, Alba Oms, Frank Oteri, Traci Parnell, Sal Piro, Leslie Quickley, Ray Ramirez, Loris Sallahian, Ilse Bass, Dawn Steinberg, Jonathan Strasser, Yvette Torres, Frank X. Vitolo, Stefanie Zimmerman. *Principal dancers:* Pat Berndt, Trady Burnett, Greg De Jean, Laura Delano, Michael DeLorenzo, Aaron Dugger, Charles Epps, Neisha Folkes, Karen Ford, Robin Gray, Hazel Green, Eva Grubler, Emera Hunt, Patrick King, Cynthia Lochard, Shana Manaker, Julian Montenaire, Alexandra Pennisi, Holly Reeve, Michelle Saran, Kate Snyder, Sallie Stadlen, Emily Stern, Meg Tilly, Louis Venosta, Philip Wright, Ranko Yokoyana, *Principal musicians and vocalists:* Adam Abeshouse, Eugene Asti, Nadine Aubort, Gregory Buchalter, Yvette D. Carrington, Fima Ephron, Anthony Evans, Shari Feder, Crystal Garner, David Glasser, Eric Goldberg, Stephanie Hatcher, Lisa Herman, Thais Hockaday, Karen Hoppe, Frankie Laino, April Lang, Richard Latimer, Lisa Lowell, Ann Marie McDermott, Kerry McDermott, Maureen McDermott, Josh Melville, Peter Rafelson, Anne Roboff, Chris Rogers, Boris Slutsky, Alan Venter, Evan Weinstein. Dir: Alan Parker. Pro: David de Silva & Alan Marshal. Screenplay: Christopher Gore. Ph: Michael Seresin. Ed: Gerry Hambling. Pro Des: Geoffrey Kirkland. Choreography: Louis Falco. M: Michael Gore. Songs 'Red Light', 'Hot Lunch Jam', 'Fame', 'Out There On My Own', and 'I Sing the Body Electric' by Dominic Bugatti & Frank Musker: 'Is It OK If I Call You Mine', by Paul McCrane. (MGM-CIC.) Rel: 24 August. 134. mins. Cert AA.

The Fan

Just to remind us that Fan is short for that anti-social creature the fanatic, this is a thriller about a young man with an obsessive adulation of stage star Sally Ross whose explosion of him leads him down the slope to psychopathic slaughter and a final murderous confrontation with the object of his love-hate desire in an empty theatre. Beautifully polished professional performances from three fine Hollywood veterans, in Lauren Bacall (as Sally), James Garner and Maureen Stapleton, some delightful musical show rehearsals – with Miss Bacall singing and dancing – and a very tense if not entirely credible climax. Rest of cast: Hector Elizondo, Michael Biehn (the psycho case), Anna Maria Horsford, Kurt Johnson, Feiga Martinez, Reed Jones, Kaiulani Lee, Charles Blackwell, Dwight Schultz, Dana Delany, Terence Marinan, Lesley Rogers, Parker McCormick, Robert Weil, Ed Crowley, Gail Benedict, D. David Lewis, Griffin Dunne, Themi Sapountzakis, Jean de Baer, Liz Smith, Haru Aki, Robin Alpert, Rene Ceballos, Clif de Raita, Edyie Fleming, Linda Haberman, Sergio Lopez-Cal, Jamie Patterson, Justin Ross, Stephanie Williams, Jim Wolfe, Thomas Saccio, Victoria Vanderkloot, James Ogden, Terri Duhaime, Donna Mitchell, Hector Orsorio, Lionel Pina, Miriam Phillips, Jack R. Marks, George Peters, Esther Benson, Eric Van Valkenburg, Ann Pearl Gary, Madeline Moroff, Leo Schaff, James Bryson, J. Nesbit Clark, Tim Elliott, Paul Hummel, Jacob Laufer. Dir: Edward Bianchi. Pro: Robert Stigwood. Ex Pro: Kevin McCormick. Assoc Pro: John Nicolella & Bill Oakes. Screenplay: Priscilla Chapman & John Hartwell; based on the novel by Bob Randall. Ph: Dick Bush. Ed: Alan Heim. Pro Des: Santo Loquasto, M: 'Hearts Not Diamonds', 'Remarkable Woman', music by Marvin Hamlisch, lyrics by Tim Rice; also 'Danger' perf by Selecter; 'It's Too Funky in Here' perf by James Brown; & 'How Sweet It Is – To Be Loved By You' perf by Jr Walker and The All Stars. (RSO Films-Paramount/Roger Stigwood-CIC.) Rel: 31 May. 95 mins. Cert X.

The Fiendish Plot of Dr Fu Manchu

Uneven comedy of some historical importance in that it marks the final screen appearance of the late Peter Sellers, who plays both the evil Chinese Doctor (now 168 years old and surviving only by means of his secret life elixir) and his Scotland Yard nemesis Nayland Smith. Some funny scenes with some flat ones between; the funniest showing something to both the Marxes and to Python; the former with King, Queen, their doubles, attendants and Yard guardians all jostling for space at the Royal Box at the opera, the latter when Smith sails his country cottage off to Manchu's Himalayan hide-out! Rest of cast: Helen Mirren, David Tomlinson, Sid Caesar, Simon Williams, Steve Franken, Stratford Johns, John Le Mesurier, John Sharp, Clement Harari, Lee Kwan-Young, John Tan, Philip Tan, Serfe Julien, Johns Rajohnson, Pralith Jngam Oeurn, Lim Bun Song, Clive Dunn, Burt Kwouk, John Taylor, Katia Chenko, David Powers, Marc Wilkinson, Grace Coyle, Jacqueline Khan, Iska Khan, George Hilsden, Rene Aranda. Dir: Piers Haggard. Pro: Zev Braun & Leland Nolan. Ex Pro: Hugh M. Hefner. Screenplay: Jim Moloney & Rudy Dochtermann. Assoc Pro: Yannoulla

Wakefield. Pro Ex: Lynne Frederick. Ph: Jean Tournier. Ed: Russell Lloyd. Pro Des: Alex Trauner. M: Marc Wilkinson. (Orion in assoc. with Playboy Productions-Warner Bros.) Rel: 31 August. 138 mins. Cert A.

The Final Countdown

Quite original if highly incredible story about a US Aircraft Carrier which after passing through a cyclonic storm finds itself sailing in pre-Pearl Harbour waters, approaching the Japanese War Fleet – giving Captain Kirk Douglas a chance to change history! Entertaining hokum with plenty of action and fascinating flying sequences. Rest of cast: Martin Sheen, James Farentino, Katherine Ross, Charles Durning, Ron O'Neal, Joe Lowry, Soon-Teck Oh, Gary Morgan, Victor Mohica, Mark Thomas, Alvin Ing, James Lawrence. Dir: Don Taylor. Pro: Peter V. Douglas. Ex Pro: Richard St Johns. Screenplay: David Ambrose & Gerry Davis. Assoc Pro: Lloyd Kaufman. Special (Storm) Visual Effects: Maurice Binder. Ex. in charge of Pro: John W. Hyde. Ph: Victor Kemper. Special Effects: Pat Elmendorf. Ed: Robert K. Lambert. Pro Des: Fernando Carrere. M: John Scott. (Bryna Co-UA.) Rel: 20 July. 105 mins. Cert A.

Fingers

A somewhat unsavoury mixture of sex and sadism in an admittedly off-beat story about an unbalanced son of a New York gangster father and insane mother who divides his time between viciously collecting his dad's overdue debts, training for his Carnegie Hall piano playing audition, irritating all and sundry by the loud pop music he plays on his portable radio that he takes everywhere with him, obtaining treatment for his misbehaving prostrate and gratifying his violent sexual appetites. With a far too mannered performance by Harvey Keitel as the candidate for the nut house, or the gallows. Rest of cast: Tisa Farrow, Jim Brown, Michael V. Gazzo, Marian Seldes, Carole Francis, Georgette Muir, Danny Aiello, Dominic Chianese, Anthony Sirico, Tanya Roberts, Ed Marino, Zack Norman, Murray Mosten, Jane Elder, Lenny Montana, Frank Pesche. Dir. & Screenplay/story: James Toback. Pro: George Barrie. Ph: Mike Chapman. Ed: Robert Lawrence. Pro Des: Gene Rudolf. M: 'Now is Forever' by George Barrie with lyrics by Sammy Kahn, sung by Jerry Vale. No Art credits. (Brut Productions Inc.-Gala.) Rel: Floating; first shown London (Scene 1) July 1980. 90 mins. Cert X.

Fire in the Water

The situation of a moviemaker running film pieces through an editing machine, while his girl-friend goes on a tour of the local countryside, allows Peter Whitehead in this Swiss production to tie together all sorts of fragments into a still fragmentary whole. Cast: Nathalie Delon, Edouard Niersman. Dir, written (with producer Marc Sursock), photographed and edited (with John Hansen) by Peter Whitehead. (Fontglow-Lorrimar.) Rel: Floating; 90 mins. No cert.

The First Deadly Sin

In his first film since his short-lived 'retirement' in 1970, Frank Sinatra plays the same kind of blasé

detective role that he so successfully performed in the late 1960s in films like *Lady in Cement* and *The Detective* and only a slight thickening of figure and puffiness of face marks the intervening decade. With only weeks to go before retirement Officer Delaney comes up with a new lead on a series of apparently senseless murders and doggedly pursues them to find and mete out his kind of justice to the psycho nut case killer. A superb performance. There's a sub-plot about the detective's dying wife which did little for the movie and some bloody opening operation shots which actually did a lot to harm it. Rest of cast: Faye Dunaway, David Dukes, George Coe, Brenda Vaccaro, Martin Gabel, Joe Spinell, Jeffrey de Munn, Anthony Zerbe, James Whitmore, Fred Fuster. Dir: Brian Hutton. Pro: George Pappas & Mark Shanker. Ex Pro: Frank Sinatra & Elliott Kastner. Screenplay: Mann Rubin; from the novel by Lawrence Sanders. Ph: Jack Priestley. Ed: Eric Albertson. Art: Woody Mackintosh. M: Gordon Jenkins. (Artanis/Cinema 7-Filmways-CIC.) Rel: 24 May. 112 mins. Cert AA.

The First Nudie Musical

About the young producer driven to make a pornographic screen revue in two weeks in order to keep his dad's film studio from being taken over by his debtors. Cast: Stephen Nathan, Cindy Williams, Bruce Kimmel, Leslie Ackerman, Alan Abelew, Diana Canova, Alexandra Morgan, Frank Doubleday, Kathleen Hietala, Art Marino, Hy Pyke, Greg Finley, Herb Graham, Rene Hall, Susan Stewart, Artie Shafer, Jerry Hoffman, Wade Crookham, Nancy Chadwick, John Kirby, Vern Joyce, Ian Praise, Eileen Ramsey, Jane Ralston, Claude Spence, Chris Corso, Alison Cohen, Susan Gelb, Kathryn Kimmel. Dir: Mark Haggard & Bruce Kimmel. Pro: Jack Reeves. Screenplay, Music & Lyrics: Bruce Kimmel. Ex Pro: Stuart W. Phelps & Peter S. Brown. Ph: Douglas H. Knapp. Ed: Allen Peluso. Art: Tom Rassmussen. (First Musical Co.-New Realm.) Rel: Floating; first shown London (Eros and Praed St Classic) February 1981. 82 mins. Cert X.

Flash Gordon

High, wide, handsome treat for the young and the young in heart; a lavish and spectacular adaptation of the famous strip cartoon and film serial, with F.G. rocketing into space to try and stop evil planet Mongo Emperor Ming from destroying the earth for the mere fun of it! And Flash finds this particular area of space peopled by a nubile Princess, a handsome Prince, a winged Hawk King and various other characters. Cast: Sam Jones, Melody Anderson, Max Von Sydow, Ornella Muti, Chaim Topol, Timothy Dalton, Brian Blessed, Peter Wyngarde, Mariangela Melato, John Osborne, Richard O'Brien, John Hallam, Philip Stone, Suzanne Danielle, Bobby Brown, Ted Carroll, Adrienne Kronenberg, William Hootkins. Dir: Michael Hodges. Pro: Dino de Laurentiis. Ex Pro: Bernard Williams. Screenplay: Lorenzo Semple Jr. Ed: Malcolm Cooke. Ph: Gil Taylor. Pro Des: Danilo Donati. Art: John Graysmark. M: 'Queen'. 2nd Unit Dir: William Kronick. Orch. score composed & arr. by Howard Blake. The story based on the original characters created by Alex Raymond. (1980 Famous Films-EMI.) Rel: 14 December. 114 mins. Cert A.

The Fog

Horror-thriller about some bloody-minded mariners who a hundred years after being deliberately wrecked by the treasure-seeking inhabitants of Antonio Bay, return to get their murderous own back on the present population, emerging in worm-crawling horror from a sea shrouded in a mysterious mist to hack at anyone who comes within their seeking arms' length! Cast: Adrienne Barbeau, Hal Holbrook, Janet Leigh, Jamie Lee Curtis, John Houseman, Tommy Atkins, Nancy Loomis, Charles Cyphers, John Goff, Ty Mitchell, George Buck Glower, Jim Jacobus, John Vick, Jim Canning, Regina Waldon, Darrow Igus, Bill Taylor, Jim Haynie, Fred Franklyn. Dir, Screenplay (with Debra Hill) & M: John Carpenter. Pro & Screenplay (with Carpenter: Debra Hill). Ex Pro: Charles B. Bloch. Ph: Dean Cundey. Co-Ed & Pro Des: Tommy Lee Wallace. Co-Ed: Charles Bornstein. (Avco Embassy-Rank.) Rel: 16 November. 90 mins. Cert AA.

For Your Eyes Only

The 007 mixture much as before, with thrills, stunts, beautiful international backgrounds superbly photographed, a silly and quite incredible story, all wonderfully polished into two packed hours of fun film, with even more hair-raising and hilarious stunts for James Bond to perform than ever previously. Cast: Roger Moore, Carole Boquet, Topol, Lynn-Holly Johnson, Julian Glover, Cassandra Harris, Jill Bennett, Michael Gothard, John Wyman, Jack Hedley, Lois Maxwell, Desmond Llewelyn, Geoffrey Keen, Walter Gotell, James Villiers, John Moreno, Charles Dance, Paul Angelis, Toby Robins, Jack Klaff, Alkis Kritikos, Stag Theodore, Stefan Kalipha, Graham Crowden, Noel Johnson, William Hoyland, Paul Brooke, Eva Rueber-Staier, Fred Bryant, Robbin Young, Graham Hawkes, John Wells, Janet Brown. Dir: John Glen. Pro: Albert R. Broccoli. Ex Pro: Michael G. Wilson. Assoc Pro: Tom Pevsner. Screenplay: Richard Maibaum & Michael G. Wilson. Ph: Alan Hume. Ed: John Grover. Pro Des: Peter Lamont. M: Bill Conti. Special Effects Sup: Derek Meddings. Pro Sup: Bob Simmonds. Pro Controller: Reginald A. Barkshire. (Eon Productions-UA). Rel: 28 June. 127 mins. Cert A.

*Forget Venice – Dimenticare Venezia

An outstanding example of true film art by Franco Brusati: a dense, intricate and subtle – and essentially literary – story of a brother and sister (he a dilettante restorer of old cars, she an opera singer dying from heart disease) and the three younger people who make up a closed little group, most of whom try to keep time at bay in the lovely old house near Venice, where memories of the past keep impinging on the present. A film of intense beauty, extending to the loving way the camera sees the proud, golden bodies of the young women, and the sense of painting which extends over the entire movie. Marvellously acted by a small cast: Erland Josephson, Mariangela Melato, Eleonora Giorgi, David Potremoli, Hella Petri, Fred Personne, Anne Caudry. Dir & Screenplay (latter with Jaja Fiastri): Franco Brusati. Pro: Claudio Gvassetti. Assoc Pro: Yves Gasser & Yves Peyvot. Pro Sup: Ennio de Meo & Vivien Boden. Ph: Romano Albani. Ed: Ruggero Mastroianni. Sets (no Art credit): Luigi Scaccianoce. M:

Benedetto Ghiglia. (Rizzoli/Action Films co-production-Connoisseur.) Rel: Floating; first shown London (Academy) June 1980. 110 mins. Cert X.

The Formula

Convoluted and confusing though very watchable thriller in which George C. Scott's investigation into the murder of his cop ex-partner leads him to a plot by an international oil cartel to keep secret a Nazi-era discovery of an easy way to make fuel from coal, holding on to it until the oil has run out thus gaining time to buy up all the coal mines in America! And Marlon Brando obviously enjoyed playing the cartel's quietly villainous headman. Rest of cast: Marthe Keller, John Gielgud, G. D. Spradlin, Beatrice Straight, Richard Lynch, John van Dreelen, Robin Clarke, Wolfgang Preiss, Calvin Jung, Alan North, David Byrd, Ferdy Mayne, Ike Eisenmann, Marshall Thompson, Dieter Schidor, Werner Kreindl, Jan Niklas, Gerry Murphy, Francisco Prado, Louis Basile, Ric Mancini, Weston Gavin, Craig T. Nelson, Herb Voland, Diane Tyler, Jim Brewer, Lavelle Roby, Albert Carrier, Ernie Feuntes, Stephanie Edwards, Nathan Roberts, Tom Hall, Reinhard Von Bauer, Janos Gönczöl, Heinz Kammer, René Kolldehoff, Martin Brandt, Paul Glawion, Emil Steinberger, (Dancers: Emily Jensen, Sandie Lawrence, Ursula Warel, Jane Faithe, Wendy Bladock), Ursula Hamann. Dir: John G. Avildsen. Pro & Screenplay: Steve Shagan; from his novel of the same title. Ph: James Crabe. Sup Ed: David Bretherton. Ed: John G. Avildsen & John Carter. Pro Des (USA): Herman A. Blumenthal. Art (Europe): Hans-Jürgen Keibach. M: Bill Conti. (Steve Shagan/CIP-MGM-CIC) Rel: 8 February. 117 mins. Cert AA.

Foxes

A somewhat sad and depressing picture of American youth in a superficial story about four teenage girl pals whose life seems confined to booze, dope and sex. Only Jodie Foster, as the 'little mother' of the four, seems to have any sense of balance or hope of a reasonably happy future. But a glimpse of the (possible?) original intention of being social comment is shown in a short but fascinating tour of weirder Hollywood, with the tarts naked under their see-through macs and dog-owners taking their pets out for 'walkies' equipped with straw hat and sun glasses. Rest of cast: Scott Baio, Sally Kellerman, Randy Quaid, Lois Smith, Adam Faith, Cherie Currie, Marilyn Kagan, Kandice Stroh, Joan Sloan, Jill Barrie Bogart, Wayne Storm, Mary Margaret Lewis, Grant Wilson, Fredric Lehne, Robert Romanus, Roger Bowen, Buddy Foster, E. Lamont Johnson, Mary Ellen O'Neill, Ben Frank, Kay A. Tornborg, Scott Garrett, Laura Dern, Michael Taylor, Gino Baffa, Charles Shull, Tony Termini, Jeff Silverman, Mae Williams, R. Scott Thomson, Ron Lombard, Steve Jones, Jon M. Benson, Tom Pletts, Ken Novick, Angel. Dir: Adrian Lyne. Pro: David Puttnam & Gerald Ayres. Assoc Pro: Geoffrey Kirkland, Michael Seresin, Joel Blasberg & Gerry Hambling. Screenplay: Gerald Ayres. Ph: Leon Bijou. Ed: Jim Coblentz. Art: Michael Levesque. M: Giorgio Moroder. (PolyGram Pictures-UA.) Rel: 26 April. 105 mins. Cert AA.

Freedom Road

Moving story of the American Deep South at the end of the Civil War and the emergence of the Ku Klux Klan. Muhammad Ali plays (with surprising restraint and a quiet dignity) an ex-soldier who leads his fellow freed-slaves in defence unto death when the corrupt local justices try to take away their legally purchased land. Rest of cast: Kris Kristofferson, Ron O'Neal, Edward Herrmann, Barbara-O Jones, Sonny Jim Gaines, Joel Fluellen, Jean Renee Foster, Grace Zabriskie, Bill Mackey, Earl D. A. Smith, Alfred Woodard, Fred Covington, Sonny Schroyer, Ernest Dixon, Syliva 'Kuumba' Williams, Tom J. Delaney, Ron Gural, William Allen Young, Erik Washington, Tony Ross, Rodney King Adams, Howard Brunner, Howland Chamberlin. Dir: Jan Kadar. Pro: Zev Braun. Co-Pro: Leland Nolan. Screenplay: David Zelag Goodman. Ph: Charles Correll. Ed: George Folsey Jr. Pro Des: Danny Lomino. M: No credit. (Enterprise Pictures.) Rel: Floating; first shown London (London Pavilion) January 1981. 100 mins. Cert AA.

*Friday the Thirteenth

Conventional, extremely gory American shocker about mad killer who one by one horrifyingly murders the new owner of a long-closed lakeside holiday camp and his several young helpers during a night of rain, storm and terror. Cast: Betsy Palmer, Adrienne King, Harry Crosby, Laurie Bartram, Mark Nelson, Jeannine Taylor, Robbi Morgan, Kevin Bacon, Peter Brouwer, Rex Everhart, Ronn Carroll, Ron Millkie, Walt Gorney, Willie Adams, Debra S. Hayes, Dorothy Kobs, Sally Anne Golden, Mary Rocco, Ken L. Parker, Ari Lehman. Dir & Pro: Sean S. Cunningham. Screenplay: Victor Miller. Assoc. Pro: Stephen Miner. Ph: Barry Abrams. Ed: Bill Freda. Art: Virginia Field. M: Harry Manfredini. (Georgetown-Warner.) Rel: 29 June 1980. 95 mins. Cert X.

Friday the Thirteenth Part II

Not knowing about the first series of horrid murders of young holidaymakers at Camp Crystal Lake in the original *Friday the Thirteenth* film, a new lot moves in for similar slaughter! Cast: Amy Steel, John Furey, Adrienne King, Kirsten Baker, Stu Charno, Warrington Gillette, Walt Gorney, Marta Kober, Tom McBride, Bill Randolph, Lauren-Marie Taylor, Russell Todd, Cliff Cudney, Jack Marks, Steve Daskawisz, Jerry Wallace, David Brand, China Chen, Carolyn Louden, Jaime Perry, Tom Shea, Jill Voight; and special appearance of Betsy Palmer as Mrs Voohees. Dir & Pro: Steve Miner. Co Pro: Dennis Murphy. Ex Pro: Tom Gruenberg & Lisa Barsamian. Assoc Pro: Frank Mancuso Jr. Screenplay: Ron Kurz. Ph: Peter Stein. Ed: Susan E. Cunningham. Pro Des: Virginia Field. M: Harry Manfredini. (Paramount-CIC.) Rel: 21 June. 87 mins. Cert X.

From the Life of the Marionettes

(Made in West Germany) Technically severe (using the close-up almost entirely and concentrating on the human face) Ingmar Bergman continues to meditate on the philosophical and psychological problems of the human condition; the conclusion that not only is God not in his heaven but the Devil has usurped his place!

Seen this time in a story about a man who commits an apparently motiveless murder of a prostitute (The Prologue) and ends up happily insane in his asylum cell (Epilogue) between which Bergman examines possible explanations without drawing any final conclusions. Intellectually stimulating; visually the opposite. Cast: Robert Atzorn, Christine Buchegger, Lola Muethel, Martin Benrath, Walter Schmidinger, Rita Russek, Heinz Bennett, Karl Heinz Pelser, Gaby Dohm, Toni Berger, Ruth Loafs. Dir & Screenplay: Ingmar Bergman. Pro: Horst Wendlandt & Ingrid Bergman. Ph: Sven Nykvist. Ed: Petra V. Oeiffen. Pro Des: Rolf Zehetbauer. Art: Herbert Strabel. M: Rolf Wilhelm. (ITC). Rel: Floating; first shown London (Academy) June 1981. 104 mins. Cert X.

The Funhouse

Another film in the cycle of Grand Guignol thrillers about teenagers meeting bloody death one by one: in this case, three of the four who for a 'dare' spend the night locked in a fair sideshow, where they are murderously stalked by a mutant horror. Nice young players in a rather nasty movie. Cast: Elizabeth Berridge, Shawn Carson, Jeanne Austin, Jack McDermott, Cooper Huckabee, Largo Woodruff, Miles Chapin, David Carson, Sonia Zomina, Ralph Marino, Kevin Conway, Herb Robins, Mona Agar, Wayne Doba, William Finley, Susie Malnik, Sylvia Miles, Sid Raymond, Larry Ross, Frank Grimes, Frank Schuller, Peter Conrad, Mildred Hughes, Glen Lawrence, Shawn McAllister, Sandy Mielke, Mike Montalvo. Dir: Tobe Hooper. Pro: Derek Power & Steven Bernhardt. Ex Pro: Mace Neufeld & Mark Lester. Screenplay: Larry Block. Ph: Andrew Laszlo. Ed: Jack Hofstra. Pro Des: Morton Rabinowitz. M: John Beal. Assoc Pro: Brad Neufeld. (Universal-CIC.) Rel: 10 May. 91 mins. Cert X.

Gates of Heaven

American documentary – made 1978 – about pets' cemeteries in that country. Dir, Pro & Screenplay: Errol Morris. Ph: Ned Burgess. Add Ph: Dyanna Taylor. Sup Ed: Charles Laurence Silver. Assoc Ed: Brad Fuller. Contributing Ed: Suzanne Fenn. Guitar M perf by Dan Harbarts. (Gates of Heaven Co-Cinegate) Rel: Floating; first shown London (Electric Cinema) February 1981. 85 mins. Cert U.

George and Mildred

Straightforward large screen adaptation of the small screen series with Yootha Joyce and Brian Murphy innocently involved in some very shady dealings. Rest of cast: Norman Eshley, Sheila Fearn, Nicky Bond-Owen, Stratford Johns, Kenneth Cope, David Barry, Neil McCarthy, Dennis Ramsden, Linda Frith, Harry Fowler, Garfield Morgan, Dudley Sutton. Dir: Peter Frazer-Jones. Pro: Roy Skeggs. Ex Pro: Brian Lawrence. Screenplay: Dick Sharples. Ph: Frank Watts. Ed: Peter Weatherley. Art: Carolyn Scott. M: Philip Martell. (Chips Prods.-Cinema Arts International-ITC.) Rel: 27 July. 93 mins. Cert A.

Germany, Pale Mother

Long, slow and gloomy German film about a marriage that is ruined by the enforced absences, abstinences and subsequent misunderstandings caused by the war; with the wife struck down by facial paralysis and only saved from committing suicide by the intervention of the not particularly loved young child. Cast: Eva Mattes, Ernst Jacobi, Elisabeth Stepanek, Angelike Thomas, Rainer Friedrichsen, Gisela Stein, Fritz Lichtenhahn, Anna Sanders, Sonja Lauer, Mirian Lauer. Dir & Screenplay: Helma Sanders-Brahms. Pro: Ursula Ludwig. Ph: Jürgen Jürges. Ed: Elfi Tillack & Uta Periginelli. Art: Götz Heymann. M: Jürgen Knieper. (Mainline Pictures.) Rel: Floating; first shown London (Screen-on-the-Hill) June 1981. 110 mins. Cert AA.

Gloria
A somewhat odd grafting of an old Hollywood gangster-era story and scene on to John Cassavetes's 'Method' style of acting and directing as he pays obvious homage to his brilliant, wife-star Gena Rowlands, as the gal on the run from the Manhattan hoods with a small boy in tow, the duo starting out by disliking each other but coming closer as the bullets fly (both ways, the gal can kill – and does so, several times). Rest of cast: Julie Carmen, Tony Knesich, Gregory Cleghorn, Buck Henry, John Adames, Lupe Garnica, Jessica Castillo, Tom Noonan, Ronald Maccone, George Yudezevich, Gary Klar, William E. Rice, Frank Belgiorno, J. C. Quinn, Alex Stevens, Sonny Landham, Harry Madsen, Shanton Granger, John Pavelko, Raymond Baker, Ross Charap, Irvin Graham, Michael Proscia, T. S. Rosenbaum, Santos Morales, Meta Shaw, Marilyn Putnam, John Finnegan, Gaetano Lisi, Richard M. Kaye, Steve Lefkowitz, George Poidomani, Lawrence Tierney, Asa Adil Oawee, Vincent Pecorella, Iris Fernandez, Jade Bari, David Resnick, Thomas J. Buckman, Joe Dabenicno, Bill Wiley, John M. Sefakis, Val Avery, Walter Dukes, Janet Rubin, Ferruccio Hrvatin, Edward Wilson, Basilio Franchina, Carl Levy, Warren Selvaggi, Nathan Seril, Vladimir Drazenovic, Edward Jacobs, Brad Johnston, Jerry Jaffe. Dir & Screenplay: John Cassavetes. Pro: Sam Shaw. Ph: Fred Schuler. Ed: George C. Villasenor. Art: Rene D'Auriac. M: Bill Conti. Assoc Pro: Steve Kesten. (Columbia.) Rel: 8 March. 121 mins. Cert AA.

Good Guys Wear Black
Minor 1977 film from America, about some cynical political plotting and killing during and after the Vietnam war, which appears at least partially produced to give many times honoured World Karate champion Chuck Norris the opportunity to show his prowess. Rest of cast: Anne Archer, James Franciscus, Lloyd Haynes, Dana Andrews, Jim Backus, Larry Casey, Tony Mannino, Soon-Teck Oh, Joe Bennett, Jerry Douglas, Stack Pierce, Michael Payne, David Starwalt, Aaron Norris, Don Pike, Ben Perry, Kathy McCullen, Michael Stark, James Bacon, Matsuo Uda, Virginia Wing, Viola Harris, Jacki Robins, Pat Johnson, Warren Smith, Dick Shoemaker. Dir: Ted Post. Pro: Allan F. Bodoh. Ex Pro: Michael Leone. Assoc Pro: Mitchell Connold. Pro Sup: Jeff Sinclair. Pro Co-Ord: Joel Westbrook. Screenplay: Bruce Cohn & Mark Medoff; from a story by Joseph Fraley. Ed: Bob Steadman. Ed: William and Millie Moore. Art: B. B. Neel. M: Craig Safan. (Action One Film Partners/Mar Vista Productions-Enterprise). Rel: 31 May. 95 mins. Cert A.

*The Great Rock 'n' Roll Swindle
Confused film which by snippets from concert and other live shows gives some idea of what punks and The Sex Pistols band were all about. Cast: Malcolm McLaren, The Embezzler, Sid Vicious, The Gimmick, Johnny Rotten, The Collaborator, Steve Jones, Paul Cook, Ronnie Biggs, Mary Millington, James Aubrey, Liz Fraser, Julian Holloway, The Blackarabs, Irene Handle. Dir & Screenplay: Julian Temple. Ex Pro: Jeremy Thomas & Don Boyd. M: Sex Pistols. (Boyds Co & Virgin Films in assoc. with Matrixbest.) Rel: 29 June. 1980. 104 mins. Cert X.

The Great Santini
A remarkable portrait of a martial martinet which at the same time paints a picture of family tensions, more particularly between the insensitive Marine US Corps war ace pilot, Col Meechum, who finds peace tiresome, and his teenage son who finds his father's natural exhibitionism hateful. Thoughtful and finely acted, especially by Robert Duvall (father), Michael O'Keefe as the son, Blythe Danner as the wife. Rest of cast: Julie Ann Haddock, Lisa Jane Persky, Brian Andrews, Stan Shaw, Theresa Merritt, David Keith, Paul Mantee, Michael Strong, Bennett Liss, Joe A. Dorsey, David Frankham, Jan Stratton, Paul Gleason, W. K. Stratton, Lew Horn, Michael Rougas, Al Garcia, Stacy MacGregor, Harold B. Bibey, Gordon Gene Jones, Harry Pickens Porth, Albert Smith, Walter Gay, Wendell Gregory, Bill Nelson, Bill Eudaly, Wayne Sharpnack, Morris Phifer, Brad Baldwin, Ronnie Cross, Timothy Norton, Richard Horsewell, Ronald Garrett Jr, Hank Chappell, Reggie Malphrus, Doyle Kelley, Larry Burke, K. C. Stiglbauer, Tom Conroy, Tony Langdale, Ray Nix, David Simmons, Randy Cauthen, Lance Snyder, Gary Towles, Chip Upchurch, Nicole Von der Heyde, Lisa Collins, Claudette Evans, Tara Hudson, Holly Malphrus, Denise Walker, Nancy Black, Kim Duncan, Carol Monson, Sandra Patterson, Sarah Sandford, Edwina Dawn Tucker. Dir & Screenplay (based on the novel by Pat Conroy): Lewis John Carlino. Pro: Charles A. Pratt. Ex in charge of Pro: John E. Pommer. Ph: Ralph Woolsey. Pro Des: Jack Poplin. Ed: Houseley Stevenson. Consulting Ed: George Folsey. M: Elmer Bernstein. (Orion-Warner.) Rel: Floating; first shown London (Gate) March 1981. 115 mins. Cert A.

Green Ice
Adventure thriller with just about everything packed into it except the humour that would have helped it to rise above its very melodramatic foundation. Ryan O'Neal as the electronics expert who gives a lift to lovely lady Anne Archer and so becomes involved with her villainous admirer Omar Sharif, whose emerald millions are housed in an impregnable fortress which O'Neal decides to crack. All highly unlikely and topped by the incredible balloon heist, but spectacular and beautifully photographed. Rest of cast: Domingo Ambriz, John Larroquette, Philip Stone, Michael Sheard, Enrique Lucero, Manuel Ojeda, Tara Fellner. Dir: Ernest Day. Pro: Jack Wiener. Assoc Pro: Colin M. Brewer. Screenplay: Edward Anhalt, Ray Hassett, Anthony Simmons & Robert de Laurentis; based on the book by Gerald Browne. Ph: Gilbert Taylor. Ed: John

Jympson. Pro Des: Roy Walker. M: Bill Wyman ('Tenderness' and 'Floating' sung by Maria Muldaur). (Lew Grade/Jack Wiener-ITC.) Rel: 14 June. 115 mins. Cert AA.

The Green Room – La Chambre Verte
Intense, personal, sombre François Truffaut film (made 1978) which, written, directed and acted by him, is the portrait of a man whose loyalty to the dead is wholly obsessive. Setting up a shrine in a restored chapel to his dead wife, his friendship blossoms with a girl who shares something of his feelings for the dearly beloved dead until she reveals her late loved one was his most hated ex-friend, so bringing about the tragic climax. A brilliant if dark piece of cinema. Cast: François Truffaut, Nathalie Baye, Jean Dasté, Jean-Pierre Moulin, Antoine Vitez, Jane Lobre, Jean-Pierre Ducos, Annie Miller, Marie Jaoul, Monique Dury, Laurence Ragon, Marcel Berbert, Guy D'Ablon, Christian Lentretien, Patrick Maléon. Dir: François Truffaut. Assoc Pro: Suzanne Schiffman & Emmanuel Clot. Screenplay: Truffaut & Jean Grualt; based on short stories – The Altar of the Dead and The Beast in the Jungle – by Henry James. Ph: Nestor Almendros. Ed: Martine Barraque-Curie. Art; Jean-Pierre Kohut-Svelko. M: Maurice Jaubert. (Les Films du Carosse/Les Productions Artistes Associes-Gala.) Rel: Floating; first shown London (ICA) July 1980. 94 mins. Cert A.

*Guyana – Crime of the Century
Fictional reconstruction of the horrific events of November 1978, when in a remote little religious colony founded by the Rev. James Johnson in Guyana nearly 800 of his followers committed mass suicide – or were killed – after the murder of a visiting congressman makes certain the exposure of the real conditions of many unhappy members of the totalitarian-ruled commune where the Rev. satisfied his sexual and dictatorial tastes. Cast: Stuart Whitman, Gene Barry, John Ireland, Joseph Cotton, Bradford Dillman, Jennifer Ashley, Yvonne de Carlo, Nadiuska, Tony Young, Erika Carlson, Robert Doqui, Hugo Stiglitz, Carlos East. Dir & Pro: René Cardona Jr. Assoc. Pro: Alfonso Lopez Negrete. Screenplay: Carlos Valdemar & René Cardona Jr.; from a story by René Cardona & Carlos Valdemar. Ph: Leopoldo Vallasenor. Ed: Earl Watson. No Art credit. M: Alfredo Diaz Ordaz & Jimmie Haskell, arr. & conducted by the latter. 'Time to Love' sung by Robertha. (Re-Al Productions International-Conacine, Mexico-Izaro Films, Spain-Care Productions S.A. Panama-Barber Rose International.) Rel: 29 June 1980. 108 mins. Cert X.

Happy Birthday to Me
Minor and unconvincing horror thriller about a series of murders – who-did-'em? Cast: Melissa Sue Anderson, Glenn Ford, Tracy Bregman, Jack Blum, Matt Craven, Lenore Zann, David Eisner, Lisa Langlois, Lawrence Dane, Frances Hyland, Sharon Acker, Michel Rene Labelle, Richard Rebiere, Lesleh Donaldson, Earl Pennington. Dir: J. Lee Thompson. Pro: John Dunning & Andre Link. Screenplay: John Saxton, Peter Jobin & Timothy Bond. Ph: Miklos Lente. Ed: Debra Karen. Pro Des: Earl Preston. M: Bo Harwood & Lance Rubin. (Columbia.) Rel: 28 June. 108 mins. Cert X.

Harlequin

Quite entertaining – if somewhat of a mish-mash – Australian-set story of crime, politics and a mysterious stranger who may have super-natural powers or be the charlatan, magician-illusionist his enemies say he is. And the film leaves it to you to make up your mind which. Robert Powell, as the Harlequinade figure who appears to cure ambitious senator David Hemmings's dying son, wins the adoration of the mother and is finally killed by the crooked, political power-seekers led by Broderick Crawford. Rest of cast: Carmen Duncan, Gus Mercurio, Alan Cassell, Mark Spain, Alyson Best, Sean Myers, Mary Simpson, Bevan Lee, Neville Teed, Mary Mackay, John Frawley, Nita Pannell, David Hough, Klaus Schultz, Peter West, Murray Ogden, Jack Ferrari, Julia Moody, Leslie Wright, Adele Cohen, Ramsay McLean. Dir: Simon Wincer. Pro: Antony I. Ginnane. Ex. Pro: William Fayman. Assoc. Pro: Jane Scott. Screenplay: Everett DeRoche. Ph: Gary Hensen. Ed: Adrian Carr. Pro Des: Bernard Hides. M: Brian May. (F.G. Film Productions Py. Ltd-Hemdale.) Rel: 7 September. 93 mins. Cert X.

Hawk the Slayer

Somewhat odd fairy story film which surely contains too much cruelty and violence to be suitable for the kids? The story of the struggle between two brothers, one good, one evil. Cast: Jack Palance, John Terry, Bernard Bresslaw, Ray Charleson, Peter O'Farrell, Morgan Sheppard, Patricia Quinn, Cheryl Campbell, Annette Crosbie, Catriona MacColl, Shane Briant, Harry Andrews, Christopher Benjamin, Roy Kinnear, Patrick Magee, Ferdy Mayne, Graham Stark, Warren Clarke, Declan Mulholland, Derrick O'Connor, Peter Benson, Maurice Colbourne, Barry Stokes, Anthony Milner, John J. Carney, Robert Putt, Stephen Rayne, Ken Parry, Lindsey Brook, Eddie Stacey, Jo England, Frankie Cosgrave, Melissa Wiltsie, Mark Cooper. Dir: Terry Marcel. Pro: Harry Robertson. Story & Screenplay: Terry Marcel & Harry Robertson. Ex Pro: Bernard J. Kingham. Ph: Paul Beeson. Ed: Eric Boyd Perkins. Art: Michael Pickwoad. M: Harry Robertson. Pro Sup: Denis Johnson Jr. (Chips-ITC.) Rel: Floating: first shown London (Odeon, Marble Arch) December 1980. 93 mins. Cert A.

He Knows You're Alone

More or less routine, shiver-striving thriller about a psychotic murderer of young girls and the one who – just about! – gets away – well, at least until her wedding day, when anything could happen after the teasing end of the movie. Cast: Don Scardino, Caitlin O'Heaney, Elizabeth Kemp, Tom Rilfing, Lewis Arlt, Patsy Pease, James Rebhorn, Tom Hanks, Dana Barron, Joseph Leon, Paul Gleason, James Carroll, Brian Byers, Curtis Hostetter, Robin Lamont, Robin Tilgham, Peter Gumeny, John Bottoms. Dir: Armand Mastroianni. Pro: George Manasse. Ex Pro: Edgar Lansbury & Joseph Beruh. Co-Pro: Robert Di Milia & Nan Pearlman. Screenplay: Scott Parker. Ph: Gerald Feil. Ed: George T. Norris. Art: Susan Kaufman. M: Alexander & Mark Peskanov. (MGM-CIC.) Rel: 9 November. 94 mins. Cert X.

Head Over Heels

Writer-Director Joan Micklin Silver (whose *Hester Street* was something of a small classic) adapts the novel *Chilly Scenes of Winter* and seems anxious to show that love and lunacy are apt bedfellows, in a story about a young man who is obsessed with a married woman and ignoring her ties to husband and child tries to woo her away from them. Warm and winning – and convincing – performances by John Heard and Mary Beth Hurt, made all this quite easy to swallow. Rest of cast: Peter Riegert, Kenneth McMillan, Gloria Grahame, Nora Heflin, Jerry Hardin, Tarah Nutter, Mark Metcalf, Allen Joseph, Frances Bay, Griffin Dunne, Alex Johnson, Beverly Rowland, Oscar Rowland, Ann Beattie, Angela Phillips, Margeressa Peach Taylor. Dir & Screenplay: Joan Micklin Silver; based on the book *Chilly Scenes of Winter* by Ann Beattie. Pro: Mark Metcalf, Amy Robinson & Griffin Dunne. Ph: Bobby Byrne. Ed: Cynthia Scheider. Pro Des: Peter Jamison. M: Ken Lauber. (Triple Play Productions-UA.) Rel: Floating; first shown London (Screen-on-the Hill) April 1981. 98 mins. Cert A.

Heart Beat

A *Jules et Jim* triangle love story set against a background of post-war America and the 'Beat' generation. Sissy Spacek as the upper-class art student drop-out who shares herself between the two men in her life, young writer John Heard and the less stable, unpredictable Nick Nolte. A rather sad yet comic picture of a period that was to prove of historical significance. Well acted. Rest of cast: Ray Sharkey, Anne Dusenberry, Margaret Fairchild, Tony Bill, Mary Margaret Amato, Kent Williams, Susan Niven, Marcia Nasatir, Mickey Kelly, Luis Contreras, Sharon Lee, Stephen Davies, Jenny O'Hara, Don Brodie, Tom Runyon, Juliana Tutak, Candy Brown, John Larroquette, John Hostetter, Billy Cross, Terry Winkless, Ray Vitte, Gary Baxley, Lloyd 'Sunshine' Parker, Garth Eliassen, Steve Allen. Dir & Screenplay: John Byrum. Pro: Alan Greisman & Michael Shamberg. Ex Pro: Edward R. Pressman & William Tepper. Ph: Laszlo Kovacs. Ed: Eric Jenkins. Pro Des: Jack Fisk, Assoc Pro: David R. Axelrod. M: Jack Nitzsche. (Orion-Warner.) Rel: Floating; first shown London (Gate) September 1980. 108 mins. Cert X.

Heartland

A masterpiece of cinema. A consistently realistic and entirely convincing adaptation of two books written by Elinore Randall about her experiences as a housekeeper-cook to and, later, wife of a dour Scots immigrant farmer on the featureless plains of Wyoming in 1910. More particularly the struggle to survive a winter in which the farmer loses half his stock and sees ten years work vanish into the bitter frosts and snows of the prairie cold. Refusing to compromise, director Richard Pearce used a warm and plump newcomer as the very convincing young widow and other players who fitted their roles to perfection. Memorable in every way. Cast: Conchata Ferrell, Rip Torn, Barry Primus, Lilia Skala, Megan Folsom. Dir: Richard Pearce. Screenplay: Beth Ferris; based on 'Letters of a Woman Homesteader' & 'Letters on an Elk Hunt' by Elinore Randall Stewart. Ph: Fred Murphy. Ed: Bill Yahraus. Art: Carl Copeland. M: Charles Gross. (Wilderness Women Co-Filmhaus-Contemporary.) Rel: Floating; first shown London (Paris-Pullman) March 1981. 95 mins. Cert A.

Hide in Plain Sight

The debut as director of James Caan, who takes the leading role in this adaptation of a true story set in the year 1967, when the US Government persuaded a small-time crook to provide damning evidence against his gangster bosses in return for dropping the case against him and providing him and his family with a new identity and life in a far-off part of the States. But they forgot the doting father of the crook's step-children, who doggedly tracks them down and finally meets up with them eight years later for an explosive climax and happy ending to the story. Plenty of integrity in both directing and playing but with a rather sadly non-involving result. Rest of cast: Joe Grifasi, Jill Eikenberry, Robert Viharo, Barbra Rae, Mary Beth Hurt, Andrew Gordon Fenwick, Heather Bicknell, Ken Sylk, Josephine Nichols, Leo Cimino, Thomas Hill, Nick Corello, Jude Farese, Kenneth McMillan, Josef Sommer, David Margulies, Anne Helm, Danny Aiello, Peter Maloney, Tom Signorelli, Chuck Hicks, Robert Gerringer, David Clennon. Dir: James Caan. Pro: Bob Christiansen & Rick Rosenberg. Assoc Pro: Fred T. Gallo. Screenplay: Spencer Eastman; based on the book by Leslie Waller. Ph: Paul Lohmann. & Bruce Hoffman. Ed: Fredric & William Steinkamp. Pro Des: Pato Guzman. M: Leonard Rosenman. (Chris-Rose-MGM-CIC.) Rel: Floating; first shown London (Ritz) June. 1980. 92 mins. Cert A.

Hollywood Boulevard

Limp little comedy (made in America 1976) weaving bits from other movies into a kind of lampoon on the whole business of film-making. Cast: Candice Rialson, Mary Woronov, Rita George, Jeffrey Kramer, Dick Miller, Richard Doran, Tara Strohmeier, Paul Bartel, John Kramer, Jonathan Kaplan, George Wagner, W. L. Luckey, David Boyle, Glen Shimada, Joseph McBride, Barbara Pieters, Sean Pieters, Sue Veneer, Charles B. Griffiths, Miller Drake, Godzina, Roberta Dean, Milt Kahn, Todd McCarthy, 'Commander Cody and the Lost Planet Airmen'. Dir: Joe Dante & Allan Arkush. Pro: Jon Davison. Assoc Pro: Terri Schwartz. Screenplay: Patrick Hobby. Ph: Jamie Anderson. Ed: Amy Jones & Allan Arkush. Art: Jack de Wolfe. M: Andrew Stein. (New World Pictures-Brent Walker.) Rel: Floating. 83 mins. No cert.

Hopscotch

Walter Matthau giving a marvellous performance as a most unlikely top CIA agent who when demoted because he won't follow the rules of the (spies) book, opts out and takes revenge by writing his explosive memoirs and mailing them, chapter by chapter prior to publication, to the Secret Services of the World and has to keep one jump ahead of his bosses' hit men, who are prepared to use a well aimed assassin's bullet to stop their idiocy and criminality becoming public knowledge. Great fun, even if all highly incredible. Rest of cast: Glenda Jackson, Sam Waterston, Ned Beatty, Herbert Lom, David Matthau, George Baker, Ivor Roberts, Lucy Saroyan, Severn Darden, George Pravda, Jacquelyn Hyde, Mike Gwilym, Terry Beaver, Ray Charleson, Christopher Driscoll, Michael Cronin, Roy Sampson, Douglas Dirkson, Ann Haney, Shan Wilson, Randy Patrick, Joe Dorsey, Candice Howard, Susan

McShayne, Yolanda King, Anthony Carrick, Osman Ragheb, Roland Frohlich, Jeremy Young, Sally Nesbitt, Susan Engel, Joanna McCallum, Laura Whyte, Larry Larson, Seab Worthy, Danny Covington, Richard Moore, Philip Voss, Jesse Wayne, Roger Creed, Richard Geary, Debra Hook, The Silversmith Band, Allan Cuthbertson. Dir: Ronald Neame. Pro: Edie & Ely Landau. Ex Pro: Otto Plaschkes. Ex in charge of Pro: Mort Abrahams. Assoc Pro: Jonathan Bernstein & Brian Garfield. Screenplay: Brian Garfield & Bryan Forbes. Ph: Arthur Ibbetson. Ed: Carl Kress. Pro Des: William Creber. M: Ian Fraser. (Ely & Edie Landau in assoc with International Film Investors Inc & Shan Productions Co Inc-Rank) Rel: 15 February. 107 mins. Cert AA.

The Howling
New and competent addition to the Werewolf cycle; about a lady TV reporter who kills her sex attacker and then starts to imagine all sorts of horrors, many of which take physical shape when she is persuaded to attend a woods-surrounded, isolated private therapy centre . . . with nasty things that bite in the night. Cast: Dee Wallace, Patrick MacNee, Dennis Dugan, Christopher Stone, Belinda Balaski, Kevin McCarthy, John Carradine, Slim Pickens, Elisabeth Brooks, Robert Picardo, Margie Impert, Noble Willingham, James Murtaugh, Jim McKrell, Kenneth Tobey, Don McLeon, Dick Miller. Dir: Joe Dante. Pro: Michael Finnell & Jack Conrad. Ex Pro: Daniel H. Blatt & Steven A. Lane. Screenplay: John Sayles & Terence H. Winkless; based on the novel by Gary Brandner. Assoc Pro: Rob Bottin. Ph: John Hora. Ed: Mark Goldblatt & Joe Dante. Art: Robert A. Burns. M: Pino Donaggio. (Avco Embassy Pictures/Daniel H. Blatt Pro-Barber International.) Rel: 17 May. 90 mins. Cert X.

The Hunter
Pretty far-fetched but fast-moving and often very funny film about a modern Bounty Hunter called 'Papa' Thorson (whose book the film is based on) who appears to have had a remarkable career bringing in – sometimes just about alive, sometimes very dead – desperate bail-jumpers while gloomily surveying his girl-friend's increasingly observable pregnancy. With Steve McQueen – his last movie before he died – as the laconic, resourceful killer-collector! Rest of cast: Eli Wallach, Kathryn Harrold, Le Var Burton, Ben Johnson, Richard Venture, Tracey Walter, Tom Rosales, Theodore Wilson, Ray Bickel, Bobby Bass, Karl Schueneman, Margaret O'Hara, James Spinks, Frank Delfino, Zora Margolis, Murray Rubin, Poppy Lagos, Dea St La Mount, Lillian Adams, Thor Nielsen. Dir: Buzz Kulik. Pro: Mort Engelberg. Screenplay: Ted Leighton & Peter Hyams; based on the book by Christopher Keane and the life of Ralph Thorson. Ph: Fred J. Koenekamp. Ed: Robert Wolfe. Pro Des: Ron Hobbs. M: Michel Legrand. (Paramount-CIC.) Rel: 19 October. 98 mins. Cert AA.

Hurricane
Dino De Laurentiis's straightforward re-make of the 1937 movie of the same title which brought stardom to the late Jon Hall (whose cousin co-wrote the original book on which both films are based). Conventional story about the almost fanatical opposition of Samoan US Naval Governor (Jason Robards) to the romance of his silly little goose of a daughter (wide-eyed Mia Farrow) with the handsome young chief (Dayton Ka'ne), with the problems all solved by the storm of the title, which spectacularly kills off everyone but the happy couple! Rest of cast: Max von Sydow, Trevor Howard, Timothy Bottoms, James Keach, Richard Sarcione, Ariirau Tekurarere, Willie Myers, Nick Rutgers, Nancy Hall Rutgers, Manu Tupou, Simplet Tefane, Piero Bushin, Noel Tepari, John Taea, Taeve Tetuamia, Bernadette Sarcione, Haunui Loyat, Daniel Taea, Miriama Tuamea, Mare Puati, Vahine Anituar, Teura Tama, Mareta Tauoura, Rota Tauratua, Ruita Tuoraa, Tairua Tetuanui, Teua Mana, Hinanui Taerea, Teriitahi, Ahmine, Lannes, Lai Chong Moe Lannes, Roo, and The Polynesian Ballet. Dir: Jan Troell. Pro: Dino De Laurentiis. Ex Pro: & Screenwriter: Lorenzo Semple Jr.; based on the novel by Charles Nordhoff and James Norman Hall. Ph: Sven Nykvist. Ed: Sam O'Steen. Pro Des: Danilo Donati. M: Nino Rota. Choreography: Coco. Art: Giorgio Postiglione. 2nd Unit Dir: Frank Clark. (Famous Films Productions NV-ITC.) Rel: Floating; first shown London (Classic, Haymarket) June. 1980. 110 mins. Cert AA.

I Want to be a Woman – Cambio de sexo
Spanish film about the trials, tribulations and final satisfactory sex-change operation of a transexual who is increasingly unhappy as a male. Serious, well made and without any sexploitation to spoil it. Sensitively acted. Cast: Victoria Abril, Bibi Andersen, Lou Castel, Fernando Sancho, Rafaela Aparicio, Montserrat Carulla, Daniel Martin, Maria Elias, Rosa Morata, Alfredo Lucchetti, Mario Gas, Victoria Peña, Juan Borrás, José Gras, Asuncion Vitória, Víctor Petit and (ie Manuel Fernandez Chica). Dir: Vincente Aranda. Pro: Jaime Fernandez-Cid. Screenplay: Joaquin Jordá & Vincente Aranda; from an idea by Carlos Durán. Ph: Nestor Almendros. Ed: Maricel. M: Ricardo Miralles (Vocalisation of Bach-Faure-Greig by Maria Fleta). (Impala-Morgana-Kruger Leisure Enterprises.) Rel: Floating; 114 mins. Cert X.

The Idolmaker
Quite fascinating glimpse of the way that Pop Stars are made, rather than born, in a story about a young New York-Italian pop-song composer who takes a couple of young waiters out of his brother's restaurant and trains and promotes them – by bribing disc jockeys and romancing lady disc-mag. editors – to the fan-screaming Big Time. And it should all be near to reality, for the 'technical adviser' was Bob Marucci, who actually did this sort of thing for several of the pop idols of the rock-and-rolling 1950s. An outstanding performance by Ray Sharkey as the star manufacturer. Rest of cast: Tovah Feldshun, Peter Gallagher, Paul Land, Joe Pantoliano, Maureen McCormick, John Aprea, Richard Bright, Olympia Dukakis, Steven Apostlee Peck, Leonard Gaines, Deney Terrio, Charles Guardino, Michael Mislove, Kenneth O'Brien, Michael Perotta, Sylvia Shemwell, Myrna Smith, Afreeka Trees, Owen C. Davis, Jamie Fallin, Larry Van Claggett, Jeffrey Tanner, Howard Gordon. Dir: Taylor Hackford. Pro: Gene Kirkwood & Howard J. Koch, Jr. Screenplay:

Edward di Lorenzo. Ph: Adam Holdender. Ed: Neil Travis. Art: David L. Snyder. Assoc Pro: R. J. Louis & David Nichols. M: Jeff Barry. (UA.) Rel: 19 April. 117 mins. Cert A.

In the Shadow of the Sun
Derek Jarman's mixture of old and new footage (centred on a piece of film about a car trip to Avebury) which was really an interesting exercise, an effort to produce an abstract surface of colour, texture and mystery. With sounds by Throbbing Gristle. Made on Super 8mm film, now blown up to 16mm. With Gerald Incandela, Christopher Hobbs, Andrew Logan. Rel: Floating; first shown London (ICA) April 1981. 60 mins. No cert.

In a Year with 13 Moons – In einem Jahr mit 13 Monden
Strange, dense Fassbinder film about the relationship with some pretty unsavoury male characters that a sex-change, man-to-woman female, Elvira, meets with. Full of symbolism and weird visual scenes. Cast: Volker Spengler, Ingrid Caven, Gottfried John, Elisabeth Trissenaar, Eva Mattes, Gunther Kaufmann, Lieselotte Lilo Pempeit, Isolde Barth, Karl Scheydt, Walter Bockmayer, Peter Kollek, Bob Dorsay, Ursula Lillig, Gunther Holzapfel, Janoz Bermez, Gernard Zwerenz. Dir, Pro, Screenplay Ed & Ph: Rainer Werner Fassbinder. M: Peer Raben. (Tango Film/Pro-ject Film/Filverlag der Autoren-Cinegate.) Rel: Floating; first shown London (The Electric Cinema) September 1980. 129 mins. No cert.

The Incredible Shrinking Woman
A quarter of a century after making *The Incredible Shrinking Man*, Universal came up with the female counterpart, although this time around instead of radiation being the cause it is supermarket detergents that reduce delightful Lily Tomlin to nothing! Helping the intermittent fun were a friendly man-in-gorilla-clothing and a slapstick climax in which the usual farce prop of a single banana skin is replaced with a load of them! Rest of cast: Charles Grodin, Ned Beatty, Henry Gibson, Elizabeth Wilson, Mark Blankfield, Maria Smith, Pamela Bellwood, John Glover, Nicholas Hormann, James McMullan, Shelby Balik, Justin Dana, Richard A. Baker. Dir: Joel Schumacher. Pro: Hank Moonjean. Ex Pro & Screenplay: Jane Wagner; suggested by Richard Matheson's novel *The Incredible Shrinking Man*. Ph: Bruce Logan. Ed: Jeff Gourson & Anthony Redman. Pro Des: Raymond A. Brandt. M: Suzanne Ciani. (Universal-CIC.) Rel: 26 April. 89 mins. Cert A.

Inferno
Overheated minor Italian thriller set in New York and about the killings of a whole string of characters after a girl finds she is living in a house formerly occupied by some very nasty characters called The Three Mothers. Cast: Leigh McCloskey, Irene Miracle, Eleonora Giorgi, Daria Nicolai, Sacha Pitoeff, Alida Valli, Feodor Chaliapin, Veronica Lazar, Gabriele Lavia, Leopoldo Mastelloni, Ana Pieroni, James Fleetwood, Rosario Rigutini, Ryan Hilliard, Paolo Paolini, Fulvio Mingozzi, Luigi Lodoli, Rodolfa Lodi, Dir, Pro & Screenplay: Dario Argento. Ex Pro: William Garroni. Pro Sup: Solly V. Bianco. Ph: Romano Albani. Ed:

Franco Fraticelli. Art: Giuseppe Bassan. M: Keith Emerson. (Produzioni Intersound for 20th Century-Fox.) Rel: Floating; first shown London (Cinecenta) September 1980. 107 mins. Cert X.

*The Inglorious Bastards – Quel maledetto treno blindato
Minor World War Two adventure from Italy, set in 1944 France, where some Americans on the way to court martial escape to become heroes. Made in 1978. Cast: Ian Bannen, Bo Svenson, Fred Williamson, Peter Hooten, Michael Pergolani, Michel Constantin, Jackie Basehart, Debra Berger, Raimund Harmstorf, Flavio Andreini, Peter Boom, Vito Fornari, Manfred Freyberger, John Loffredo, Mike Morris, Donald O'Brian, Gerard Schwarz, Brian T. Rostron, Massimo Vanni, William Vanders, Mauro Vestri. Dir: Enzo G. Castellari. Pro: Alfonso Ligata & Sylvia Gaperna. Ex Pro: Roberto Sbaragia. Screenplay: Sandro Continenza, Sergio Grieco, Romano Migliorini, Laura Toscana & Franco Marotta. Ph: Giovanni Bergamini. Ed: Gianfranco Amicucci. Art: Aurelio Crugnola & Pierluigi Basile. M: Francesco de Masi. (Film Concorde-Entertainment.) Rel: 22 June 1980. 90 mins. Cert AA.

Inside Moves
Rather rambling and sometimes seemingly interminable story of a group of happy cripples, more especially of two of them who become pals and then fall out over a girl; the background, a New York bar where they all foregather and which in part is owned by some of them. And, sadly, none of the characters emerge as sympathetic or even particularly credible. Cast: John Savage, David Morse, Diana Scarwid, Amy Wright, Jack O'Leary, Harold Russell, Bert Remsen, Bill Henderson, Arnold Williams, Steve Kahan, Tony Burton, Harold Sylvester, Pepe Serna, George Brenlin, Shirley Carroll. Dir: Richard Donner. Pro: Mark Tanz & R. W. Goodwin. Screenplay: Valerie Curtin & Barry Levinson; based on the novel by Todd Walton. Ph: Laszlo Kovacs. Ed: Frank Morriss. Pro Des: Charles Rosen. M: John Barry. (Goodmark Productions/Richard Donner-Barber International.) Rel: Floating; first shown London (Odeon, St Martin's Lane) March 1981. 113 mins. Cert AA.

The Island
Lively if entirely fanciful adventure thriller with nosey newsman Michael Caine and pesky small son as captives of an island community of pirates who have continued their bloody trade through the centuries undetected and undeterred by the march of civilisation and so fed the myths about the vanishing ships in the 'Bermuda Triangle'. Written by 'Jaws' author Peter Benchley and made by the producers of that famous film – though hardly up to that fortune-making standard. Rest of cast: David Warner, Angela Punch McGregor, Frank Middlemass, Don Henderson, Dudley Sutton, Colin Jeavons, Zakes Mokae, Brad Sullivan, Jeffrey Frank, John O'Leary, Bruce McLaughlin, Jimmy Casino, Suzanne Astor, Susan Bredhoff, Reg Evans, Steve Gladstone, David Hart, Robert Hirschfeld, Cary Hoffman, George Marshall Ruge, John Macchia, Ricky Rincon, Robert Thomas Salmi, William Schilling, Stewart Steinberg, Bob Westmorland, Mark Westwood. Dir: Michael Ritchie. Pro: Richard D. Zanuck & David

Brown. Screenplay: Peter Benchley; based on his own novel. Ph: Henri Decae. Ed: Richard A. Harris. Pro Des: Dale Hennesy. M: Ennio Morricone. (Zanuck/Brown-Universal-CIC.) Rel: 16 November. 115 mins. Cert X.

Jaguar Lives
Rip-roaring action melodrama about a pretty lethal chap, known in the Special Agents business as 'The Jaguar', who is lured out of peaceful retirement by the chance to get even with the killers of his old buddy and working partner. Cast: Joe Lewis, Christopher Lee, Donald Pleasance, Barbara Bach, Capucine, Joseph Wiseman, Woody Strode, John Huston, Gabriel Melgar, Anthony de Longis, Sally Faulkner, Gail Grainger, Anthony Heaton, Luis Prendes, Simon Andreu, James Smilie, Oscar James, Ray Jewers, Ralph Brown. Dir: Ernest Pintoff. Pro: Derek Gibson. Ex Pro: Sandy Howard. Screenplay: Yabo Yablonsky. Assoc Pro: Quinn Donoghue. Ph: John Cabrera. Ed: Angelo Ross. Art: Adolfo Cofino. Pro Sup: Adrian Hughes. M: Robert O. Ragland: Songs: 'Jug of Wine' written & performed by Elliot Redpearl; 'Smokin'' written by Rob Walsh & Gerry Gibson, performed by The Fuller Avenue Band. (Jaguar Prods-Rank Org.) Rel: Floating. 90 mins. Cert AA.

Jane Austen in Manhattan
Another unusual contribution from the always interesting, invariably original-thinking James Ivory-Ismail Merchant-Ruth Prawer Jhabvala moviemaking team. This time the departure point was the sale a few years back, at Sotheby's, of the manuscript of a play Miss Austen wrote when she was twelve. Upon this fact the trio have built an imaginative screenplay about the American Cultural Foundation purchasers being initially undecided whether to give permission for the piece's staging, along with the financial grant to make it possible, to either a poseur-led *avant garde* group who want to do it as a Punch-and-Judy-style production, or the rival set-up, led by the poseur's ex-mistress, which wants to do it in the form of a Mozartian opera. Cast: Anne Baxter, Robert Powell, Sean Young, Kurt Johnson, Katrina Hodiak, Tim Choate, Nancy New, Chuch McCaughan, John Guerrasio, Michael Wager. Dir: James Ivory. Pro: Ismail Merchant. Screenplay: Ruth Prawer Jhabvala. Ph: Ernst Vincze. Set Designs (no Art credit): Michael Yeargan. M: Richard Robbins: with some songs sung by Miss Hodiak (Miss Baxter's daughter) and composed by her. (Merchant Ivory Productions in assoc. with Polytel International – Contemporary.) Rel: Floating; first shown London (Everyman, Hampstead) July 1980. 108 mins. Cert A.

The Jazz Singer
A re-make (the second, first starred Danny Thomas in 1953) of the 1927 film which astounded everyone with its singing-talking Al Jolson on a screen hitherto silent. Now American top pop star Neil Diamond is the young Cantor who longs to get away from *Kol Nidre*, family tradition and the synagogue and sing his own more modern numbers to less inhibited audiences. With Laurence Olivier as the rigidly orthodox old Jewish poppa who is only brought round to approval with the

advent of a grandson. Diamond sings the songs he wrote (both words and music for the most part) in a pleasing deep-brown voice and puts across a nice, warm personality. Rest of cast: Lucie Arnaz, Catlin Adams, Franklyn Ajaye, Paul Nicholas, Sully Boyar, Mike Kellin, James Booth, Luther Waters, Oren Waters, Rod Gist, Walter Janowitz, Janet Brandt, John Witherspoon, Dale Robinette, David Coburn, Judy Gibson, Hank Garrett, Ernie Hudson, James Karen, Tim Herbert, Ed Jahnke, Hugh Gillin, Jill Jaress, Victor Paul, Cantor Uri Frenkel, Rex Cutter, Mike Pasternak, Sandy Helberg, Brion James, Douglas Nigh, (The Neil Diamond Band): Dennis St John, Richard Bennett, Alan Lindgren, Reinie Press, Doug Rhone, Tom Hensley, King Errisson, Linda Press, Vince Charles). Dir: Richard Fleischer. Pro: Jerry Leider. Assoc Pro: Joel Morwood. Screenplay: Herbert Baker (Screenplay adaptation by Stephen H. Foreman; based on the stage play by Samson Raphaelson). Ph: Isidore Mankofsky. Sup Ed: Frank Urioste. Ed: Maury Winetrobe. Pro Des: Harry Horner. Art: Spencer Deverill. Incidental M: Leonard Rosenman. M Pro: Bob Gaudio. (EMI.) Rel: 22 February. 115 mins. Cert A.

Joe Albany . . . A Jazz Life
Documentary about the well-known jazz pianist who, coming back from a five-year jail sentence for drugs, climbed – via a period of playing in a London 'topless' club – back to success in his native America. Dir & Pro: Carole Langer. No Screenplay credit. Ph: Jonathan Smith. Add Ph: Carole Langer & Ken Murray. Ed: Michael Schenkein. Assoc Ed: Michael Gersh. M Dir: Bert Goldblatt. (Cinegate.) Rel: Floating; first shown London (Electric) February 1981. 60 mins. No cert.

*Jungle Burger
Self-confessed 'lewd, crude and outrageously rude' but also often amusing feature cartoon – a French-German co-production – which starts off by poking fun at Tarzan but then veers off towards various other targets. With the voices of Johnny Weissmuller Jr. and John Belushi. Dir: Picha (Jean-Paul Walravens) & Pierre Bartier. Pro: Boris Szulzinger. Ex Pro: Jenny Gérard & Michel Gast. Screenplay: Picha (Jean-Paul Walravens) & Pierre Bartier. American Version (as shown in GB): Michael O'Donoghue & Anne Beatts. Original character designs by Picha (Jean-Paul Walravens). Ph: Raymond Burlet. Animators: Vivien Miessen, Claude Monfort, Kjeld Simonsen, Alan Ball, Malcolm Draper, Jack Stokes, Arthur Button, Richard Cox, Tom Barker, Michael Stuart, Denis Rich. Songs: Marc Moulin, Teddy Lasry & Louise Gikow. American lyrics: Michael O'Donoghue & Anne Beatts. (SND-Valisa Films-Entertainment Film Distributors.) Rel: 22 June 1980. 72 mins. Cert X.

A Jury of her Peers
Masterly half-hour film which in perfect short story terms uses the murder of a farmer as an oblique comment on the unhappy position of women on farms in rural America at the turn of the century. Made on 16mm film. Cast: Diane de Lorian, Dorothy Lancaster. Dir, Pro, Screenplay & Ed: Sally Heckel. Adapted from the (1917) story by Susan Glaspell. No other credits available. (Contemporary.) Rel: Floating; first shown London (Paris-Pullman) March 1981. 30 mins. Cert A.

Releases of the Year in Detail

Kagemusha – The Shadow Warrior
A major classic from Japan, made by Akira Kurosawa. Set in late sixteenth century Japan, a time of ambitious war lords and constant clan struggles, it tells a story about powerful clan leader Takeda and the man, a thief saved from crucifixion, who looks so much like him that he is trained to carry on a masquerade if and when milord dies in or away from battle, and does just that very successfully (after a sniper has killed Takeda) until the fake is discovered and he is disgraced and expelled from throne, palace and town. Marvellous visual effects of armies marching and fighting; of shadowy battles in the night; of bloody aftermath; in all of which Kurosawa uses colour and sound with tremendous artistry and terrific effect. Long, not always easy to follow but utterly fascinating and consistently brilliant. Cast: Tatsuya Nakadai, Tsutomu Yamazaki, Kenichi Hagiwara, Kohta Yui, Shuji Otaki, Hideo Murata, Takayuji Shiho, Osamu Sugimori, Noboru Shimizu, Koji Shimizu, Sen Yamamoto, Jimpachi Nezu, Kai Ato, Yotaka Shimaka, Eiichi Kanakubo, Yugo Miyazaki, Mitsuko Baisho, Kaori Momoi, Kumeko Otowa, Naruhito Iguchi, Daisuke Ryu, Tetsuo Yamashita, Yasuhito Yamanaka, Masayuki Yui, Yasushi, Doshida, Noboru Sone, Norio Matsui, Toshihiko Shimizu, Takashi Shimura, Francis S. Sercu, Alexander Kairis, Jean-Pierre Carlini, Kamatari Fujiwara, Toshiaki Tanabe, Yoshimitsu Yamaguchi, Takashi Ebata, Fujio Tokita, Akihiko Sugizaki, Naeko Nakamura, Sumire Aoki, Al Matsubara, Kuni Nanase, Senkichi Omura, Masatsugu Kuriyama. Dir: Akira Kurosawa. Ex Pro: Akira Kurosawa & Tomoyuki Tanaka. Assoc Pro: Teruyo Nogami. Pro Co-Ord: Inoshiro Honda. Screenplay: Akira Kurosawa & Masato Ide. Script Sup: Teruyo Nogami. Ph: Takao Saito & Masaharu Ueda. Cinematographers: Kazuo Miyagawa & Asaichi Nakai. No Ed. credit. Art: Yoshiro Muraki. M: Shinichiro Ikebe. Ex Pro. of the International Version of the film: Francis Ford Coppola & George Lucas. (Toho/Kurosawa-Fox.) Rel: Floating; first shown London (Gates at Camden and Notting Hill) November. 1980. 159 mins. Cert A.

The Kidnapping of the President
Coincidentally remarkably topical thriller – its London premiere came just a couple of days after the March 1981 attempt on President Reagan's life – about a South American terrorist who, quoting politics, in fact is just after wealth for himself as he and his girl accomplice force the President out of his Canadian Parade, while on a State Visit to that country, and into a lethal van of triggered explosives, holding him there on threat of death while the bargaining goes on. Maybe unlikely, but certainly possible, and a fine performance by Hal Holbrook as the Presidential victim. Rest of cast: William Shatner, Miguel Fernandes, Maury Chaykin, Cindy Girling, Van Johnson, Ava Gardner, Michael J. Reynolds, Elizabeth Shepherd, Gary Reineke, Murray Westgate, Michael Kane, Jackie Burroughs, Aubert Pallascio, Virginia Podesser, Elias Zarov, Larry Duran, Patrick Brymar, Gershon Resnik, John Stocker, Chappelle Jaffe, John Romaine. Dir & Pro: George Mendeluk. Ex Pro: Joseph Sefel. Pro: John Ryan. Screenplay: Richard Murphy; based on the novel by Charles Templeton. Ph: Richard Malloy. Ed: Michael

McLaverty. Art: Douglas Higgins. M: Paul J. Zaza. (Bordeaux Films.) Rel: 10 May. 114 mins. Cert X.

King of the Gypsies
Screen adaptation of the Peter Maas novel about a young gipsy lad in America who is not at all keen to accept his heritage, runs away, roughs it, but finally is persuaded to reluctantly accept the crown. Cast: Sterling Hayden, Shelley Winters, Susan Sarandon, Judd Hirsch, Eric Roberts, Brooke Shields, Annette O'Toole, Annie Potts, Michael V. Gazzo, Antonia Rey, Stephen Mendillo, Daniel Spira, Joe Zaloom, Lou Cevetillo, Svee Scooler, Corey Einbinder, Matthew Laborteaux, Danielle Brisbois, Tiffany Bogart, Marc Vahanian, Chris Manor, John Oppenheim, C. A. R. Smith, Kathi Moss, Mary Louise Wilson, David Rounds, Anthony Holland, Tom Quinn, David Little, Martin Rosenblatt, Fred Coffin, Michael Higgins, Macintyre Dixon, Marc Victor, James Shannon, Paul Sparer, Mark Weston, Joe Maruzzo, Alice Drummond, Bernie McInerney, Franklin Scott, Jay Norman, Artie Cavallo, Glen Gianfrancisco, William Duell, Roy Brocksmith, Harris Laskaway, Tom Mason. Dir & Screenplay: Frank Pierson – script suggested by the book of the title by Peter Maas. Pro: Federico de Laurentiis. Assoc Pro: Anna Gross. Ex. in charge of Pro: Fred C. Caruso. Ph: Sven Nykvist. Ed: Paul Hirsch. Pro Des: Gene Callahan. Art: Jay Moore. M: David Grisman (Violin by Stephane Grappelli). Dino De Laurentiis – Paramount-CIC.) Rel: 1 June 1980. 113 mins. Cert AA.

The Lady in Red
'Roaring 20s' story about a farm lass who, becoming innocently involved in a bank stick-up – and belted by her sadistic old dad in consequence – runs away to become a sweat shop machinist, dance hall hostess, is sent to a brutal jail for soliciting, comes out only to be forced into a brothel, where she meets Public Enemy No. 1 John Dillinger and, when he dies at her side in a hail of FBI bullets, attempts a bank hold-up with her own pretty inept amateur gang. Good atmosphere and a good performance by Pamela Sue Martin as the girl. Rest of cast: Robert Conrad, Louise Fletcher, Robert Hogan, Laurie Heineman, Glenn Withrow, Rod Gist, Peter Hobbs, Christopher Lloyd, Dick Miller, Nancy Anne Parsons, Alan Vint, Milt Kogan, Chip Fields, Buck Young, Phillip R. Allen, Ilene Kristen, Joseph X. Flaherty, Terri Taylor, Peter Miller, Mary Wonorov, Jay Rasumny, Michael Cavanaugh, Arnie Moore, John Guitz, Saul Krugman, Blackie Dammett. Dir: Lewis Teague. Pro: Julie Corman. Co-Pro: Steven Kovacs. Screenplay: John Sayles. Ph: Daniel Lacambre. Ed: Larry Bock, Ron Medico & Lewis Teague. Pro Des: Jac McAnelly. Art: Philip Thomas. M: James Horner. (New World Pictures-Barber Rose International.) Rel: 1 February. 93 mins. Cert X.

The Last Embrace
Mystery thriller, with Roy Scheider finding himself threatened by an unseen foe who follows him from his Greenwich Village home to Princeton University, and a final confrontation against a backdrop of Niagara Falls where everything at last becomes clear. Rest of cast: Janet Margolin, John Glover, Sam Levene, Charles Napier, Christopher Walken, Jacqueline Brookes,

David Margulies, Andrew Duncan, Marcia Rodd, Gary Goetzman, Lou Gilbert, Mandy Patinkin, Max Wright, Sandy McLeod, Burt Santos, Joe Spinell, Jim McBride, Cynthia Scheider, Sasha von Scherler, George Hillman, Gary Gunter. Dir: Jonathan Demme. Pro: Michael Taylor & Dan Wigutow. Assoc Pro: John Nicolella. Screenplay: David Shaber; based on the novel *The Thirteenth Man* by Murray Teigh Bloom. Ph: Tak Fujimoto. Ed: Barry Malkin. Pro Des: Charles Rosen. M: Miklos Rosza. (Taylor/Wigutow-UA.) Rel: 15 March. 101 mins. Cert X.

Last Feelings
Sad little Italian film about a fourteen-year-old family reject who gets the chance to swim in the European championships and wins just as his terminal illness takes over. Cast: Carlo Lupo, Vittoria Galeazzi, Fiorenzo Fiorentini, Angela Goodwin, Jacques Sernas, Luigi Siberti, Alfio Androuer, Emilio Delle Piane, Luigi Pagnani Fusconi, Richard Raynsford, Anna Maria Savagnone, Gianni Solaro. Dir: Ruggero Deodato. Pro: Roberto Gandus & Tito Carpi. Ex Pro: Giorgio Carlo Rossi. Screenplay: Roberto Gandus & Tito Carpi. Ph: Claude Cirillo. Ed: Daniele Alabiso. Pro. Des: Carmelo Patrono. M: Ubaldo Continiello. (Song, 'Feeling' comp, & sung by Morris Alpert). (Tritone Cinematografica-GTO Films.) Rel: 28 September. 98 mins. Cert A.

The Last Flight of Noah's Ark
Thoroughly enjoyable addition to Disney's warm and charming family films: a familiar story about a penniless pilot, pretty missionary, two cute kiddies and a farm-full of animals wrecked on a South Seas island where with the two Japanese survivors from the war (they don't know it has ended) they miraculously convert the old plane into a boat and sail into fair winds and foul towards a universally happy landing. And there's some witty lines among the fun. Cast: Elliott Gould, Genevieve Bujold, Ricky Schroder, Tammy Lauren, Vincent Gardenia, John Fujioka, Yuki Shimoda, John P. Ryan, Dana Elcar, Ruth Manning, Arthur Adams, Austin Willis, Pete Renaday, Bob Whiting. Dir: Charles Jarrott. Pro: Ron Miller. Co-Pro: Jan Williams. Screenplay: Steven W. Carabatsos, Sandy Glass & George Arthur Bloom; from a story by Ernest K. Gann. Ph: Charles F. Wheeler. Ed: Gordon D. Brenner. Pro Des: Preston Ames. Art: John B. Mansbridge. M: Maurice Jarre. (Song, 'Half of Me' sung by Alexandra Brown; lyrics by Hal David). (Disney.) Rel: 3 August. 98 mins. Cert U.

The Last Metro – Le Dernier Metro
Francois Truffaut's multi-Cesar (France's premier award) winner (ten) and holder of the L'Academie Francaise Grand Prix. A story of the struggle to keep a small Parisian theatre alive (and its Jewish director hidden) during the German Occupation which gave Truffaut the chance to fulfil several long-cherished dreams: to capture the back-stage atmosphere, to evoke the strange climate of the Occupation, and to give Catherine Deneuve the role of a sensible, responsible woman. The sideboard of prizes illustrate how far he achieved his object and at the same time produced his greatest commercial success. Cast: Catherine Deneuve, Gérard Depardieu, Jean Poiret, Heinz Bennent, Andrea Ferreol, Paulette Dubost, Sabine Haudepin, Jean-Louis

Richard, Maurice Risch, Jean-Pierre Klein. Dir: François Truffaut. Screenplay: François Truffaut, Suzanne Schiffman & Jean-Claude Grumberg. Ph: Nestor Almendros. Ed: Martine Barraque. Art: Jean-Pierre Kohut Svelko. M: Georges Delerue. (Les Films Du Carosse/Sedif SA/TF1/Soc Francaise de Prod-Gala Films.) Rel: Floating; first shown in London (Curzon) June 1981. 132 mins. Cert A.

The Life – La Dérobade
French adaptation of the Jeanne Cordelier book about five years in the life of a young girl who becomes a Paris prostitute and has to suffer the clients' perversions, periodical beatings by her pimp, the ill-treatment and degradation which are all part of the job. Cast: Miou-Miou, Marie Schneider, Daniel Duval, Niels Arestrup, Brigitte Ariel, Jean Benguigui, Martine Ferriere, Marie Pillet, Regis Porte, Michel Berto, Yvon Brexel, Bernard Cazassus, Henri Djanik, Jacques Doniol-Valcroze, Albert Dray, Jean Claude Dreyfus, Guy Kerner, Max Morel, Marc Adjadji, Dominique Alavoine, Mireille Alguacil, Solange Ancona, Marie-Claude Benoit, Luc Bergerac, Monica Botero, Véronique Brisset, Betty Bros, Patricia Bros, Jeane Carre, France Lise Celestine, Beatrice Champanier, Chouska, François Colaiani, Christian Delangre, François Deldick, Patrick Depeyrrat, Roland Deronzier, Carole Deterrer, Armelle Duche, Michel Duchezeau, Deddy Dugay, Suzanne Dupré, Paola Esturgeon, Serge Fabris, Hughette Fargeas, Herbert Fiala, Alain Frerot, Yves Gabrielli, Manuela Gouvary, Joelle Guillaud, Gérard Guit, Murielle Helary, Catherine Henry, Maaike Jansen, Jean-Claude Jay, Nadia Kaci, Marylene Koja, Patrice Laclau, Gérard Lardeur, Katia Lando, Noelle Leiris, Ludmille Magin, Alexandra Manet, René Marquant, Viviane Mathieu, André Mathis, Isabelle Mergault, Lucifugus Merklen, Gladys Melka, Patricia Millardais, Guillemette Morichere, Maite Nahyr, Betty Nocella, Maya Panni, Caroline Paretti, Thérèse Quentin, Adelita Requena, Anne Sacket, Odile Schmitt, Benjamin Simon, Frank Stuart, Brigitte Sy, Micjelle Thuilliez, Christiane Tissot, Maria Verdi, Daniel Verite, Henri Viscogliosi, Anne Rosa Vourron, Marina Yvart, Ania Zabielak. Dir: Daniel Duval. Pro: Benjamin Simon & Gérard Lorin. Pro Ex: Bernard Simon. Assoc Pro: Gerard Crosnier. Pro Sup: Louis Trinquier & Odette Hainsseln. Screenplay: Christopher Frank; based on the book by Jeanne Cordelier. Ph: Michel Cenet. Sup Ed: Jean-Bernard Bonis. Pro Des: François Chanut. M: Vladimir Cosma. (ATC 3000/Société Nouvelle Prod-Watchgrove.) Rel: Floating; first shown London (several cinemas) October. 1980. 114 mins. Cert X.

Little Darlings
Kristy McNichol and Tatum O'Neal as poor and rich girl competitors in a well-backed race to the loss of their virginity while staying at a summer camp. Nice kids in a not such a nice story. Rest of cast: Armand Assante, Matt Dillon, Maggie Blye, Nicolas Coster, Krista Errickson, Alexa Kenin, Abby Bluestone, Cynthia Nixon, Simone Schachter, Jenn Thompson, Troas Hayes, Mary Betten, Marianne Gordon, Paige Connor, Edith Ivey, J. Don Ferguson, Laura Whyte, Suzanne Hlavacek, Scott Macellan, Martha Wollbrinck, Bill

Gribble, Cathy Larson. Dir: Ronald F. Maxwell. Pro: Stephen J. Friedman. Assoc Pro: Kimi Peck. Screenplay: Kimi Peck & Dalene Young; from the former's story. Ph: Fred Batka. Ed: Pembroke J. Herring. Pro Des: William Hiney. M: Charles Fox. (Kings Road-Paramount-CIC.) Rel: 6 July. 95 mins. Cert AA.

Little Lord Fauntleroy
Third filming (first, starring Mary Pickford, in 1921, second in 1936) of the famous Frances Hodgson Burnett story about the angelic little lad living with his ma on the edge of poverty in the New York Bronx who is suddenly told that he is Lord F. and heir to the Earl of Dorincourt, who requests he come to England to be trained for his inheritance. A quite outrageously sentimental tale made into outstanding movie by brilliant performances, marvellously balanced and witty direction, a literate script and fine overall polish. A superb performance by Alec Guinness as the ogre-Earl won over to warm humanity by the golden-hearted, loving charms of his grandson, played with amazing maturity by little Ricky Schroeder. Rest of cast: Eric Porter, Colin Blakely, Connie Booth, Rachel Kempson, Carmel McSharry, Antonia Pemberton, Rolf Saxon, John Cater, Peter Copley, Patsy Rowlands. Dir: Jack Gold. Pro: Norman Rosemont. Pro Sup: Peter Manley. Assoc Pro: William Hill. Ph: Arthur Ibbetson. Ed: Keith Palmer. Pro Des: Herbert Westbrook. Art: Martin Atkinson. M: Allyn Ferguson. (Rosemont-GTO Films.) Rel: 12 April. 103 mins. Cert U.

Little Miss Marker
Fourth version of Damon Runyon's delightful story (previous movies: *Little Miss Marker* with Shirley Temple in 1934; *Sorrowful Jones* with Bob Hope in 1949; *Forty Pounds of Trouble* with Tony Curtis in 1963, who also plays in the present film, though in a different role) about a stingy, grumpy old New York bookmaker who is turned into a warm and caring human being by the cute seven-year-old kid left with him by her father as guarantee against his defaulting on a debt, and the sunny wiles of Julie Andrews, who quickly spots the man beneath the shell. A beautifully made and wonderfully well acted sentimental comedy with Walter Matthau as the bookie, Sara Stimpson as the kid, Tony Curtis as the gangster and Miss Andrews. Rest of cast: Bob Newhart, Lee Grant, Brian Dennehy, Kenneth McMillan, Andrew Rubin, Joshua Shelley, Randy Herman, Nedra Volz, Jacquelyn Hyde, Tom Pedi, Jessica Rains, Henry Slate, Alvin Hammer, Don Bexley, Jack de Leon, John P. Finnegan, Ralph Manza, Jack Mullaney, Mark Anger, Lennie Bremen, Maurice Marks, Colin Gilbert, Wynn Irwin, Joseph Knowland, Stanley Lawrence, Louis Basile, Ed Ness, H. B. Newton, Stanley E. Ritchie, Willian Ackridge, Alan Thomason, Charles A. Vanegas, Sharri Zak, Robert E. Ball, Simmy Bow, Jorge B. Cruz, Leonard Iniguez, Arthur F. Lobato, Dennis Bond, Pat Seeley, Ray York, Bob Marley, Dir & Screenplay: Walter Bernstein (based on a story by Damon Runyon). Pro: Jennings Lang. Ex Pro: Walter Matthau. Ph: Philip Lathrop. Ed: Eve Newman. Pro Des: Edward C. Carfagno. M: Henry Mancini. (Universal-CIC.) Rel: 3 August. 103 mins. Cert U.

The Long Good Friday
Very well made if violent London gangland piece, filmed entirely on London locations. Bob Hoskins as the racketeer boss who on the edge of an enormous multi-million part American financed scheme to develop a large part of derelict dockland, finds unpleasant things start to happen, such as the blowing up of his Rolls, the murder of his partner, the bombing of his favourite restaurant where he is to dine and various other little things which disturb his USA backer. Whodunnit it all? One learns in time for the bloody climax. Rest of cast: Helen Mirren, Eddie Constantine, Dave King, Bryan Marshall, George Coulouris, Derek Thompson, Bruce Alexander, Paul Barber, Pierce Brosnan, Charles Cork, Bill Cornelius, Stephen Davis, Alan Devlin, Christopher Driscoll, Dexter Fletcher, Alan Ford, Paul Freeman, Brian Hall, Ruby Head, Karl Howman, Nigel Humphries, Paul Kember, Trevor Laird, Patti Love, Kevin McNally, Pauline Melville, Bill Moody, P. H. Moriarty, Daragh O'Malley, Dave Ould, George Phillips, Olivier Pierre, Tony Rohr, Nick Stringer, Kim Taylforth, Robert Walker, Shelley Borkum, Brenda Cavendish, Robert Hamilton, Brian Hayes, James Ottaway, Mary Sheen, Trevor Ward, James Wynn. Dir: John Mackenzie. Pro: Barry Hanson. Assoc Dir: Chris Griffin. Screenplay: Barrie Keeffe. Ph: Phil Meheux. Ed: Mike Taylor. Art: Vic Symonds. M: Francis Monkman. (Handmade Films.) Rel: 29 March. 114 mins. Cert X.

The Long Riders
Hard, sinewy and grimly realistic Western in the style of *The Wild Bunch*, re-telling the old story of the exploits of the outlaw James, Younger, Miller and Ford brothers, who joined up to rob banks and trains until they made an error of judgment and bloodily suffered the results. With plenty of the style but little of the magic which made so many big old Westerns classics of the screen. An intriguing gimmick is to use real life kin-folk as the various brothers: David, Keith & Robert Carradine as Cole, Jim & Bob Younger; James & Stacy Keach as Jesse and Frank James; Dennis & Randy Quaid as Ed & Clell Miller. Rest of cast: Kevin Brophy, Harry Cary Jr., Christopher Guest, Nicholas Guest, Shelby Leverington, Felice Orlandi, Pamela Reed, James Remar, Fran Ryan, Savannah Smith, Amy Stryker, James Whitmore Jr., John Bottoms, West Buchanan, Edward Bunker, Martina Deignan, Allan Graf, Chris Mulkey, Thomas R. Myers, Marlise Pieratt, Glenn Robards, Tim Rossovich, Lin Shaye, Gary Watkins, Peter Jason, Steve Chambers, Duke Stroud, William Traylor, J. Don Ferguson, Hugh McGraw, Prentiss E. Rowe, Stuart-Mossman, Michael Lackey, Mitch Greenhill, Bill Bryson, Tom Sauber, Jimmy Medearis, Edgar McLeod, Luis Contreras, Kalen Keach, R. B. Thrift. Dir: Walter Hill. Pro: Tim Zinnemann. Ex Pro: James & Stacy Keach. Screenplay: Bill Bryden, Steven Phillip Smith & Stacy & James Keach. Ph: Ric Waite. Ed: David Holden. Pro Des: Jack T. Collis. Art: Peter Romero. M: Ry Cooder. (Huka-UA.) Rel: 12 October. 100 mins. Cert X.

*Long Shot
An interesting film about film-making; the story of a producer (played by an actual, Scots, moviemaker, Charles Gormley) trying to set up a feature film and

finding it pretty hard-going! Cast: Charles Gormley, Neville Smith, Ann Zelda, Mary Maddox, Jill Beck, David Stone, Suzanne Danielle, Ron Taylor, Wim Wenders, Stephen Frears, Jim Haines, Jacqui Byford, Maurice Bulbulian, William Forsyth, Richard Demarco, Alan Bennett, Sarah Boston, Mel Calman, Susannah York, Dennis Sellinger, Sandy Lieberson, John Boorman. Dir & Pro: Maurice Hatton. Screenplay: Eoin McCann & The Players, from a story by Maurice Hatton. Ph: Michael Davis, Michael Dobbs, Ivan Strasburg, Maurice Hatton & Teo Davis. Ed: Howard Sharp. Art: None. M: Terry Dougherty (recorded music by Vivaldi). (Mithras Films.) Rel: Floating; first shown London (Everyman, Hampstead) June 1980. 86 mins. Cert AA.

*Long Weekend
Atmospheric Australian thriller about a squabbling young couple – arrogant husband, resentful wife; both characters drawn in some depth – who spend a camping weekend on a lonely beach. Several initial incidents, such as the killing of a kangaroo and losing the way, start up the atmosphere of tension and terror which builds steadily to the ironical conclusion of the deadly holiday. Like so many Aussie films, this one shows the male as uncouth, hard-drinking, callous, selfish and otherwise entirely anti-social. Cast: John Hargreaves, Briony Behets, Mike McEwen, Michael Aitkins, Roy Day, Sue Kiss von Soly. Dir & Pro: Colin Eggleston. Ex Pro: Richard Brennan. Screenplay: Everett de Roche. Ph: Vincent Monton. Ed: Brian Kavanagh. Pro Dir: Larry Eastwood. M: Michael Carlos. (Dugong-Bordeaux Films International.) Rel: Floating; first shown London (Odeon, Kensington and Swiss Cottage) June 1980. 97 mins. Cert AA.

Loophole
Initially quite brilliantly engineered and fascinating but finally highly unsatisfactory crime thriller about a very specialised, small gang led by the affluent-living 'brains' Albert Finney (a polished performance) whose plan it is to travel through the old Fleet river tunnel and then smaller sewers to the bank of their choice and then break into the strong-room through the floor, thus circumventing the many safety devices operating. But then an unexpected thunderstorm catches them on their way out and washes them away to death? . . . at which point comes an anti-climax to leave a myriad of important questions in the air, unanswered. Rest of cast: Martin Sheen, Susannah York, Colin Blakely, Jonathan Pryce, Alfred Lynch, Christopher Guard, Robert Morley, Terrence Hardiman, Bridget Brice, Ian Howarth, Harriet Collins, Gwyneth Powell, Tony Doyle, Jerry Harte, James Grout, Clive Graham, Donna Reading, Timothy Bateson, Lisa Coleman, Amy Dagley. Dir: John Quested. Pro: David Korda & Julian Holloway. Ex Pro: George A. Walker & Edward D. Simons. Screenplay: Jonathan Hales; based on the book by Robert Pollock. Ph: Michael Reed. Ed: Ralph Sheldon. Pro Des: Syd Cain. Art: Maurice Cain. M: Lalo Schifrin. (Brent Walker.) Rel: 15 March. 105 mins. Cert A.

Loulou
French. Unappealing story of a silly little sleep-around slut who works to keep her lazy, work-shy lover happy,

all rather a wasted effort by obviously very talented director Maurice Pialat, a recruit from the documentary and television film fields. Cast: Isabelle Huppert, Gérard Depardieu, Guy Marchand, Humbert Balsan, Bernard Tronczyk, Christian Boucher, Frédérique Cerbonnet, Jacqueline Dufranne, Willy Safar, Agnès Rosier, Patrick Playez, Patricia Coulet, Jean-Claude Meilland, Gerald Garnier, Catherine de Guirchitch, Jean van Herzeele, Patrick Poivey, Xavier Saint Macary. Dir: Maurice Pialat. Ex Pro: Klaus Hellwig, Yves Gasser & Yves Peyrot. Screenplay: Arlette Langmann (dialogue by Langmann & Pialat). Ph: Pierre William Glenn & Jacques Loiseleux. Ed: Yann Dedet & Sophie Coussein. Art: Max Berto. (Gaumont/Action Films-Artificial Eye.) Rel: Floating; first shown London (Camden Plaza & Chelsea Classic) January 1981. 105 mins. Cert X.

Lover Boy – L'Amant de Poche
Dubbed (into sometimes unfortunate Americanisms by ill-fitting American voices) French film with a light and sometimes amusing story about a high-class Call Girl who spontaneously picks up a sixteen-year-old, innocent, schoolboy and finds herself increasingly involved with him. And it all becomes rather moving at the end. Nice performances by Mimsy Farmer as the pretty prostitute and Pascal Sellier as the boy. Rest of cast: Andréa Ferréol, Serge Sauvion, Bernard Fresson, Madeleine Robinson, Stéphane Jobert, Eva Ionesco, Vèronique Delbourg, Pascale Audret, Roger Hanin, Robert Hossein, Philippe Lemaire, Jacques Spiesser. Dir & Screenplay (the latter with Pierre Pèlegri): Bernard Queysanne; based on the novel by Voldemar Lestienne. Ex Pro: Christine Gouze-Renal. Ph: Alain Levent. Ed: Agnès Molinard. Art: No credit. M: Laurent Petitgirard. (Progéfi/SFP/Gaumont – Gala.) Rel: Floating; first shown London (Odeons at Kensington & Swiss Cottage) July 1980. 90 mins. Cert X.

Manila
1975 Philippines film now getting its British premiere. Romantic story of a boy who follows his girl to the town and finds her in a brothel there. Cast: Rafael Roco, Hilda Koronel. Dir: Lino Brocka. (Cinegate). Rel: Floating; first shown London (Gate 3) April 1981. 125 mins. Cert X.

McVicar
Story – factual with lots of overlaid fictional trimming – of the notorious criminal who broke out of Durham – high security risk – jail, continued his professional crime career until re-captured by the police, when he turned to education and when paroled began writing as a career! What emerges is a picture of wonderfully disciplined warders standing up to endless provocation from their moronic charges; some pretty lax supervision that allows McVicar to tunnel his way to freedom from the washroom; and some slow work by the CID which allowed the escapee to return and live openly with his wife and family and carry out violent crimes. Historically correct? A background of often near-shrieking musical numbers contributed by The Who. Cast: Roger Daltrey, Adam Faith, Cheryl Campbell, Steven Berkoff, Brian Hall, Jeremy Blake, Leonard Gregory, Peter Jonfield, Anthony Trent,

Matthew Scurfield, Joe Turner, Terence Stuart, Charlie Cork, Ronald Herdman, Tony Haygarth, Tony Rohr, Ralph Watson, Richard Simpson, Allan Mitchell, Stanley Lloyd, Mikki Margorian, James Marcus, Georgina Hale, Anthony May, Malcolm Tierney, Raymond Skipp, Billy Murray, John Rolfe, Ricky Parkinson, David Beames, Robert Walker, Jamie Foreman, Ian Hendry, Malcolm Terris, Charles Cork, Paul Kember, Stephen Bent, Harry Fielder, Michael Feast. Dir: Tom Clegg. Pro: Bill Curbishley, Roy Baird & Roger Daltrey. Ex Pro: David Gideon Thomson & Jackie Curbishley. Screenplay: John McVicar, Tom Clegg. Ph: Vernon Layton. Ed: Peter Boyle. Art: Fred Carter. M: Jeff Wayne. (Who Films Ltd-Brent Walker.) Rel: 31 August. 120 mins. Cert X.

Maîtresse
1975 French film which understandably, in view of its content, only now reaches the British screen (and then without any censor's certificate). Extremely unpleasant story about a wealthy man's wife whose sideline is a highly lucrative cellar where she caters for every possible sadomasochistic whim of her clients, including nailing their testicles to a board, putting them on the rack and running pins in their nipples, all shown in revolting close-up. Bulle Ogier as the Madame and Gérard Depardieu as her moronic, ill-attired lover who is drawn into the nasty business for both money and, apparently, sadistic satisfaction. Rest of cast: André Rouyer, Nathalie Keryan, Roland Bertin, Tony Taffin, Holger Lowenadler, Anny Bartanovsky, Serge Berry, Richard Caron, Pierre Devos, Jeanne Herviale, Michel Pilorge, Cécile Pochet. Dir & Screenplay (the latter with Paul Voujargol): Barbet Schroeder. Production Director: Pierre Andrieux. Ph: Nestor Almendros. Ed: Denise de Casabianca. Art: Roberto Plate. M: Carlos d'Alessio. (Les Films du Losange/Gaumont-Lagoon Associates Productions Ltd.) Rel: Floating; first shown London (Screen on the Hill) July 1980. 112 mins. No cert.

A Man, A Woman and a Bank
Minor, pleasant little bank heist comedy-thriller which never quite makes it in either department; although the original idea, the story of the crooks building their own particular 'fail' system into the fail-safe system going into a new bank is full of promise. Cast: Donald Sutherland, Brooke Adams, Paul Mazursky, Allan Magicovsky, Leigh Hamilton, Nick Rice, Peter Erlich, Paul Rothery, Elizabeth Barclay, Leanne Young, Tibbi Landers, Sharon Sourrell, Annette Marie Dupuis, Walter Marsh, Jackson Davies, Alex Willows, Robert Forsythe, Alex Kliner, Cam Lane, Fred Latremouille, Ken Chamberlain, Debbie Wakeham, Allan Anderson, Lili Franks, Robert Stalmach, Harry Nicols, Fernando Antumes, Bob Vernon, George Milliaris, Anne Kidder, Dir: Noel Black. Pro: John B. Bennett & Peter Samuelson. Assoc Pro: Maurice Dunster. Screenplay: Raymond Gideon, Bruce A. Evans & Stuart Margolin; from a story by the former two. Ph: Jack Cardiff. Ed: Carl Kress. (Additional editing by Gail Yasunaga). Pro Des: Anne Pritchard. M: Bill Conti. (Bennettfilms in assoc. with McNichol-Avco Embassy-Rank Film Dist.) Rel: 23 November. 111 mins. Cert AA.

Marigolds in August

Movingly real South African film about poverty; the militant reactions of a kindly old part-time gardener working in a Whites' seaside holiday hamlet when a young rival appears on the scene and threatens to take some of his jobs. And the realistic comments on the feud by the 'coloured' snake-catcher who brings understanding of the youngster's plight to the old man. This movie completes the trilogy begun by *Bosman and Lena* and continued with *The Guest*, with each film focusing on 'an important dimension of South African realities'. Cast: Winston Ntshona, John Kani, Athol Fugard, Joyce Hesha, Mabel Ntshinga, Dudu Nene, Zola Marwanqa, Nomonde Mhlobiso, Tata U-Ngesi. Dir: Ross Devenish. Pro: Jonathan Cohen & Mark Forstater. Screenplay: Athol Fugard. Ph: Michael Davis. Ed: Lionel Selwyn. Art: None. M: None. (Serpent Southern Productions/R M Productions – Contemporary.) Rel: Floating; first shown London (Paris-Pullman) July 1980. 87 mins. Cert A.

The Marriage of Maria Braun – Die Ehe der Maria Braun

Rainer Werner Fassbinder's most commercial and possibly best film yet (made 1979); about a girl who marries during a Berlin bombing raid towards the end of the war only to have her husband called off to the Russian front the following day. He does eventually return – to find his wife in bed with a negro, leading to a fight, the negro's death and a rather confected series of events. Cast: Hanna Schygulla, Klaus Löwitsch, Ivan Desny, Gottfried John, Gisela Uhlien, Günther Lamprecht, Hark Bohm, George Byrd, Elizabeth Trissenaar, Rainer Werner Fassbinder, Isolde Barth, Peter Berling, Sonja Neudorfer, Lieslotte Eder, Volker Spengler, Karl-Heinz von Hassel, Michael Ballhaus, Christine Hopf de Loup, Dr Horst-Dieter Klock, Günther Kaufmann, Bruce Low, Claus Holm, Anton Schirsner, Hannes Kaetner, Martin Häussler, Norbert Scherer, Rolf Bohrmann, Arthur Glogau. Dir: Rainer Werner Fassbinder. Pro: Michael Fengler. Screenplay: Peter Märthesheimer & Pia Fröhlich. Ph: Michael Ballhaus. Ed: Juliane Lorenz. No Art credit. M: Peer Raben. (Albatros Film, Trio Film & Westdeutscher Rundfunk in assoc. with Filmverlag der Autoren-Miracle International.) Rel: Floating; first shown London (Odeon, Kensington, Screen on the Hill & Cinecenta) September 1980. 120 mins. Cert AA.

Middle Age Crazy

Comedy about the forty-year itch suffered by a successful Houston businessman (Bruce Dern) who meets his dream girl in Dallas. But after a great deal of aggro the crazy man finds there's no place like home and nobody quite like a wife of some twenty years. Rest of cast: Ann-Margret, Graham Jarvis, Eric Christmas, Helen Hughes, Geoffrey Bowes, Michael Kane, Diane Dewey, Vivian Reis, Patricia Hamilton, Anni Lantuch, Deborah Wakeham, Gina Dick, Thomas Baird, Norma Dell'Agnesi, Shirley Solomon, Elias Zarou, Michele Chiponski, Victor Sutton, Jack Mather, Jim Montgomery, John Facenda. Dir: John Trent. Pro: Robert Cooper & Ronald Cohen. Ex Pro: Sid & Marty Krofft. Screenplay: Carl Kleinschmitt. Co-Pro: John M. Eckert. Ph: Reginald Morris. Ed: John Kelly. Pro Des:

Karen Bromley. Art: Jill Scott. M: Matthew McCauley. (M & Lyrics for 'Where Did the Time Go' and 'Just Friends' by Burt Bacharach & Carole Bayer Sager). (Sid & Marty Krofft-R. Cooper & R. Cohen-Barber International.) Rel: 22 March. 92 mins. Cert AA.

The Mirror Crack'd

Highly entertaining adaptation of an Agatha Christie murder mystery set in an English village and Stately Home taken over by an American movie-making unit. Miss Marple – Miss Christie's matronly sleuth – solves the not particularly credible crime almost by remote control, through her Scotland Yard Inspector nephew. Lots of polished performances and plenty of witty lines in a wryly amusing, perceptive script. Cast: Angela Lansbury (Miss M.), Geraldine Chaplin, Tony Curtis, Edward Fox, Rock Hudson, Kim Novak, Elizabeth Taylor, Marella Oppenheim, Wendy Morgan, Margaret Courtenay, Charles Gray, Maureen Bennett, Carolyn Pickles, Eric Dodson, Charles Lloyd-Pack, Richard Pearson, Thick Wilson, Pat Nye, Peter Woodthorpe. Cast of the introductory interpolated mini-murder mystery: Anthony Steel, Dinah Sheridan, Oriane Grieve, Kenneth Fortescue, Hildegard Neil, Allan Cuthbertson, George Silver, John Bennett, Nigel Stock. Dir: Guy Hamilton. Pro: John Brabourne & Richard Goodwin. Screenplay: Jonathan Hales & Barry Sandler; based on the novel by Agatha Christie. Ph: Christopher Challis. Ed: Richard Marden. Pro Des: Michael Stringer. M: John Cameron. (EMI.) Rel: 22 March. 106 mins. Cert A.

Model

Documentary about the making of TV commercials and the models who feature in them; the whole model business in fact. Dir, Screenplay Ed, & Pro: Frederick Wiseman. Ph: John Davey. (Zipporah Films-Cinegate.) Rel: Floating; first shown London (Electric) March 1981. 120 mins. In black-and-white. No cert.

Monster

Minor thriller about some experimental salmon which escape into the sea and turn into vaguely manlike creatures who have a violent hatred for humans and savage them to death whenever they can get their claws on them. Cast: Doug McClure, Ann Turkel, Vic Morrow, Cindy Weintraub, Anthony Penya, Denise Galik, Lynn Theel, Meegan King, Breck Costin, Hoke Howell, Don Maxwell, David Strassman, Greg Travis, Linda Shayne, Lisa Glaser, Bruce Monette, Shawn Erler, Frank Arnold, Amy Barrett, Jo Williams & her Whitewater Boys (Jo Williams, Henry T. Williams, Lyle Isom, Jonathan Lehan). Dir: Barbara Peeters, Pro & Story (the latter with Frank Arnold): Martin B. Cohen. Screenplay: Frederick James. Co-Pro: A. Hunt Lowry. Ph: Daniel Lacambre. Ed: Mark Goldblatt. Art: Michael Erler. M: James Horner. Humanoids created by Rob Bottin. (New World-United Artists.) Rel: 7 December. 81 mins. Cert X.

The Monster Club

A jolly little horror spoof with smooth vampire Vincent Price relating three macabre stories and explaining the Draculean hierarchy to his friendly victim and teller-of-horrid-tales John Carradine. An amusing mix

of horror, fun and, very loud, punk-pop music. A sort of holiday for Hammerites! Rest of cast: Donald Pleasence, Stuart Whitman, Warren Saire, Richard Johnson, Britt Ekland, Barbara Kellerman, Simon Ward, James Laurenson, Anthony Valentine, Neil McCarthy, Anthony Steel, Lesley Dunlop, Patrick Magee. Dir: Roy Ward Baker. Pro: Milton Subotsky. Ex Pro: Bernard J. Kingham. Assoc Pro: Ron Fry. Screenplay: Edward & Valerie Abraham; based on the novel by Ronald Chetwynd-Hayes. Ph: Peter Sinclair. Ed: Peter Tanner. Art: Tony Curtis. M: performed by: B. A. Robertson, Night, The Pretty Things, The Viewers, John Williams, UB40 and Expressos. (Chips Productions-Sword and Sorcery Production-ITC.) Rel: 24 May. 97 mins. Cert A.

More American Graffiti

A follow-up of the original, 1974, *American Graffiti* film: two years older now (in 1964) the group of youngsters are facing up to more adult problems, including the Vietnam war, the anti-war demonstration riots, and more domestic matters such as the right of the young wife (and mother) to go back to work. With, as in the original, a musical background of the chart-toppers of the period. Cast: Paul Le Mat, Ken Place, Anna Bjorn, Mary Kay Place, Charles Martin Smith, Richard Bradford, Bo Hopkins, Jay Jacobus, John Vella, James Houghton, Candy Clark, John Lansing, John Brent, Scott Glenn, Monica Tenner, Ralph Wilcox, Cindy Williams, Ron Howard, Will Seltzer, Carol-Ann Williams, Wolfman Jack. Dir & Screenplay: B. W. L. Norton. Pro: Howard Kazanjian. Ex Pro: George Lucas. Ph: Caleb Deschanel. Ed: Tina Hirsch. Art: Ray Storey. M Ed: Gene Finley (Numbers performed by Country Joe and the Fish, Doug Sahm and Electric Haze, Cindy Williams with Naomi Judd and Leslie Gay Leace & recorded performances by The Supremes, The Miracles and many other groups). (Universal-CIC.) Rel: 1 March. 102 mins. Cert AA.

Motel Hell

Ghoulish little shocker about a motel owner and his sister who mix some of their clients with animal flesh to give that extra special flavour to their renowned smoked delicacies! And they store their victims till wanted (with vocal cords carefully cut!) up to their necks in the earth. Cast: Rory Calhoun, Paul Linke, Nancy Parsons, Nina Axelrod, Wolfman Jack, Elaine Joyce, Dick Curtis, Monique St. Pierre, Rosanne Katon, E. Hampton Beagle, Everett Creach, Michael Melvin, John Ratzenberger, Marc Silver, Victoria Hartman, Gwil Richards, Toni Gillman, Shaylin Hendrixson, Dick Curtis, Margot Hope, Barbara Goodson, Kim Fowler. Dir: Kevin Connor. Pro & Screenplay: Steven, Charles & Robert Jaffe. Ex Pro: Herb Jaffe. Ph: Thomas del Ruth. Ed: Bernard Gribble. Assoc Pro: Austen Jewell. Art: Joseph M. Altadonna. M: Lance Rubin. (Camp Hill-UA.) Rel: 15 March. 102 mins. Cert X.

The Mountain Men

Trapper Charlton Heston fighting Redskin Stephen Macht over the Blackfoot beauty Victoria Racimo after he has acquired her as the result of a battle with her tribe. And Brian Keith as Heston's fellow-trapper and companion steals most of the few honours going. Rest of cast: Seymour Cassel, John Glover, David Ackroyd, Cal Bellini, Bill Lucking, Ken Ruta, Victor Jory, Danny Zapien, Tim Helderman, Buckley Norris, Daniel Knapp, Michael Greene, Stewart East, Terry Leonard, Steve D. Chambers, Bennie Dobbins, Suzanna Trusillo, Melissa Sylvia, James Ecoffey. Dir: Richard Lang. Pro: Martin Shafer & Andrew Scheinman. Ex Pro: Richard R. St Johns. Assoc Pro: Cathleen Summers. 2nd Unit Dir: Joe Canutt. Screenplay: Fraser Clarke Heston. Ph: Michael Hugo. Ed: Eva Ruggiero. Pro. Des: Bill Kenney. M: Michael Legrand. (Martin Ransohoff-Columbia.) Rel: 9 November. 105 mins. Cert AA.

My American Uncle – Mon oncle d'Amérique
Brilliant Alain Resnais film which manages to smoothly blend what amounts to a lecture on human behaviourism by famous French professor Henri Laborit with fascinating fictional illustrations, the story of three characters and their relationship with each other. It all adds up to a quite magnificent and original achievement. Cast: Gérard Depardieu, Nicole Garcia, Roger Pierre, Marie Dubois, Nelly Borgeaud, Pierre Arditi, Gérard Darrieu, Philippe Laudenbach, Prof. Henri Laborit, Véronique Silver Lescot, Geneviève Minich, Maurice Gautier, Guillaume Boisseau, Ina Bedart, Ludovic Salis, Francois Calvez, Stéphanie Loustau, Monique Mauclair, Damien Boisseau, Gaston Vacchia, Bertrand Lepage, Jean-Philippe Puymartin, Catherine Frot, Valérie Dréville, Briggite Rouan, Max Vialie, Yves Peneau, Jean-Bernard Guillard, Laurence Février, Charlote Bonnet, Jean Dasté, Ann-Christine Joinneau, Sébastien Drai, Marjorie Godin, Liliane Gaudet, Isabelle Ganz, Maria Laborit, Albert Médina, Laurence Badie, Carène Ferrey, Sabine Thomas, Catherine Serre, Jacques Rispal, Hélèna Manson, Serge Feuillard, Gilette Barbier, Dominqie Rozan, Michel Muller. Dir: Alain Resnais. Pro: Philippe Dussart. Pro Sup: Michel Faure. Screenplay: Jean Gruault; based on the works of Prof Henri Laborit. Ph: Sacha Vierny. Ed: Albert Jurgenson. Art: Jacques Saulnier. M: Arié Dzierlatka. (Andrea-Films/TFI-Gala.) Rel: Floating; first shown London (Academy) September. 1980. 126 mins. Cert A.

My Bloody Valentine
Yet another film in which during a teenagers' jollification a psychotic killer murders one after the other of them in particularly horrible and bloody ways, after previously announcing his presence in the community by a murder in which he tears out his victim's heart and sends it, in suitably red-ribboned package, to the sheriff! All very eye-averting. Cast: Paul Kelman, Lori Hallier, Neil Affleck, Keith Knight, Alf Humphreys, Cynthia Dale, Helene Udy, Rob Stein, Tom Kovacs, Terry Waterland, Carl Marotte, Jim Murchison, Gina Dick, Peter Cowper, Don Francks, Patricia Hamilton, Larry Reynolds, Jack Van Evera, Jeff Banks, Pat Hemingway, Graham Whitehead, Fred Watters, Jeff Fulton, Pat Walsh, Marguerite McNeil, Sandy Leim, John MacDonald. Dir: George Mihalka. Pro: John Dunning, Andre Link & Stephen Miller from a story concept by John Beaird. Pro: Lawrence Nesis. Pro Sup: Bob Presner. Ph: Rodney Gibbons. Ed: Jean Lafleur. Art: Penny Hadfield. M: Paul Zaza. (CIC.) Rel: 10 May. 91 mins. Cert X.

My Bodyguard
Quite pleasant film about a fifteen-year-old schoolboy who after his initial private school education finds 'public' (in the American sense) school a far less pleasant place, with its bullies, gangs and extortion rackets. So he hires one of the more respected pupils to protect him, a scheme which works well until the bully boys put a sadistic thug on their payroll. Something here of both *The Blackboard Jungle* and *Tom Brown's Schooldays!* Nice performances by Chris Makepeace as the lad, an impressive one by bodyguard Adam Baldwin, and Ruth Gordon contributing one of her now all too familiar portraits of a dotty, man-mad old girl. Rest of cast: Matt Dillon, Paul Quandt, Joan Cusack, Dean R. Miller, Tim Reyna, Richard Bradley, Denise Baske, Hank Salas, Vicky Nelson, Tom Rielly, Paul Charbonneau, Laura Salenger, Bert Hoddinott, Jonathan Turk, Cindy Russ, Laurie McEathron, Lori Mandell, Dean Devlin, Martin Mull, John Houseman, Craig Richard Nelson, Kathryn Grody, Richard Cusack, Dorothy Scott, Angelo Buscaglia, Kitt York, Marge Kotlisky, Tim Kazurinsky, Bill Koza, Vivian Smolen, Bruce Jarchow, Andrea Dillon, Leonard Mack, George Wendt, Jerome Myers, Freddy Moss, Joseph Cohn, Patrick Billingsley, Barbara Hoddinott, Eddie Gomez. Dir: Tony Bill. Pro: Don Devlin. Ex Pro: Melvin Simon. Assoc Pro: Phillip Goldfarb. Screenplay: Alan Ormsby. Ph: Michael D. Margulies. Ed: Stu Linder. Pro Des: Jackson de Govia. M: Dave Grusin. (Market Street-Melvin Simon-Fox.) Rel: 22 February. 96 mins. Cert A.

Nela, The Story of a Painter
Austrian feature documentary made by H. C. Fischer, father of a twenty-two year-old girl who died from blood cancer. After giving several public piano recitals in her earliest teens she turned to art and proceeded to turn out paintings until she died. (Fischer Films/Teleclassic – Academy.) Rel: Floating; first shown London (Fischer Films/Academy) October. 1980. 90 mins. Cert U.

Nighthawks
Sylvester Stallone and Billy Dee Williams (as a sort of unconventional Starsky-and-Hutch-type cop couple who make the night-time Bronx a little less dangerous by trapping the muggers and drug-pedlars) suddenly assigned the capture of an international terrorist who reckons to demonstrate his destructive prowess on their patch. Fast, rugged and brutally effective. Rest of cast: Lindsay Wagner, Persis Khambatta, Nigel Davenport, Rutger Hauer, Hilarie Thompson, Joe Spinell, Walter Mathews, E. Brian Dean, Caesar Cordova, Charles Duval. Dir: Bruce Malmuth. Pro: Martin Poll. Ex Pro: Michael Wise & Franklin R. Levy. Screenplay: David Shaber; from a story by him & Paul Sylbert. Ph: James A. Contner. Ed: Christopher Holmes. Pro Des: Peter Larkin. M: Keith Emerson. (Universal-CIC.) Rel: 7 June. 100 mins. Cert X.

Nijinsky
Lovely-to-look-at production which with superb Edwardian decor and consistent good taste relates the events that led up to, and the final break-up of, the long-standing love affair between the great dancer and his mentor, the ballet impresario Diaghilev, when the former presumed too far on the indulgence of the latter and demanded more opportunities to stage his controversial choreography. The end result was a disastrous marriage to a member of the *corps de ballet* and a rapid decline towards the madness which was to confine Nijinsky in an insane asylum for the last thirty years of his life. Smooth performances from most of the cast, with an outstanding one by Alan Badel (as the patron of the arts who is a self-confessed 'bitch'); a thoughtful one by Alan Bates as the maestro and an interesting debut by George de la Pena in the title role. Rest of cast: Leslie Browne, Carla Fracci, Colin Blakely, Ronald Pickup, Ronald Lacey, Vernon Dobtcheff, Jeremy Irons, Frederick Jaeger, Anton Dolin, Janet Suzman, Stephen Chase, Henrietta Baynes, Sian Phillips, Charles Kay, Tomas Milian Jr., Monica Mason, Valerie Aitken, Genesia Rosato, June Brown, Blaise Mills, Kim Miller, Dean McMillan, Mart Crowley, Olga Lowe, Geoffrey Hughes, Patricia Ruanne, Ben Van Cauwenbergh. Dir: Herbert Ross. Pro: Nora Kaye & Stanley O'Toole. Ex Pro: Harry Saltzman. Assoc Pro: Howard Jeffrey. Pro Sup: Al Burgess. Screenplay: Hugh Wheeler: based on *Nijinsky* by Romola Nijinski and *The Diary of Vaslav Nijinsky*. Ph: Douglas Slocombe. Ed: William Reynolds. Art: George Richardson. Set Dec: Peter James. M: adapted & conducted by John Lanchbery & played by the Los Angeles Philharmonic. Ballet sequences danced by The London Festival Ballet. (Saltzman-Paramount-CIC.) Rel: Floating; first shown London (ABC) June 1980. 125 mins. Cert AA.

Nine to Five
Somewhat loosely contructed but generally delightfully amusing comedy (which never quite decides whether it wants to be just that or to be just a semi-serious attack on male chauvinism) about three girls who work for a satirically overdrawn boss, who relies upon his efficient office manageress, makes passes at his secretary and hypocritically lectures the new girl: three grand performances by Lily Tomlin, Dolly Parton and Jane Fonda. His actions finally drive the girls into kidnapping him and holding him prisoner in his own home while they wait for what they hope will be incriminating evidence against him. Rest of cast: Dabney Coleman, Sterling Hayden, Elizabeth Wilson, Henry Jones, Lawrence Pressman, Marian Mercer, Ren Woods, Norma Donaldson, Roxanna Bonilla-Giannini, Peggy Pope, Richard Stahl, Ray Vitte, Edward Marshall, Alan Haufrect, Earl Boen, Jeffrey Douglas Thomas, Tom Tarpey, Michael Delano, Barbara Chase, David Price, Gavin Mooney, Peter Hobbs, Terrence McNally, Esther Sutherland, Helene Heigh, Vicki Belmonte, Jerrold Ziman, Jessica Badovinac, Eric Mansker, Shirley Anthony, Michael Hehr, Gary Bisig, Brad David Stockton, Terry Jackson House, Raymond O'Keefe, Vanna Salviati. Dir: Colin Higgins. Pro: Bruce Gilbert. Screenplay: Colin Higgins & Patricia Resnick; from the latter's story. Ph: Reynaldo Villalobos. Ed: Pembroke J. Herring. Pro Des: Dean Mitzner. M: Charles Fox (song 'Nine to Five' written and performed by Dolly Parton). Art: Jack Gammon Taylor. (Fox.) Rel: 5 April. 110 mins. Cert AA.

The Ninth Configuration
William Peter ('Exorcist') Blatty's first effort at direction (of his own story) shows he might be well

advised to stick to the pen. An odd story about some Vietnam war maniacs kept in what appears to be Count Dracula's Castle assaulted by a constant thunderstorm, and the arrival there of a new psychiatrist who is finally unveiled – after he has mass-murdered a group of 'Devil's Angels' who unbearably humiliate him – as a famous martial killer. Cast: Stacy Keach, Scott Wilson, Jason Miller, Ed Flanders, Neville Brand, George Dicenzo, Moses Gunn, Robert Loggia, Alejandro Rey, Tom Atkins. Dir, Pro & Screenplay: William Peter Blatty. Ex Pro: William Paul. Assoc Pro: Tom Shaw. Ph: Gerry Fisher. Sup Ed: Peter Taylor. Ed: T. Battle Davis, Peter Lee-Thompson & Roberto Silvi. Pro Des: Bill Malley & J. Dennis Washington. M: Barry DeVorzon. (Lorimar-ITC.) Rel: Floating; first shown London (Odeon, St Martin's Lane) February 1981. 105 mins. Cert X.

No Nukes
Straightforward recording of several concerts and a final open-air mass rally (attended by nearly a quarter-of-a-million fans) staged to raise money for a campaign against nuclear power in the United States, with the artists concerned performing for free to help the cause. Performers: Jackson Browne; Crosby, Stills and Nash; The Doobie Brothers; John Hall; Graham Nash; Bonnie Raitt; Gil Scott-Heron; Carly Simon; Bruce Springsteen; James Taylor; Jesse Colin Young. Dir: Julian Schlossberg, Danny Goldberg & Anthony Potenza. Pro: Schlossberg & Goldberg. Ph & Documentary footage: Haskell Wexler. Madison Square Garden/Battery Park Rally: Barbara Kopple. (Muse-[Musicians United for Safe Energy]-Film-Mainline Pictures). Rel: Floating; first shown London (Odeon, Kensington) March 1981. 103 mins. Cert A.

The Nude Bomb
A sort of pretty wild James Bond thriller spoof with Don Adams as the bumbling secret agent with three very pretty 'Angels' assistants (including Sylvia Kristel), assigned the task of thwarting the villainous KAOS plot to bring into operation a secret weapon which will dissolve all the world's fabrics and leave the people bare! Rest of cast: Rhonda Fleming, Dana Elcar, Pamela Hensley, Andrea Howard, Norman Lloyd, Bill Dana, Gary Imhoff, Sarah Rush, Vittorio Gassman, Walter Brooke, Thomas Hill, Ceil Cabot, Joey Forman, Patrick Gorman, Earl Maynard, Alex Rodine, Richard Sanders, Vito Scotti, Byron Webster, Horst Ehrhardt, Lawrie Osag, Robert Karvelas, David Adnopoz, Adam Anderson, Kevin Donnelly, Gary Douris, Gary Young, Robert Ball, Robert Bralver, Hap Lawrence, Ashley Cox, Beverly Hart, Edgy Lee, Nick Dimitri, Fred Lerner, Bond Gideon, Chere Bryson, Greg Elam, Glynn Rubin, Dick Durock, James Gavin, Ross Reynolds, James McInnes, Bobby M. Porter, Richard Washington, Anthony Herrera. Dir: Clive Donner. Pro: Jennings Lang. Screenplay: Arne Sultan, Bill Dana & Leonard B. Stern; based on characters created by Mel Brooks & Buck Henry. Ph: Harry L. Wolf. Ed: Walter Hannemann. Pro Des: William Tuntke. M: Lalo Schifrin. (Universal/in assoc with Time-Life Films/CIC.) Rel: Floating; first shown London (Ritz) December 1980. 94 mins. Cert A.

1 + 1 = 3
Mildly amusing, meandering 1979 West German comedy about an unconventional young woman and her association with various men. Cast: Adelheid Arndt, Christoph Quest, Dietrich Leiding, Kelle Riedl, Charlotte Witthauer, Dominik Graf, Helga Storck, Ira & Daniel Genee, Florian, Greta Kelwing, Karin Kussauer. Dir & Screenplay: Heidi Genee: Pro: No credit. Ph: Gernot Roll. Ed: Helga Beyer. Art: No credit. M: Andrea Kubner. (Contemporary.) Rel: Floating; first shown London (Paris-Pullman) June 1981. 85 mins. Cert AA.

Ordinary People
Actor Robert Redford making an outstanding job of his first film direction (acknowledged by his being awarded the 1981 Best Direction Oscar), producing a sensitive, finely acted, leisurely and polished examination of explosive family tensions after it has experienced tragedy and trauma, with the death by drowning of the beloved elder son and the guilt complex of the younger one that leads to his attempting suicide and his subsequent sojourn in a mental hospital. A very superior effort indeed. Cast: Donald Sutherland, Mary Tyler Moore, Judd Hirsch, Timothy Hutton, M. Emmet Walsh, Elizabeth McGovern, Dinah Manoff, Fredric Lehne, James B. Sikking, Basil Hoffman, Quinn Redeker, Mariclare Costello, Meg Mundy, Elizabeth Hubbard, Adam Baldwin, Richard Whiting, Scott Doebler, Carl Di Tomasso, Tim Clarke, Ken Dishner, Lisa Smuth, Ann Eggert, Randall Robbins, Cynthia Baker Johnson, John Stimpson, Liz Kinney, Steve Hirsch, Rudy Hornish, Clarissa Downey, Cynthia Burke, Jane Alderman, Paul Preston, Gustave Lachenauer, Marilyn Rockafellow, Don Billett, Ronald Solomon, Virginia Long, Paula Segal, Estelle Meyers, Stuart Shiff, Rose Wool, Douglas Kinney, Constance Addington, Edwin Bederman, Bobby Coyne, Michael Creadon. Dir: Robert Redford. Pro: Ronald L. Schwary. Screenplay: Alvin Sargent, based on the novel by Judith Guest. Ph: John Bailey. Ed: Jeff Kanew. Art: Phillip Bennett & J. Michael Riva. M: Marvin Hamlisch. (Wildwood Enterprises-Paramount-CIC.) Rel: 5 April. 125 mins. Cert AA.

The Orlovs – Suprugi Orlovy
Charming Russian adaptation of some of Maxim Gorky's stories: how a no-good drunken wife-beater finds temporary fulfilment by working in a hospital during a cholera outbreak but after it reverts to type, while his wife in helping him finds real happiness, first as nurse and then as schoolteacher, rejecting her husband's final efforts towards reconciliation. All pastel colours and period atmosphere and fine leading performances. Cast: Nina Ruslanova, Anatoly Semyonov, Sergei Tegin, Daniil Sagal, Pyotr Merkuriev, Yuri Kamorny, Pavel Vinnik. Dir: Mark Donoskoi. Screenplay: Mark Azov; Mark Donskoi & Valery Mikhailovsky; based on stories by Maxim Gorky. Ph: Viachesiav Egorov. Pro Des: Olga Kravchenya. Ed: O. Bachorunoi. M: Raphail Khozak. (Central Gorki Studios of Children and Youth Films Production – Rank Film Dist.) Rel: Floating; first shown London (Everyman, Hampstead) November. 1980. 90 mins. Cert AA.

Papa les Petits Bateaux
Mildly amusing French comedy (with black streaks!) made, circa 1971, by Nelly Kaplan which presents Sheila White with the opportunity to give a remarkable performance as the apparently silly but in fact endlessly devious heiress who, abducted by a very inept kidnap gang, neatly arranges for their demise one by one so that she ends up with the ransom money paid by her dad. Rest of cast includes Michel Bouquet, Michel Lonsdale, Judith Ma Magre, Sydney Chaplin, Bernard Musson. Dir: Nelly Kaplan. No other technical details. (Scala.) Rel: Floating; first shown London (Scala) February 1981. 107 mins. No cert.

Penitentiary
Tough prison melodrama about a young negro unjustly convicted of murder (of a white man), who literally fights his way to parole freedom. Plenty of brutal fistic battles and interleaved sex scenes, with a mostly coloured cast: Cast: Leon Isaac Kennedy, Thommy Pollard, Hazel Spear, Badja Djola, Gloria Delaney, Chuck Mitchell, Wilbur (Hi-Fi) White, Donovan Womack, Floyd Chatman, Chuck Mitchell, Cepheus Jaxon, Dwaine Fobbs, Ernest Wilson, Will Richardson, Elijah Mitchell, Tony Andrea, Darrell Harris, Lonnie Kirtz, Ray Wolfe, Charles Young, Ellsworth Harrell, Cornelius Desha, Michael Melvin, Steve Eddy, Irene Stokes, Bill Murry, Terri Hayden, Herman Cole, Carl Erwin, Irving Parham, Warren Bryant, Lorri Gay, Thomas Earl Stiratt, Walter Gordon, Joaquin Leal, David Carter, Hassan Abdul-Ali, Marcus Guttierrez, Zee Howard, Gwynn Pineda, Ann Hutcherson, Cardella Demilo, Beverly Wallace, Onja Fenee, Deloris Figueroa, Zeola Gaye, Jackie Shaw, Brenda Joy Griffin, Renee Armanlin, Sarah Jaxon, Barbara Torres, Irene Terrell, Lisa Visco, Shelli Hughes, Tony Rapisarda, Casey J. Littlejohn, Edgardo Williams, Tyrone S. B. Thompson, Sam Olden, Roderic Williams, Dominic Giusto, William Bey, Shawn Davis, Johnny Jones, Robert Wayne Cornelius, Quitman Gates. Dir Pro & Screenplay: Jamaa Fanaka. Ph: Marty Ollstein. Ed: Betsy Blankett. Art: Adel Mazen. M: Frankie Gaye. (Jerry Gross Organisation-Eagle Films.) Rel: Floating; first shown London March 1981. 98 mins. Cert X.

Peppermint Soda – Diablo Menthe
Remarkably mature, witty and warmly human first film, made on a very modest budget without any stars (though with some delightful and talented youngsters) by Diane Kury, who fifteen years after leaving her école Jules Ferry returned with a camera and a script to make this fascinating record of a year in the lives of two sisters in and out of the classroom. A small classic, it deserved its winning of the coveted French Louis Delluc award for the best motion picture of the year. Cast: Eléonore Klarwein, Odile Michel, Anouk Ferjac, Michel Puterflam, Coralie Clément, Marie-Véronique Maurin, Valérie Stano, Dora Doll, Arlette Bonnard, Dominique Lavanant, Tsiliia Chelton. Dir & Screenplay: Diane Kurys. Pro: Armand Barbault. Ph: Philippe Rousselot. Ed: Joëlle van Effenterre. Art: Bernard Madelenat. M: Yves Simon. (Les Films de L'Alma/Alexandre Films-Gala.) Rel: Floating; first shown London (The Minema) October 1980. 97 mins. Cert AA.

Phobia
A psychological thriller about an experimenting psychiatrist whose prison-released patients each in turn die violent deaths when their 'cure' appears to have failed. A film which evolves into a whodunnit, solved not by the nasty, violent cop, but by the doctor's girl-friend. Lots of unexplained matters and not one of John Huston's more distinguished efforts, with 'Starsky & Hutch' star Paul Michael Glaser failing to make any particular impact in his first major movie role. Rest of cast: Susan Hogan, John Colicos, David Bolt, Patricia Collins, David Eisner, Lisa Langlois, Robert O'Ree, Alexandra Stewart, Neil Vipond, Marian Waldman, Kenneth Welsh, Gwen Thomas. Dir: John Huston. Pro: Zale Magder. Ex Pro: Larry Spiegel & Mel Bergman. Screenplay: Jimmy Sangster, Lew Lehman & Peter Bellwood; from a story by Gary Sherman & Ronald Shusett. Ph: Reginald H. Morris. Ed: Stan Cole. Pro Des: Ben Edwards. Art: David Jaquest. M: Andre Gagnon. (Borough Park-Barber Rose International.) Rel: 22 March. 90 mins. Cert X.

Popeye
A near-miss translation to screen terms of the famous old comic-strip cartoon, with cluttered but amusingly Disneyish backgrounds, generally very good performances (with Shelley Duvall's 'Olive Oyl' being outstanding) and reasonably attractive musical numbers. Robin Williams as the athletic, mumbling but rather too restrained spinach-powered tar. Good fun which might have been great fun if the film had more of the sharpness and one-dimensional comicality of cartoonist creator Elzie Segar's work. Rest of cast: Ray Walston, Paul Dooley, Paul L. Smith, Richard Libertini, Donald Moffat, Macyntyre Dixon, Roberta Maxwell, Donovan Scott, Allan Nicholls, Wesley Ivan Hurt, Bill Irwin, Peter Bray, Linda Hunt, Geoff Hoyle, Wayne Robson, Larry Pisoni, Carlo Pellegrini, Susan Kingsley, Michael Christensen, Ray Cooper, Noel Parenti, Karen McCormick, John Bristol, Julie Janney, Patty Katz, Diane Shaffer, Nathalte Blossom, Dennis Franz, Carlos Brown, Ned Dowd, Hovey Burgess, Roberto Messina, Pietro Torrisi, Margery Bond, Judy Burgess, Saundra MacDonald, Eve Knoller, Peggy Pisoni, Barbara Zegler, Paul Zegler, Pamela Burrell, David Arkin. Dir: Robert Altman. Pro: Robert Evans. Ex Pro: C. O. Erickson. Screenplay: Jules Feiffer; based on the cartoon character created by E. C. Segar. M: Giuseppe Rotunno. Sup Ed: Tony Lombardo. Ed: John W. Holmes & David Simmonds. Add Ed: Raja R. Gosnell. Pro Des: Wolf Kroeger. M & Lyrics: Harry Nilsson & Van Dyke Parks. Add M: Tom Pierson. (Disney-Paramount.) Rel: 19 April. 97 mins. Cert U.

Portrait of Teresa – Retrato de Teresa
1979 Cuban film. Cast: Daysi Granados, Adolfo Llaurado. Dir: Pastor Vega. (Cinegate.) Rel: Floating; first shown London (Gate 3) June 1981. 103 mins. No cert.

The Postman Always Rings Twice
Fourth, and arguably best, certainly most sensual, filming of the famous James M. Cain story (previous: Tay Garnett in 1946, Visconti in 1942 and a French version), with Jack Nicholson the drifter with a prison record who is persuaded by the sexually hungry wife of the Greek owner of a wayside cafe to join her in murdering her husband; their failure, success and the court case which follows in which they accuse each other but are finally set free by a technicality; and the ironic retribution that follows. Sexually explicit but not deliberately exploitably so; a minutely studied but fascinating performance by Nicholson and a smouldering, excellent one by Jessica Lange – the girl in King Kong's paw in the recent re-make of that movie! Rest of cast: John Colicos, Michael Lerner, John P. Ryan, Anjelica Huston, William Traylor, Tom Hill, Jon Van Ness, Bryan Farrel, Rayleigh Bond, William Newman, Albert Henderson, Ken Magee, Eugene Peterson, Don Calfa, Louis Turenne, Charles B. Jenkins, Dick Balduzzi, John Furlong, Sam Edwards, Betty Cole, Joni Palmer, Ron Flagge, Lionel Smith, Brion James, Frank Arno, Virgil Frye, Kenneth Cervi, Chris P. Rellias, Theodoros A. Karavidas, Basil J. Fovos, Nick Hasir, Demetrios Liappas, James O'Connell, William H. McDonald, Elsa Raven, Kopi Sotiropulos, Tom Maier, Glenn Shadix, Tani Guthrie, Carolyn Coates, Jim S. Cash, Alan Gibbs, Tom Elliott, Christopher Lloyd. Dir: Bob Rafelson. Pro: Charles Mulvehill & Bob Rafelson. Ex Pro: Andrew Braunsberg. Assoc Pro: Michael Barlow. Screenplay: David Mamet; based on the book by James M. Cain. Ph: Sven Nykvist. Ed: Graeme Clifford. Pro Des: George Jenkins. M: Michael Small. (Lorimar-ITC.) Rel: 7 June. 121 mins. Cert X.

Private Benjamin
Uneven but often very funny comedy which sets the old cliché story about the trials and tribulations of an Army recruit on its head by having that recruit a gal! And not any gal – delightful Goldie Hawn, as a pretty, wealthy young Jewish widow who finds more satisfaction with the martial than with men who, it is suggested, even including those foreign, hand-kissing Gallic charmers, are all more or less male chauvinist pigs! And it wouldn't be half as funny without Miss Hawn and her very able supporting cast: Eileen Brennan, Armand Assante, Robert Webber, Sam Wanamaker, Barbara Barrie, Mary Kay Place, Harry Dean Stanton, Albert Brooks, Alan Oppenheimer, Estelle Marlov, Everett Covin, Robert Hanley, Lee Wallace, James Dybas, Gretchen Wyler, Maxine Stuart, Lillian Adams, Sandy Weintraub, Tim Haldeman, Kopi Sotiropulos, Stu Nahan, J. P. Bumstead, Hal Williams, Toni Kalem, Damita Jo Freeman, Alson Aherne, P. J. Soles, Craig T. Nelson, James R. Barnett. Ray Oliver, Robin Hoff, Ed Lewis, Carrol Davis Carson, Clayton D. Wright, Danny Wells, Keone Young, George Roberts, Helen Baron, Paul Marin, Mimi Mayhard, Alice Hirson, Wil Albert, Richard Herd, Sally Kirkland, Denise Halma, Lilyan Chauvin, David Olivier, Elie Liardet, Gina Picerni. Dir: Howard Zieff. Pro & Screenplay: Nancy Meyers, Charles Shyer & Harvey Miller. Ex Pro: Goldie Hawn. Ph: David M. Walsh. Ed: Sheldon Kahn. Pro Des: Robert Boyle. Art: Jeff Howard. M: Bill Conti. (Warner.) Rel: 1 March. 110 mins. Cert AA.

Prom Night
Corpse-strewn thriller about the bloody revenge taken during their college's annual big dance occasion, because of a long-held grudge by one of the students. Cast: Leslie Nielsen, Jamie Lee Curtis, Casey Stevens, Eddie Benton, Antoinette Bower, Michael Tough, Robert Silverman. Pita Oliver, David Mucci, Jeff Wincott, Marybeth Rubins, George Touliatos, Melanie Morse MacQuarrie, David Gardner, Joy Thompson, Sheldon Rybowski, David Bolt, Beth Amos, Sonia Zimmer, Sylvia Martin, Liz Stalker-Mason, Pam Henry, Ardon Bess, Lee Wildgen. The children: Brock Simpson, Debbie Greenfield, Tammy Bourne, Dean Bosacki, Leslie Scott, Karen Forbes, Joyce Kite. Dir: Paul Lynch. Pro: Peter Simpson. Assoc Pro: Richard Simpson. Screenplay: William Gray; from a story by Robert Guza Jr. Ph: Robert New. Ed: Brian Ravock. Art: Reuben Freed. M: Carl Zittrer & Paul Zaza. Ex in charge of Pro: Deanne Judson. (Avco Embassy/Simcon Productions-Barber Rose International.) Rel: 8 February. 93 mins. Cert X.

Prostitute
Serious, socially conscious story of a Birmingham street prostitute with ambitions who goes to London to make the big money but soon finds herself involved in the more unpleasant side of the business. And behind it all is a plea to amend the laws about prostitution. Cast: Eleanor Forsythe, Kate Crutchley, Kim Lockett, Nancy Samuels, Richard Mangan, Phyllis Hickson, Joseph Senior, Ann Whitaker, Paul Arlington, Carol Palmer, Pat Manning, Brigid Mackay, Barbara Rosslyn, Jackie Thompson, Philippa Williams, Colin Hindley, Count Prince Miller, Sultan Akbar, Howard Dickenson, Heather Barrett, Kim Durham, Suzanne Francis, Mary Newell, Vincent Osborne, Mary Waterhouse, Kym Goodwin, Gillian Hawser, John Evans, Terry Pearson, Anne Beverley, Elizabeth Revill, Paul Moriarty, David Landberg, Lloyd McGuire, Yxanne Churchman, Bill Boazman, Clive Rickhards, Jackie Abbey-Taylor, Paul Ridley, Maureen O'Donnell, Paul McCleary, Edward Clayton. Dir, Pro & Screenplay: Tony Garnett. Pro Ex: Bobby Blues. Ph: Charles Stewart & Diane Tammes. Ed: Bill Shapter. Art: Martin Johnson. M: played by The Gangsters (Songs: 'Big Brother' by Jonathan Dewsbury & 'A Woman That Understands' by Ray King). (Mainline Pictures.) Rel: Floating; first shown London (Screen, Classic, Chelsea & Cinecenta, Leicester Sq) February 1981. 96 mins. Cert X.

Raging Bull
Martin Scorsese's powerful and unrelentingly harshly realistic film based on the autobiographical book of the same title by Jake La Motta, a Bronx Italian with an ungovernable temper who brutally fought his way to winning the middleweight championship of the world, was dethroned by Sugar Ray Robinson, opened a nighterie, was sent to prison, and then started to make a new career as a night club raconteur. Robert De Niro's portrait of the 'Bronx Bull' who distrusts everyone, including his brother, and periodically beats up his wife, is remarkably impressive.* The fight sequences, though actually taking up very little of the film's 129 minutes are terrifyingly bestial in both sight and sound. Rest of cast: Joe Pesci, Cathy Moriarty, Frank Vincent, Nicholas Colasanto, Theresa Saldana, Frank Adonis, Mario Gallo, Frank Topham, Lori Anne Flax, Joseph Bono, James V. Christy, Bernie Allen, Bill Mazer, Bill

Hanrahan, Rita Bennett, Mike Miles. Also, the fighters: Johnny Barnes, Kevin Mahon, Ed Gregory, Louis Fartis, Johnny Turner. Dir: Martin Scorsese. Pro: Irwin Winkler & Robert Chartoff. Pro in assoc with Peter Savage. Assoc Pro: Hal W. Polaire. Screenplay: Paul Schrader & Mardik Martin; based on the book 'Raging Bull' by Jake La Motta with Joseph Carter & Peter Savage. Ph: Michael Chapman. Ed: Thelma Schoonmaker. Pro Des (New York): Gene Rudolf. Art (Los Angeles): Alan Manser & Kirk Axtell. M. Ed: Jim Henrickson. (Chartoff/Winkler-UA.) Rel: 29 March. 129 mins. Cert X. Black-and-white (with colour sequences).

*It brought him the 1980–81 Best Actor Oscar.

Raise the Titanic
Pretty fanciful but quite fascinating tale about the Americans bringing the famous wreck to the surface in order to obtain some mysterious mineral power-source supposedly secretly hidden on board and being taken to the US when the ship went down. And how the Russians try to snatch the spoils – which turn out to be a lot less powerful than was thought, leading to a neat little tail-twist to tidy the story up. Spectacular scenes above and below the ocean, nice performances, reasonably good entertainment. Cast: Jason Robards, Richard Jordan, David Selby, Anne Archer, Alec Guinness, J. D. Cannon, Bo Brundin, M. Emmet Walsh, Norman Bartold, Elya Baskin, Dirk Blocker, Robert Broyles, Paul Carr, Michael C. Gwynne, Harvey Lewis, Charles Macaulay, Stewart Moss, Michael Pataki, Marvin Silbersher, Mark L. Taylor, Maurice Kowalewski. Dir: Jerry Jameson. Pro: William Frye. Ex Pro: Martin Starger. Screenplay: Adam Kennedy; based on the novel by Clive Cussler adapted by Eric Hughes. Ex in charge of Pro: Richard O'Connor. Ph: Matthew F. Leonetti. Ed: J. Terry Williams & Robert F. Shugrue. Pro Des: John F. DeCuir. Art: John F. DeCuir Jr. M: John Barry. (Marble Arch-ITC Films.) Rel: 18 January. 113 mins. Cert A.

Reggae Sunsplash
West German. Within the context of the 1979 Montego, Jamaica, Bay Festival with its succession of reggae stars, something of the story of this 'rebel' music with its political and social roots. Stars include Burning Spear, Third World, Peter Tosh and Bob Marley. Dir: Stefan Paul. Pro: Kino Arsenal Tubingen. Ph: Hans Schalk, Rainer Heinzelmann & Peter Rees. Ed: Hildegarde Schroder (UFO Productions-Osiris Films.) Rel: Floating; first shown London (Odeon, Westbourne Grove) April 1981. 107 mins. Cert AA.

The Reign of Naples – Neapolitanische Geschwister
West German-Italian film (made 1978) which tries too hard to reduce the entire post-war history of the working-class in Italy to within its two meandering and left-slanted hours. Cast: Liana Trouche, Romeo Giro, Tiziana Ambretti, Antonio Orlando, Renata Zamengo, Dino Mele, Margarethe Clementi, Raul Gimenez, Cristina Donadio, Ida di Benedetto, Patrizia Rispo, Maria Antonietta Riegel, Laura Sodano, Gerardo D'Andrea, Percy Hogan. Dir, Ed & Screenplay/Story: Werner Schroeter. Pro: Christoph Hotch. Ex Pro: Peter Berling. Assoc Pro: Michelangelo Ciafre. Ph: Thomas Mauch. Art: Franco Calabrese. M: Roberto Pregadio.

(Dieter Geissler Filmproduktion, Munich/PBC Spa, Rome/in assoc with Zweites Deutsches Fersehen, Mainz-Cinegate.) Rel: Floating; first shown London, (Electric Cinema) February 1981. 125 mins. No cert.

*Les Rendez-vous d'Anna
Strangely static but almost hypnotically fascinating Belgian-French-German co-production, written and directed by Chantal Akerman, about a young woman film director visiting several German towns in order to publicise her latest production and her several encounters *en route*. A portrait of a withdrawn, lonely woman seen against a background of train-window landscapes and coldly impersonal hotel rooms and foyers. Cast: Aurore Clément, Helmut Griem, Magali Noël, Lea Massari, Hanns Zischler, Jean-Pierre Cassel. Dir & Screenplay: Chantal Akerman. Pro: Alain Dahan. Ph: Jean Penzer. Ed: Francine Sandberg. Art: Philippe Graaf & André Fonteyne Coyotte. No M. credit. (Paradise Films, Brussels/Hélène Films, Unité Trois Paris/ZDF, Mainz – The Other Cinema.) Rel: Floating; first shown London (ICA) May 1980. 122 mins. Cert AA.

A Respectable Life
1979 Swedish film, a follow up of a 1967 documentary about young people who take drugs and break the law. All seen with a disappassionate eye. Dir Pro & Screenplay: Stefan Jarl. Ph: Per Kallberg. Ed: Anette Lykke-Lundberg, Jan Persson, Badis Andersson. Art: No credit. M: Ulf Dageby. (Stefan Jarl Films-Darvill Associates). Rel: Floating; first shown London (Moulin) March 1981. 102 mins. Cert X.

Resurrection
A generally remarkably well balanced and carefully non-committal movie on the divisive subject of Faith Healing, avoiding the religious implications in a story about a down-to-earth Kansas widow who cures her own paralysis by faith and gritty determination and then finds she can do the same for others. Not without its faults (such as sci-fi-like tunnel death sequences) but triumphantly held together by the marvellously sincere performance of Helen Burstyn, finely supported by some other impressive players like Eva La Gallienne, who won an Oscar nomination with her Granny Pearl role. Rest of cast: Sam Shepard, Richard Farnsworth, Roberts Blossom, Clifford David, Pamela Payton-Wright, Jeffrey De Munn, Lois Smith, Madeleine Thornton-Sherwood, Richard Hamilton, Carlin Glynn, Lane Smith, Penelope Allen, Ebbe Roe Smith, John Tillinger, Trazana Beverley, Ralph Roberts, George Sperdakos, Bernard Behrens, Sylvia Walden. Dir: Daniel Petrie. Pro: Reneé Missel & Howard Rosenman. Screenplay: Lewis John Carlino. Ph: Mario Tosi. Ed: Rita Roland. Pro Des: Paul Sylbert. Art: Edwin O'Donovan. M: Maurice Jarre. Special Visual Sequences: Richard and Robert Greenberg. (Universal-CIC.) Rel: 8 March. 109 mins. Cert AA.

Riding High (called *Heavy Metal* in America)
Story about a British motor cycle messenger who accepts the challenge to compete against the 'world champion stunt rider' at the awesome 'Devil's Leap'. Cast: Eddie Kidd, Irene Handl, Murray Salem, Marella Oppenheim, Bill Mitchell, Zoot Money, Paul Humpoletz, Lynda Bellingham, Daniel Peacock, Owen

Whittaker, Claire Toeman, Ken Kitson, Vivienne McKone, Saiward Green, Peter Whitman, Angela Crowe, April Olrich, Oliver Smith, Patricia Hodge, Alan Dudley, Allan Warren, Diana Weston. Dir & Screenplay (from a story by Derek Ford): Ross Cramer. Pro: Michael Klinger & Tony Klinger. Assoc Pro: Robert Sterne & Derek Ford. Ph: Brian Tufano. Ed: John Jympson. Pro Des: Keith Wilson. (Enterprise Pictures.) Rel: 31 May. 96 mins. Cert A.

Rock Show
A recording of a concert given to 70,000-plus fans in the King Dome, Seattle, by Paul McCartney's 'Wings' Group as a finale to a 1976 tour which took in ten countries. The Group: Linda McCartney, Denny Laine, Jimmy McCulloch, Joe English. Horn Section: Tony Dorsey, Howie Casey, Steve Howard Jr, Thaddeus Richard. Pro: Tom Priestley & Richard Dunford. Ed: Robin Clarke & Paul Stein. Ph: Jack Priestley. (MPL-Miracle.) Rel: Floating; first shown London (Classic) April 1981. 143 mins. Cert U.

Rough Cut
Lightly amusing crook comedy with Burt Reynolds as the lush-living diamond thief who is tempted by Chief Inspector David Niven's blackmailed, beautiful bait Lesley-Ann Down into attempting a £15 000 000 heist which the Inspector hopes will lead to achieving his final ambition of beating the heister. But there's an unexpected and witty twist in the tail. Rest of cast: Timothy West, Patrick Magee, Al Matthews, Susan Littler, Joss Ackland, Isobel Dean, Wolf Kahler, Andrew Ray, Julian Holloway, Douglas Wilmer, Geoffrey Russell, Ronald Hines, David Howey, Frank Mills, Roland Culver, Alan Webb, Cassandra Harris, Sue Lloyd, Hugh Thomas, Paul McDowell, Stephen Reynolds, David Eccles, Stephen Moore, Peter Schofield, Jonathan Elsom, Ron Pember, Cyril Appleton, John Slavid, Brian Tipping, Carol Rydall. Dir: Donald Siegel. Pro: David Merrick. Screenplay: Francis Burns, based on the novel 'Touch the Lion's Paw' by Derek Lambert. Ph: Freddie Young. Ed: Doug Stewart. Pro Des: Ted Haworth. M: Scored and adapted from the works of Duke Ellington by Nelson Riddle. (Paramount-CIC.) Rel: 7 September. 112 mins. Cert AA.

Rough Treatment – Bez Znieczulenia (Without Anaesthetic)
Andrzej Wajda's remarkably, openly critical, political comment (made 1978) which of all the single-party countries could only have been allowed in Poland. The story of an honest journalist and foreign correspondent who in a TV interview gives some highly unpopular and critical comments and then finds, on returning from abroad, that the effect of this integrity is disastrous to his personal life: his foreign newspapers are withheld, his next assignment abroad is cancelled, the TV producer is castigated by his superiors, the journalist's civil servant friend is demoted and sent to a small post in a far country, and his wife sues for divorce; his final humiliation – and illumination – coming in the court case presided over by a blatantly biased magistrate and packed with a counsel-less list of lying witnesses. A strong, absorbing movie. Cast: Zbigniew Zapasiewicz, Ewa Dalkowska, Andrzej Seweryn, Krystyna Janda, Emilia Krakowska, Roman Wilhelmi, Kazimierz Kaczor, Aleksandra Jasienska, Marta Salinger, Stefania

Iwinska, Iga Mayr, Halina Golanka, Jerzy Stuhr, Magda Teresa Wojcik, Danuta Balinska-Satanowska. Dir: Andrzej Wajda. Pro: Barbara Pec-Slesicka. Screenplay: Agnieszka Holland & Andrzej Wajda. Ph: Edward Klosinski. Ed: Halina Prugar. Art: Allan Starski. (Film Polski Unit X Production-Artificial Eye.) Rel: Floating; first shown London (Camden Plaza) April 1981. 115 mins. Cert AA.

Savage Weekend
A highly unpleasant last weekend spent by a group of New Yorkers whose country holiday ends in various horrid ways, such as by chain-saw, hatpin, rope, impalation, etc. Whodunnit? Cast: Christopher Allport, James Doerr, Marilyn Hamlin, Kathleen Heaner, David Gale, Devin Goldenberg, Jefrey David Pomerantz, William Sanderson. Dir, Pro & Screenplay: David Paulsen. No other credits. (Entertainment Film Distributors.) Rel: 1 February. 76 mins. Cert X.

Scanners
Rather nasty though clever and well directed, macabre thriller which starts off with a bursting head and ends with a duel of wills which results in veins swelling to leaking point and eyes popping out from sockets! About a nutty professor who plans to breed and train an elite of killer-willers so he can take over the earth. Cast: Stephen Lack, Jennifer O'Neill, Patrick McGoohan, Lawrence Dane, Charles Shamata, Adam Ludwig, Michael Ironside, Victor Desy, Mavor Moore, Robert Silverman, Louis del Grande, Lee Broker, Terry Coady, Steve Michael, Malcolm Nelthrope, Don Buchsbaum, Dave Patrick, Neil Affleck, Babs Gadbois, Griff Brewer, Karen Fullerton, Victor Knight, Elijah Siegler, Tom Kovacs, Harriet Stein, Rollie Nincheri, Mikhail Berkut, Danny Silverman, Louis Draper, Bob Peters, Fred Doederlein, Graham Bachelor, Elizabeth Mudry, Jerome Tiberghien, Barry Blake, Sonny Forbes, Lee Murray, Dean Hagopian, Alex Stevens, Danny Hausmann, Ken Umland, Anthony Sherwood, Nick Kilbertus, Kimberly McKeever, Geza Kovacs, Tim Webber, Sam Stone, Domenico Fiore. Dir & Screenplay: David Cronenberg. Pro: Claude Heroux. Ex Pro: Pierre David & Victor Solnicki. Ph: Mark Irwin. Ed: Ron Sanders. Art: Carol Spier. M: No credit. (Filmplan International- New Realm.) Rel: 3 May. 103 mins. Cert X.

The Sea Wolves
Larger-than-life (though based on a quite incredible, true story of World War Two), lavish, exciting and generally well made adventure melodrama telling the story of the extraordinary mission of a group of old-stager members of the Calcutta Light Horse regiment (which had not seen action since the Boer War) recruited by HM Government to carry out the dangerous and delicate mission of sinking a German spy ship interned in neutral Portugal's Goa harbour, where it was sending accurate information about British shipping to the lurking U-boats. A carefully contrived and controlled mixture of thrills, laughs, romance, spectacle and star parade; adding up to splendid entertainment. Cast: Gregory Peck, Roger Moore, David Niven, Trevor Howard, Barbara Kellermann, Patrick Macnee, Patrick Allen, Bernard Archard,

Martin Benson, Faith Brook, Allan Cuthbertson, Kenneth Griffith, Donald Houston, Glyn Houston, Percy Herbert, Patrick Holt, Wolf Kahler, Terence Longdon, Michael Medwin, John Standing, Graham Stark, Jack Watson, Moray Watson, Brook Williams, George Mikell, Jurgen Anderson, Morgan Sheppard, Edward Dentith, Clifford Earl, Victor Langley, Mark Zuber, Robert Hoffmann, Dan Van Husen. Dir: Andrew V. McLaglen. Pro: Euan Lloyd. Ex Pro: Chris Chrisafis. Assoc Pro: Harold Buck. Co Pro: Jorge L. Araneta. Screenplay: Reginald Rose: based on the novel 'The Boarding Party' by James Leasor. Ph: Tony Imi. Ed: John Glen. Pro Des: Syd Cain. Art: Maurice Cain. M: Roy Budd: song 'The Precious Moments' with Richard Addinsell's 'Warsaw Concerto' music, lyrics by Leslie Bricusse, sung by Matt Monro. (Lorimar-Rank.) Rel: 14 September. 120 mins. Cert A.

The Secret Policeman's Ball
Straightforward film record of an Amnesty International charity stage show, with constant cut-ins of shots of an obviously highly amused audience. A mixture of contrasting, and highly variable, words and music with some items good (John Williams with his guitar, Rowan Atkinson's piano recital) and some a lot less! Starring: John Cleese, Peter Cook, Billy Connolly, Michael Palin, Terry Jones, Rowan Atkinson, Eleanor Bron, Pete Townshend, John Williams, Tom Robinson, Clive James, The Ken Campbell Roadshow. Guest appearances by: Anna Ford, Mike Brearley & Clive Jenkins. Stage show dir. by John Cleese. Ph: Clive Tickner, Pascoe Macfarlane, Ernest Vincze, Joe Hidderley, Steve Tickner & Mike Metcalfe. Ed: Thomas Schwalm & Andy Attenburrow. Pro: Roger Graef & Thomas Schwalm. Ex Pro: Peter Walker & Martin Lewis. Dir: Roger Graef. (Amnesty International-Tigon Films.) Rel: 17 August. 95 mins. Cert AA.

Seems Like Old Times
Delightful Neil Simon comedy (written this time especially for the screen rather than a play adaptation to it) which wittily follows the complicated life of pretty lawyer Goldie Hawn when ex-husband and-innocent-suspected bank-robber Chevy Chase turns up asking for succour at a time when her current hubbie Charles Grodin is about to be elected Attorney General of the State of California. Five dogs of assorted size and a kitchen staff of lawbreakers – ex-clients kept out of prison by her employment of them – all add to the fun. Rest of cast: Robert Guillaume, Harold Gould, George Grizzard, Yvonne Wilder, T. K. Carter, Judd Omen, Marc Alaimo, Bill Zuckert, Jerry Houser, David Haskell, Chris Lemmon, Ed Griffith, Joseph Running Fox, Ray Tracey, Fay Hauser, Carolyn Fromson, Sandy Lipton, Herb Armstrong, Natividad Rios Kearsley, Dolores Aguirre, Rosanna Huffman, Edmund Stoiber, Alice Sachs, Ann Cooper, Shirley Anthony, Denise Franc, Roberta Storm, John Moio. Stunt People: Bruce Barbour, Alan Oliney, Roger Creed, Conrad Palmisano, Jim Gavin, Glynn Rubin, Bill Hart, Rick Seaman, Larry Holt, Mike Tillman, Bob Hoy, Richard Washington, Fred Lerner, James Winburn, Sally Mason. Dir: Jay Sandrich. Pro: Ray Stark. Ex Pro: Roger M. Rothstein. Screenplay: Neil Simon. Ph: David M. Walsh. Ed: Michael A. Stevenson. Assoc Pro

& Supervising Ed: Margaret Booth. Pro Des: Gene Callahan. M: Marvin Hamlisch. Art: Pete Smith. (Columbia.) Rel: Floating; first shown London (Warner) February 1981. 102 mins. Cert A.

Une Semaine de Vacances
Delightful, intelligent and delicate comedy, by Bertrand Tavernier, with a serious theme. The story of a dedicated teacher who, indecisive and near breakdown, takes a week off to consider and decide her future. Haunted by a feeling of failure she drifts through the days; visiting her parents in the country; getting comfort from a middle-aged cafe owner (who falls in love with her); examining her relationships with family, friends and unruly pupils – and her lover – finding all the sadness of life but finally emerging with renewed courage. Beautifully acted by Nathalie Baye, Michel Galabru and Philippe Noiret, and others against a haunting background of wintry Lyons. Rest of cast: Flora Fitzgerald, Gérard Lanvin. Dir: Bertrand Tavernier. Screenplay: Bertrand Tavernier, Marie-François Hans, Colo Tavernier. Ex Pro: Louis Grav. Deputy Pro: Alain Sarde. Ph: Pierre William Glenn. Ed: Armand Psenny. Sets: Jean Baptiste Poirot. M: Eddy Mitchell & Pierre Papavermanndies. (Sara/Antenne 2/Little Bear Curzon Films.) Rel: Floating; first shown London (Curzon) August 1980. 100 mins. Cert AA.

The Shining
Stanley Kubrick's venture into the realm of the supernatural thriller with a story about an increasingly crazy caretaker of a large, isolated, snowed-up hotel, who eventually rolls right off his trolley and goes stalking his wife and son with an axe and a murderous intent. A somewhat ambiguous and subtle mixture of good old-fashioned blood-and-thunder and sly innuendo; with the main theme of reincarnation veiled, and a suggestion that all the apparitions may after all be only in the minds of their beholders. Cast: Jack Nicholson, Shelley Duvall, Danny Lloyd, Scatman Crothers, Barry Nelson, Philip Stone, Joe Turkel, Lia Beldam, Billie Gibson, Barry Dennen, David Baxt, Manning Redwood, Lisa Burns, Louise Burns, Alison Coleridge, Kate Phelps, Norman Gay. Dir, Pro & Screenplay (the last with Diane Johnson): Stanley Kubrick; based on the novel by Stephen King. Ex Pro: Jan Harlan. Ph: John Alcott. Ed: Ray Lovejoy. Pro Des: Roy Walker. M: Bela Bartok con. Herbert von Karajan. (The Producer Circle Co/Robert Fryer, Martin Richards & Mary Lea Johnson-Peregrine Films-Hawk Films Ltd-Warner Bros.) Rel: 5 October. 119 mins. Cert X.

Shock – Shock Transfer-Suspence-Hypnos
Small, stylish Italian thriller (made 1977). When seven years after the death of her previous husband the lady returns to the house in which they lived (and he died) strange and bizarre things start to happen until her son finds the ex-hubby's body in the cellar and all becomes explained! Cast: Daria Nicolodi, John Steiner, David Colin Jr., Ivan Rassimov. Dir: Mario Bava. Pro: Juri Vasile. Assoc Pro: Ugo Valenti. Screenplay: Lamerto Bava, Francesco Barbieri, Paolo Brigenti & Dardano Sacchetti. Ph: Alberto Spagnoli. Ed: Roberto Sterbini. Art: Francesco Vanorio. M: I. Libra. (Laser Films-Eagle.) Rel: 17 August. 95 mins. Cert X.

Simon

Amiable little comedy with Alan Arkin as the college professor selected by a scientists' think-tank and brainwashed into imagining he's a visitor from another planet. They then sit back to see what the American public's reaction will be! Rest of cast: Austin Pendleton, Judy Graubart, William Finley, Jayant, Max Wright, Madeline Kahn, Wallace Shawn, Fred Gwynne, Adolphe Green, Keith Szarabajka, Ann Risley, Pierre Epstein, Roy Cooper, Rex Robins, David Warrilow, Hetty Galen, David Gideon, David Susskind, Dick Cavett, Remak Ramsay, Hansford Rowe, Yusef Bulos, Jerry Mayer, Sol Frieder, William Griffis, Frank J. Lucas, George Riddle, Tom Kubiak, Al Cerullo Jr, Barbara Mougin, Paula Gibson, Jim Saxon, Jay Lowman, Barbara Bergen, Bonnie Deroski, Leslie Frances Williams, Ed Karvoski, Richard Bassett, Isam Culver, Stephanie Segal, Mary Donnet, Nikki Kollins, Regina Rodwell, Tina Austin, Jeffrey Bacon, Joan Adams, Michael Earl, Steven Nash, Joyce Adams, Kathryn Cordes, Nick Pippins, Mary Lou Kleinbach, Phil Witt, Rich Murray, Max Goff, Don Stitt, Jenny Gault, Schorling Schneider, Billie Perkins, Elizabeth Wingate, Lisa Maurer. Dir, Story & Screenplay (with Thomas Baum): Marshall Brickman. Pro: Martin Bregman. Ex Pro: Louis A. Stroller. Ph: Adam Holender. Ed: Nine Feinberg. Pro Des: Stuart Wertzel. M: Stanley Silverman, with classical music extracts by Lobos, Mozart, Stravinsky, etc. (Orion Picture-Warner Bros.) Rel: Floating; first shown London (Warner) September 1980. 97 mins. Cert A.

Sir Henry at Rawlinson End

British film of Vivian Stanshall's words-and-music creation which after being serialised on radio, made into a record album and stage play reached the screen at the same time as the book was published. Crazy, often crude, series of incidents impossible to capsulate reasonably into a brief synopsis. With Trevor Howard making more than the best of his leading role. Rest of cast: Patrick Magee, Denise Coffey, J. G. Devlin, Harry Fowler, Sheila Reid, Vivian Stanshall, Suzanne Danielle, Daniel Gerroll, Ben Aris, Liz Smith, Jeremy Child, Susan Porrett, Gary Waldhorn, Simon Jones, Michael Crane, Nicholas McArdle, Toni Palmer, Vernon Dudley, Bowhay Nowell, Talfryn Thomas, Ian McDiarmid, Eiji Kusuhara, Tony Sympson, Jim Cuomo, Peter Moss, Julian Smedley. Dir: Steve Roberts. Assoc Pro & Pro Sup: Peter Smith. Pro: Tony Stratton Smith. Ex Pro: Martin Wesson. Writer/Composer: Vivian Stanshall. Ph: Martin Bell. Pro Des: Alistair Bowtell. Art: Jim Acheson. Ed: Chris Rose. (Charisma Films.) Rel: Floating; first shown London (Paris Pullman) October 1980. 72 mins. Cert AA.

Sitting Ducks

Henry Jaglom – who both wrote and directed this generally slaphappy comedy – overlays on to his often perfunctorily treated plot (about two glaringly diverse amateur crooks who steal a cash fortune from the Mafia boss of one of them and then set off for a safe haven in Costa Rica with two girls whose undercover job it is to kill them and recover the cash) a series of sharply satirical observations and amusing comments on today's sexual and other mores. And there's an amusing return to the plot for the film's unexpected ending. Cast: Michael Emil, Zack Norman, Patrice Townsend, Irene Forrest, Richard Romanus, Henry Jaglom. Dir & Screenplay: Henry Jaglom. Pro: Meira Attia Dor. Ph: Paul Glickman. Ed: No credit. Art: No credit. M: Richard Romanus. (Sunny Side Up Corp-ICA/Contemporary.) Rel: Floating; first shown London (ICA & Paris-Pullman) January 1980. 90 mins. Cert AA.

Skip Tracer

Modest but excellent, award-laden – circa 1977 – Canadian film made for only £61,000 in twenty-two days! A lean, always visual and well observed story about a ruthless, successful young debt collector who is brought to full realisation of what his job is all about when after relentlessly hounding a client the man kills his family and commits suicide. A fine, spare performance by David Peterson. Rest of cast: John Lazarus, Rudy Szabo, Mike Grigg, Al Rose, Sue Astley, Jack Leaf, Mark Acheson. Dir, Screenplay & Ed: Zale Dalen. Pro: Laara Dalen. Ph: Ron Orieux. Art: Elinor Barg. M: J. Douglas Dodd. (Highlight Prods.-Contemporary Films.) Rel: Floating; first shown London (Paris-Pullman) June 1980. 92 mins. Cert AA.

Slow Motion – Sauve Qui Peut (La Vie)

After several years involved with television, Jean-Luc Godard returns to the cinema with a typical, almost incomprehensible celluloid rag-bag of ideas, obsessions, political allusions and whatever – including a long and disgusting sequence in which a prostitute obeys the humiliating demands of her business-man client – presented in a technically wilful way embracing slow and stop motion photography. Swiss/French made. Cast: Isabelle Huppert, Jacques Dutronc, Nathalie Baye, Anna Baldaccini, Cécile Tanner, Paule Muret, Michel Cassaghe, Fred Personne, Roland Amstutz, Catherine Freiburghaus, Serge Maillard, Dore de Rosa. Dir: Jean-Luc Godard. Pro: Alain Sarde & Jean-Luc Godard. Screenplay: Jean-Claude Carrière, Anne-Marie Miéville & Jean-Luc Godard. Ph: William Lubtchansky, Renato Berta & Jean-Bernard Menoud. Ed: Anne-Marie Miéville & Jean-Luc Godard. Art: Romain Goupil. M: Gabriel Yared. (Sara Films/MK2/Saga Production/Sonimage/CNC/ZDF/SSR/ORF-Artificial Eye.) Rel: Floating; first shown London (Camden Plaza) October 1980. 87 mins. Cert X.

Smokey and the Bandit Ride Again

Something very like a re-make of the original *Smokey* success, with the same players in more or less the same routines, leading to one of those now fashionable silly mass car smashes. Sheriff Jackie Gleason chasing 'Bandit' driver Burt Reynolds as he tries to earn the £200 000 fee for delivering an elephant to the Republican Convention in Dallas by opening day. Rest of cast: Sally Field, Jerry Reed, Dom DeLuise, Paul Williams, Pat McCormick, David Huddleston, Mike Henry, John Anderson, Phil Balsley, Lew DeWitt, Don Reid, Harold Reid, Mel Tillis, Don Williams, Terry Bradshaw, 'Mean' Joe Greene, Joe Klecko, Nancy Lenehan, Brenda Lee. Dir: Hal Needham. Pro: Hank Moonjean. Screenplay: Jerry Belson & Brock Yates; story by Michael Kane based on characters created by Hal Needham & Robert L. Levy. Ph: Michael Butler. Ed: Donn Cambern & William Gordean. Art: Bernie Cutler. Pro Des: Henry Bumstead. M: Snuff Garrett. (Rastor/Mort Englebert-Universal-CIC.) Rel: 21 December. 101 mins. Cert AA.

Soldier Girls

A quite remarkable, well polished documentary feature about the basic training of a group of United States Women soldier volunteers under the tuition of a sadistic, moronic Vietnam war veteran sergeant whose excuse for his treatment of the girls is that he lost his 'soul', and all hope of loving or being loved, in that unfortunate business against the Viets! Those taking part include Joann Johnson, Jackie Hall, Clara Alves, Sgt Abing, Sgt Berting and Sgt Taylor. Made by Nick Broomfield & Joan Churchill (on 16mm film). (Contemporary Films.) Rel: Floating; first shown London (Paris-Pullman) June 1981. 87 mins. Cert AA.

Somewhere in Time

Charming, romantic story of a young man who falls in love with a photograph of a girl and travels back through time to find her. All quite beautifully presented, with 'Superman' Christopher Reeve as the determined lover. Rest of cast: Jane Seymour, Christopher Plummer, Teresa Wright, Bill Erwin, George Voskovec, Susan French, John Alvin, Eddra Gale, Audrey Bennett, W. H. Macy, Laurence Coven, Susan Bugg, Christy Michaels, Ali Matheson, George Wendt, Steve Boomer, Patrick Billingsley, Ted Liss, Francis X. Keefe, Taylor Williams, Noreen Walker, Evans Ghiselli, Barbara Giovannini, Don Franklin, David Hull, Paul M. Cook, Victoria Michaels, William P. O'Hagan, Maud Strand, Bo Clausen, James P. Dunnigan, Sean Hayden, Hal Frank, Hayden Jones, Val Bettin, Bruce Jarchow, Ed Meekin, Erin Tomcheff, J. J. Butler, Chukuma, Michael Woods, Jerry Kaufherr. Don Melvoin, Ann K. Irish, Jo Be Cerny, Richard Matheson, Audrie Neenan, Tim Kazurinsky, Bob Swan. Dir: Jeannot Szwarc. Pro: Stephen Deutsch. Assoc Pro: Steven Bickel. Screenplay: Richard Matheson; based on his own novel, *Bid Time Return*. Ph: Isadore Mankofsky. Pro Des: Seymour Klate. Ed: Jeff Gourson. M: John Barry. (Universal/MCA-Rastar/Stephen Deutsch-CIC.) Rel: Floating; first shown London (Ritz) January 1981. 104 mins. Cert A.

Special Treatment – Poseban Tretman

Delightful ironic Yugoslavian comedy, with serious moral undertone, about a hypocritical doctor at a clinic for alcoholics who takes a group of his 'cured' patients to a brewery (where the staff nearly all have a drinking problem) to present an illustrated lecture there but which turns into chaos as while he has been secretly drinking, and seducing a woman secretary, his patients get drunk and drive the audience out of the hall. Superbly directed and acted. Cast: Ljuba Tadic, Milena Dravic, Dusica Zegarac, Danilo Stojkovic, Petar Kralj, Milan Srdoc, Radmila Zivkovic, Boroa Todorovic, Predrag Bijelic. Dir: Goran Paskaljevic. Screenplay: Dusan Kovacevic, in collaboration with Filip David & Goran Paskaljevic. Ph: Aleksander Petrokovic. Ed: Olga Skrigin. Art: Dragoljub Ivkov. M: Vojíslav Kostic. No other credits. (Cental Films, Yugoslavia/Dan Tana Productions, USA-Cinegate.) Rel: Floating; first shown London (Gate, Notting Hill) October 1980. 94 mins. Cert AA.

The Sphinx
Desert sands thriller which gets wilder and unavoidably funnier as it goes along towards its highly melodramatic climax. A story about a fabulous, hitherto unseen tomb, the lethal black market in antiquities which springs from it, and the determinedly enquiring, lovely young lady Egyptologist from America who gets mixed up with the murderous goings-on! Well – sometimes nicely ironically – observed backgrounds of Cairo and Luxor; plenty of thrills; good performances add up to a superior 'fun' film. Cast: Lesley-Anne Down, Frank Langella, Maurice Ronet, John Gielgud, Vic Tablian, Martin Benson, John Rhys-Davies, Nadim Sawalha, Tutte Lemkow, Saeed Jaffrey, Eileen Way, William Hootkins, Mark Kingston, James Cossins, Victoria Tennant, Cengiz Saner, Kevork Malikyan, Ismat Rafat, Yashar Adem, Ahmed Abdel Wareth, Ahmed Hegazi, Abdullah Mahmoud, Mohammed Metwalli, Seif Allah Mokhtar, Behrouz Vossoughi, Abdel Rehiem El Zorkani, Abdel Salem Mohamed. Dir & Ex Pro: Franklin J. Schaffner. Pro: Stanley O'Toole. Screenplay: John Byrum; based on the novel of the same title by Robin Cook. Ph: Ernest Day. Ed: Robert Swink & Michael F. Anderson. Pro Des: Terence Marsh. Supervising Art Dir: Peter Lamont. Art: Gil Parrondo. M: Michael J. Lewis. (Schaffer/O'Toole-Orion-Warner.) Rel: 29 March. 118 mins. Cert AA.

Spiderman – The Dragon's Challenge
Spiderman Nicholas Hammond assigned the task of helping Chinese Minister Benson Fong to track down the former US Marines who will be able to substantiate his claim that he is innocent of the charge that he betrayed his country in the Second World War. And about the villains prepared to murder him if that's the only way they can prevent him from giving the building contract they want to outside contractors! Lots of Hong Kong backgrounds and Kung Fu fights. Rest of cast: Robert F. Simon, Ellen Bry, Chip Fields, Myron Healey, Rosalind Chao, Hagan Beggs, Richard Erdman, Anthony Charnotta, George Cheung, Tony Clark, Ted Danson, Michael Mancini, Robert Mayo, Arnold F. Turner, Herman Tweeder, John Milford, Zara Brierley, W. K. Lam, Peter Wong, Suzanne Vale, Joel Laykin, Hudson Lueng, Michael Chan, Eric Wile. Dir & Screenplay (based on the Marvel Comics character) Don McDougall. Pro: Lionel F. Siegel. Ex Pro: Charles Fries & Daniel R. Goodman. Pro Ex: Malcolm Stuart & W. P. Owens. Ph: Vince Martinelli. Ed: Edwin Dumbrille & Fred Roth. Art: Julian Sacks. M: Dana Kaproff. (Danchuk-Columbia.) Rel: 10 August. 96 mins. Cert U.

Stalker
Extremely complex, leisurely (sometimes almost static) Andrei Tarkovsky film, a sort of symbolic science-fiction tale with endless psychological, sociological and ethical content as it follows the journey of three men – the stalker, or self-appointed guide (Aleksandr Kaidanovsky), the Professor (Nikolai Grinko) and the Writer (Anatoly Solonitsyn) – into the forbidden 'Zone' (in which whole armies have been entirely destroyed) and towards The Room, where wishes come true – but not always in the way anticipated. And all this photographed in a greenish-sepia: outside the Zone all mud and mist and misery, within it a complete windless stillness broken only by the call of a cuckoo. A very strange, absorbing film which asks for intelligence and imagination (and patience!) from the viewer but in return offers limitless possibilities for assumption, argument and wonder. Rest of cast: Alisa Freindlich (as the Stalker's wife). Dir: Andrei Tarkovsky. Screenplay: Arkady & Boris Strugatsky; based on their book 'Roadside Picnic'. Ed: L. Feiginovoi. Ph: Aleksandr Kniazhinsky. Design: Andrei Tarkovsky. M: Eduard Artemiev. Poems by F. I. Tiutchev & Tarkovsky. (Connoisseur/Contemporary.) Rel: Floating; first shown London (Academy) February 1981. 161 mins. Cert A.

Stardust Memories
Intermittently visually and verbally witty, but often sour and somewhat petulant Woody Allen film, in black-and-white, which bites the hand that feeds it by attacking most bitterly the very people who have brought him to his present film fame; critics, adulatory public, and others who come into his orbit. Loosely constructed story which once again somewhat self-indulgently delves into his own experience, artistic agony and hatred of being just a comic! Cast: Woody Allen, Charlotte Rampling, Jessica Harper, Marie-Christine Barrault, Tony Roberts, Daniel Stern, Amy Wright, Helen Hanft, John Rothman, Anne de Salvo, Joan Neuman, Ken Chapin, Leonardo Cimino, Eli Mintz, Bob Maroff, Gabrielle Strasun, David Lipman, Robert Munk, Jaqui Safra, Sharon Stone, Andy Albeck, Robert Friedman, Douglas Ireland, Jack Rollins, Howard Kisell, Max Leavitt, Renee Lippin, Sol Lomita, Irving Metzmah, Dorothy Leon, Roy Brocksmith, Simon Newey, Victoria Zussin, Frances Pole, Bill Anthony, Filomena Spagnuolo, Ruth Rugoff, Martha Whitehead, Judith Roberts & Barry Weiss (singer & dancer of 'Three Little Words'), Robin Ruinsky, Adrian Richards, Dominick Petrolino, Sharon Brous, Michael Zannella, Doris Dugan Slater, Michael Goldstein, Neil Napolitan, Stanley Ackerman, Noel Behn, Candy Loving, Denice Danon, Sally Demay, Tom Dennis, Edward Kotkin, Laura Delano, Lisa Friedman, Brent Spiner, Gardenia Cole, Maurice Shrog, Larry Robert Carr, Brian Zoldessy, Melissa Slade, Paula Raflo, Jordan Derwin, Tony Azito, Marc Murray, Helen Hale, Carl Don, Victoria Page, Bert Michaels, Deborah Johnson, Benjamin Rayson, Mary Mims, Charles Lowe, Marie Lane, Gustave Tassell, Marina Schiano, Dimitri Vassilopoulos, Judith Crist, Carmin Mastrin, Sylvia Davis, Joseph Summo, Victor Truro, Irwin Keyes, Bonnie Hellman, Patrick Daly, Joe Pagano, Wayne Maxwell, Ann Freeman, Bob Miranti, Cindy Gibb, Manuella Machado, Judith Cohen, Madeline Moroff, Maureen P. Levins, E. Brian Dean, Marvin Peisner, Robert Tennenhouse, Leslie Smith, Samuel Chodorov, Philip Lenkowsky, Vanina Hosasek, Michel Touchard, Kenny Vance, Iryn Steinfink, Frank Modell, Anne Korzen, Eric Van Valkenburg, Susan Ginsburg, Ostaro, Wade Barnes, Gabriel Barre, Charlie Riggs III, Geoffrey Riggs, Martha Sherrill, Ann Risley, Jade Bari, Marc Geller, Daniel Friedman, James Otis, Judy Goldner, Rebecca Wright, Perry Gewertz, Larry Fishman, Liz Albrecht, Sloane Bosniak, James Harter, Henry House, Largo Woodruff, Jerry Tov Greenberg, Mohammed Nabi Kiani, Alice Spivak, Armin Shimerman, Edith Grossman, Jacqueline French, John Doumanian, Jack Hollander. Dir & Screenplay: Woody Allen. Pro: Robert Greenhut. Ex Pro: Jack Rollins & Charles H. Joffe. Ph: Gordon Willis. Ed: Susan E. Morse. Pro Des: Mel Bourne. Art: Michael Molly. (UA.) Rel: 8 March. 89 mins. Black-and-white. Cert AA.

Stir Crazy
And a pretty crazy, four-letter-word proliferating, gag-strewn comedy, built on the fun rapport of the two stars, Gene Wilder and Richard Pryor; in a story about their conviction to 120-year sentences in 'stir' (or jail) for a hold-up committed by two other characters. And about their subsequent – needless as it transpires – prison break-out. Rest of cast: Georg Stanford Brown, Jobeth Williams, Miguelangel Suarez, Craig T. Nelson, Barry Corbin, Charles Weldon, Nicholas Coster, Joel Brooks, Jonathan Banks, Erland Van Lidth de Jeude, Lewis Van Bergen, Lee Purcell, Karmin Murcelo, Franklyn Ajaye, Estelle Omens, Peter Looney, Cedrick Hardman, Doug Johnson, Henry Kingi, Joseph Massendale, Herman Poppe, Luis Avalos, Esther Sunderland, Pamela Poitier, James Lee Oscar, Rod McCary, Claudia Cron, Bill Bailey, Donna Benz, Grand Bush, Alvin Ing, Thomas Moore, Danna Hansen, Gwen Van Dam, Herb Armstrong, Herbert Hirschman, Don Circle, Madison Arnold, Gene Earle, Tracey Lee Rowe, Essex Smith, Kenneth Menard, Billy Beck, John Ashby, Kerrie Cullen, Chuck Henson, Larry McKinney, Stoney Neufang Jr., Scott Raftery, Gene Walker. Dir: Sidney Poitier. Pro: Hannah Weinstein. Ex Pro: Melville Tucker. Assoc Pro: Francoise de Menil. Screenplay: Bruce Jay Friedman. Ph: Fred Schuler. Ed: Harry Keller. Pro Des: Alfred Sweeney. M: Tom Scott; songs sung by ('Crazy') Gene Wilder, ('Eat Your Heart Out') Leata Galloway, ('Love') Randy Goodrum, ('The Love of a Cowboy') Mary Gregory, ('Watch Her Dance') Leroy Gomez, and ('Nothing's Going To Stop Us Now') Kiki Dee. (Columbia.) Rel: 29 March. 111 mins. Cert AA.

The Stunt Man
Slightly uneven, intermittently brilliant and consistently entertaining Richard Rush movie which in the course of taking a satirical look behind the camera and what goes on there during the making of a movie, produces a marvellously subtle portrait in depth of an almost maniacally egotistical, devious director – a role played with great delight and to marvellous effect by Peter O'Toole. It is he who shelters a young criminal on the run in return for the fugitive's acceptance of replacing the director's No. 1 stuntman, who has tried one stunt too many. Rest of cast: Steve Railsback, Barbara Hershey, Allen Goorwitz, Alex Rocco, Sharon Farrell, Adam Roarke, Philip Bruns, Chuck Bail, John Garwood, Jim Hess, John B. Pearce, Michael Railsback, George D. Wallace, Dee Carroll, Leslie Winograde, Don Kennedy, Whitey Hughes, Walter Robles, A. J. Bakunas, Gregg Berger, Ross Reynolds, Robert Caruso, Frank Avila, Stafford Morgan, John Alderman, James Avery, Leigh Webb, Frank Beetson,

Jack Palinkas, Garrett McPherson, Nelson Tyler, Larry Dunn, Deanna Dae Colman, Louie Gartner, Gordon Ross, Marion Wayne, William Joseph Arno. Stuntmen: Phil Adams, Whitey Hughes, A. J. Bakanus, Gray Johnson, Greg Barnett, John Michael Johnson, Gary Baxley, Alton Leo Jones, Norm Blankenship, Tom Morga, Hank Calia, Reggie Parten, Eric Cord, Don Pulford, Ted Duncan, Walter Robles, Larry Dunn, Dick Warlock, Kenny Endoso, James B. Winborn (Stunt Co-ordinator: Gray Johnson). Also Ross Reynolds, Jim Appleby, Wayne Berg, John Kazian, Dean Westgaard. Dir & Pro: Richard Rush; who also adapted the Paul Brodeur novel on which the screenplay by Lawrence B. Marcus is based. Ex Pro: Melvin Simon. Assoc Pro: Paul Lewis. Ph: Mario Tosi. Ed: Jack Hofstra & Caroline Perriol. Art: James Schoppe. M: Dominic Frontiere (Song: 'Bits & Pieces'; music by Frontiere, lyrics by Norman Gimbel, sung by Dusty Springfield). (Melvin Simon Productions-Fox.) Rel: 15 February. 131 mins. Cert X.

Sunday Daughters – Vasárnapi Szülök
Hungarian film about a sixteen-year-old delinquent who is always breaking out of her reformatory to re-join members of her family, from whom she receives short shrift when she turns up. Her few small moments of happiness are always followed by retribution, but she goes on trying . . . Cast: Julianna Nyakó, Melinda Szakács, Julianna Balogh, Andrea Blizik, Erzsi Pásztor, Ági Kakasi, Sergei Elistratov. Dir: János Rózsa. Screenplay: Istvan Kardos. Ph: Elemér Ragályi. M: Levente Szörényi – The Fonográf Group. (Objektiv Studio, Budapest/Hungarofilm-Cinegate.) Rel: Floating; first shown London (Gate 2) April 1981. 100 mins. Cert AA.

Superman II
Very much a continuation of the comic-strip character's adventures started in *Superman* No. 1 (and promised to extend into No. 3) with Christopher Reeve as the all-powerful hero occasionally emerging, in times of great stress, from his normal shy journalist shell. On this occasion he is called upon to confront three nasty characters who arrive from outer space and decide to take up residence in – and in fact take over – the earth. With their personal flight powers, laser-beam eyes and hands that casually brush aside shot, shell and flame, they seem likely to achieve their aims – until Superman takes them on with their own weapons. Still good fun if now lacking the spectacular novelty impact of the original. Rest of cast: Gene Hackman, Ned Beatty, Jackie Cooper, Sarah Douglas, Margot Kidder, Jack O'Halloran, Valerie Perrine, Susannah York, Clifton James, E. G. Marshall, Marc McClure, Terence Stamp, Leueen Willoughby, Robin Pappas, Roger Kemp, Roger Brierley, Anthony Milner, Richard Griffiths, Melissa Wiltsie, Alain Dehay, Marc Boyle, Alan Stuart, John Ratzenberger, Shane Rimmer, John Morton, Jim Dowdell, Angus McInnes, Anthony Sher, Elva May Hoover, Hadley Kay, Todd Woodcroft, John Hollis, Gordon Rollings, Peter Whitman, Bill Bailey, Dinny Powell, Hal Galili, Marcus D'Amico, Richard Parmentier, Don Fellows, Michael Shannon, Tony Sibbald, Tommy Duggan, Pamela Mandell, Peter Martin, Eugene Lipinski, Cleon Spencer, Carl Parris. Dir: Richard Lester. Pro: Pierre Spengler. Ex Pro: Ilya

Salkind. Screenplay: Mario Puzo, David & Leslie Newman; from Puzo's story. Ph: Geoffrey Unsworth. Ed: John Victor-Smith. Pro Des: John Barry & Peter Murton. M: Ken Thorne; from original material comp. by John Williams. Ph Dir: Bob Paynter. Miniature Photography Dir: Paul Wilson. Superman created by Jerry Siegel & Joe Shuster. (International Films Pro Inc/Alexander Salkind-Alexander & Ilya Salkind Pro-Warner.) Rel: 12 April. 127 mins. Cert A.

Terror
Macabre little thriller with lots of violent deaths, a bevy of suspects and an eerie solution. Cast: John Nolan, Carolyn Courage, James Aubrey, Sarah Keller, Tricia Walsh, Glynis Barber, Rosie Collins, Michael Craze. Dir: Norman J. Warren. Pro: Les Young & Richard Crafter. Assoc Pro: Moira Young. Screenplay: David McGillivray. M: Ivor Slaney. No Art or Ed credits. (Entertainment Film Distributors Ltd.) Rel: 1 February. 84 mins. Cert X.

Terror Train
Routine thriller about a psycho transsexual killer loose on a steam train hired for a special party by a group of college students all dressed up in various disguises, making it easier for the killer to pick off his victims undetected! Cast: Ben Johnson, Jamie Lee Curtis, Hart Bochner, David Copperfield, Derek Mackinnon, Sandee Currie, Timothy Webber, Anthony Sherwood, Howard Busgang, Steve Michaels, Greg Swanson, D. D. Winters, Joy Boushel, Victor Knight, Don Lamoureux, Charles Biddles Sr., Elizabeth Cholette, Thomas Haverstock, Peter Feingold, Richard Weinstein, John Busby, Roland Nincheri, Andrea Kenyon, Elaine Lakeman, Gerald Eastman, Charles Biddles Jr., Nadia Rona; The Band: Larry Cohen, Brenda Gagnier, Phil Albert. Dir: Roger Spottiswoode. Pro: Harold Greenberg. Ex Pro: Lamar Card. Screenplay: T. Y. Drake. Ph: John Alcott. Ed: Anne Henderson. Pro Des: Glenn Bydwell. M: John Mills-Cockle. Pro Ex: Don Carmody. (Triple T-Fox.) Rel: 23 November. 97 mins. Cert X.

Tess
Roman Polanski's hybrid but remarkably effective adaptation to the screen of Thomas Hardy's strongest and, at its time, most controversial novel *Tess of the d'Urbervilles*, with its typical Hardy theme of the inevitability of fate and the story about the unfortunate young girl who is seduced and 'ruined' by the rich young milord, is subsequently rejected by the husband she loves, and has to pay with her life for the few stolen hours of happiness she enjoys in an otherwise totally unsatisfactory life – thanks largely to the Victorian code of morals which Hardy so bitterly attacked in the book. Long, leisurely, but stunning in visual impact (the film won 1981 art direction, costume and cinematography Oscars) while strongly capturing the spirit and atmosphere of the novel. Cast: Nastassia Kinski, Peter Firth, Leigh Lawson, John Colin, Tony Church, Brigid Erin Bates, Jeanne Biras, John Bett, Tom Chadbon, Rosemary Martin, Geraldine Arzul, Stephane Treille, Elodie Warnod, Ben Reeks, Jack Stephens, Lesley Dunlop, Marilyne Even, Jean-Jacques Daubin, Sylvia Coleridge, Jacob Weisbluth, Peter Benson, Jacques

Mathou, Veronique Alain, Richard Pearson, Fred Bryant, John Barrett, Ann Tirard, Carolyn Pickles, Suzanna Hamilton, Caroline Embling, Josine Comellas, Arielle Dombasle, David Markham, Pascale de Boysson, Gordon Richardson, Patsy Smart, Dicken Ashworth, Jimmy Gardner, Reg Dent, John Gill, Forbes Collins, Keith Buckley, John Moore, Patsy Rowlands, Lina Roxa, Graham Weston. Dir: Roman Polanski. Pro: Claude Berri. Co-Pro: Timothy Burrill. Assoc Pro: Jean-Pierre Rassam. Ex Pro: Pierre Grunstein. Screenplay: Gerard Brach, Roman Polanski & John Brownjohn; based on the Thomas Hardy novel *Tess of the d'Urbervilles*. Ph: Geoffrey Unsworth & Ghislain Cloquet. Ed: Alastair McIntyre & Tom Priestley. Pro Des: Pierre Guffroy. Art: Jack Stephens. Costume Des: Anthony Powell. M: Philippe Sarde. (Renn Productions, France/Burrill Productions, England-Societe Francaise de Production-Columbia.) Rel: 31 May. 171 mins. Cert A.

The Third Generation – Die Dritte Generation
Fassbinder (West German) film which satirises terrorism (and outrageously suggests it is a necessary ingredient of the modern State), taking the opportunity of poking fun at the bourgeois left-wingers. Cast: Volker Spengler, Bulle Ogier, Hanna Schygulla, Harry Baer, Vitus Zeplichal, Udo Kier, Margit Carstensen, Gunther Kaufman, Eddie Constantine, Raul Gimenez, Y Sa Lo, Hark Bohm, Claus Holm, Lilo Pempeit, Jurgen Draeger. Dir: Pro & Screenplay: Rainer Werner Fassbinder. Ph: Hans Gunther Bucking & Fassbinder. Ed: Juliane Lorenz. Art: Raul Gimenez. M: Peer Raben. (Tango Films, Berlin/Pro-ject Filmprodukteion/Filmverlag der Autorem-Cinegate.) Rel: Floating; first shown London. 111 mins. Cert X.

Times Square
Youth-aimed story of two teenage girl rebels – one a sleazy sixteen-year-old slut from the slums, the other a wealthy politician's daughter – who join forces to poke a joint snoot at Society. The moral values may be a bit confused, and the four-letter word proliferation may be inexcusable, but the girls themselves, both newcomers, are brilliant enough to suggest they are bound for the starry top: Trini Alvarado and Robin Johnson as 'The Sleaze Sisters'. The film, with its many rock/pop numbers soundtrack, was made on location in or around the Square. Rest of cast: Tim Curry, Peter Coffield, Herbert Berghof, David Margulies, Anna Maria Horsford, Michel Margotta, J. C. Quinn, Miguel Pinero, Ronald 'Smokey' Stevens, Billy Mernit, Paul Sass, Arti Weinstein, Tim Choate, Elizabeth Pena, Kathy Lojac, Susan Merson, George Morfogen, Charles Blackwell, Bill Anagnos, Tammas J. Hamilton, Franklyn Scott, Jane Solar, Victoria Vanderkloot, Steve W. James, Jay Acovone, Alice Spivak, Calvin Ander, Peter Lacangelo, Michael Riney, Louis Belero, Gerald Kline, Ben Slack, Aaron Hurst, Sean Hust, Peter Lopiccolo, Roger Camcaho, Steve Pabon, Daniele Tiletnick, Donna Sirota, Tulane Howard 11, Karen Evans, Rodi Alexander, Ramon Franco, Riki Colon, Melanie Henderson, Larry Silvestri, Paul Naples, Mandy Cameron, Scott P. Sanders, Tiger Haynes, Cammi Lynn Buttner, Sarah Dougherty, Amy Gabriel, Sandra Lee Goga, Pamela Gotlin, Shuna Lydon, Kelly

McClory, Marlena Seda. Dir: Alan Moyle. Pro: Robert Stigwood & Jacob Brackman. Ex Pro: Kevin McCormick & John Nicolella. Screenplay: Jacob Brackman; from a story by Alan Moyle & Leanne Unger. Assoc Pro: Bill Oakes. Ph: James A. Contner. Ed: Tom Priestley. No Art credit. Groups and musical performers: Suzi Quatro, The Pretenders, Roxy Music, The Cars, Gary Numan, Marcy Levy & Robin Gibb, Talking Heads, Joe Jackson, XTC, The Ramones, Robin Johnson & Trini Alvarado, The Ruts, D. L. Byron, Lou Reed, Desmond Child & Rouge, Garland Jeffreys, The Cure, Patti Smith, David Johansen & Robin Johnson, Blue Weaver. (RSO-EMI.) Rel: 18 January. 111 mins. Cert AA.

A Touch of Zen
1969 Hong-Kong/Taiwan production telling a story of romance and adventure – introducing a considerable amount of martial arts exposition – during the Ming (AD 1368 – 1644) dynasty. Cast: Hsu Feng Shih Chun, Pai Ying, Hseuh Han Roy Chiad, Chang Ping-Yu, Han Ying-Chieh, Tien Peng, Miad Tien, Chia Lu-Shih, Tsao Chien, Wang Jui, Men Chu-Hua, Chang Yun-Wen, Liu Chu, Chen Shi-Wei, Tu Wei-Ho. Dir Ed & Screenplay: King Hu; based on the story 'The Magnanimous Girl' by Pu Sung-Ling. Pro: Sha Jung-Feng. Ph: Hua Hui-Ying & Chou Yeh-Hsing. Art: King Hu. M: Ng Tai-Kong. (Union Film Co, Taipei-International Film Co-Osiris Films.) Rel: Floating; first shown London (Gate 2) July 1980. 175 mins. Cert AA.

Tribute
Another magnificent performance by Jack Lemmon in the screen adaptation of his big stage success, playing a Broadway press agent whose laughing life style has won him legions of friends, but lost him his wife and estranged him from his more serious son, gets a terrible jolt when he is told a blood disorder means death in a few weeks, or months, or, just possibly, years. A wittily wise-cracking comedy which when the mask cracks and the tears rivulet it, becomes a moving human drama, climaxed by one marvellous scene of revealment shared by Lemmon and Lee Remick as his wonderfully serene ex-wife. Rest of cast: Bobby Benson, Colleen Dewhurst, John Marley, Kim Cattrall, Gale Garnett, Teri Keane, Rummy Bishop, John Dee, Bob Windsor, Eileen Lehman, Andrew Foot, Trevor Daley, Sid Smith, Jennifer Goldie, Bill McMann, Gaylyn Britton, Peter Peers, Ron Marino, Tony Powers, Bob Scarantino, Michael Monet. Dir: Bob Clark. Pro: Joel B. Michaels & Garth H. Drabinsky. Ex Pro: The Turman-Foster Company & Richard S. Bright. Assoc Pro: Hannah Hempstead. Screenplay: Bernard Slade; based on his own stage play. Ph: Reginald H. Morris. Ed: Richard Halsey. Pro Des: Trevor Williams. Art: Reuben Freed. M: Kenn Wannberg (Song: 'We still have time', words by Jack Feldman & Bruce Sussman, music by Barry Manilow – who also sings it: 'It's all for the best', words & music by Jack Lemmon & Alan Jay Lerner). (Kudos-Paramount-Fox.) Rel: 1 March. 125 mins. Cert AA.

Union City
Neat little thriller with something of a Poe-ish touch: about a man who traps and kills – it appears – the tramp who steals his morning milk, in a panic hides the body in the adjoining apartment, and then waits in mental agony for the inevitable moment when his crime will be discovered. Co-stars are fine Shakespearean actor Dennis Lipscomb and former pop group star Blondie, Deborah Harry, here making her acting debut. Rest of cast: Irina Maleeva, Everett McGill, Sam McMurray, Terina Lewis, Pat Benatar, Tony Azito, Paul Andor, Taylor Mead, Cynthia Crisp, Charles Rydell. Dir & Screenplay (based on the story *The Corpse Next Door* by Cornell Woolrich): Mark Reichert. Pro: Graham Belin. Assoc Pro: Ron Mutz. Ph: Edward Lachman. Art: George Stavrinos. M: Chris Stein. (Mainline Pictures.) Rel: Floating; first shown London (Cinecenta) April 1981. 90 mins. Cert A.

Urban Cowboy
John Travolta as the Texas farm boy who comes to town (Houston) for the big money, hopefully from the petrol business, meets girl, marries girl, loses girl and finally learns his lesson. A quite pleasing performance, plenty of rowdy backgrounds and country-and-western musical interludes. Rest of cast: Debra Winger, Scott Glenn, Madolyn Smith, Barry Corbin, Brooke Alderson, Cooper Huckabee, James Gammon, Mickey Gilley, Johnny Lee, Bonnie Raitt, The Charlie Daniels Band, Betty Murphy, Ed Geldart, Leah Geldart, Keith Clemons, Howard Norman, Sheryl Briedel, Sean Lawler, Gator Conley, Minnie Elerick, David Ogle, Bret Williams, Tamara Matuesian, Becky Cinway, Sherwood Cryer, Jerry Hall, Cyndy Hall, Lucky Mosley, Zetta Ranay, Ellen March, Gina Alexander, Steve Chambers, Anne Travolta, Anson Downs, W. P. Wright 111, Steve Strange, Norman Tucker, Debie Tucker, Jessie La Rive, Bettye Fitzpatrick, Jim Gough, Connie Hanson, Glenn Hlotzman, Christopher Saylors, Daniel Heintschel Jr., Ben F. Brannon 3rd. Dir: James Bridges. Pro: Robert Evans & Irving Azoff. Ex Pro: C. O. Erickson. Screenplay: James Bridges & Aaron Latham, from the latter's story. Ph: Ray Villalobos. Ed: Dave Rawlins. Pro Des: Stephen Grimes. Music Co-ordinator: Betty Shargo; score adapted by Ralph Burns. Art: Stewart Campbell. (Paramount-CIC.) Rel: 14 September. 135 mins. Cert AA.

The Valiant Ones
(Original title: *Chung-Lieh Tu*).
King Hu film made in Hong Kong in 1974, with Mandarin Chinese dialogue; a very superior Martial Arts movie about the struggle of a loyal band of the Emperor's soldiers trying to smash the Japanese/Chinese gangs of pirates devastating the coastal villages of the Kwangtung Province during the early years of the Ming Dynasty. Beautifully photographed and stylised balletic (and bloodless!) sequences of armed and unarmed conflict between goodies and baddies, all quite captivating, and sometimes lightly amusing. Cast: Roy Chiao, Pai Ying, Hsu Feng, Chao Lei, Tu Kunang-Chi, Chu Yuan-Lung, Han Yang-Chieh, Yuen Hsiao-Tien, Hao Lu-Jen, Wu Chia-Hsiang, Li Wen-Tai, Wu Ming-Tsai, Tao Wei, Liu Chiang. Dir & Screenplay: King Hu (whose Chinese name is Hu Chin-Chuan). Ph: Chen Ching-Chu. Ed: Hsiao Nan & King Hu. Art: King Hu. M: Wan Chung-Tung. Martial Arts Choreographers: Chu Yuan-Lung & Han Ying-Chieh. (King Hu Film Productions-Osiris Films.) Rel: Floating; first shown London (Gate 2) August 1980. 105 mins. Cert AA.

When a Stranger Calls
Somewhat superior if slightly meandering thriller about an escaped insane murderer who having terrified a baby-sitter and killed her two small charges, after a seven year lapse threatens the now married baby-sitter's own two children. Restraint, balance and good character drawing all help to lift the movie out of the blood-and-guts rut. Cast: Charles Durning, Carol Kane, Colleen Dewhurst, Tony Beckley, Rachel Roberts, Ron O'Neal, Steven Anderson, Rutanya Alda, Carmen Argenziano, Kirsten Larkin, Bill Boyett, Heetu, Michael Champion, Joe Reale, Ed Wright, Louise Wright, Carol O'Neal, Dennis McMullen, Wally Taylor, John Tobyansen, Sarah Dammann, Richard Bail, Lenora May, Randy Holland, Trent Dolan, Frank Di Elsi, Arell Blanton, De Forest Covan, Charles Boswell. Dir: Fred Walton. Pro: Doug Chapin & Steve Feke. Ex Pro: Melvin Simon & Barry Krost. Screenplay: Steve Feke & Fred Walton. Ph: Don Peterman. Ed: Sam Vitale. Pro Des: Elayne Barbara Ceder. M: Dana Kaproff. Assoc Pro: Larry Kostroff. (Melvin Simon-UA) Rel: 7 December. 97 mins. Cert AA.

When You Comin' Back Red Ryder
Psychological thriller set against a background of a snack-bar-restaurant in a lonely part of New Mexico and the storm of mental and physical violence that occurs there one Sunday when a manic arrival (with a load of cocaine in his parked van) begins to go to vicious work on the cafe's other customers. Cast: Marjoe Gortner, Hal Linden, Peter Firth, Lee Grant, Pat Hingle, Bill McKinney, Audra Lindley, Stephanie Feracy, Candy Clark. Dir: Milton Katselas. Pro: Marjoe Gortner. Ex Pro: Melvin Simon. Co-Pro: Paul Maslansky. Screenplay: Mark Medoff – based on his own stage play. Ph: Jules Brenner. Ed: Richard Chew. No Art credit. M: Jack Nitzsche (song 'No One Knows Better Than You' written by Nitzsche & Alan Gordon, sung by Tammy Wynette & Freddy Fander). (Barber International.) Rel: 22 March. 92 mins. Cert X.

Wholly Moses!
Following on the British, 'Monty Python' effort in this direction, the Americans have some fun with the Bible stories, with Dudley Moore writing the Ten Commandments for Moses to bring down the mountains . . . Rest of cast: Laraine Newman, James Coco, Paul Sand, Jack Gilford, Dom DeLuise, John Houseman, Madeline Kahn, David L. Lander, Richard Pryor, John Ritter, Richard B. Shull, Tanya Boyd, William Watson, Sam Weisman, Jeffrey Jacquet, Howard Mann, Charles Thomas Murphy, Hap Lawrence, David Murphy, Tom Baker, Andrea Martin, Stan Ross, Sandy Ward, Lee Wilkof, Maryedith Burrell, Ruth Manning, Rod McCary, Brion James, Lois Robbins, Shelley Johnson, Michael Champion, Lauren Frost, Ion Teodorescu, Nick Mele, Danny Goldman, Larry Gelman, Alexander Lockwood, Walker Edmiston. Stunt Persons: Richard Drown, Bob Bass, May Boss, Victor Paul, Bob Terhune, Steve Boyum, Jim Burk, Bennie Moore, Richard Butler, Steve Chambers, Gilbert Combs, Andy

Epper, Loren Janes, Wayne King, John L. Meier, Walter Wyatt. Dir: Gary Weis. Pro: Freddie Fields. Ex Pro: David Begelman. Screenplay: Guy Thomas. Ph: Frank Stanley. Ed: Sidney Levin. Pro Des: Dale Hennesy. M: Patrick Williams. (Columbia.) Rel: 2 November. 103 mins. Cert AA.

The Wildcats of St Trinians
Fifth in the series of British comedy films based on the little hockey-stick horrors originally created by artist-cartoonist Ronald Searle. And not exactly the funniest of the five in spite of lovely character cameos by Thorley Walters, Michael Hordern & Julia McKenzie. Rest of cast: Sheila Hancock, Joe Melia, Rodney Bewes, Maureen Lipman, Luan Peters, Deborah Norton, Ambrosine Phillpotts, Rose Hill, Diana King, Barbara Hicks, Rosalind Knight, Patsy Smart, Bernadette O'Farrell, Sandra Payne, Francis Ruffell, Hilda Braid, Hilda Gridley, Veronica Quilligan, Miranda Honnisett, Eileen Fletcher, Anna Mackeown, Sarah Jane Varley, Theresa Ratcliff, Lisa Vanderpump, Debbie Linden, Sandra Hall, Eliza Emery, Suzanna Hamilton, Danielle Corgan, Nicholas McArdle, Eric Kent, Ballard Berkeley, Melita Clarke, Sarah Lam, Tony Wredden, Jeremy Pearce, Matthew Smith, Jason Anthony, Alfie Curtis. Dir & Screenplay: Frank Launder. Pro: E. M. Smedley-Aston. Pro Consultant: Sidney Gilliat. Ph: Ernest Steward. Ed: Tony Gibbs. Art: John Beard. M: James Kenelm Clarke. (Wildcart-Enterprise Pictures.) Rel: 21 December. 92 mins. Cert A.

Willie and Phil
Another variation on the *Jules et Jim* situation, set in modern America, where a girl from Kentucky, a high school teacher of English and a Jewish movie cameraman love and are loved in a confused triangle of emotional relationships which ends, inevitably, in growing up and breaking up. Not anything like as charming as the gallic original, but with a certain subdued charm, humour and reasonably appealing performances, by Margot Kidder, Michael Ontkean and Ray Sharkey. Rest of cast: Jan Miner, Tom Brennan, Julie Bovasso, Louis Guss, Kathleen Maguire, Kaki Hunter, Kristine DeBell, Alison Cass Shurpin, Christine Varnai, Laurence Fishburne III, Walter N. Lowery, Jerry Hall, Helen Hanft, Sol Frieder, Ed Van Nuys, Jill Mazursky, Donald Muhich, Anne E. Wile, Hubert J. Edwards, Allen C. Dawson, Alvin Alexis, Robert Townsend, Cynthia McPherson, Karen Montgomery, Tom Noonan, Ginny Ortix, Lionel Pina Jr, Louis Cappeto, Karen Ford, Stephan Hart, Kitty Muldoon, Eivand Harum, Nikolas K. Irizarry, Madeline Moroff, R. M. Wexler, Mary-Pat Green, Natalie Wood. Dir & Screenplay: Paul Mazursky. Pro: Paul Mazursky & Tony Ray. Ph: Sven Nykvist. Ed: Donn Cambern. Pro Des: Pato Guzman. M: Claude Bolling. (Fox.) Rel: Floating; first shown London (Odeon, Kensington) February 1981. 116 mins. Cert X.

The Wishing Tree – Drevo Zhelanya
Classical Georgian-Russian film (made 1976) about life in a small village at the turn of the century, observed with gentle irony at first, as it surveys the local eccentrics, but turning to increasing bitterness as it follows the human sacrifice tradition demands, and gets, when a young wife, married to a man she did not want, is found in the arms of her returned, original lover. Cast: Lika Kavzharadze, Soso Dzhachvliani, Zaza Kolelishvili, Kote Daushvili, Sopiko Chiaureli, Kahi Kavsadze, Erosi Mandzhgaladze, Otar Meghvinetuhutsesi, Ramaz Ch'hikvadze, Giorgi Gegechkori, Sesilia Tagaishvili, Giorgi Hobua, Dzemal Ghaghashidze, Boris Tsipuria, Ia Hobua, Mzia Mahviladze, Temina Kuaeva, Dato Abashidze, Tina Burbutashvili, Shota S'hirtladze. Dir: Tengiz Abuladze. Screenplay: Revaz Inanishvili & Tengiz Abuladze; based on the stories of Giorgi Leonidze. Ph: Lomer Ahvlediani. Ed: Gulnara Omadze, Revaz Mirzashvili. Art: M. Kartvelishivili, Dzh. Abuashvili. M: Bidzina Kvernadze & Yakov Bobohidze. No Pro. credit. (Grusiafilm, Tbilisi-Artificial Eye.) Rel: Floating; first shown London (Camden Plaza) August 1980. 105 mins. Cert A.

*The Wobblies
American feature documentary about the IWW (Industrial Workers of the World), one of the country's first trade unions, which, founded in 1905, more or less ceased to exist during the first World War. Dir & Pro: Stewart Bird & Deborah Shaffer. Narrated by Roger Baldwin. (The Other Cinema.) Rel: Floating; first shown London (ICA) June 1980. 89 mins. No cert.

Xanadu
Olivia Newton-John (in her second movie) as a Greek Goddess who comes down to earth to fulfil the dreams of young and restless record-album-cover artist Michael Beck, and older and frustrated business man Gene Kelly, who longs for the old days when he had his own band in a night club. Mild little musical. Rest of cast: James Sloyan, Dmitria Arliss, Katie Hanley, Fred McCarren, Ron Woods, Sandahl Bergman, Lynn Latham, Melinda Phelps, Cherise Bate, Juliette Marshall, Marilyn Rokuda, Yvette Van Voorhees, Teri Beekerman, Marty Davis, Bebe Drake-Massey, Mickey McMeel, Aharon Ipale, Lise Lang, Melvin Jones, Matt Lattanzi, Ira Newborn, Jo Ann Harris, Cindy Leake, Patty Keene, John 'Fee' Waybill, Stephen Pearlman, Church Ortiz, Randy T. Williams, David Tress, Madison Arnold, Wilfred Hyde-White, Coral Browne, Maria V. Langston and the Xanadu Dancers. Dir: Robert Greenwald. Pro: Larence Gordon & Joel Silver. Ex Pro: Lee Kramer. Assoc Pro: Terry Nelson. Screenplay: Richard Christian Danus & Marc Reid Rubel. Ph: Victor J. Kemper. Ed: Dennis Virkler. Assoc Ed: Tina Hirsch. Pro Des: John W. Corso. M: Barry DeVorzon. (Universal-CIC.) Rel: 12 October. 96 mins. Cert A.

*Zombies – Dawn of the Dead
Repellently bloody thriller which beneath all the desperate efforts to shock (cannibalism in close-up) has quite a nice sense of suspense and a real ability to show fast action. Caused by 'molecular mutation', the recent dead reel out of their graves and – looking remarkably tidy – go searching somewhat haphazardly for the living bodies which offer them their only means of sustenance. And they take over the lower floors of the supermarket where a quartet of human survivors are holed-up hoping for some solution to their life-and-death problem to turn up. Cast: David Emge, Ken Foree, Scott Reiniger, Gaylen Ross, David Crawford, David Early, Richard France, Howard Smith, Daniel Dietrich, Fred Baker, Jim Baffico, Rod Stouffer, Jese del Gre, Clayton McKinnon, John Rice, Ted Bank, Randy Kovitz, Patrick McCloskey, Joe Pilato, Pasquale Buba, Tom Savini, Tony Buba, Marty Schiff, 'Butchie', Joe Shelby, Dave Hawkins, Taso Stravrakis, Tom Kapusta, Nick Tallo, Rudy Ricci, Larry Vaira, Sharon Ceceatti, Pam Chatfield, Bill Christopher, Clayton Hill, Jay Stover, George Romero. Dir Ed & Screenplay: George A. Romero. Pro: Richard P. Rubinstein. Ph: Michael Gornick. Set Decor: Josie Caruso, & Barbara Lifsher. M: The Goblins & Dario Argento. (Laurel Group Productions for Dawn Associates-Target International.) Rel: 29 June 1980. 127 mins. Cert X.

The Children's Film Foundation

The somewhat gloomy forebodings I expressed in this feature last year have proved all too sadly real. With only one new production completed during the year – as against the more than usual half-dozen or even more – and with not much hope of any further finance for the future, things look very black indeed for the Children's Film Foundation.

After all the marvellous work the Foundation has done in the past, producing grand little movies on very modest budgets; usefully employing a lot of technicians and players; and giving chances to newcomers in both fields, the present situation is a tragedy. I can only hope that even at this late hour something turns up to secure in some way or another the future of one of Britain's less well known but consistently high class producers of essentially British movies. The one new film was called *4D Special Agents* and full details of it are as follows.

4D Special Agents
Thriller about a group of children who become suspicious of a small cruiser in a disused dockland area and investigate; leading to a kidnapping of one of the kids and a chase down the river after the fleeing crooks. Cast: Lisa East, Dexter Fletcher, Sarah Jenkins, Paul Medford, Philip Cook, Soice (the dog), Bryan Marshall, James Coyle, Ken Shorter, Neil Hallett, Paul Luty, Mark Jones, Stewart Bevan. Dir: Harold Orton. Pro: H. Orton & Caroline Neame. Screenplay: H. Orton & Peter Frances-Browne. Ph: Ray Orton. Ed: Gordon Grimward. Art: Michael Pickwoad. M: Harry Robertson. Made on location in and around The Isle of Dogs. (Eyeline Films for the CFF.) 60 mins. Cert U.

After finding some stolen jewellery Dexter Fletcher and the other children escape from the deserted warehouse by shinning down a rope in *4D Special Agents*.

The Film Books of the Year

Reviewed by Ivan Butler

Recession or no recession, the outflow of books on the cinema has remained remarkably constant, and this year has seen some notably interesting ones, particularly in the reference section. In the previous two issues I have included a mention of specialist publishers or distributors whose titles may not be readily available from bookshops outside the large centres. This year I draw attention to the Tantivy Press. This enterprising House specialised in books on antiques until 1963, when Peter Cowie acquired the name from his father and started the annual *International Film Guide*. Tantivy's first monograph was by Cowie – entitled *Antonioni-Bergman-Resnais*. This was followed, among others, by Peter Graham's very successful (but now, sadly, out-of-date and out-of-print) *A Dictionary of the Cinema* and Robin Wood's *Hitchcock's Films*, one of the best of all Hitchcock studies. At the end of the decade Tantivy joined forces with A. S. Barnes, US, a move which enabled it

to produce a far greater number of film books. By the close of the 1970s the combination had yielded over 200 titles.

The range is wide, from textbooks such as *Directing Motion Pictures* and *Practical Motion Picture Photography* to surveys of the Cinema of individual nations, directors and stars. One of its most notable undertakings was a series of histories of Hollywood by decades, later produced in a single volume. It has also produced a number of more specialist studies, such as *Dutch Cinema* and *Animation in the Cinema*. *The International Film Guide* remains its centrepiece, and readers of these columns past and present will need no further recommendation of this essential reference treasure-house. Catalogues and information about Tantivy books can be obtained from: The Tantivy Press, Magdalen House, 136–148 Tooley Street, London SE1 2TT.

It may be of interest to note that LSP Books, referred to at length last year, now also distribute over here a number of books from the well-known and prolific Arlington House.

Among the Film Books of the Year in this issue are a few titles which are strictly Film Books of a Few Years Ago. These are mainly American publications which have only recently become readily available in Britain, generally through specialised distributors, and which – because of their value (in particular as reference books) – should be brought to the notice of anyone interested in the cinema.

BIOGRAPHY, MEMOIRS

The Cinema of Sidney Poitier: Lester J. Keyser and Andre R. Ruszkowski; Tantivy Press, £3.95.
An informative and readable account of the star's career, well documented, fully illustrated and with a detailed chronology. Welcome for Sidney Poitier's many admirers and good value as a glossy paperback. Two photographs of a much made-up Harry Belafonte in *Uptown Saturday Night* show an astonishing resemblance to Citizen Kane.

The Eighth Veil: Ann Todd; William Kimber, £8.50.
In this very engaging autobiography, Ann Todd describes her not-too-happy childhood, her training at the Central School of Speech Training (for a teacher) during which she played in class in W. B. Yeats' *The Land of Heart's Desire* – in which, if I may insert a personal note, at the age of eighteen I appeared as her father – and the way in which this led to her first professional performance in the same verse drama. From there she quite swiftly rose to prominence, culminating in the triumph of the film *The Seventh Veil* – a triumph which has dogged her relentlessly ever since. In the early 1960s she embarked on a completely new career as producer of a number of travel drama-documentaries – the *Thunder of . . .* series – set in various exotic places. En route to these achievements she suffered a car accident, being 'repaired' by the renowned surgeon Sir Archibald MacIndoe, and a brutal coshing by two louts on the seafront at Brighton.
   At one time she was married to David Lean, who directed her in *The Passionate Friends, Madeleine,* and *The Sound Barrier*. All this, and much more, is told in a frank, modest and often humorous style in this brief but enjoyable book, which is illustrated by personal snapshots and photographs.

Elvis, The Final Years: Jerry Hopkins; W. H. Allen, £6.95
The Presley cult is one of the least comprehensible of all such aberrations. However, it undeniably exists – to date, at any rate – and this reasonably sane and objective, very detailed account of his last seven years will undoubtedly appeal to its adherents. The book is divided into headed sections covering each two or three months: it has a number of illustrations, but no index.

Errol Flynn – The Untold Story: Charles Higham; Granada Publishing, £7.50.
So the idol has not only feet of clay, but is clay most of the way up. Flynn has often been referred to as a liar and braggart, amoral, dishonest and promiscuous: he was also, it appears from this book, a thief, a drug trafficker, an anti-Semite, and a major Nazi spy! Mr Higham brings up a formidably convincing wealth of documentation to back his sensational claims and his book makes engrossing, if not particularly edifying, reading.

Garbo – A Portrait: Alexander Walker; Weidenfeld & Nicolson, £10.
By going back for much of this material to the ultimate source – the day-to-day transactions recorded in the MGM archives – Mr Walker has collected a mass of fresh detail and fascinating sidelights, and has incorporated these into a full account and survey of the

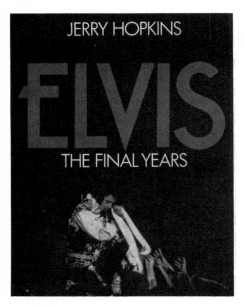

known facts to produce a glittering mosaic. Among the numerous interesting points are figures relating to the costs of the films, which are given in the filmography, together with comparative pound/dollar equivalents through the years. A fresh light is thrown on the Mauritz Stiller/*Temptress* débâcle; and some truly astonishing comments made by the Swedish historical adviser on *Queen Christina* are reported – advice which, the author says, was cheerfully ignored by the director Rouben Mamoulian.

The hundreds of illustrations are magnificent, ranging from Garbo's parents to revealing shots of the star grabbed by ruthless photographers in recent years. There are dozens of stills, frame enlargements and publicity shots. Those of *The Temptress* are particularly interesting: Garbo and Antonio Moreno at rehearsal with Stiller, he moustachioed and she in a costume she did not wear in the particular sequence, dancing with Moreno – which she did not do. A subsequent page shows her with H. B. Warner (who did not appear in the final print) and a still moustacheless Moreno (not Roy D'Arcy, as in the captions).

Gregory Peck: Michael Freedland; W. H. Allen, £6.95.
A pleasant biography of a most engaging personality. Gregory Peck has proved in a dozen and more films that he is more than a film star, he is a film *actor* (and from his early years an experienced stage actor as well). Despite the inevitable occasional slip his career presents a gratifyingly smooth progress from success to success – crowned perhaps by the unforgettable *To Kill a Mockingbird*. A fine and much respected worker both in his professional life and for the motion picture industry, he is also, and most strongly, a 'family man'. All this is brought out in Mr Freedland's readable and entertaining biography. The illustrations are excellent, the filmography complete as to titles but otherwise skimpy, and the index non-existent despite blank pages to spare.

Ingrid Bergman – My Story: Ingrid Bergman and Alan Burgess; Michael Joseph, £9.95.
Written by Alan Burgess as biography but with lengthy first-person interpolations by Ingrid Bergman, this is a great deal more satisfactory than the more usual 'with . . .'-type autobiographies, where the personality of the original subject is so often obscured by the 'with' writer. The present arrangement, in fact, works very well indeed, resulting in a long (about 450 pages), full, gracious and richly rewarding story of the notable Swedish star's life and career. The first sixty pages or so give an interesting account of her early years and work in Sweden, before coming on to the better-known events that followed the success of her first American film, *Intermezzo*. More personal recollections include a full story of her relationship with Roberto Rossellini. There are four generous sections of illustrations, a good index, and a combined chronology of stage, screen and television appearances.

Jane Fonda – All-American Anti-Heroine: Gary Herman and David Downing; Omnibus Press, dist. Book Sales Limited, £2.95.
This 'appraisement' of Jane Fonda's life is a good deal more solid than a quick glance at its paperback format might suggest. It is, in fact, a full and well researched

account both of her film career and of her more controversial activities as a political firebrand. Each aspect is covered with authority, and is set against the background of the other. Though the 140 pages are crammed with illustrations (many of them rare and interesting) the text itself is full and detailed. There is a concise filmography – but unfortunately no index.

The Last Hero – Gary Cooper: Larry Swindell; Robson Books, £7.50.
We have had to wait a long time for a full and authoritative life of Gary Cooper, but the wait has been worth while, for this is among the best biographies of the year – warm, perceptive, frank (without descent into sensationalism for sensationalism's sake, for which relief much thanks) – a soundly written history of a large part of cinema through one of its most famous figures. The span of Cooper's career was great. His first actual film part was in 1925 (he had played an unknown number of 'extra' roles previously), his last in 1961. It is surprising to realise how late in the list his most famous film comes – *High Noon* is number eighty in the book's excellent filmography, and the last film, *The Naked Edge*, number ninety-five.
The Last Hero is an apt title for Mr Swindell's biography. *The Naked Edge* appeared some twenty years ago but no-one has really filled the place left by Gary Cooper. All in all, we shall not see his like again, and more's the pity.

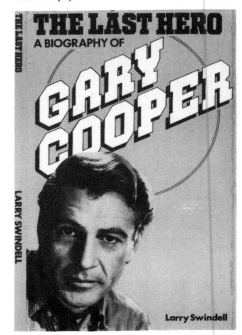

Laurence Olivier, Theater and Cinema: Robert L. Daniels; The Tantivy Press, £8.95.
Despite its subtitle this is a filmic rather than a theatrical survey, the latter being confined to a twelve-page list – useful as a summary but a small part of the book's 313 pages. The main section gives a very full coverage of Olivier's cinema career, following the usual form of technical credits, commendably full cast lists, reviews and comments for each film. In addition there are biographical details, lists of television appearances, recordings, music from the films, awards, notes and bibliography. It is fully illustrated, though some of the stills are of variable quality: they also include, quite unnecessarily, a number in which Olivier does not appear at all. All in all, however, a useful, enthusiastic and possibly standard record of a great career.

Loving Lucy: Bart Andrews and Thomas J. Watson; Robson Books, £7.95.
Subtitled 'An Illustrated Tribute to Lucille Ball', this is a lively and entertaining picture book. The biographical text covers her life and career in straightforward and comprehensive detail, but it is the illustrations that are the highlights of the presentation. Her early days as a fashion model, her film debut in 1933 (in two intriguingly contrasted pictures – Eddie Cantor's *Roman Scandals* and Zola's *Nana*), her later starring vehicles, radio appearances and of course her greatest successes on television – are recorded in lavish and very attractively set out photographs. An obvious essential for all the thousands who have Loved Lucy.

My Side of the Road: Dorothy Lamour; Robson Books, £7.50.
This as an 'as-told-to . . .' autobiography (Dick McInnes) – a hybrid which sometimes leaves the reader wondering how much the 'author's' personality has been diluted in the process. However, when the result is as successful as in this warm and lively book, to criticise on this score would be merely to cavil. Dorothy Lamour will always be remembered with affection by all those who recall her essential and delightful contributions to the evergreen Hope-Crosby 'Road' series, but she also partnered many other famous names in a great period. The story of her film career as well as her personal life – war service, happy family, the tragedy of the death of her husband William Howard – is told fully, amusingly and at times movingly. One is left with the sure knowledge that there is much more to Dorothy Lamour than a sarong.

An Open Book: John Huston; Macmillan London, £8.95.
This is a thoroughly good, straightforward biography, an engrossing portrait of a creative craftsman at work, full of good stories but with greater prominence given than is sometimes the case, to the job in hand – the actual business of making films. The list of such films is imposing. Particularly interesting here are the pages on *The Treasure of the Sierra Madre, The Misfits* (where he explodes a myth concerning Clark Gable's death), *The African Queen* and – not for any quality of this unwieldy 'epic' itself but for Huston's share in it and his handling of the animals – the Noah section of *The Bible* . . .

Above all there is the (tantalisingly brief) section on *The Red Badge of Courage,* arguably his masterpiece, unforgettable even in its mutilated form, the failure of which was a sad reflection on the taste and sensitivity of the audiences at the time. On the personal side a highlight is the heart-warming story of his relationship with his father and the moving account of the latter's death. There are three generous sections of illustrations: no filmography but a good and full index.

Repulsion – The Life and Times of Roman Polanski: Thomas Kiernan; New English Library, £7.95.
In his introduction the author reveals that he tried to persuade Roman Polanski to agree to the writing of his 'life', but the director declined as he was about to write it himself. When this project fell through Mr Kiernan decided to go ahead on his own, without his subject's co-operation, and produce an 'unauthorised biography'. In doing so he received a 'wealth of knowledgeable and intimate insights into the man', but respected the wishes of his informants, in many cases, to conceal their names. He starts off with a lurid, unnecessarily detailed and highly sensational account of the scandal over the thirteen-year-old girl (unnamed), based, he says, on grand jury testimony, police reports and interviews – containing details which only the girl and Polanski could have known ('Polanski released a guttural laugh', 'Polanski's eyes glinted in appreciation'), and which were frequently denied by Polanski himself.
The lack of full documentation, here and elsewhere, is bound to raise doubts as to the authenticity of some statements throughout the book – especially after the style of the opening section – and this is a pity, for much of it, particularly that concerned with Polanski's appalling boyhood and youth in war-ravaged Poland, is riveting and moving. This is a very 'personal' life and the films themselves get only brief mention. The book shows signs of being rather hastily written, and is index-less.
In reviewing it, it is perhaps only right that I should reveal myself as the author of a book on Polanski, published a few years ago and the only one, until now, in English; written from a totally different viewpoint, with only a brief biographical sketch, but detailed analyses of the films up to *Rosemary's Baby;* containing interviews with Polanski himself, and with several people who have worked with him, and who expressed the highest opinions not only of his professional skill but of his loyalty, enthusiasm, humour, patience and warmth.

Screen Writer – Nunnally Johnson: Tom Stempel; Tantivy Press/Barnes, £6.95.
The first title in Nunnally Johnson's filmography is *Rough House Rosie* (Clara Bow, 1927), the last *The Dirty Dozen* (1967). During the forty-year span he wrote a few major scripts such as *The Grapes of Wrath* and *The Woman in the Window,* and a host of efficient, light-weight movies, produced one of the best Gregory Peck films (*The Gunfighter*), and directed and wrote *The Three Faces of Eve.* Mr Stempel has written a good, thorough account of the life and work of a good, thorough Hollywood writer, concentrating rewardingly on his professional rather than private activities, dealing with information rather than gossip. He examines in

more detail than is often done in similar books the role of the writer in the making of a movie. Mr Johnson (who, strangely, failed in the 'live' theatre) can be caustic at times – read him on Marilyn Monroe and Vincent Price – and there is a sharp little chapter on the Un-American Activities affair. The filmography is excellent.

Shelley: Shelley Winters; Granada Publishing, £7.95.
A spirited and often endearing account of an accomplished actress determined to win for herself the parts she considered worthy of her, and to which – when she was successful – she almost invariably did justice: eg *A Place in the Sun, The Night of the Hunter, A Patch of Blue* and others, even, as far as possible, when miscast as Mrs Haze in the generally mistaken *Lolita.* If at times the style is a bit slap-happy this is no doubt suitable to a lively personality and an eventful career. Miss Winters has appeared in a large number of films in a large number of locales: it is a pity no filmography is provided – and a greater pity that there is no index.

Sparks Fly Upwards: Stewart Granger; Granada Publishing, £7.95.
A thoroughly entertaining and often vastly amusing autobiography, with plenty of prominence given to the actual business of moviemaking. In his long career Stewart Granger has always given the impression of a star who knows every trick of the film actor's trade – a sound performer in his very best sense. One remembers with pleasure such films as the early *Waterloo Road,* and the action-packed costume pieces, *Saraband for Dead Lovers, Scaramouche,* the 1952 remake of *The Prisoner of Zenda,* and other romantic adventures – doubly welcome when they appear on television now that such enjoyments are rarely to be seen in the contemporary cinema. There is also to be found in the book, of course, plenty about colleagues, film personalities, a devastating portrait of Howard Hughes, accounts of his marriages to Elspeth March and Jean Simmons.

Susan Hayward – A Star is a Star is a Star!: Christopher P. Andersen; Robson Books, £7.50.
Susan Hayward's tempestuous life is well told in this vigorous biography. Often underrated as an actress (with, admittedly, an undeservedly large proportion of mediocre films in her total of sixty-seven), she does not appear in many lists of Big Names; yet in the period of her career – 1935–1972 – she gave many sound and a few quite memorable performances. Her private life was as hectic as any of her films, incorporating frequent conflicts with her colleagues, marital unheavals, an attempted suicide and a ghastly, agonising death. Her determination and courage during this final dreadful time was beyond praise.
In many ways, as indicated in the title of this book, her story is a scenario for what is often thought of as the Life of a Film Star: Mr Andersen does it justice. A filmography is provided, but – sadly – no index.

Swanson on Swanson: Gloria Swanson; Michael Joseph, £9.95.
Gloria Swanson is, for certainty, the supreme example of the Film Star. Even to the unlucky majority who today are too young to have seen her films as they illuminated the screen in her heyday, the name itself

conjures up all the glittering glamour of the golden age. Behind the glamour, as this large and handsome book reveals, was an astute business woman, a staunch fighter for her rights, a witty and undeluded observer of the frenetic world around her. From her disastrous marriage to Wallace Beery (very frankly told), her relationship with Joseph P. Kennedy, her career as actress and as producer, through to her uniquely successful comeback as ex-star Norma Desmond – and beyond – the story of those days and films (in particular *Rain* and *Queen Kelly*) is all here, told in a style which shows she has never lost sight of the fact that she was a Star, and worthy of recognition as such, yet never loses its warmth, humour and humanity.

There are plenty of illustrations, and an index, the usefulness of which is lessened by the absence (except in the case of the main subject) of any sub-entries.

Tyrone Power – The Last Idol: Fred Lawrence Guiles; Granada Publishing, £8.95.
Though Mr Guiles's subtitle may be open to question (Tyrone Power died, after all, in 1958) there is no question that the aura, ambience – or what fashionable word you will – that surrounded the star is not to be found circulating about the film/television players of today. Familiarity through the home screen breeds – not contempt, perhaps – but certainly a less worshipful attitude.

This is a warm, appreciative but frank biography, solidly researched and affectionately presented, of one of Hollywood's most likeable figures from the great days. There is much also on his relatives, friends and associates – notably his first wife, Annabella – and an interesting chapter on the famous Tyrone Powers 1 and 2. A busy career is followed in detail up to Power's horrifyingly sudden death during the making of *Solomon and Sheba*, in which he was replaced by Yul Brynner. An excellent filmography and good index round off a worthy tribute.

Up in the Clouds, Gentlemen Please: John Mills; Weidenfeld & Nicolson, £8.50.
Sir John's long career opened in the theatre in 1929, and on screen in 1933, achieving on the way an imposing number of awards. It is all covered in one of the most enjoyable autobiographies of the year, full of anecdotes, presenting a vivid picture of both theatre and cinema over forty years, and set down with urbanity, humour, and a warm generosity towards colleagues and friends. There is also plenty, of course, about his famous theatrical family – daughters Hayley and Juliet, and authoress wife Mary Hayley Bell.

A couple of slips: the famous Cockney actor in *Britannia of Billingsgate* was Gordon Harker, not Parker: and the name of Sir John's agent in the early years was Vincent Erne, not Earne – this I remember because he was my agent also!

HISTORY, CRITICISM, ANALYSIS

Art and Animation – The Story of The Halas and Batchelor Animation Studio: Roger Manvell; Tantivy Press, £8.25.
An essay on animation, a brief history of the famous partnership, a massive list of titles and credits by decades, followed by the main section – a lavish display of illustrations, not only from the cartoons themselves, but also production stills and portraits. Obviously this is the 'definitive' work on H. & B., and essential for any animation enthusiast. Many people may be surprised at the extent of the range, from shorts for the Ministry of Information and other official bodies to language teaching and similar educational series, comedies, satires, fairy tales, large-scale works (including opera) and experimental productions – all crowned by their most famous achievement, *Animal Farm*. The only qualification is the small proportion of colour stills, always so advantageous in books on animated film: for the price, one might have expected a larger number.

The Art of the Great Hollywood Portrait Photographers: John Kobal; Allen Lane, £15.00.
A lavish and beautifully produced volume of pictures taken by the portrait photographers of Hollywood's great era, 1925–1940. A long general survey is followed by portfolios on selected photographers with introductory notes. It is odd to realise that these marvellous works of art, reproduced here from the *original* negatives or prints, were regarded merely as publicity items, to be handed out to magazines, newspapers and fans who wrote into their favourites. Not unexpectedly, women predominate, but the male stars are represented also, eg Douglas Fairbanks, Jr., John Wayne, Joel McCrea. Here are the young Mae West, and Clara Bow before and after Hollywood treatment. Readers (or viewers) in search of their own particular choices may find a disproportionate share of attention given to Garbo, Hepburn, Crawford and Dietrich to the exclusion of others: but this is, after all, a study of the photographers rather than of their subjects, and as such it is superb.

Cathedrals of the Movies: David Atwell; Architectural Press, £12.95.
This well produced and lavishly illustrated book, *A History of British Cinema and their Audiences,* nicely mingling scholarship and nostalgia, is also one of the most heartrending imaginable: a sorry, indeed a disgraceful record of mindless destruction and mutilation of often marvellously imaginative buildings. Commercial vandalism and greed have taken a terrible toll. Indiscriminate 'twinning' or 'tripling' has wholly ruined original finely calculated proportions, bingo or even worse has destroyed all atmosphere. (See the really dreadful illustrations on pages 167 and 171.) One can only be thankful for recent efforts (however belated and often feeble) to preserve some of the remaining 'Picture Palaces' from the same fate; and grateful also that the details, plans and excellent photographs in Mr Atwell's book will at least help to keep alive some memories of the great days. Dozens of cinemas are here, old and new, large and small – though not, inevitably, the many modest (and often, frankly, somewhat shabby) little houses that gave so much pleasure to so many people in the past.

Some readers are bound to regret the omission of a favourite cinema – the long-destroyed Capitol, Haymarket in London, for instance, one of the most comfortable and attractive of all the earlier Palaces, gets only the barest of mentions. Nevertheless this is a very valuable and authoritative record, with useful appendices and a good index.

Cliffhanger: Alan G. Barbour; A & W Publishers, BCW, LSP Books, £5.95.
A Pictorial History of the (sound) Motion Picture Serial, divided into seventeen sections of illustrations, stills and publicity photographs, each preceded by a brief introductory note. It will no doubt provide a nostalgic feast for the serial buff, particularly as the illustrations are very well produced and refreshingly unfamiliar. At the end of the book is a complete list of sound serials (1929–1956), arranged chronologically by studio, giving the star, but – unhappily – no further reference material. In so complete an account a list of casts and credits would have been welcome.

Crime Movies: Carlos Clarens; Secker & Warburg, £7.97.
This magnificently illustrated book is a 'study in depth' of the American gangster movie – a worthy companion to the same author's book on the horror film – except that the latter also included a useful filmography. Mr Clarens sets the films firmly in the context of the real-life crime and gangster situations of the period, making a strong point that they are not merely isolated escapist thrillers but both reflect and derive from contemporary conditions and outlooks. His range is chronologically complete – from Griffith's *Musketeers of Pig Alley* (1912) to *Black Sunday* (1977). The 'greats' – *Scarface, The Godfather* etc – are afforded the major space, but many films slightly down the ladder – *Quick Millions, Death Wish,* and dozens more – are also discussed in detail.

As already indicated, the illustrations are first-rate: not only in the rarity of many of the stills, but also in their reproduction, which is crystal clear. Documentary and 'actual' photographs of crime and criminals are also included. To sum up – probably as good a review of the crime *genre* as any we are likely to see.

Fifty Great American Silent Films: (1912–1920): Anthony Slide and Edward Wagenknecht; Dover, dist. Constable & Co., £4.05.
Interest in the silent film has increased considerably over the past few years, thanks to the widening studies of cinematic history and to the screening of such programmes as the magnificent Thames Television series on Hollywood, *The Pioneers.* In this most attractively and stoutly produced paperback two of the leading enthusiasts of the early silent period survey a selection of its finest productions, starting with *From the Manger to the Cross* and concluding with *The Kid.* Famous films such as *The Spoilers, Birth of a Nation, Intolerance, Stella Maris, The Miracle Man, Dr Jekyll and Mr Hyde* (John Barrymore) and *The Mark of Zorro* are not unexpectedly included, but there are many equally memorable if lesser known titles. Each is given production details, cast, synopsis and lively, informative commentary, as well as – in all – over 200 splendid stills. This fine collection must surely appeal not only to those who have treasured memories, but to anyone interested in the early great days of the cinema.

The Film in History: Pierre Solin; Basil Blackwell, £9.95.
An interesting and original approach to the study of the representation of history in fictional films; scholarly and serious but stimulating and eminently 'readable'. After opening sections of general interest the author deals

mainly with five major historical events: the French Revolution, the American Civil War, the Italian Risorgimento, the Russian Revolution and the Italian Resistance in World War II. Films such as *La Marseillaise*, *Napoleon Bonaparte*, *Birth of a Nation*, *Gone With the Wind*, *The Red Shirts*, *The End of St Petersburg* and *Rome – Open City* are taken as key subjects, with many others referred to in passing. Copious notes, a bibliography and two indexes round off a well-researched and authoritative book.

Film Noir: ed. Alain Silver and Elizabeth Ward; Secker & Warburg, £15.

The *Film Noir genre* may be described as roughly parallel to the French *Série Noire* – a type of detective or crime fiction notable for its atmosphere of darkness, menace, helplessness and underlying pessimism. It flourishes mainly – with numerous excellent films – from the mid-1940s to the late 1950s, though including a number of films from the silent *Underworld* (1927) to *The French Connection II* and *Taxi Driver* of the late 1970s.

In this truly magnificent study its whole range is examined with a thoroughness which makes the film student long for such treatment to be extended to every cinematic *genre*. More than 300 films are covered with a synopsis, notes and criticism, credits, and a cast list of unequalled detail, down to the smallest 'bit' parts. A most valuable series of appendices includes an extended essay, a chronological list of films, break-ups of players, directors, writers, cameramen, producers and releasing companies. There is an extensive bibliography and an enormous index, together with some seventy-five illustrations.

In such a detailed work the odd slip is bound to occur – *Forces (Force) of Evil*, Sylvia Sydney (Sidney), Colleen (Coleen) Gray, *Cross Cross (Criss Cross)* – but the only serious one is that the compilers have evidently not read Patrick Hamilton's novel *Hangover Square*: the film was a ghastly travesty, and this could have been pointed out. Otherwise there can be little but praise for an obvious labour of love, painstakingly researched and beautifully produced.

Film Score: Tony Thomas; Barnes/Yoseloff, £6.95.

The indefatigable Mr Thomas here presents a series of essays on twenty great film composers – Copland, Rozsa, Waxman, Tiomkin, Herrmann, Mancini, Addison, etc – written with his usual style, and prefacing the views of the subjects on their work. The result is unfailingly interesting and highly recommended. A photograph of each composer is provided, and a 'discography since 1970' is included as an appendix. Record lists are apt to have a distressingly short life before becoming out of date, but these remain a useful guide to some of the composers' film scores.

The Films of Bela Lugosi: Richard Bojarski; Citadel, dist. LSP Books, £11.50.

Bela Lugosi is so closely bound to Dracula that it is probably not widely realised that he actually appeared in over sixty films. True, most of them were distinctly less than memorable – tired, mechanical rehashes of stale horror formulae – *The Bodysnatcher* being a rare exception. All are gathered here in this handsomely produced volume, together with an exhaustive list of his

many stage appearances as a young actor in Hungary – starting in the year 1902. The illustrations are exceptionally interesting, particularly the early ones (Bela as Christ in 1916; as Armand in *The Lady of the Camellias* in 1910) and some of the informal and production photographs. One is left with a slight feeling of sadness – a suspicion that a much better actor was too often wasted dealing out snarls, threats, clutching claws and general monstrosities.

The book has a bonus in the form of an introduction by the enchanting Carroll Borland – the vampire of all vampires, to whose attentions one would willingly submit: but who on earth was responsible for passing the spelling of her Christian name as 'Carroll' in the text and 'Carol' (prominently, twice) on the jacket? (And which is correct?)

The Films of Charles Bronson: Jerry Vermilye; Citadel, dist. LSP Books, £11.50.

Mr Vermilye – author of the excellent *The Great British Films* reviewed previously – has produced a very good and full account of the great He-Man, particularly strong on the cast lists. It is intriguing to trace the development of that seamed and rugged face from the early Charlie Buchinsky days to the present. Mr Vermilye contributes an interesting character study, noting for instance Bronson's extreme reserve. There is a list of television credits (which one hopes will not one day be called a 'teleography') and illustrations are up to standard both in quality and quantity.

The Films of Charlton Heston: Jeff Rovin; Citadel, dist. LSP Books, £5.95.

This follows the usual format of the 'Films of . . .' series, except that the accounts of many of the movies are much longer than usual – *Ben Hur*, for instance, covers some sixteen pages! Heston himself is quoted extensively. Illustrations are, as usual, excellent, and include interesting shots of the young actor in the 16 mm *Julius Caesar* made by David Bradley.

The Films of Ginger Rogers: Homer Dickens; Citadel, dist. LSP Books, £5.95.

The paperback edition of one of the more lavish books in the series, this is particularly good on the reference material, including notes on the early shorts and a stage chronology. The main filmography contains seventy-three titles. The usual features are included – biographical section, portrait gallery, lavish array of stills and other illustrations. In addition, a very welcome bonus, is a large selection of photographs of the famous Rogers/Astaire dances.

The Films of Hedy Lamarr: Christopher Young; Citadel, dist. LSP Books, £5.95.
The Great British Films: Jerry Vermilye; Citadel – dist. LSP Books, £5.95.

Paperback versions of two books reviewed (in hardback) in the 1979–80 *Film Review*. The first was recommended in particular for its photographic and reference sections; the second as a warm and generous tribute to the British cinema, charmingly 'covered' in red, white and blue, lavishly illustrated with excellent stills, and by no means concentrating solely on the major productions in a survey which extends from *The Private Life of Henry VIII* to *The Go-Between*.

The Films of Myrna Loy: Lawrence J. Quirk; Citadel, dist. LSP Books, £11.50.

By the time she appeared in *The Thin Man*, aged twenty-nine, Myrna Loy had, incredibly, played in some eighty films: the total to 1980 being over 120. Mr Quirk deals with them all with admirable conciseness-plus-completeness. Within the normal limits of this series every film, from the earliest to the latest, from the important to the less important, is given full cover, with plenty of space left available for the usual lavish supply of illustrations. *The Best Years of Our Lives* is probably the most notable of Miss Loy's movies, with the 'Thin Man' series proving equally durable: but what would one not give for a chance to see her (or to see her again) in some of her early vamp parts – minor productions though they may be!

Mr Quirk has been able, perhaps, to save a little space in the biographical side, because of his subject's known reserve in regard to her personal life; though even here he provides a full account of a full career. All in all – a warm-hearted tribute to one of the most enduring, and endearing, of Hollywood's major stars.

The Films of Ronald Reagan: Tony Thomas; Citadel, dist. LSP Books, £11.50.

'In 1980 the Republicans selected Ronald Reagan as their candidate for President. The result . . . that's another story. This one is about an actor and his films.' So writes Mr Thomas at the end of his biographical introduction. Even so, it is perhaps a little more than mere coincidence that this book, a good one, should appear just at the present time! As lavishly illustrated as the other titles in this long-lasting series, it presents a most likeable personality. Many people may be surprised at the number of Reagan's films – no fewer than fifty-three. Many of them may be forgettable, but the list contains one masterpiece, *Kings Row* – still very effective today – and at least two very worthy runners-up, *The Voice of the Turtle* and *Storm Warning*. Mr Thomas deals with them all in his usual informative and very readable style.

The Films of Sherlock Holmes: Chris Steinbrunner and Norman Michaels; Citadel, dist. LSP Books, £5.95.
In general, Sherlock Holmes on the screen has been a sorry saga of travesty and distortion. Hardly any of the dozens of films made convey with accuracy the atmosphere of Victorian London, and England, which is a main part of his fascination. Holmes in the cinema is woefully misrepresented, dragged out of period, lumbered with ludicrous – often impossible – stories. Oddly enough, despite their faults the old silents, plentifully illustrated here, have probably dealt best with the unfortunate detective. All is faithfully preserved in this well-illustrated book – though the authors are far too kind to their material. One is left full of indignation at the sins committed, and sadness at the opportunities missed.

The Films of Shirley Maclaine: Christopher Paul Denis; Citadel, dist. LSP Books, £11.50.
It becomes increasingly difficult for a conscientious reviewer to find variants in writing about this almost unfailingly successful series, and readers will appreciate that to describe a newcomer as 'well up to standard' – as can be done here – is a high recommendation. The introductory biography affords an interesting picture or two of the young brother, Warren Beatty: the films section follows the customary layout, from Hitchcock's *The Trouble with Harry* (1955) to *Being There* (1979). Chapters follow on her television work, an interview with Ed Murrow, a brief survey of stage appearances and night club shows. Illustrations include dozens of stills, numerous poses (some of them a bit coy) and a fascinatingly diverse portrait gallery.

The Films of the Sixties: Douglas Brode; Citadel, dist. LSP Books, £11.50.
Following on the heels of the 1940s and the 1950s, this forms a useful record of the period. From each year half-a-dozen to a dozen important films are selected and given a commentary, a concise cast list and a collection of stills. One or two foreign language movies which have made the sea crossing (eg *La Dolce Vita*) are included. The survey provides interesting proof of the excellence of much cinema of the 1960s: a decade which can claim such films as *Psycho, Lawrence of Arabia, David and Lisa, Dr Strangelove, Belle de Jour (De Joup* in the Contents list), *The Pawnbroker* and *Blow-Up* – to name just a handful – can hold up its head among any. May we now hope for a backward look to the 1930s, and even the 1920s?

The Films of Warren Beatty: Lawrence J. Quirk, Citadel, dist. LSP Books, £5.95.
The Films of Montgomery Clift: Judith M. Kass, Citadel, dist. LSP Books, £5.95.
The paperback editions of two books reviewed in

hardback in the *1980–1981 Film Review*. Both were recommended, particularly as regards illustrations, as worthy members of this very good series.

Glorious Technicolour: Fred E. Basten; Tantivy Press, £13.95.
A full and lavish history of the most famous and long-lasting of all film colour processes, the first appearance of which (a fact which will surely surprise many people) was as long ago as 1917 in 'a modest venture' entitled *The Gulf Between*. This was followed in 1920 by sequences from *Way Down East* and a year or two later by sequences from De Mille's *The Ten Commandments*. Mr Basten's account is full, lively and authoritative both historically and, in an appendix, technically. Another very useful appendix contains a comprehensive filmography of twenty-five large pages. Illustrations are plentiful, though, oddly, considerably more in black-and-white than in colour. The latter show up rather cruelly the crudities of the early efforts: and indeed not only the early efforts – see the mauve horses of the 1959 *Ben Hur* and the frequent effect of an all-pervading blue. As so often, the coloured cartoons come off best on the page. Taken all in all, this is an important book – the only surprise being that it took so long for one on the subject to appear.

Gone Hollywood: Christopher Finch and Linda Rosenkrantz; Weidenfeld & Nicolson, £8.95.
Interest in all aspects of Hollywood during its great years seems insatiable, but to produce a really original book on it is quite an achievement. This the authors have managed to do very successfully: an entertaining sort of super-gossip-column ingeniously blending the seriously informative and the chattily intriguing. Their book is divided alphabetically into a large number of headings covering almost every activity of the film colony, starting with 'About Hollywood' and concluding with 'A Week in the Life of a Hollywood Bachelor'. A few of the headings may give some idea of the scope of the work: Agents, Children, Contracts and Billing, Gambling, Investments, Keeping Fit, Pets, Politics, Publicity, Recreations, San Simeon. Also included are a number of lengthy lists, such as False Starts, Nicknames, Parental Professions, and Salaries. An added attraction is the large number of unique illustrations – candid camera shots, publicity photographs, stars at work and at play. An index and a large bibliography round off this enjoyably nostalgic journey back to an irrecoverable era.

The Great Adventure Films: Tony Thomas; Citadel, dist. LSP Books, £5.95.
In his introduction Mr Thomas explains the restrictions he imposed on making what must have been a difficult choice of films for his book, 'adventure' covering so wide a field. Even so, he ranges from *The Mark of Zorro* (1920) to *Henry V*, from *Tarzan and His Mate* to *War and Peace*, from Keaton's *The General* to *The Man Who Would Be King*. In his lively comments he manages to make us appreciate his enthusiasms, even where we might not always share them! There are dozens of excellent stills: the third figure on p. 11, uncredited, is one of the finest character actresses of the earlier years, Emily Fitzroy.

Grierson on the Movies: Ed. Forsyth Hardy; Faber & Faber, £7.25.
The publishers have done a considerable service in making available this collection of film reviews and articles by John Grierson. The vast majority of them deal with films produced around the time when the cinema was undergoing the painful transition from the polished art of the final silent period to the fumbling beginnings of sound (which Grierson did not at first welcome) and many of such films are, sometimes undeservedly, forgotten today. It is salutary to read the contemporary opinions of an informed and sensitive man of the cinema – to see, for instance, a film such as Lubitsch's *The Man I Killed* afforded the appreciation it merited. In places Mr Grierson's political bias may somewhat cloud his judgement, but on the whole these are brief but lucid, well written, penetrating and often humorous pieces. *Note:* The film title of J. M. Barrie's *The Admirable Crichton* was, of course, *Male and Female*, not 'Woman to Woman': an odd slip in so knowledgeable a writer, and one which it is surprising the editor did not spot.

Hollywood Film Acting: Theodore Noose; Tantivy Press, £6.95.
Though aimed primarily at the hopeful American professional, there is much in this eminently practical little handbook to interest any filmgoer anxious to know 'how it is done' – or, indeed, 'what it is like'. There are chapters on characterisation, on simulating moods and emotions, on how to face the grimness of auditions. The second part of the book deals with the business side – such as agents and casting directors, and finally with an average workday on the set. Specimen script pages, contracts, etc, are reproduced. Of particular interest are the details of working in television commercials: perhaps knowing a little of what goes into their making might make them a little more tolerable when they break into a favourite programme.

The Hollywood Professionals – Vol 6: Allen Estrin; Tantivy Press, £6.95.
The latest volume in the series, in its larger, hardback format, deals with Frank Capra, George Cukor and Clarence Brown. Each is given a critical essay and a very full filmography, together with a number of good stills. Capra and Cukor need no introduction here. Brown is probably best remembered for his Garbo films (*Flesh and the Devil, Anna Christie, Anna Karenina*, etc) but he also made a number of other famous movies during his long sojourn with MGM, including the silent spectacular *The Trail of '98* – referred to as a 'lost' film, but by no means lost in the memory of those, like myself, fortunate enough to have seen it. Together with the earlier volumes this book helps to form an intelligent, useful and convenient gallery of portraits and reference material.

The Hollywood Professionals, Vol. 7: Leland A. Poague; The Tantivy Press, £6.95.
This useful series has expanded considerably in format since its early days. The present volume, of some 320 pages, deals with two directors: Billy Wilder and Leo McCarey, surveying their career and analysing their films in two lengthy and perceptive essays. These are followed by comprehensive filmographies, that on

McCarey, in particular, being exceptionally detailed and invaluable for reference. There are many stills, but unfortunately they are often of poorer quality than one is accustomed to expect these days – smudgy and apparently at times seen through a murky fog: a pity that so generally admirable a book should be let down in this important field.

Indian Film: Erik Barnouw and S. Krishnaswamy; Oxford University Press, £3.25.
A paperback reissue of a study which first appeared in 1963, this is the more welcome in view of the greatly increased market for Indian cinema now existing in Britain. It traces its history and development from the earliest days, with additional pages to bring it up to the late 1970s, and is derived from a very large number of interviews. Addenda include production statistics, a chronology, and a useful map of places referred to in the text. There are nearly 300 illustrations. The historical, social and political backgrounds of the film industry are set against the artistic development of an art form. A filmography of important productions would have been an added attraction, but in other respects this is a valuable handbook.

John Wayne – In the Camera Eye: Sam Shaw; Hamlyn, £4.95.
Marlon Brando – In the Camera Eye: Sam Shaw, Hamlyn, £4.95.
Sophia Loren – In the Camera Eye: Sam Shaw, Hamlyn, £4.95.
Marilyn – In the Camera Eye: Sam Shaw, Hamlyn, £4.95.
Each of the above four books consists of an extended 'photographic essay' of some one hundred pages, with a brief chatty text and illustrations taken by the author, candid-camera type and studio portraits, followed by a brief biographical section and a concise but complete filmography with stills. The illustrations in the main section – which are the real *raison d'être* of the books are lively, often amusing and at times rather moving – for example in the case of John Wayne, where the compilation has been made into a memorial. Though primarily picture books, each contains a good deal of useful reference material also. In all, an attractive and very reasonable priced quartet.

The Limits of Infinity: Vivian Carol Sobchack; Barnes/Yoseloff, £7.00.
To discover a fresh approach to the science-fiction film is quite an achievement in itself. In this 'attempt to re-evaluate and rework its traditional definitions' Miss Sobchack has produced an interesting and stimulating (though occasionally somewhat tortuous) study which really does enable the cinemagoer to view the sci-fi scene from a different angle. Of particular interest is her third section, which is concerned with the *sound* of the films – dialogue, music, effects. This is quite new ground when dealt with in such detail. The book is very well illustrated and indexed, and fully documented. Despite an occasional liking for the long and obscure word when the short and simple one would do, and some really hideous split infinitives, this is a well-written book – more entertaining and less formidable than a brief glance might suggest.

The Musical – From Broadway to Hollywood: Michael B. Druxman; Barnes/Yoseloff, £8.95.
Not just one more history of the *genre,* but an interesting account of the problems and attitudes involved in the transference of the musical from stage to screen, concentrating on twenty-five major productions from *On the Town* (1949) to *Jesus Christ Superstar* (1973) and *A Little Night Music* (1977). Many others are briefly discussed on the way. Illustrations are plentiful and good, and the book concludes with a 'Musical Gallery' of stills. Comparative stage and film credits would have been a useful addition.

The Proust Screenplay: Harold Pinter; Eyre Methuen, £2.95.
At present it seems unlikely that this adaptation of *À la Recherche du Temps Perdu* will be transferred from page to screen in the near future, but to the increasing number of filmgoers who can derive enjoyment from reading filmscripts this paperback edition is undoubtedly an important event, in addition to affording a good demonstration of the author's supreme skill in condensing (or, more properly, transforming) so enormous a work into a manageable potential example of the art of the film.

Spaghetti Westerns: Christopher Frayling; Routledge & Kegan Paul, Cloth £15.95, paperback £8.95.
It might be considered that this peculiar phenomenon, the Italian Western, hardly merits a major full-length study, but Mr Frayling (in this book in the new Cinema and Society Series) presents a brave case for such a scrutiny. The films of Sergio Leone (*alias* Bob Robertson), Sergio Sollima (*alias* Simon Sterling) and others with their quaint adopted names are treated in depth – even more, perhaps, being read into their work than was intended. The many illustrations (frame blow-ups, stills, etc) are interesting: the contrasting photographs of the 'good' Henry Fonda in *My Darling Clementine* and the 'bad' one (placed next to it) in *Once Upon a Time in the West,* for instance. Appendices include a critical filmography, box office receipts, and a list of the cut sequences in Leone's Westerns. There are two indexes and a large bibliography. One can only salute the care and work which have obviously gone into so complete a survey, written in a style genuinely lively and only occasionally heavy-handed. Over 400 such films, we are told, were produced between 1964 and 1970, but a doubt remains. How many have left a mark?

Theories of Authorship: Ed. John Caughie; Routledge & Kegan Paul, £11.95 cloth, £5.95 paperback.
In the earlier part of this book, a collection of essays and articles on the role of the author (or the *auteur*) in film, there are a number of interesting and illuminating pieces – eg Lindsay Anderson – on Ford's *The Searchers.* As we reach the second half, however, sadly, we find ourselves sinking deeper and deeper into the mass of sludgy verbiage in which so much of the 'higher criticism' of the cinema seems to enjoy floundering. In a sort of endlessly circling in-game of pretentious obscurity the general aim seems to be to avoid at all costs the lucid in favour of the involved, the precise in favour of the vague. Much of the writing style is, frankly, appalling. To take but one example: what, briefly and clearly, is the writer getting at in the

following scintillating sentence – 'The festishization of the "direct" can, in the last instance, be understood only as the mark of a division into fictional field/socio-historical exterior of this field, where one of the terms of the division is not made the object of a literal inscription since it is ideologically implied as the precise historical moment of the shooting of the film, a moment of which the spectators are presumed to have made the political analysis: the absent field of "direct cinema" is in effect the place of a spectator presumed to have already produced the analysis of the relations between the scene of the film and its exterior, and between this scene (as site of the production of the symptoms which affect it) and the discourse which he is supposed to hold on these symptoms.' Is the filmgoer's understanding and appreciation of the film really increased and deepened by such outpourings?

The World of Fantasy Films: Richard Meyers; Tantivy Press, £8.95.
This survey concentrates in the main on the output of the past four or five years, but within that time limit covers a wide field of science-fiction-fantasy and horror-fantasy films, and even extends to – for instance – Polanski's *The Tenant* at one extreme and *Monty Python and the Holy Grail* at the other. Special sections, covering a longer time span, deal with cartoons and television productions.
There is an excellent account of the splendid *Carrie* (Brian De Palma), and a devastating exposé of the second *King Kong* version. A useful review, very well illustrated and indexed, but with no further reference material.

REFERENCE

The Award Movies: Roy Pickard; Muller, £10.95
The indefatigable Mr Pickard has compiled another useful and entertaining reference book. Following arrangements similar to his earlier books for easy fact-hunting, in Part One he lists, in alphabetical order, the top 'best picture' winners of the past fifty years as awarded by the most influential critical bodies and several of the leading Film Festivals. Each film is given a brief note, followed by cast, credits and running time. In Part Two he provides details of all the awards of the chosen Academies, etc for best film, best actor, actress and director. A postscript ('compiled for fun') gives a breakdown of the most awarded actors, actresses and directors, the fifty films that 'nearly made it', and the award movie box office hits which brought in over four million dollars.
As he says in his preface, critics and historians tend to dismiss the compilation of 'ten best' lists as parlour games. Maybe, but they are endlessly fascinating – a collection of Desert Island Movies. Some of the information, of course, is readily available elsewhere (eg the American Academy 'Oscars'), but some is not – and in any case it is very convenient to have them collected together in so handy a form. Two indexes and several sections of good stills round off a most attractive volume.

Cinema – The Magic Vehicle, Journey One: The Cinema Through 1949
Cinema – The Magic Vehicle, Journey Two: The Cinema in the Fifties:
Adam Garbicz and Jacek Klinowski; The Scarecrow Press, dist. Bailey Bros & Swinfen, £14.35 (Vol 1), £17.50 (Vol 2)
The second of these volumes appeared during the current year, the first in 1975, though it has only now come my way. The purpose of the books is 'to give a panoramic view of the achievement of the cinema through the film-to-film approach'. It succeeds admirably. Selected films, arranged year by year, are given a critical comment, brief synopsis, cast list and credits. The first volume extends from *The Student of Prague* (1913) to *On The Town* (1949), totalling some 450 productions in all. The silent film gets a good showing. The second volume, covering a single decade, runs to about 350 films, and also includes a number of illustrations. Each book is prefaced by a short outline of main events of the period, and concludes with an index of directors and full general index. A useful embellishment is a comparison of lengths (in metres and feet) and running times – in the first book for sixteen and twenty-four frames a second, in the second for cinema and television screenings. Particular care has been taken to check the accuracy of the cast-and-credit lists. The selection of titles naturally includes many 'big names', but a point has been made of incorporating lesser known ones which, in the opinion of the authors, have particular artistic value. There is a good coverage of foreign-language films which have had distribution in the USA and Britain.
Having given a full description of these important – indeed indispensable – books, it only remains to add that the critical comments are short, sharp and to the point, the standard of presentation fully up to the high quality of other reference volumes from Scarecrow, and that the books are most attractive to handle. Highly recommended.

The Entertainers: Ed. Clive Unger-Hamilton; Pitman House, £12.50.
This magnificent, superbly illustrated book (with foreword by Sir John Gielgud) contains brief biographies of over one thousand celebrities from the sixth century to the present day, together with numerous special features on theatrical history, mime, puppet shows, audiences, etc. Though concerned with the 'live' theatre rather than the cinema, numerous famous names from the screen (Olivier, Gielgud, Glenda Jackson, Richardson, the Redgraves, Spencer Tracy, *et al* are included. For this reason – and because acting is acting, players are players, drama is drama throughout the whole sphere of the art of entertainment, it has its place in these columns. Equally valuable for study or casual enjoyment, it is beautifully produced, and research is made easy by two indexes and a (somewhat elementary) glossary.

Film Directors Guide – Western Europe: James Robert Parish; Scarecrow Press, dist. Bailey Bros & Swinfen, £7.70.
A companion volume to *Film Directors – A Guide to their American Films* (1974), this 1976 book covers full-length productions (over four reels) of those whose 'major

reputation was first obtained in Europe'. Where the directors made American films as well, these are also included here. The research is formidable, and the completeness of these lists admirable. To take just two examples from many: Maurice Elvey receives over 140 credits (starting from 1915); and Michael Curtiz around 170 (from 1912) including about seventy before he arrived in America. Dates and places of birth and death are given in most cases, and there are numerous illustrations – portraits or photos of directors at work. A list of European countries *not* covered includes Sweden, Greece and Norway, but otherwise Western Europe is very fully presented. For the serious researcher or historian this is an indispensable book – part of an attractively produced series.

The Filmgoer's Companion (7th edition): Leslie Halliwell; Granada Publishing, £15
The seventh edition of this monumental work has some 1000 extra entries, yet manages to be about eighty pages shorter. This has been achieved by omitting the stills of the previous edition – not a loss to be greatly deplored (some of them were of less than perfect quality) and the gain of so large a number of entries is more than adequate compensation. There are plenty of illustrations – crystal-clear reproductions of old posters and advertisements, much more enjoyable than over-familiar stills.
One of the charms of Mr Halliwell's two reference volumes (the present one, and the *Film Guide*) is the

stimulatingly personal approach. For this reason one may regret the omission of his Hundred Favourite Films – which only took up a couple of pages. Otherwise this marvellous compilation reaches its seventh edition with undiminished glory: 740 pages packed with information, an increased number of complete filmographies, about 6000 corrections and extensions, and the 'grand opening' of the Halliwell Hall of Fame.

Films on Film History: Anthony Slide; Scarecrow Press, dist. Bailey Bros & Swinfen, £8.40.
A very useful handbook, the title of which, as the author states, is self-explanatory, aiming to list all films – features and shorts – on the history of the cinema. Film compilations such as those made by Robert Youngson, are included, as also are the generally dire 'star biographies' (Monroe, Harlow, Keaton, etc) but not those on actual film-making. Each title is given details such as length, running time, content, cast and credit lists where applicable, notes and, where possible, availability on 16mm. A subject index is provided, together with an address list of film companies and distributors – almost wholly American.
Here is another indispensable specialist book for the student/researcher from the valuable Scarecrow-Bailey Bros reference list.

Forgotten Films to Remember: John Springer; Citadel, dist. LSP Books, £11.50
This is surely a 'must' for every film historian, film buff, or even nostalgia addict. Each single year from 1929–1959 is covered by (a) a brief survey of important 'remembered' movies, (b) a selection of memorable 'forgotten' ones in separate paragraphs and (c) an annotated list of others. It concludes with a warning list of 1960 and 1970 films which may go the same way. The author aims to draw attention to, or keep alive the memory of, those hundreds of English language productions which, though having often considerable value, are seldom seen even on television, either through deliberate destruction (movie vandalism), bad luck, or some quirk of fate. And what a mine of treasures he uncovers! Older filmgoers – or to put it more kindly, mature filmgoers – must often feel sympathy for those whose accident of birth has prevented them from realising just how much they have missed. Old books, old music records, even old plays in printed form are available for years. A film once lost has gone for ever. This fact makes an informed, enthusiastic collection such as this all the more valuable.
Even for the Citadel series, the illustrations are outstanding – page after page of rare stills, many with interest outside the actual film (eg Sidney Lumet as a boy actor) and all fully captioned. Perhaps one might suggest that quite a number of the films covered are not really (thanks to television) 'forgotten' – some indeed can be seen fairly regularly – and that an index of 'forgotten' titles might have been an asset; but these are small points in a quite remarkable and delightful book.

The Funsters: James Robert Parish and William T. Leonard; Arlington House, dist. LSP Books, £14.95
Deserving better than its somewhat facetious title, this huge book is a serious (in the best sense) and informed survey of no fewer than sixty-two Hollywood

comedians. Though understandably concentrating mainly on the sound era, several well-known silent cinema figures (in addition, of course, to the Big Four – Keaton, Chaplin, Lloyd, Langdon) also appear, eg Thelma Todd, Ben Turpin, Charley Chase. The life and career of each comedian is given in some ten double-column pages, with stills and a complete list of feature films, and the book is rounded off with a massive fifty-page index. The text is concise, lively and always interesting, full of such intriguing matters as Thelma Todd's mysterious suicide and the occasional sharp exchanges between Stan Laurel and Oliver Hardy. Illustrations, often full-page, are excellent. A listing of important short films would have been welcome (but many are referred to in the text) and, as in any collection of this kind, somebody's favourite name may have been omitted – but over sixty players is a surprisingly large number to find presented in such detail in a single volume. Much of the information is, of course, obtainable elsewhere, but it has certainly never been made available in so convenient – and at today's prices so reasonable – a form. Highly recommended.

The Great Movie Stars – The International Years: David Shipman; Angus & Robertson, £15.
In the previous issue of *Film Review* I expressed the hope that this revised edition might be published in time for inclusion with its sister volume, *The Golden Years.* It arrived too late by some months, but can now be warmly welcomed here. The original appeared (from the same publisher) in 1972: it has been enlarged, revised and updated, and now appears as a matching pair with its companion. The same guiding principles are followed in this prodigious work – every feature film (even in the case of 'foreign' players) being recorded in the course of a concise biography of some 230 stars who flourished roughly from the immediate post-war years. Some, eg Jean Gabin, had been famous for some years previously. Each biography is accompanied by several stills, very well reproduced, and the whole text is written in a stimulating sharp and witty style. Many new names are added, and an explanatory introduction gives clear information both on the procedure adopted and on the incontestable reasons for what must have been agonising decisions on whom to include and whom to omit. Perhaps the saddest exclusions, which Mr Shipman himself laments, are the members of the great Ingmar Bergman repertory company. To include everyone's choice, however, would have made the project impossibly unwieldy – and expensive. As it is, with its 632 double-column pages, plus a list of title changes, handsomely printed and bound, this book is a bargain at its price, and an essential addition to any reference collection.

The Great Songwriters of Hollywood: Warren Craig, Tantivy Press, £7.95.
This is a well researched and full reference book covering thirty-two composers and/or lyric writers of the American musical film. Each is given a brief biographical sketch, followed by an exhaustive list of songs from each film, chronologically arranged and covering overall the earliest days of sound, up to the present time. Illustrations consist of a portrait, stills and a selection of sheet music covers in each case. There is a short, pleasant introduction by veteran Harry Warren.

Three excellent indexes – of songs, film titles and personal names – round off a reference book essential to all students of film history.

The Guinness Book of Film Facts and Feats: Patrick Robertson; Guinness Superlatives, £8.95
This crammed cornucopia is surely the cinema list book to end all list books. Even a list of the lists it contains would require several pages. They range from the more-or-less expected, such as Academy Awards, Top Moneymakers, Shakespeare (and Dracula) on film, to the delightfully surprising, such as Twins Who Have Played Together, Worst Film Awards, and Film Fans, Famous and Infamous. Grave statistics are nicely mixed with light-hearted trivia. There is an entertaining section, 'Out-Takes', on assorted oddities and a selection of blunders made by directors, producers or unobservant script-girls. All this is embellished with many rare illustrations (black-and-white and colour) and a first-rate index.
Such a compilation of facts is, of course, a challenge to the reader. Mr Robertson refers on p. 114 ('Tallest screen artistes') to Johann Aason, 7ft 2 in, who entered films in 1928. Is he related, one wonders, to John Aasen, who appeared with Harold Lloyd in *Why Worry?* in 1923, in *Legionnaires in Paris* and *Two Flaming Youths* in 1927, died in 1938, and measured, reportedly, 8 ft 9½ in?

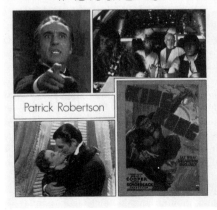

Hollywood on Hollywood: James Robert Parish, Michael R. Pitts and Gregory W. Mank; Scarecrow Press, dist. Bailey Bros & Swinfen, £12.25.
Hollywood has always been as fascinated by itself as

filmgoers are fascinated with Hollywood. Here is a survey (published 1978) of the films made in various ways about it – the adventures of movie-making, the tribulations or triumphs of fictional film aspirants, and those dreadful 'biopics' of the real stars, such as Harlow, Keaton, Gable and Lombard. Each film is given the full treatment of cast lists, technical credits, synopsis, notes and comments. The latter are often satisfyingly trenchant in particular about the above-mentioned 'true' biographies. There are also a number of good illustrations.

Horror and Science Fiction Films – A Checklist: Donald C. Willis; Scarecrow Press, dist. Bailey Bros & Swinfen, £13.30.
This enormous compilation (published in 1972) is surely the most complete list of movies in the particular *genre* which has been (or is ever likely to be) available. The main section of almost 550 packed pages contains some 4,400 titles, from all over the world and from early days to 1971, together with much relevant information even down to comment and a one-sentence synopsis. Addenda include brief details of 1971/72 productions; shorts from 1930; and a fifty-page 'Out List' of borderline cases and others omitted from the main section. Useful introductory notes attempt that most difficult of problems – a definition of what is horror (or science fiction) and what is not.

The International Film Encyclopedia: Ephraim Katz; Macmillan London, £15
It is almost impossible to believe that this vast, all-embracing book could be the love-labour of a single man. In 1266 packed pages, hundreds of players, directors, composers, designers and others are given concise, intelligent biographies and comments together with often complete and always commendably full film credits. In addition, there are sections on companies, countries, etc, and dozens of explanations of technical terms. Prominence, as may be expected, is given to English language productions, but there is a wealth of information too on foreign films and personalities. The silent era has full recognition. Not only are stars and leading players featured, but also many who are less well known: not only Loretta Young but also her equally charming sister Sally Blane; not only Sydney Greenstreet but also Lucien Littlefield.
Wisely, the author has omitted two items in order to devote all available space to other considerations – stills and comments on individual films. Both are readily available elsewhere and their inclusion would have made this already enormous volume altogether too unwieldy (and expensive). Highly recommended as an essential addition to the reference shelf.

International Film Guide 1981: Ed. Peter Cowie; Tantivy Press, £4.95
542 pages this year and, though inevitably higher in price, still astounding value: a world survey of cinema from Afghanistan to Yugoslavia: records of every side of the film world, festivals, awards, music, bookshops and book reviews, etc, and an excellent section on animation. The year's Big Five directors are Berlanga, Keslowski, Olmi, Roeg and Yates. Particular mention should be made about the unfailingly good reproduction, throughout the whole series of Guides, of

the stills and other illustrations, whether in colour or black-and-white. As has been lamented previously, this cannot help being a very tantalising treasury, with its notes and illustrations on so many movies most of us are never likely to see (a pity a fifth TV channel cannot be launched devoted solely to such films) – but at least it is an annual revelation of just how exciting and flourishing the worldwide cinema continues to be.

Movies Made for Television, 1964–1979: Alvin H. Marill; LSP Books, £14.95.
In general this Book Review section is concerned with the cinema rather than television, but the boundary between the films made for the first and those for the second is becoming so vague, and the interchange between the silver screen and the small one so frequent, that this magnificently complete reference book of the American output must certainly be included. Quite a number of the movies (*Duel*, for instance, to name only one) have been seen in both the cinema and the home. Over one thousand titles are to be found here (with some 300 illustrations) in 400 large pages; each is given full cast list, technical credits and a brief synopsis or note. A useful attempt to define the 'telefilm' as against the cinema film is made in a foreword by producer Quinn Martin. There are detailed checklists of players and directors, and an index of titles. In the main body of the book the films are arranged chronologically. In a smaller section (the Mini-Series) will be found productions such as *Washington – Behind Closed Doors*, *Holocaust*, *Jesus of Nazareth* and *Centennial* (all of twenty-six and a half hours, this last one).
The frequency with which American TV movies reach our British screens make such a detailed guide very valuable indeed. Now may we hope for a similar volume dealing with the British output?

The Oscar Directors: I. G. Edmonds and Reiko Mimura; The Tantivy Press, £7.95.
Details of the American Oscar Awards are fairly fully covered by the cinema booklist, but this deals with a special part of the subject somewhat differently, offering a thumbnail career sketch of every director of the winning *film* from the start (1927 – Frank Borzage for *Seventh Heaven* to 1979 – Robert Benton for *Kramer vs Kramer*). It thus compresses two useful facets into one volume – a study of some forty directors (allowing for repeats) and a brief account of the winning movies. Mention is made in each case of other memorable films by the respective directors, together with stills (some of them a bit smudgily reproduced) and a photograph of the director in question. A useful addition to the reference shelf. *Note:* The lady in the still from *Midnight Cowboy* is Sylvia, not Sarah, Miles.

Reel Facts: Cobbett Steinberg; Penguin Books, £2.95.
This giant Book of Lists, first published in USA, must be one of the best value-for-money offers of the year. In its 590 pages are to be found lists of Awards, lists of 'The Best Ten', lists of money-making productions, pocket histories of the big studios, top box-office stars, salaries, etc. Brief but very useful histories of the various award-making bodies precede each section. In the American Academy (Oscar) Awards are not only full details, but nominations as well as winners – a welcome enlargement of the usual lists. The often hilarious (if

sometimes tediously facetious) Harvard Lampoon 'Movie Worsts Awards' are included, together with such extras as award comparisons and a final section on the various American Production Codes. Much of this information is, of course, available elsewhere – but not in so compact, convenient and inexpensive a form. For its price and conciseness this is a splendid bargain.

The Screen Image of Youth: Ruth M. Goldstein and Edith Zornow; Scarecrow Press, dist. Bailey Bros & Swinfen, £14.
A somewhat specialised book in the first-class Scarecrow reference library, this is a 'serious' study, 'concerned not with films *for* children, but with films that have something to tell us *about* children'. Some 350 films are included in the main body of the book, generally from the 1950s on, but extending to such classics as *The Kid*, *Zéro de Conduite* and others that one might expect to find. Some omissions are understandably lamented because of non-availability of prints, notably the unforgettable *Poil de Carotte*. Each film is given brief production details followed by in some cases quite lengthy synopsis and commentary. Stills are here, but in somewhat sparse number.
Though aimed, perhaps, at sociologists and the serious student rather than the 'ordinary' cinemagoer, this should appeal to anyone interested in the subject, or indeed in the film in general. As always with books from this source, it is very well set out, easy to find one's way around (with title index, lengthy 'category' index, bibliography and directory of film companies) and pleasant to handle.

Screen World 1980: John Willis; Muller, £8.95.
This perennially popular annual starts off its fourth decade showing no sign whatever of the withering of age or the staling of custom. Once again it contains a mass of information, biographical and technical data, splendidly full cast lists, excellently reproduced stills and portraits, and a truly colossal index of names and titles. It is, indeed, a complete record of the American cinema year of 1979, including releases, obituaries, awards, 'top stars', etc.

Shoot-Em-Ups: Les Adams and Buck Rainey; Arlington House, dist. LSP Books, £15.95
The subtitle of this massive volume – 'The Complete Reference Guide to Westerns of the Sound Era' – is more apposite than the rather jokey main title, for this is a comprehensive record of the entire field: 3,339 cast-and-credit lists of American Westerns, plus a checklist of the exotic, or Continental, ones from Spain, Italy, etc. After a short section on the silent film, the years 1928–1977 are divided into ten sections with descriptive headings such as the Boon Years, the Golden Years, the Cynical Years, etc. In each case a critical/historical preface, embellished with rare stills, is followed by a filmography arranged year by year. At the end, an enormous index makes any particular title easy to trace. This index in itself makes pleasant reading with its half-a-column of 'Riders of . . .' titles, three-quarters-of-a-column of 'Texas . . .', etc.
The authors claim their work to be a 'record of *every* American sound Western', and this appears very probable: even such borderline films as *Shenandoah* and

The Red Badge of Courage – Civil War stories rather than Westerns – are included. The convenient layout and arrangement of this fine book – definitive, surely – is one of its most attractive assets.
Two slips in the photo captions: the actor on p. 26 (*Tumbleweeds*) is not Lucien Littlefield; that on p. 586 (*The Treasure of Silver Lake*) is not Herbert Lom.

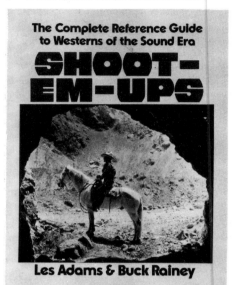

The Complete Reference Guide to Westerns of the Sound Era
SHOOT-EM-UPS
Les Adams & Buck Rainey

Universal Pictures – A Panoramic History: Michael E. Fitzgerald; Arlington House, dist. LSP Books, £14.95
With this gargantuan volume (over 750 large pages) Universal joins those Hollywood companies which have recently issued books with casts, credits, stills and synopses of their entire output, in this case from 1930 to 1976. Here also are included a 120-page history (profusely illustrated), lists of awards and a 60-page biographical section on Universal stars, from Abbott and Costello to John Wayne. A good index makes research easy. The layout is attractive, and photograph reproduction mainly very good. It is, one must admit, a pity that the record was not made complete by the inclusion of the silent era – years when Universal was very active indeed. However, apart from this limitation, here is a real whale of a book, a compulsory purchase for all those interested, historically or nostalgically, in the cinema.

Index

Page numbers in italics indicate pictorial references; titles in italics indicate reference to books.